PLATO'S INTRODUCTION OF FORMS

Scholars of Plato are divided between those who emphasize the literature of the dialogues and those who emphasize the argument of the dialogues, and between those who see a development in the thought of the dialogues and those who do not. In this important book, Russell Dancy focuses on the arguments and defends a developmental picture. He explains the Theory of Forms of the *Phaedo* and *Symposium* as an outgrowth of the quest for definitions canvased in the Socratic dialogues, by constructing a Theory of Definition for the Socratic dialogues based on the refutations of definitions in those dialogues, and showing how that theory is mirrored in the Theory of Forms. His discussion, notable for both its clarity and its meticulous scholarship, ranges in detail over a number of Plato's early and middle dialogues, and will be of interest to readers in Plato studies and in ancient philosophy more generally.

R. M. DANCY is Professor of Philosophy at Florida State University. He is the author of *Sense and Contradiction: A Study in Aristotle* (1975) and *Two Studies in the Early Academy* (1991), and editor of *Kant and Critique* (1993).

PLATO'S INTRODUCTION OF FORMS

R. M. DANCY

Florida State University, Tallahassee

CAMBRIDGE
UNIVERSITY PRESS

PUBLISHED BY THE PRESS SYNDICATE OF THE UNIVERSITY OF CAMBRIDGE
The Pitt Building, Trumpington Street, Cambridge, United Kingdom

CAMBRIDGE UNIVERSITY PRESS
The Edinburgh Building, Cambridge, CB2 2RU, UK
40 West 20th Street, New York, NY 10011–4211, USA
477 Williamstown Road, Port Melbourne, VIC 3207, Australia
Ruiz de Alarcón 13, 28014 Madrid, Spain
Dock House, The Waterfront, Cape Town 8001, South Africa

http://www.cambridge.org

First published 2004

Printed in the United Kingdom at the University Press, Cambridge

Typeface Adobe Garamond 11/12.5 pt.   *System* LaTeX 2_ε [TB]

A catalogue record for this book is available from the British Library

ISBN 0 521 83801 0 hardback

For Margaret

Contents

Preface

In the spring of 1966, Gregory Vlastos invited me (among others) to submit a paper for consideration for an issue of the *Monist* he was editing. I did. Gregory did not accept the paper, but generously (as was his way always) provided me with detailed comments. One of those comments was: "To do this, you'd have to write a book." Here it is.

Along the way I have incurred an enormous number of intellectual debts. There is no possibility of my thanking all of those who have helped; for one thing, I would have to include all the students in seminars who have asked penetrating questions and made perceptive comments. So I'll confine myself to the oldest debt, that owed to Gregory Vlastos, and the most recent ones.

Michael Ruse sat through the better part of a seminar I gave on the book in 2002–2003, was obstreperous (often helpfully), and got me to submit the manuscript to Cambridge University Press. I won't say that without his prodding the book would never have got out, but I won't deny it either.

Hilary Gaskin, of Cambridge University Press, also pushed me to submit it. She has been unfailingly encouraging throughout the entire process.

She had it sent on to two referees, who gave me further reason to push on. One of them, Eric Brown, gave me very extensive comments indeed. Among other things, the book was far too long, and he had a lot of suggestions for ways to shorten it (one of the most important was to stop short of the *Republic*, which was part of the original design; another was to curtail references to the secondary literature).

Angela Blackburn did the copyediting, and was at all times understanding and helpful. She uncovered more errors than I'll admit to; if any remain, mea culpa.

Lastly, my wife Margaret has been unflagging in editing, transferring computer files from one word processing system to another, asking questions such as, "Do you really need to say this?" and so on. The book is accordingly dedicated to her, although, quite possibly, she may never want to see it again.

Note on the text

Translations from the Greek are mine unless otherwise noted.

Square brackets ([ ]) enclose material that is in manuscripts or standard editions of the Greek that should not be there.

Angle brackets (< >) enclose material that is missing from manuscripts and standard editions of the Greek.

Curly brackets ({}) enclose translator's supplements, as well as the Greek where this is cited within the translation. I have also used curly brackets to enclose words of my own when I have included them in quotations from other authors.

In matters of logic, initial universal quantifiers whose scope is the whole formula are mostly suppressed. Frequently I flag a conclusion that is intermediate – one drawn on the way to a further conclusion – with an "L" – "(L1)," for example. The "L" stands for "Lemma."

Abbreviations

DK H. Diels, *Die Fragmente der Vorsokratiker*, ed. W. Kranz, 9th edn., Berlin 1960
LSJ H. G. Liddell, R. Scott, H. S. Jones, *A Greek–English Lexicon*, Oxford 1996.

CHAPTER I

Introduction

There are lots of divisions among Plato scholars, but two of the biggest are these.

Some think that Plato's dialogues proceed from a single view throughout: that there is no question of a *development* in Plato's thought. Their opposite numbers think that there is development to be seen in the dialogues. The first view is sometimes referred to as "unitarian,"[1] and the second could be labeled "developmental."[2]

Then again, some scholars see in the dialogues dramatic creations, and so the technique they favor in understanding them is literary analysis. *Their* opposite numbers see in the dialogues a lot of abstract argumentation, and so their favored technique is that of logical analysis. The first of these two approaches we may call "literary," and the second "analytic."[3]

This latter opposition would be unreal if either position were understood as exclusive of the other: obviously the dialogues contain both drama and argument. The question of which approach to take is, then, one of emphasis. But there are extremes, and the extremes are in opposition.

This book is a defense of a developmental view with an analytic emphasis.[4]

It is confined to the dialogues commonly regarded as early plus the *Phaedo* and *Symposium*, and to what in those latter dialogues pertains to a certain metaphysical theory, commonly referred to as the "Theory of Forms."

---

[1] As far as I know, the first printed use of the term is in Owen (1973) 349 = Owen (1986) 138; but as Owen there defines the term, it applies to the middle-period dialogues and later, and I am thinking of it more broadly, so that it covers the early to middle dialogues as well. This use has become fairly standard: see, e.g., Teloh (1981) 1 and *passim*, Prior (1985) 2, Ledger (1989) 73 n. 10, Rutherford (1995) 24.

[2] The standard label in the literature is "revisionist," but this is potentially misleading. Mostly, the terms "revisionist" and "unitarian" have their homes in discussions of the late sequence of dialogues, with which I am not here concerned. But cf. Dancy (1984).

[3] A description of this opposition, with passionate advocacy of the literary approach, may be found in the introduction to Stokes (1986) 1–35.

[4] That emphasis does not necessarily lead to "developmentalism": for a carefully argued alternative see Penner (1987).

The idea that a development can be discerned in Plato from a stage in which the Theory of Forms is not in play to a later stage in which it is in play is not a new idea.[5] But it has come under attack recently,[6] so much so that "developmentalism" has become a term of reproach.[7] What is missing in the literature is a detailed defense of this two-stage theory. This book provides such a defense, by considering certain arguments of the dialogues assigned to the first stage to show how, from them, the arguments that appear in dialogues of the second stage emerged.

Even a purely "literary" approach would lack a good deal if it did not take account of the arguments: the dialogues contain a lot of (more or less abstract) argumentation that is an essential part of the literature.[8]

There are, however, many other aspects of the literature contained in Plato's dialogues: the dialogues are dramatic, employing many different characters, in many different settings; there are images, stories, myths; there is humor. It is perfectly possible to study these and pay less attention to the arguments, and to say interesting and important things.[9]

But the arguments are the part of the literature on which this book concentrates, somewhat fiercely. No objection is being raised against the literary approach. The reader will find very little of that in this book – not because it isn't interesting or shouldn't be done: it just is not being done here.[10]

Frequently, representatives of the literary approach emphasize that Plato wrote, not treatises, but dialogues, and that he does not himself take a part in those dialogues. More often than not, the lead character is Socrates. But, the *literati* rightly point out, the idea that Socrates is speaking for Plato is an inference.[11] Some who are aware of this are prepared to make the inference.[12]

---

[5] See, e.g., Teloh (1981), where further references can be found.   [6] See, e.g., Nails (1995).

[7] Press (2002) 252 n. 1, for example, says of Schmid (1998) that it "is a detailed and sensitive interpretation marred by commitment to Platonic chronology and developmentalism."

[8] So also Frede (1992) 202.

[9] As do, for example, Stokes (1986) and Rutherford (1995).

[10] And I'm not saying that understanding the arguments is a magic key for unlocking all of Plato. Rosen (1968) xiv–xv = (1987) xlii–xliii nominates the "problem of irony" as *"the central problem in the interpretation of Plato"* (his italics). I doubt that there is any such animal.

[11] See, e.g., Edelstein (1962), Rosen (1968) xiii–xiv = (1987) xli–xlii, Weingartner (1973) 1–7, Tigerstedt (1977) 93–94, 96–98, Stokes (1986) 1–35, Rutherford (1995) 7–8. See also Kahn (1981a) 305, Kahn (1996) 36–37. Sometimes *Phaedrus* 275c–277a and *Seventh Letter* 341a–345c (in both of which the author condemns philosophical writing) are brought in as well, and often then as part of a case for the so-called "unwritten doctrines": see, e.g., Krämer (1959) 392–404, Gaiser (1963) 3–5 with nn., Szlezák (1985) 1–23, 331–405, Richard (1986) 50–58; for accounts in English, see Watson (1973) 7–14, Krämer (1990) 65–74.

[12] E.g., Kraut (1992a) 25–30.

I see no very good reason not to make it.[13] But I do not take it as a presupposition that Socrates is Plato's "mouthpiece." The train of thought I want to bring out coheres in a way that makes it extremely difficult to believe that it is not Plato's. So this book is a sort of argument in favor of the inference in the case of this train of thought rather than one that presupposes it.

That does not mean that absolutely everything Socrates says in every dialogue is precisely what Plato was thinking at the time of writing. First, Plato no doubt thought more than he wrote, and the dialogues would be unreadable if in them he had recorded every reaction he had to every argument put in the mouth of Socrates. And second, many of the presuppositions that we shall uncover may have been ones of which Plato was unaware, so, in that sense, he may have thought less than he wrote.

So when I speak of "Socrates" I shall mean the character in the dialogue under discussion, not Plato.

A related point has to do with the "Socratic question": do the supposedly "early" dialogues represent the thought of Socrates? It seems to me that the evidence of Aristotle (§ 1.2 below) makes it quite plausible that they do.[14] Things seem different to others.[15] I need not commit myself on this score to get what I want across. So, for yet another reason, by "Socrates" I shall mean the character in the dialogue under discussion (except in § 1.2) as opposed to the historical Socrates.

As for the question of development, with at least one caveat everyone would agree that the dialogues were written in a certain order. The caveat is that Plato may have gone back to rewrite earlier efforts after later insights. Besides, there may have been overlapping writing. But, broadly speaking, the chances are that he worked on the dialogues in some order or other.

To unitarians, that doesn't matter. Each dialogue is a partial view of the block of thought that is Plato's philosophy; there are no ineliminable discrepancies.

---

[13] It sometimes sounds as if the *literati* think that it would be inexplicable why Plato wrote dialogues rather than treatises if he did not intend to distance himself from the views expressed by the characters (including Socrates). But there are alternative explanations: see, e.g., Kraut (1992a) 26–27, Rutherford (1995) 8–9.

[14] This does not mean that I am tempted by the doctrine Kahn (1981a) 305 is attacking (cf. Kahn [1996] 38–39), to the effect that Plato's object in the Socratic dialogues was "primarily historical: to preserve and defend the memory of Socrates as faithfully as possible." The *Second Letter* 314c4 describes the Socrates of the dialogues as "a Socrates who has become beautiful and young"; if the letter is to be condemned as spurious, it is not because it says this.

[15] E.g., to Charles Kahn: see Kahn (1981a) *passim*, Kahn (1992) 235–40, Kahn (1996) 71–100 (esp. 79–87).

Sometimes it is made to sound as if there were some a priori reason for favoring such a view: as if there were a principle of methodology that dictated that charity required explaining away apparent discrepancies. Sometimes it is made to sound as if Plato would be inferior as a philosopher if he ever altered his views about anything.[16] I think, on the contrary, that changing one's mind often is something any self- and other-respecting philosopher can be expected to do: the questions are far too difficult.

I.I. THE DIALOGUES

This book is concerned with a development in Plato's thought. But it does not depend on a particular chronological scheme.[17] The development in question is in the first instance a logical one. The most natural way of thinking of this development is as a chronological one as well, and I know of nothing against this, but if Plato's biography turns out to be more complex, so be it.

Socrates in certain dialogues produces arguments to defeat proposed definitions without committing himself to the idea that the things being defined are to be found in an eternal, unchanging, and ontologically pure realm. In other dialogues definition takes more of a back seat, and Socrates does commit himself to that metaphysical view. The metaphysical view is the Theory of Forms.

The dialogues I am going to consider[18] fall into two groups: they are those frequently (see n. 17) taken to be the "early" and "middle" dialogues,

---

[16] For an extreme statement of this sort of view, over a century old but still influential, see Shorey (1903) 3–4.

[17] Most scholars, whether unitarian, developmental, or uncommitted, suppose that there are three identifiable groups of dialogues: earlier ones in which Socrates plays a predominantly question-raising role, "middle-period" ones in which Socrates has a lot more by way of answers, and later ones, in which Socrates mostly takes a back seat. See, e.g., Field (1967) 64–76, Stefanini (1932/35) I lxii–lxxxi (esp. lxxix, where there are four groups), Ross (1951) 1–10, Crombie (1962/63) I 9–14, Guthrie (1975) 41–54, Vlastos (1991) 46–47, Vlastos (1994) 133, Kahn (1996) 42–48. More detail and references may be found in Thesleff (1982) pt. I (esp. 8–17). For stylometry, see Brandwood (1990) 249–52 (Brandwood [1992] for a more summary account, and Brandwood [1976] xvii for a comprehensive table) and Ledger (1989) 170–226 (esp. 224–25). Two review articles, Robinson (1992) and Young (1994), are very sobering (the latter has a useful comparative table on p. 240).

[18] The cases against the authenticity of certain dialogues need to be reexamined: earlier scholars relied altogether too much on arguments resting on more or less subjective evaluations (e.g., Shorey [1933] 429 on the *Theages*, Lamb [1927] 276 on the *Hipparchus*). For the *Clitophon* see Slings (1999) 215–34 and *passim* (arguing for tentative acceptance); for the *Theages* Joyal (2000) 121–32 and *passim* (for rejection), and for *Alcibiades I* Denyer (2001) 14–26 and *passim* (for acceptance, and see also Gordon [2003]; some of Joyal's case against *Theages* would carry the *Alcibiades* with it: see Joyal [2000] 98–99, 154–55). But these doubtful dialogues have little bearing on my theme.

but, since I am emphasizing argument rather than date, I have preferred the labels "Socratic" and "doctrinal." Both labels could be misleading: the first because it suggests that the historical Socrates is in view and the second because it suggests that things are written in stone. Neither implication is intended here.

The groups in question are as shown in the table below. I am not going to be trying to discern development, whether logical or chronological, within the group of Socratic dialogues.[19]

	Socratic[a]	Doctrinal[b]
Definitional	Nondefinitional	
Charmides	*Apology*	*Meno*
Euthyphro	*Crito*	*Phaedo*
Hippias Major	*Euthydemus*	*Symposium*
Laches	*Hippias Minor*	
Lysis	*Ion*	
	Menexenus	
Republic I	*Protagoras*	
	Gorgias	

[a] Within each of the two groups, in alphabetical order (except for the *Gorgias*: see below).
[b] Alphabetical by coincidence: see below on the *Meno*.

The dialogues that count as "Socratic" and "definitional," as I am using the terms,[20] are those in which

---

[19] Such attempts have been made: see, e.g., Vlastos (1983) n. 2 pp. 27–28 (= Vlastos [1994] 135), 57–58 (= Vlastos [1994] 29–31), 27 n. 2: "I take the *Lysis, Euthydemus*, and *Hippias Major* to be the latest of these . . . {*sc.* of the Socratic dialogues, including *Republic* I}, falling between the *Gorgias* (which I take to be the only one of the earlier dialogues to precede this trio) and the *Meno*, which I take to mark the point of transition from the earlier to the middle dialogues." (The comment in parentheses contradicts the rest of the paragraph; Vlastos must have intended to say that he takes the *Gorgias* to be last of the earlier dialogues, immediately preceding the *Lysis, Euthydemus*, and *Hippias Major*.) See also Vlastos (1985) n. 1, pp. 1–2 (not reprinted in Vlastos [1994]), where *Republic* I "down to 354a11" is taken as preceding the *Lysis* et al., and Beversluis (1987) 221 n. 4.

Kahn (1981a) 309 gives a quite different ordering (partially retracted in Kahn [1996] 48): the *Apology, Crito, Ion, Hippias Minor, Gorgias*, and *Menexenus* count as "Early or 'pre-systematic' dialogues"; the *Laches, Charmides, Lysis, Euthyphro, Protagoras, Euthydemus*, and *Meno* as "Pre-middle or 'Socratic'."

The chronology adopted in Vlastos (1983), Vlastos (1985), and Beversluis (1987) would have some impact on the discussion of what I shall be calling the "Intellectualist Assumption."

[20] See also Vlastos (1991) 47–49, Penner (1992) 125–31; they operate with somewhat more elaborate criteria than I do, but the upshot is roughly the same.

(1) Socrates is the main speaker;
(2) the main task is that of defining something, with the object of resolving some practical issue (not simply for the sake of pursuing a theoretical puzzle);
(3) that task is not performed by the time things are done; and
(4) Socrates professes no significant positive view other than one or another of the "Socratic paradoxes" (and in particular nothing by way of metaphysics).[21]

By the "Socratic paradoxes" I mean the following interrelated claims:

(SP1) No one does wrong voluntarily (or knowingly, or intentionally);
(SP2) the supposedly distinct virtues (courage, self-control, justice, etc.) are really one;
(SP3) virtue is knowledge (or wisdom).

These claims will often be at the margin of subsequent discussions in this study. A great deal has been written about them,[22] but all we need here is a rough grasp of the interrelationships among them. So, briefly: (SP3) tells us that knowing what to do is all there is to being virtuous, which means that the one thing that all the supposedly separate virtues are is knowledge, which is (SP2), and that departure from virtue can only come of ignorance, which is (SP1).

The important part of feature (4) is not its positive part but what it denies: typically, Socrates professes no doctrine; indeed, he often professes to know nothing about the matters into which he inquires. In *Theaetetus* 149a–151d, he describes himself as a philosophical midwife, and midwives, he says, are barren:[23] he has no ideas of his own, but is an assistant at the birth of the ideas of others. The characterization of Socrates as a midwife occurs nowhere else in the dialogues, but within this passage, in 150e–151a, he seems to be referring to the conversation dramatized in the *Laches* as one in which he played that role, and the characterization certainly fits with what Socrates is made to say of his "teaching" activity in *Apology* 21b–24b. So it is natural to generalize this to the other Socratic dialogues, and I shall call feature (4) the "midwife requirement."[24]

---

[21] If Irwin (1995) (or [1977b]) is right, there is a fair amount of ethical doctrine to be found in the dialogues I want to classify as "Socratic" under this criterion. But, at any rate, it is not metaphysics, and I should be inclined to say that it all hinges on these paradoxes.

[22] See, e.g., Santas (1966), Santas (1964), Vlastos (1971/72), Penner (1973), Forrester (1975), Vlastos (1981), Irwin (1977b) 86–90 and *passim*, Ferejohn (1983/84), Ferejohn (1984), Wakefield (1987), Devereux (1992), Devereux (1995), Brickhouse and Smith (2000) 157–83.

[23] See Dover (1968a) xliv = Dover (1971) 62.

[24] Of course this carries with it no answer to the question whether the "midwife" metaphor goes back to the historical Socrates: see here Burnyeat (1977a), Tomin (1987).

In determining whether a certain dialogue satisfies the midwife requirement, I am going to take Socrates at his word. If he ends a dialogue without endorsing a position, that does it. It may be that we can see, there or elsewhere, reason why Socrates or Plato might have preferred to adopt one of the positions discussed. But if Socrates doesn't actually adopt it, I shall pass him on the midwife requirement.[25]

We are concerned primarily with the development of Plato's metaphysics, so it is in particular this subject on which Socrates' failure to commit himself is important for our purposes. And, more particularly, the doctrine to watch for is the metaphysical one that comes to dominate the *Phaedo, Republic,* and others: the Theory of Forms.

The dialogues that share features (1)–(4) are those in the first column plus the *Theaetetus.* But the *Theaetetus* is very much a special case.[26] In fact, it would make little difference to my story if we counted the *Theaetetus* among the Socratic definition dialogues. But it would make a difference to a subsequent story I'd like to tell, so I've left it out. That at least shortens the work.

Certain entries in that first column are no doubt more controversial than the others.

The *Hippias Major* has been rejected as spurious by eminent scholars,[27] but I find their reasons less than compelling. So I shall follow current

---

[25] So the *Laches* passes, despite Vlastos (1971/72) 230–31 n. 24 in the reprint in Vlastos (1973b); its final definition, which Vlastos takes Socrates to be accepting (courage is "the knowledge of things to be avoided and {things} to be embarked on in war and in all other things"), is followed by a refutation, and Socrates concludes that refutation by saying "So we have not found out what courage is" (199e11). Vlastos's grounds for overriding that are inadequate (the definition is not, *pace* Vlastos, accepted by Socrates in the *Protagoras,* and it does not straightforwardly derive from Platonic doctrine). Similar considerations lead me against, e.g., Heidel (1900) 170–71 or Heidel (1902) 20–21 on the *Euthyphro,* and Schmid (1998) 40–42 on the *Charmides.*

[26] Among other things, it is pretty much locked into place between the *Parmenides* and the *Sophist: Theaetetus* 183e refers back, along with *Sophist* 217c, to the *Parmenides; Sophist* 216a refers back to the closing line of the *Theaetetus.* And the *Sophist* fills quite definite lacunae left by the *Theaetetus:* at *Theaetetus* 180de, Socrates mentions the Eleatic partisans of unity and immobility, and suggests quite strongly that an examination of their views is in order (see 180e–181b), and then, when called on this suggestion by Theaetetus, he puts the examination on the shelf (183c–184a: it is in the course of this that the reference to the *Parmenides* occurs). And later he suggests that it would be an aid in answering the question "what is knowledge?" if we could understand how false belief is possible (187c–e), but then elaborately fails to achieve the latter understanding, and shelves the problem again (200cd). The *Sophist* takes both of these matters down off the shelf, and (purportedly) resolves them.

See Bostock (1988) 2–3 (reservations in 10–14). Guthrie (1978) 61–62 follows a twentieth-century tradition in assigning an absolute date of 369 or after to the *Theaetetus,* but this date is not stable: see Nails (2002) 276.

[27] Notably by Dorothy Tarrant and C. H. Kahn: see Tarrant (1920), Grube (1926), Tarrant (1927), Tarrant (1928), Grube (1929). See Malcolm (1968) and esp. Woodruff (1982) (esp. 94–103), in defense of its genuineness. Contra, cf. Kahn (1985) 267–73, but Kahn's rejection relies on an appeal (see esp. p. 268) to a sense of Plato's style that I do not share.

orthodoxy, and count in the *Hippias Major*. That raises another problem: according to some commentators,[28] it contains some substantive meta-physics, and so would fail to meet the midwife requirement. Others too would fail it under this sort of interpretation,[29] but I am going to be reject-ing such interpretations.

Book I of the *Republic* has often been thought to have originated as a separate dialogue,[30] which would have been called *Thrasymachus*[31] in the absence of the sequel, which was attached later. I find this view quite attractive. But it is not important here that it be correct; what is important is the fact that *Republic* I, regarded on its own, does not require completion by *Republic* II–X any more than any of the other dialogues in our group requires completion. And there is a startling break in continuity between I and II–X.

Book I shows us a Socrates with a massive midwife complex: since he does not know, at the end of that book, what justice is, he doesn't even know whether it is a virtue, much less whether someone who has it is happy or not (which question dominated the latter half of the book). This is what he says at 354bc. But then, after Glaucon and Adeimantus have in book II elaborately motivated the question whether justice brings happiness, Socrates does *not* say (at 368c): "By the dog, Glaucon and Adeimantus, admiring your zeal for discussion as I do I can feel nothing but dismay over the incredible weakness of your intellects. Either you weren't paying attention or you've forgotten in the space of a Stephanus page: I just went out of my way to explain that I don't know this, since I don't know what justice is." Rather, for book after book he tells them and us what justice is and why it makes its possessor a happy man. The questions are still those of book I: II–X are trying to show us what book I apparently did not, but it is a different Socrates who has taken over.[32] Unlike that of the Socratic dialogues, this Socrates has the definitions in his back pocket, and

---

[28] E.g., Tarrant (1928) lx–lxviii, Allen (1970) refs. to *Hippias Major* on 69 and ff., and in Allen (1971) *passim*, but esp. 329–30. To a lesser degree, Malcolm (1968).

[29] Cf. Prior (1985) 1: "The Theory of Forms receives its first real treatment in the *Euthyphro*."

[30] A view apparently first expressed by Hermann (1839) 538–39 (the sentence begins on 537). See further references in Kahn (1993) 131–32 (Kahn goes on to argue against the idea that book I was originally a separate dialogue).

[31] According to Diès (1932) xviii and Friedländer (1958/69) II 305 n. 1, this title comes originally from Dümmler (1895)(and cf. 305–6 for further references).

[32] Vlastos (1991) 248–51 similarly argues on the basis of his criteria that *Republic* I is an earlier dialogue. Kahn (1993) 136–40 lists passages in books I and II–X that, in his view, "show that Book I contains massive anticipation of the following books" (136). But what would you expect, if II–X were written with an eye to answering the main problem raised in I? No one who thinks I was originally a separate dialogue is maintaining that II–X are simply *irrelevant* to its concerns.

produces them. And there is no shortage of other doctrines over which he waxes enthusiastic: in particular, the Theory of Forms.

And lastly, in the leftmost column above, the *Lysis* is counted as a definition dialogue, although it is borderline:[33] half of it (203a–212a) is preamble to the main question, and when that question is raised, it is not in the characteristic form of a definition question, but reads (212a8–b2): "When someone loves {φιλῇ} someone, which becomes the lover of which, the one who loves of the one who is loved, or the one who is loved of the one who loves? Or does it make no difference?" Still, at the end of the dialogue, Socrates says (223b7–8): "we've turned out unable so far to find out what the lover {ὁ φίλος} is," and that gives it the form of a definition question.[34] Going on the latter formulation, I have included the *Lysis* among the definition dialogues, although the connection between the two questions is not terrifically clear.[35] I think there is not a great deal at stake here.

The second column lists dialogues that closely resemble the definition dialogues but fail to pursue singlemindedly the task of defining something, and so lack features (2) and (3). But they often accord crucial roles to definitions: it is not difficult to recognize the Socrates of the definition dialogues in *Protagoras* 360e–361d. So we might say: we encounter attenuated versions of features (2)–(3) in these dialogues.

The *Crito* comes in only for incidental mention in what follows; that is fortunate, since it signally fails the midwife requirement by propounding a theory of political obligation of some complexity.[36] The fact that this theory is put in the mouth(s) of the Laws of Athens may mean that, formally speaking, the *Crito* passes the test,[37] but this is too much a surface consideration even for me. Still, there is not a trace of metaphysics in the theory propounded. So I have classed it where most people would, among the Socratic dialogues.

---

[33] See Robinson (1953) 49, Szlezák (1985) 118 n. 4, Watt (1987a) 121–23, and Bordt (1998) 76–78 (with further references).

[34] Sedley (1989) 107 dismisses this passage as "a humorous parting shot, not intended to be squeezed too hard for precise philosophical content." His main argument (108) for refusing to classify the dialogue as definitional is actually the claim that if it is, Socrates is "committing the cardinal sin of failing to maintain the very distinction between definitional and non-definitional questions whose importance he himself stresses in such well known passages as *Euthyphro* 11a and *Meno* 71b." But: (a) This makes it sound as if that distinction were to be found in many other passages throughout the Socratic dialogues. It is not, and it is a rather subtle distinction. (b) Sedley assumes that the question "who comes-to-be the friend of whom?" cannot be construed as a definition question, and that begs the question. Suppose the answer were "the one who loves and is loved in return becomes the friend of the one he loves." Why should that not be tantamount to a definition for "*x* is a friend of *y*"?

[35] See Santas (1979) 155. [36] See especially Woozley (1979), Allen (1980), Kraut (1984), Young (1997).

[37] So Irwin (1979) 6.

The *Gorgias* is a rather more interesting case. Plato "brings Socrates on in the *Gorgias* asserting and making the answerer agree with his questions," says the anonymous Neoplatonist who wrote the *Prolegomena to Platonic Philosophy*,[38] and he or she is right. Like the *Crito*, the *Gorgias* shows us a Socrates relatively unembarrassed about expressing convictions, and so gets a low grade in midwifery. For the most part, the views Socrates expresses are, like those expressed in the *Crito*, untainted by metaphysical considerations. But there is some strong language, metaphysically speaking, and this we shall have to look into, if only in passing. Besides, Socrates here plumps for the immortality of the soul, which surely does count as a piece of metaphysics and is elsewhere closely associated with the Theory of Forms. In fact, Socrates' attitude toward this issue in the *Crito* had shown a bit more in the way of positive thinking than the optimistic agnosticism registered in the *Apology*.

For this reason, I am inclined to think that the *Gorgias* ought to be classed as a "transitional" dialogue along with the *Meno*.[39] But the tradition of thinking of the dialogue as Socratic is strong. So I have compromised, and placed it, out of alphabetical order, at the end of the Socratic group.

The Socratic dialogues contrast with the *Meno*, and, more sharply, with the *Phaedo* and *Symposium*. In each of the latter, Socrates is the main speaker (but this characterization is a bit of a stretch in the case of the *Symposium*). But none of them has as its primary object the obtaining of a definition. And in each of the latter two, Socrates is made to express a metaphysical doctrine, most importantly, the Theory of Forms.

The *Meno* begins as a definition dialogue whose question is "what is virtue?" But this attempt aborts at 79e–80e, at which point Socrates launches into an exposition of and argument for a doctrine.

This doctrine is not the Theory of Forms,[40] but the "Doctrine of Recollection," to the effect that what we call "learning" is really recollecting things we already knew. The only piece of metaphysics this theory

---

[38] Westerink (1962) II.17–18. The author is trying to show that Plato was not a skeptic but a "dogmatist."

[39] See also Dodds (1959) 18–34, Irwin (1979) 5–8.

[40] According to Shorey (1903) 32, with regard to the argument in the *Meno* for the theory of recollection: "The *Phaedo* distinctly refers to this argument as a proof of the reality of ideas, and the myth in the *Phaedrus* describes the ante-natal vision of the pure, colorless, formless, essences of true being. It follows that, though the ideas are not there explicitly mentioned, the reminiscence spoken of in the *Meno* must refer to them." But: (a) it does not follow, and would not follow even if these paraphrases of the *Phaedo* and *Phaedrus* were correct; (b) that is not at all what the *Phaedo* says (the reference is to 72e–73a, where the argument is used to support the claim that our souls preexisted, and the Theory of Forms is introduced as part of another argument to the same effect). The reference to the *Phaedrus* is simply irrelevant. Still, we shall consider an argument internal to the *Meno* that points toward the Theory of Forms.

directly involves is the claim that the soul existed before embodiment. But the theory of recollection is going to be connected closely with the Theory of Forms in the *Phaedo*. So, just as the *Gorgias* stands, in my ordering, at the end of the Socratic group, the *Meno* stands at the beginning of the doctrinal group.

One final reflection on logic and chronology: when I deny (as I shall) that the *Euthyphro* has a "Theory of Forms," I do not suppose that I am commenting on what was or was not in Plato's mind at the time he wrote the *Euthyphro*. I am talking only about what is required by the argument of the *Euthyphro*. The *Euthyphro* is not here being used as a clue to be put with the other clues provided by the dialogues to reconstruct Plato's inner life. It, and the other dialogues, are difficult enough without that. The problem is understanding their arguments, and the theories required by those arguments.

Once again, what matters here is the surface of the text. That is not going to preclude a fairly detailed logical analysis of that surface. But that analysis is not intended to tell us what was really going on in Plato's mind: he knew nothing of first-order predicate logic.[41]

1.2. THE GENESIS OF THE THEORY OF FORMS: ARISTOTLE'S ACCOUNT

In various passages, especially in the *Metaphysics*,[42] Aristotle tells us about the development of the theory of forms: these passages are the concern of this section. After a summary, one subsection deals with some difficulties in understanding Aristotle's account and a pattern of argument that underlies it, the "Argument from Flux" (the reason for the label will be obvious). A final subsection anticipates an argument whose gradual emergence in the dialogues will be our chief concern in the rest of the book, the "Argument from Relativity" as I shall call it, and considers the fit between it and the Argument from Flux.

---

[41] In a review of Nehamas (1999), a collection of Nehamas's essays, Prior (2001) expresses his frustration in reading them, saying (183): "Time and again I asked myself how Vlastos managed to convince so many of us that in these highly technical issues lay the key to understanding such a creative philosopher and literary artist as Plato." There is no such thing as "the key to understanding" Plato. We do the best we can with what we have. For some of us this involves "highly technical issues." And Vlastos wasn't the only influence.

[42] A 6. 987^a29-^b14, M 4. 1078^b12-32, M 9. 1086^a24-^b4. My treatment of these passages is in many respects similar to that in Fine (1993) 44–65. We diverge when it comes to the question whether Plato's Socrates should be construed as having a Theory of Forms: Fine thinks he does (49–54).

Here, then, is a composite sketch of the three main passages (A 6, M 4 and 9) and others.[43]

Socrates had been concerned with the universal, seeking for definitions (τὸ καθόλου, ὁρισμοί, etc.: *Metaphysics* A 6. 987^b2–4, M 4. 1078^b18–19, 28–29, M 9. 1086^b3), confining the inquiry to matters of "ethics" (τὰ ἠθικά, 987^b1) or "the ethical virtues" (τὰς ἠθικὰς ἀρετάς, 1078^b17–18); in particular, he paid no attention to "nature as a whole" (περὶ δὲ τῆς ὅλης φύσεως οὐθέν, 987^b2) or "natural {matters}" (τὰ φυσικά: cf. 1078^b19; with these passages compare *De Partibus Animalium* A 1. 642^a13–31, esp. 28–31). But, although Socrates sought definitions for evaluative terms, he apparently did not offer any himself; see here *Sophistici Elenchi* 34. 183^b7–8:[44] "Socrates used to ask but used not to reply; for he would concede that he did not know."

But Plato had earlier been influenced by Cratylus (*Metaphysics* A 6. 987^a32) and Heraclitean views ($^a32$–33, M 4. 1078^b13–14) to the effect that everything perceptible is in constant flux (ἁπάντων τῶν αἰσθητῶν ἀεὶ ῥεόντων, 987^a33–34, 1078^b14–15; τῶν αἰσθητῶν . . . ἀεί γε μεταβαλλόν-των, 987^b6–7; cf. M 9. 1086^a37–$^b1$), and consequently nothing perceptible could be known (987^a34, 1078^b15), since there is no knowledge of things in flux (1078^b32). So there could be no definition for anything percep-tible (987^b6–7), and Plato took the questions Socrates was raising about definitions to pertain to a realm of objects different from the ones we perceive (987^b5–6, 1078^b15–16, 1086^a25, 36, $^b1$–2). He set the "universal" (καθόλου) for which Socrates had been seeking (987^b3; cf. 1078^b19, 1086^b1) "apart from" (παρά) the things we perceive (1078^b16, 1086^a25, and possi-bly[45] 987^b8); he made them "separate" (χωριστά) where Socrates had not (1078^b30–31, 1086^a33–34, $^b3$–4). Aristotle also speaks of the objects Plato separates but Socrates does not simply as "definitions" (ὁρισμοί: 1078^b31, 1086^b3–4): this sounds like a "use-mention" error, but I doubt that anything turns on it.

---

[43] More or less similar composite accounts are to be found in Ross (1924) I xxxiii–xlviii, Vlastos (1991) 91–98, Penner (1992) 122–23 and 147–48 n. 2, Rutherford (1995) 56–58.

[44] Bolton (1993) 142 assumes that this comment is based on Plato's dialogues.

[45] Ross (1924) I 161 would take παρὰ ταῦτα in 987^b8 differently: perceptible things, on his under-standing, would be "called after" the ideas. But παρά in 97^b14 means "apart from," and on Ross's interpretation of $^b8$–9 (τὰ δ' αἰσθητὰ παρὰ ταῦτα καὶ κατὰ ταῦτα λέγεσθαι, which Ross para-phrases "and he said the sensibles were called after these and were called what they were called by virtue of their relation to these") there is some pointless repetition. This is disguised somewhat by the padding in Ross's paraphrase (in fact, as he construes the clause, it would translate "and {he said} the sensibles were called after these and by virtue of these"). It seems to me that "the sensibles were spoken of apart from these and by virtue of these" is preferable.

It is these objects that Plato speaks of as "ideas" (ἰδέαι, 987ᵇ8, 1078ᵇ32; cf. 1086ᵃ27, 31, 33) or "forms" (εἴδη, 987ᵇ10, 1078ᵇ12).⁴⁶ What is special about Plato's view is that he makes these forms *distinct* from perceptible things (see A 6. 987ᵇ5, M 4. 1078ᵇ15, M 9. 1086ᵃ25, 36, ᵇ1–2), which is at least part⁴⁷ of what Aristotle means by saying that Plato "separated" the forms from the perceptibles.

At 987ᵇ13–14, Aristotle says of Plato (and of the Pythagoreans, whom I here gloss over): "But what the participation in or imitation of forms might be they left to be investigated in common" (τὴν μέντοι γε μέθεξιν ἢ τὴν μίμησιν ἥτις ἂν εἴη τῶν εἰδῶν ἀφεῖσαν ἐν κοινῷ ζητεῖν). "Investigation in common" here is "dialectical discussion":⁴⁸ Plato did not have a settled view as to the nature of the relation of "participation" or "imitation" – Socrates is made to say as much in *Phaedo* 100d4–8 – but left that for determination in open discussion.

This picture of Aristotle's, as far as his comments on Socrates go, fits the Socratic dialogues quite well.⁴⁹ And if we take the Socrates of the doctrinal dialogues to be the spokesman for Plato, the "separation" of the forms and the talk about perceptible things in constant change fit those dialogues fairly well, too.⁵⁰ We shall shortly turn to the dialogues with this in mind. Let us first stop over a few details in Aristotle's picture.

⁴⁶ Cherniss (1959/60) 278 n. 1 "can see no advantage and many disadvantages" in using the term "forms" instead of the "traditional designation 'ideas'." (Shorey [1930/35] II 421 n. *f* is perhaps to be compared here.) Gadamer (1988) 259 also speaks of "the unfortunate Aristotelian translation 'forms' . . . as if Plato knew of 'matter'." My intuitions are precisely the opposite; the reminder that Aristotle also used the term εἶδος is salutary, and the Lockean translation "idea," which points toward thoughts, is misleading (so also Burnet [1914] 154 n. 1, Allen [1970] 29, Guthrie [1975] 114). So I generally speak of "forms." But in translating I have adhered to the above scheme: εἶδος is always translated "form" and ἰδέα always "idea."

⁴⁷ As we shall see when we turn to the dialogues, what Aristotle is referring to is not just a matter of the forms being distinct from perceptible things, but of their being, we might say, *radically* distinct from them.

⁴⁸ Cf. Hicks (1907) 265 *ad De Anima* A 4. 407ᵇ29, and note Plato, *Protagoras* 330b6, *Gorgias* 498e10, 506a4.

⁴⁹ Skeptics such as Kahn find the fit too good to be true; Kahn (1981a) 310 n. 13 says Aristotle's "account of Socrates' position . . . seems largely based upon a reading of the Platonic dialogues as historical documents." (See also 314–15; Kahn [1992] 235–40; Kahn [1996] 79–87.) Aristotle's twenty years in the Academy while Plato was still alive and presumably able to answer questions apparently did him no good at all. Kahn (1996) 82: "what we do know of Plato as a writer does not suggest any readiness to speak openly about his intellectual development." Nor, as far as I can see, does it suggest any reluctance to speak about that.

⁵⁰ Ilting (1965) 381 tells us that Aristotle's account is "demonstrably false." The demonstration turns on various assumptions I am not prepared to make. For example, Ilting infers from the fact that no dialogue before the *Cratylus* (his chronology is roughly my own, although he is quite a bit more certain of things, right down to dates, than I am: see his p. 381 n. 19) refers to the theory of flux that Plato could not have accepted the theory while writing the earlier dialogues. This portrays the dialogues as progress reports from the Platonic Academy, which seems to me absurd: there is no reason whatever to believe, and good reason to deny, that Plato's activity was primarily literary. And Ilting tells us (383–84) that, since Socrates would have nothing to do with natural philosophy, if

1.2.1. Forms and definitions: The Argument from Flux

In the composite sketch in the preceding section, it is possible to discern, not just a biographical account, but an argument for the existence of separate Forms. To do this, we have to read out the Academic jargon in which the argument is phrased,[51] and we have to read out Aristotle's negative comments on this view.[52]

The terms "universal" and "particular" are no part of the vocabulary of the Socratic dialogues. The terms "idea" (ἰδέα) and "form" (εἶδος) do appear in those dialogues, as does a term translatable as "define" (ὁρίζεσθαι). I shall be suggesting in § 2.1 that "define" may not be the best translation for that word in those dialogues, but, provided we are aware that we are describing Socrates' activity in terms that may not have been available to Plato when he wrote those dialogues (much less to Socrates himself), we may characterize him as seeking definitions.

And when Aristotle states that Plato's position separates the forms from the particulars (M 9. 1086^{b}3–4), but still makes them *particulars* (1086^{a}32–34), that is part of Aristotle's case against the position. This is a claim for which Aristotle would need to argue: he is in no position simply to lift it out of the dialogues.

Then one way of putting the position is this: the forms are distinct from perceptible things. But we want to be able to use Socrates' quest for definitions as part of the premises for the argument to come, so perhaps it is better to put the projected conclusion in terms of what can be defined. It might, then, read as follows:

What can be defined ≠ anything perceptible,[53]

where we know that we can replace "what can be defined" with "a form."

It is clearly a presupposition of the whole enterprise that there are things to be defined. And, just as clearly, the argument underlying Aristotle's account contrasts such things with perceptibles on the ground that the former are stable and the latter are in flux (where "stable" and "in flux" are

---

Plato had accepted Heracliteanism before his association with Socrates, "he would have had to give it up as soon as he became a Socratic." This picture of card-carrying Socratics with confessions of faith is only appropriate to comedy.

[51] Incidentally, this does not mean that we must accuse Aristotle of distorting Plato's views; in this case, I think he is not. But he is stating those views in a vocabulary that is rather more sophisticated than anything to be found in the dialogues we shall be studying.

[52] Which does not mean his comments are unjustified. But we are here trying to get back to the beginnings of the Theory of Forms, not to criticize it.

[53] I.e., $(x)(y)(x$ can be defined & y is perceptible $\rightarrow x \neq y)$.

understood as contradictory). So the argument, an "Argument from Flux," AF, falls out as follows:

> (AFE) There is something that can be defined.
> (AFP) Everything perceptible is in flux.
> (AFD) What can be defined is stable.
> ∴ (AFC) What can be defined ≠ anything perceptible.

Here (AFE) is an Existential presupposition of the Argument from Flux, (AFP) a premise about Perceptibles, and (AFD) one about what's Definable. Clearly more needs to be said about (AFP) and (AFD).

Premise (AFD) is motivated by:

> (a) Nothing in constant change is knowable.

And then we can see that we need something else, which is only implicit in the passages cited but explicit elsewhere (see *Metaphysics* Z 1. 1028^{a}36–37, 6. 1031^{b}6–7, etc.):

> (b) To know a thing is to have its definition.

That gives us a valid argument to get us as far as (AFD). Unfortunately, validity is not everything an argument needs: it is also supposed to have true premises. And none of these premises, read straightforwardly, passes that test.

First consider (b), which has the best chance of the lot. This is because it is the hardest to read straightforwardly. (Aristotle himself has trouble with it: cf. *Metaphysics* M 10. 1086^{b}32–37, 1087^{a}10–25, Z 15. 1039^{b}20–1040^{a}7, etc.) What is it to know a thing in the first place? The problem is not the incredibly deep one of the nature of knowledge in general, but the incredibly shallow one of understanding what someone might mean by asking "do you know that coffee-pot?" On the face of it, the best one can do is take him to mean "do you recognize it? Is it yours?" But suppose he tried to explain his question by saying "I mean, can you define that coffee-pot?" This is explaining the obscure through the yet more obscure. So what does (b) mean?

It is tempting to say: the claim has nothing to do with that coffee-pot; it is about universals, and tells us that knowing a universal is being able to define it. Perhaps a modern-day platonist would say this. But it is not much help. First, the grammar of "do you know coffee-pot-hood?" (or "do you know whiteness?" or "do you know bravery?" to take less ridiculous-sounding examples) is not much better than that of "do you know that coffee-pot?" Second, and more important, this is not a claim that Aristotle's Plato can make in this context. For that Plato is giving us an argument to the effect that particulars, perceptible, mundane things, cannot be known. He is in no position to introduce a premise that explains "to know a thing" and restricts itself to knowing "universals." Besides, those of us who are not already convinced platonists are looking at this material in part in order to gain an understanding of such things as forms and universals. The argument we have here is one that establishes the existence of a domain of such objects. The terms Aristotle uses, "universals" and "definitions," are his own (coined, presumably, by Academics);[54] we do not understand them in advance, and if we hope to shed light on the background for the theory of forms, we should not pretend that Plato understands them in advance, either.

A "definition," in Aristotle (cf. *Posterior Analytics* B 3. 91^{a}1, 10. 93^{b}29, etc.), is supposed to give the answer to the question "what is it?" And that is the way we are using the terminology when we describe Socrates as seeking definitions: he asks "what is the beautiful?" and we say: he's after a definition. So it is the ability to answer this question that (b) fixes on as knowledge of the thing.

We can ask "what is it?" about mundane objects such as this coffee-pot and that cabbage. And once we have it that what this is is a coffee-pot and what that is is a cabbage, we can repeat the question: what, in general, is a cabbage? What is a coffee-pot? The answers to questions at this second level are universal answers (and are, properly speaking, the only definitions: cf. *Metaphysics* Z 11. 1036^{a}28–29, for example). Many of the troubles Aristotle gets into have to do with the relation between this and the preceding level. So do many of the troubles Plato gets into. But the trouble here is antecedent to those. For here Aristotle's Plato, who sounds a lot like the author of the Socratic and Doctrinal dialogues, is not so much having difficultly relating the two levels of question as boggling over the first one. His Heracliteanism is leading him to say that there simply are no answers on that level.

There is, according to Aristotle's Plato, because he accepts (AFP) and (a)–(b), no way of saying what this coffee-pot or that cabbage is: these things do not have stable identities. This is what (AFC) says, once the word "define" has been translated out of it. If there were only such things as coffee-pots and cabbages, Plato would have been forced to follow Cratylus all the way:

---

[54] The term "universal" (καθόλου) does not occur at all in Plato, and the prepositional phrase from which it derives occurs only once (unelided, κατὰ ὅλου, "in general," at *Meno* 77a6).

it was Cratylus who "thought he ought to say nothing, but only moved his finger" (*Metaphysics* Γ 5. 1010ᵃ13–14), and it is not really clear how he could have justified moving his finger, either (not, presumably, by moving his finger). But Plato was, apparently, antecedently assured of the possibility of defining things: it is this assurance that underlies the move to (AFC), which carries with it the existential claim of (AFE), that there are things to be defined.

Why is it that things that do not have stable identities cannot be defined or known? This brings us to (a). Straightforwardly read, it is false. John, suppose, is a bachelor. There is a definition (notoriously) for "bachelor." Suppose now that John is in constant change: considered deadpan, this is what Heracliteanism is telling us about everything. Plato is supposed to be going from this (alleged) fact to the conclusion that John cannot be defined or known. But, on the face of it, there is no problem here: John's marital status is no secret, and he comes under the definition of "bachelor": he is, we may suppose, known to be an unmarried male adult.

There is an ancient and hoary argument that comes in here, as follows.

As long as John remains a bachelor, there is a respect in which he is not changing. And that is what Heracliteanism is supposed to rule out: according to that doctrine, everything here below is constantly changing in every respect. So it is that there can be no defining or knowing such things; for, if something were constantly changing in every respect, it would have to be changing in that respect by virtue of which it is supposed to come under the definition or be known. Thus John would have to be a bachelor now, and not later, and again a bachelor yet later, and so on. And while he is not a bachelor, he does not come under the definition and cannot be known to be a bachelor. And while he is a bachelor, he is becoming a nonbachelor. So you cannot talk or think fast enough to get the definition off before he slips out from under it. So there is no defining or knowing him qua bachelor or qua anything else.

It seems to me that we should not ascribe this train of thought to anyone we like unless we absolutely have to.

First, of course, things are not constantly changing in every respect. If that is what (AFP) is to mean, (AFP) is false. John's marital habits may show many signs of flightiness, but if that is the way he is, it is not metaphysics that makes him so; there is no piece of abstract argumentation whose conclusion is that John is forever marrying and divorcing. Anyway, he could hardly perform the ceremonies and sign the papers fast enough to satisfy the demands, for we are here requiring that there be no stretch of time as long as it takes to say "he's a bachelor" over which he is a bachelor.

But then, even if there were no such stretch of time, that would not stop us from correctly claiming and even knowing that John was a bachelor. Suppose (although the supposition is quite insane) we can never say "John was a bachelor from t_1 to t_2," because for no duration however short is it true that John was a bachelor from its beginning to its end. He will, in any duration, be vacillating. Still, what he is vacillating between is being and not being a bachelor. So at some of the times between 4:00 and 4:30 he was a bachelor; he was one, say, at 4:10. There is no harm in saying so now, and we have all sorts of time in which to say it. So, for all that has been said so far, John might have, and might be known to have, come under the definition of bachelor at 4:10.

So, on a straightforward reading, both (AFP) and (a) are false. And (b) is confusing.

If we now turn to the dialogues, we shall see some ways of reading these premises less straightforwardly: "change" in particular is much more slippery than we have been supposing. Let us take a preliminary look at how the Argument from Flux looks in more Platonic garb.

I.2.2. *The Argument from Relativity: A forward glance at the dialogues*

The pattern of argument we shall see emerging from the Socratic dialogues and made explicit in *Phaedo* 74a–c, whose upshot is to contrast forms and perceptible objects, is the following, which I shall refer to as the "Argument from Relativity," AR:

> (ARE) There is such a thing as the *F*.
> (ARO) Any ordinary *F* is also con*F* (fill in here the predicate
>   contrary to "*F* ").
> (ARF) The *F* is never con*F*.
> ∴ (ARC) The *F* is not the same as any ordinary *F*.

Premise (ARE) is the Argument from Relativity's Existential presupposition, (ARO) a premise about Ordinary *F*s, (ARF) one about the Form, the *F*, and (ARC) the conclusion.

It is immediately obvious that there is a structural similarity between AR and AF. But there is more than that: the two arguments are identical.

Throughout AR, "*F* " is a term of the sort for which Socrates sought definitions. The first premise then expresses Socrates' presupposition that there were things to be defined. So it is (AFE) in different dress.

Interlocutors in Socratic dialogues sometimes concede (ARE) as a preliminary to discussing the *F*: in a definition dialogue, that might mean as a preliminary to defining the *F*. The concession by itself is not a piece of metaphysics, but simply a matter of fixing the topic for discussion. We shall consider cases of this kind below.

But the rest of the argument is intended to bring out what, in the estimation of the Socrates of the *Phaedo*, we committed ourselves to in conceding the truth of (ARE): the Theory of Forms.

Although the Argument from Relativity first appears in the *Phaedo*, the materials for its construction are to be found in the Socratic dialogues. Premise (ARF) figures as a criterion of adequacy for a correct definition, and instances of (ARO) are used in showing that various proposed definitions fail to meet that criterion. And (ARO), it will emerge, is what Aristotle is pointing to when he ascribes (AFP) to Plato. Flux as it appears in Plato is not straightforward change as you and I conceive it:[55] baldly put, flux is relativity. And then AR is simply another version of the Argument from Flux.

But what we want to do now is approach the Theory of Forms, not through Aristotle, but through Plato's dialogues. We shall have to examine the Socratic dialogues with attention to what Socrates demands of definitions (Part I). We can then see what led Plato to the Theory of Forms, and consider the impact that has on the theory's structure (Part II).

---

[55] And this is something of which scholars have been aware at least since Irwin (1977a).

A Socratic theory of definition

CHAPTER 2

Socrates' demand for definitions

Socrates, Aristotle says, was the first to fix attention on definitions, and the Socrates of the Socratic dialogues does that. But he does not simply say: let's define (say) piety. He doesn't have the word "define": this is discussed in § 2.1.

Nor does he simply look for definitions as an abstract intellectual enterprise. He expects definitions to solve certain problems. So we must look at the problems (§ 2.2), and at the reason Socrates thinks definitions are required for solving them (§ 2.3).

2.1. PRELIMINARY: ON THE VOCABULARY FOR "DEFINING"

The Socratic dialogues do not consistently employ terms for "define" or "definition." Aristotle has a technical terminology here, but this is after the arteries have hardened considerably. Some of his words appear in the Socratic dialogues. His favored noun, ὁρισμός, does not appear anywhere in Plato, but an alternative, ὅρος, does, as does the associated verb ὁρίζειν. All these words have to do originally with (spatial) boundaries, and the transition to technical philosophical terminology is only just under way in the Socratic dialogues. Of the six occurrences of ὅρος in these dialogues,[1] that in the first book of the *Republic* is the one for which the translation "definition" is the most comfortable. There Socrates, having raised the question (331c1–3) "whether we are to say that this itself, justice, is, without qualification, truthfulness and giving back what one has taken from someone," gives a counterexample, and says (331d2–3): "So this is not {a} definition of justice, saying the truth and giving back what one has taken." Even here, "boundary stone" would preserve the metaphor, which is hardly dead yet.[2] And the other Socratic occurrences come through better as "boundary" or

---

[1] *Lysis* 209c7, *Hippias Major* 283b2, *Gorgias* 470b10, 488d1, *Menexenus* 238d8, *Republic* I 331d2.
[2] So also Robinson (1953) 55.

"mark": in almost all cases, "definition" is plainly wrong. Similarly the verb ὁρίζεσθαι, in its fifteen occurrences in these dialogues[3] (examples below), is most often better translated as "mark off," "separate," or "bound" than as "define."[4]

Aristotle thinks of a definition as something that can replace the term defined (cf., e.g., *Topics* Z I. 139^{a}25–26, ^{a}31–32 on how a proposed definition may be defeated), and hard-nosed philosophical usage is no less demanding. That is, where w is the term to be defined (the *definiendum*) and d the proposed definition (the *definiens*), we expect that

$$\text{(S)} \ w =_{\text{df}} abc \rightarrow (\ldots w - \leftrightarrow \ldots abc -).$$

Here and in the sequel "... x —" is intended to represent any sentence containing x, and syntactic transformations of x such as "$x$ness" or "the x" are allowed. So "Socrates is brave," "bravery is admirable," and "the brave does not yield to fear" are all instantiations of "... brave —." And then (S) is telling us that, if abc adequately defines w, a sentence containing w will be true if and only if the sentence you get by replacing occurrences of w by abc is true; translated, partially anyway, into Latin: the *definiens* must be substitutible for the *definiendum salva veritate*. I'll refer to the requirement as "Substitutivity"; hence the label "(S)."

Anyway, Socrates has no words that indicate unambiguously to his hearers or himself that he is demanding even this much. Consider a few occurrences of ὁρίζεσθαι from the list of fifteen above.

At *Laches* 194c7–8, Nicias says: "You people have seemed to me for a while not to be defining {ὁρίζεσθαι} courage properly," and he goes on to recite something he says he has heard Socrates saying that is then turned into a formula which is held up against something like the requirement above. So here there is nothing, on the face of it, wrong with the translation "define," except that it is likely to suggest to the philosophically minded that Nicias is aware of the philosophical task of defining and what is needed to perform it. Perhaps he is,[5] but his use of this word is no sign of that awareness, as the other cases show.

At *Gorgias* 470b1–c3, the following interchange occurs, in Irwin's translation:[6]

---

[3] *Charmides* 163d7, 171a5, a9, 173a9, *Laches* 194c8, *Euthyphro* 9c7, d5, *Republic* I 345c2, *Gorgias* 453a7, 470b10, 475a3 (*bis*), 491c1, 513d5, *Menexenus* 239e4 (this one actually has to do with land boundaries).

[4] Two passages in which "define" is natural are *Charmides* 173a9 and *Laches* 194c8.

[5] Laches certainly isn't: see 188e–189a; and note that what Nicias says about his familiarity with Socratic procedures in 187d–188c includes nothing specifically about definitions.

[6] Irwin (1979) 40.

SOCRATES: . . . Don't we agree that it is sometimes better to do the things we were mentioning just now, to kill, expel, and expropriate people, and sometimes not?

POLUS: Quite.

SOC: Then this apparently is agreed both by you and by me.

POL: Yes.

SOC: Then when do you say it's better to do these things? Tell me what definition you define {εἰπὲ τίνα ὅρον ὁρίζῃ}.

POL: No – you answer that, Socrates.

SOC: Well, Polus, if it pleases you to hear it from me, I say – whenever someone does these things justly, it's better, and whenever unjustly, worse.

Here there is, in fact, no particularly good candidate for a term to be defined, and better than Irwin's "tell me what definition you define" would be "tell me what distinction you distinguish"[7] – or, to eliminate the pleonasm that seems to have been pleasing to Greek ears but grates on ours, "tell me what distinction you draw."

Similarly, in *Euthyphro* 9c7–8 Socrates says: "For the pious and the impious were just now shown not to be distinguished {ὡρισμένα} by this, for the god-hated was shown to be also god-loved." Here the translation "defined" is quite common,[8] but the force of the objection is precisely that being loved by the gods fails to *separate* things pious from things impious. And the immediately subsequent appearance (9d5) of ὡρίσθαι gets its force from this.

The vocabulary by itself tells us nothing about how the distinguishing is to be done. We are to provide what Aristotle or any other philosopher would recognize as a definition, but the notion of definition is here in the process of construction. It is what Socrates goes on to say, and in particular what he will say by way of rejecting the answers his interlocutors offer to his questions, that makes his quest a quest for definitions. We shall soon see that (S) is involved: but Socrates has to explain it, and no use of ὅρος or its relatives would have shortened the work.

The central question that Socrates turns into a request for a definition is "what is so-and-so?" It is this question whose treatment in the Socratic dialogues will concern us now.

---

[7] Zeyl, in Cooper (1997) 814: "Tell me where you draw the line." See also Beversluis (2000) 327 n. 26. The note in Irwin (1979) 148 *ad* 470b seems to show that we do not disagree over the substantial point here.

[8] E.g., in Grube's translation, Cooper (1997) 9.

None of the dialogues generally accepted as genuine[9] begins with a question of this form;[10] instead, where such a question occurs, there is a more or less elaborate build-up to it. So let us first attend to the stage setting (in the remainder of this chapter and the next), and then consider what happens to attempts to answer the question (in subsequent chapters).

2.2. DEFINING AND LIVING RIGHT

In the definition dialogues, it is natural to see the main philosophical import in the failed attempt at definition. In the bulk of my discussion of these dialogues, that will be where the emphasis lies. But this is misleading; it is a product of a particular interest in those dialogues that is certainly not as broad as Plato's own. For in the Socratic dialogues the demand for definition is always subordinate to another question, or other questions. The amount of attention given to these other questions makes it impossible to read these dialogues merely as exercises in the methodology of defining, or as essays in preparation for metaphysics. The Socrates we meet here is looking for definitions in order to determine how one ought to live, as he says at *Republic* I 352d.[11]

2.2.1. Laches

A striking case of the subordination of definition questions to questions of how to carry on is provided by the *Laches*.[12] Here the defining question "what is courage?" (or "manliness" or "bravery": ἀνδρεία) is only brought

---

9 But *De Justo* begins "Can you tell us what the just {τὸ δικαῖον} is?" (372a1), *Hipparchus* "Well, then, what is the gain-loving {τὸ φιλοκερδές}?" (τί γὰρ τὸ φιλοκερδές; 225a1, with a connecting particle: cf. Friedländer [1958/69] II 119–20), and *Minos* "What shall we say law {ὁ νόμος} is?" (313a1). Perhaps this is a reason for treating them as Academic exercises: so Thesleff (1982) 231 on *De Justo*.

10 The single most common opening question is "where are you coming from?" (*Ion, Protagoras, Menexenus, Phaedrus,* and cf. *Theaetetus*). The first order of business is usually a matter of locating the speakers (cf. *Charmides, Euthyphro, Hippias Major, Lysis, Republic* I, *Euthydemus, Gorgias, Symposium, Parmenides, Sophist,* and *Laws* I 625a–c). But even after this locating is done with, the "what is it?" question is deferred (when it occurs at all).

11 And see *Gorgias* 500c, but this is not in the context of definition seeking.

12 Cf. Rutherford (1995) 83: "It is obvious that the *Laches* is not composed solely, or even primarily, for the sake of the brief and flimsy 'philosophical' arguments used to support these definitions." But he says nothing to support the claim that the "philosophical" (why the scare quotes around "philosophical," anyway?) arguments are flimsy, and appears not to notice that few of them are in *support* of a definition in the first place. In fact, although these "'philosophical' arguments" occupy the final, culminating, third of the dialogue, Rutherford says nothing much about them at all. Contrast the extensive treatment of the *Laches* in Stokes (1986) 36–113, which deals with the arguments in detail as well as the characters.

in at 190d7–8, over two-thirds of the way through the dialogue.[13] At that point, answering it is expected to resolve a disagreement between two of the interlocutors as to the value of learning to fight in heavy armor, which Nicias has been recommending and Laches condemning. In asking his question, Socrates focuses the disagreement on Nicias' claim (182c5–7) "that for every man in war, this knowledge will make him more daring and more manly than himself,[14] to no small degree" and Laches' counterclaim (184b3–c4) that possession of this alleged art will at most induce daring in someone cowardly to begin with, and may simply lend ludicrous ostentation to a person who is already courageous. To decide whether learning to fight in heavy armor, or anything else for that matter, will help in acquiring excellence, "virtue," and in particular that part of excellence which fighting in armor might be expected to help induce, namely, courage, we must first determine what courage is (190c–e).

But not even the disagreement between Nicias and Laches is an abstract intellectual one: it arises from the leading question of the dialogue, which is put to Laches and Nicias by two others, Lysimachus and Melesias. These latter confess that they themselves, by contrast with their fathers, have not acquired fame for noble deeds (καλὰ ἔργα), and they do not wish their own sons to turn out "no-accounts," "men of no repute" (ἀκλεεῖς, 179d4). They want to know whether they should have their sons trained to fight in heavy armor. It is an assumption unquestioned by anyone, including Socrates, that the acquisition of "virtue," "excellence," carries with it glory in the public eye.[15] It is apparently an assumption on the part of Laches

---

[13] A point often made: see, e.g., Kahn (1986) 12, Benson (2000) 24. It leads Kohák (1960) 124 to say that the subject of the *Laches* is education rather than courage; Nichols (1987) 269 also sees the long preamble to the question about courage as "situating" it "within the larger context of questions about education to virtue." This is clearly true. But Kohák goes on to say (131) that courage "is the existential form of the power of being. Thus it cannot be given a definition." This is not intelligible, and the word "thus" is unsupportable.

Nichols (1987) 269, 271 also supposes that the lengthy preamble shows us something about the characters of Laches and Nicias relevant to understanding the whole dialogue. But the most important points he tries to make about these characters are derived from the discussion of definitions, not the preamble: e.g., on the basis of 195d–196b, with the help of Thucydides, he tells us that "Nicias' flaw" is "that he is in fact superstitious" (275), and then that "Nicias' deepest trait is anxiety about future events" (277).

A more convincing discussion of the *Laches*, that actually deals with the arguments as well as the characters, is Devereux (1977a) 133–37. There is a review of "single-minded interpreters" of the dialogue in Guthrie (1975) 130–31. See also Sprague (1973) 3–4, Lane (1987) 70–79.

[14] "Than himself" is a bleakly literal translation of αὐτοῦ in c7; Nichols (1987) 244 translates it so. Jowett (1953) I 77 = Hamilton and Cairns (1961) 127 simply leaves it untranslated, which may be best. The sense is either "braver . . . than he was before" (Sprague [1973] 18–19 = Cooper [1997] 668) or "braver . . . than he would otherwise be" (Lane [1987] 88).

[15] On the importance of fame and reputation, see Dover (1974) 226–29.

and Nicias, who are military men, and of Lysimachus and Melesias, who, along with everybody else, have been brought up on Homer, that about all there is to "virtue" or "excellence" is courage,[16] and Socrates does call this assumption into question, when he singles out courage as the *part* of virtue to be defined (with 190cd cf. 198ab, 199e).

This is elaborate, but otherwise typical. The definition is expected to resolve questions that are practical and concrete: should *these* individuals do *this, now*?

2.2.2. Protagoras

The *Protagoras* provides an even more elaborate introduction to a demand for definition, and then comes to a stop without making the attempt. At 360e–361d, just before the end of the dialogue, Socrates locates the source for the confusing reversal of positions that has taken place between himself and Protagoras in their failure to determine what virtue (or excellence) is: Protagoras had begun by claiming that excellence (virtue) was teachable (cf. 328c4) in the face of Socrates' doubts (cf. 319ab); now Socrates is arguing that virtue is knowledge, and so must be teachable, in the face of Protagoras' doubts (cf. Socrates' summary of the situation in 361a–c). The thing to do, according to Socrates, is start over, with the question "what is excellence?" (360e8, 361c5). But everybody, including Socrates, has something else to do (361d–362a) – despite the importance Socrates attaches to the enterprise (361d3–5): "it is by way of having forethought for my own entire life that I busy myself with all these things."

In this dialogue, just as in the *Laches*, the initial question is quite concrete: a certain Hippocrates,[17] excited by the prospect of studying under Protagoras, has gone to Socrates hoping for an introduction (see 310e). Socrates has qualms: these initiate a small-scale definition dialogue on the question "what is a sophist?" leading Hippocrates to the state of puzzlement normally induced by Socrates (311a–313c). Socrates essays a partial definition (313c), but leaves unanswered the crucial question whether study with Protagoras would be any good for Hippocrates, and with that question they go to Protagoras.

---

[16] There is no separate word in Homer for "courage": the word ἀγαθός, "good," often just means "courageous" (e.g., *Iliad* I 131, XVII 632; more subtly put, in the context of Homeric poetry, a man's goodness has as its leading ingredient courage). The idea that courage is pretty much all that counts in virtue survives in the fifth and fourth centuries: see Adkins (1972) 60–72, Dover (1974) 160–63, 164–65, Irwin (1977b) 19.

[17] About whom little is known: cf. Taylor (1976) 65 *ad* 310a9, but see now Nails (2002) 169–70.

As Socrates describes Hippocrates' goals to Protagoras, they are just those sought by Lysimachus and Melesias for their sons: success and acclaim (316b), and it is this that Protagoras translates into talk about excellence or virtue, which he professes to be able to teach. So the question here is almost exactly that of the *Laches*: there the question was whether the art of fighting in heavy armor would help someone achieve excellence and so public success, and here it is whether the art of fighting in heavy intellectual armor (to employ a Socratic way of putting it: see, e.g., *Euthydemus* 271c5–272b1, *Hippias Minor* 364a) is of any use in that direction.

2.2.3. Gorgias

Outside the *Protagoras* and the definition dialogues proper, no Socratic dialogue[18] comes to focus on a defining question, but there is one that pretends to have such a question as its focus: the *Gorgias*, cited in Thrasyllus' canon (Diogenes Laertius III 59) as "*Gorgias, or On Rhetoric.*"[19] "On Rhetoric" is a very inadequate guide to the content: the dialogue certainly begins with a build-up (447a–449a) to the defining question "what is rhetoric?" (under discussion from 449cd) via the question "what is Gorgias?" answered (at 449a) as "a rhetorician." But the question "what is rhetoric?" very nearly drowns. The dialogue, in effect, reverses the procedure of the *Protagoras*: where the *Protagoras* had worked toward the question "what is excellence?" the *Gorgias* works out from the question "what is rhetoric?" into the question "what sort of man should one be, and what should one take up, and how far?" (487e9–488a1), "in what way should one live?" (500c3–4),[20] for which we do not seem to require a prior definition of rhetoric.

It is possible to see other questions central to the *Gorgias*' treatment of living right as definition questions: the refutation of Callicles' identification of pleasure and the good (495d–499b) has a structure shared by many Socratic refutations of definitions. Similar comments could be made about definition questions or near-definition questions in many Socratic dialogues (cf., e.g., *Gorgias* 474d–475b, *Hippias Minor* 365b, *Euthydemus* 277e–278a). But the pattern I am discussing, of channeling real-life issues into a request

---

[18] But see n. 9. The *Amatores* asks "what is philosophy?" (133bc), the *Theages* "what is wisdom?" (121d, 122e, 123d: as Joyal [2000] 20 notes, this isn't quite the same), and the *Sisyphus* "what is deliberation?" (387d).

[19] More fully, "*Gorgias, or On Rhetoric*: refutative" (Γοργίας ἢ περὶ ῥητορικῆς, ἀνατρεπτικός, Long [1964] I 145.25–26, Marcovich [1999] I 9–10). Thrasyllus was court astrologer to Tiberius, who died in AD 36: see Tarrant (1993) 7–11.

[20] See Dodds (1959) 1–5.

for definition, is most clearly illustrated by the definition dialogues. I now return to them.

2.2.4. Charmides

The *Charmides* leads up to a series of attempts by Charmides and his uncle Critias to answer the question "what is temperance?" (or "self-control" or "moderation": σωφροσύνη, 159a3).[21] Here the concrete provoking question is whether Charmides himself is self-controlled or temperate.

It is hard, and I think it might be an error,[22] to read this in abstraction from the career of the "tyranny of the thirty" (404–403 BC), of which Charmides became an associate[23] and Critias an actual member: the thirty and their fellows were, it appears, notorious for their intemperance. The author of *Letter* VII is very big on the need for temperance in a statesman (see the letter's use of σώφρων: 326c4, 332e2, 336b1, c3, 351d2), and condemns these people in terms that suggest their lack of this virtue (see 324b–325a). Critias, if Xenophon is right (cf., e.g., *Hellenica* II 3. 50–56), was the worst of the thirty;[24] Xenophon is explicit and long-winded (*Memorabilia* I 2. 12–18, 24–38) about the contrast between Socrates and Critias on the score of temperance.

Even within the dialogue, Socrates, despite extreme provocation, is able to contain himself (see 155c–e), and Critias is not (162cd). And Chaerephon, who speaks the first words of the dialogue (which Socrates is narrating), is in

---

[21] I should have preferred the translation "self-control" (with Watt [1987b]: see esp. his pp. 165–66 with n. 5), but "self-control" has the drawback of including a direct reference to the self; nothing in the Greek suggests this, and particularly in this dialogue we must take great care over references to oneself. "Self-control" also makes for difficulty when we come to the word ἐγκράτεια, especially in the phrase ἐγκράτεια ἑαυτοῦ (*Republic* III 390b3), which has to be translated as "control of oneself" or "mastery of oneself": at IV 430e6–7 Socrates says that σωφροσύνη is a sort of ἐγκράτεια. Aristotle distinguishes ἐγκράτεια, "control," from σωφροσύνη, "temperance" (*Nicomachean Ethics* H 9. 1151^{b}32–1152^{a}3) on the ground that the former involves having base appetites and desires but controlling them, while the latter does not. Contrast, perhaps, Antiphon DK 87B58 (II 364.6–9; see Dover [1974] 118–19), where σωφροσύνη is described in terms that strongly suggest self-control (cf. Pendrick [2002] 405–6). For further discussion, see, e.g., Tuckey (1951) 8–9, Dover (1974) 66–69, Irwin (1977b) 20, Dover (1980) 110 *ad* 188a4 and 106 *ad* 186c1.

[22] See also Tuckey (1951) 14–17, 95–96, Santas (1973) 105–8, Rutherford (1995) 93–96, Schmid (1998) 10–14.

[23] He was, according to Xenophon, not one of the thirty, *pace* Jowett (1953) I 4, Sprague (1973) 54, Teloh (1986) 57 (referring to Santas [1973] 105: but Santas has it right), Watt (1987b) 167, Cooper (1997) 639, Wolfsdorf (1998) 130, Beversluis (2000) 135, 157 (further references in Nails [2002] 92). In *Hellenica* II 3. 2 Xenophon gives the list of thirty, and Charmides is not on it, although Critias is. But in *Hellenica* II 4. 19 he makes Charmides "one of the ten who ruled in the Piraeus."

[24] Cf. Nestle (1940) (1941 ed.) 400–420, Guthrie (1969) 298–304, Rankin (1983) 70–74, Nails (2002) 108–13.

a frenzy, as always (μανικὸς ὤν, 153b2; cf. *Apology* 21a3),[25] in the face of the monumental calm of Socrates (note the exchange between Chaerephon and Socrates at 153b4–c7), who has just returned from the grueling (see Thucydides I 63) fighting at Potidaea. Socrates enjoyed, in fact, a certain notoriety for his temperance (cf. Alcibiades in *Symposium* 216de and 219d, immediately followed by Alcibiades' description of Socrates' behavior at Potidaea, 219e–220e). And yet this presents something of a paradox: here is Socrates, whose expressed views include the idea that virtue is knowledge, but who never claims to know anything except when to avoid claiming knowledge. It is, I take it, no accident that the *Charmides*' most extended attempt to define this Socratic virtue works in terms of self-knowledge and the ability to distinguish what one doesn't know from what one does know (in 164d–175a).

This is a dialogue whose focus, the definition of temperance, is intended to shed light on the characters themselves. Its overarching question, to which the task of defining is subordinated, is explicit in the case of Charmides and implicit in the case of others: is this person temperate?

The *Laches* and *Protagoras* emphasized what we might call "worldly success" in the pursuit of virtue, and that puts in a brief appearance here (*Charmides* 157d–158d), although the virtue of self-control or temperance is considerably less showy than courage.

2.2.5. Euthyphro

The *Euthyphro* opens (2a–5d) with an obvious illustration of the practical aim of its attempt to define piety: Euthyphro claims his prosecution of his father for murder is an act of piety; Socrates is incredulous (4de), and asks Euthyphro to tell him what piety is (more detail in § 2.3.1).

2.2.6. Hippias Major

The *Hippias Major* is less obviously an example of the transition from practical questions to a request for definition than any of the definition dialogues, at least in many translations.[26] But the difficulty in seeing the pattern here is, in fact, mostly a difficulty in translation. The Greek word καλός and its cognates do not have natural translations into English that can be used uniformly.[27] In discussing the *Hippias Major*, I shall mostly

---

[25] For references on Chaerephon see Dodds (1959) 6, Nails (2002) 86–87.
[26] A notable exception is that of Woodruff (1982) 1–7, in Cooper (1997) 899–905.
[27] See Dover (1974) 69–73, Woodruff (1982) 109–11, Waterfield (1987) 217–18.

use "beautiful"; although that will, at times, make quite barbaric English, it will leave no question as to the relevance of Socrates' finally (at 286d1–2) springing on Hippias the question "what is the beautiful?"[28]

For, reviewing the preamble to that question (281a1–286d1), what we find is this.[29] The first words of the dialogue are: "Hippias, the beautiful and wise" (281a1: Ἱππίας ὁ καλός τε καὶ σοφός). At 282b1–2, Socrates says of Hippias' preceding words, "You seem to me to be phrasing it and conceiving it beautifully (καλῶς)." At d6, Hippias refers to "the beautiful {things}" (τῶν καλῶν) about being an itinerant teacher: he goes on to talk about how much money he makes at it. At e9, Socrates speaks of this as "*beautiful* (καλόν γε) . . . testimony" to Hippias' wisdom, and repeats the phrase at 283a8. At 284a3 he speaks of Hippias as "knowing most beautifully of men" (κάλλιστ' ἀνθρώπων ἐπίστασαι) how to impart virtue, and this phrase is picked up again in a4 and 285b8. And then, with less than a page to go before the question is popped, the occurrences of the word get dense: Hippias has a discourse put together "all-beautifully" (286a5, παγκάλως) on the subject of the "beautiful practices" (a3–4 περί γε ἐπιτηδευμάτων καλῶν, b1 καλὰ ἐπιτηδεύματα) which one ought to take up, including a list of "all-beautiful rules" (b4 νόμιμα . . . πάγκαλα) delivered by Nestor; his mention of this reminds Socrates "at a beautiful moment" (c5, εἰς καλόν) of a recent occasion on which he was extolling certain discourses as "beautiful" (c7) but was stopped by someone who wanted to know how he knew which things were "beautiful" (d1), and asked him if he could say what the beautiful was (d1–2, τί ἐστι τὸ καλόν). Socrates enlists the aid of Hippias, and we are off.

This passage by itself would be enough to show that in καλός we are dealing with an adjective of commendation with a high degree of generality. As a translation, "beautiful" is no good; but "good," which the *Oxford English Dictionary* notoriously characterizes as "the most general adjective of commendation, implying the existence in a high, or at least satisfactory, degree of characteristic qualities which are either admirable in themselves or useful for some purpose," is spoken for by ἀγαθός. There are questions

---

[28] Tarrant (1928) says (44 *ad* 286d τί ἐστι τὸ καλόν): "The main problem is at last stated; and its entry is felt to be somewhat abrupt, in spite of the repeated καλά in various forms that have come before." I cannot agree. For a better characterization, see Woodruff (1982) 43.

[29] The translation of this passage in Jowett (1953) I 565–71 (Hamilton and Cairns [1961] 1534–39), not Jowett's original, makes it impossible for the English reader to follow: the καλ- words and phrases here cited are translated as "beautiful," "fine," "charms," "better than anyone else," "great," "honorable," "in the nick of time." Perhaps the Jowett editors' note on Greek expressions for beauty and the beautiful (Jowett [1953] I 563–64) is supposed to rectify this (in fact it does not), but even that note is missing from Hamilton and Cairns (1961).

of great difficulty and moment here. For the most part, they are ethical questions, and we can edge past them. But a little must be said.

The word "beautiful" is a lousy translation for καλός. I do not find "fine," the translation of choice these days,[30] that much better. The words "admirable," "commendable," and "praiseworthy" are quite a bit better, to my ear, and they will come in for use occasionally in the sequel (mostly outside the discussion of the *Hippias Major*). But they are all misleading in the same way: they build into the word an implicit reference to a third person, doing or potentially doing some admiring, commending, or praising, and there is nothing in the morphology of the original word to correspond to this. Still, this is not as misleading as it might be, for the word καλός *does*, in Plato, point toward evaluation from a third-person point of view, while ἀγαθός, "good," points more toward evaluation from the point of view of the agent.[31]

If that is so, some of the things Socrates says that seem innocent at first sight are in fact substantive claims. At *Lysis* 216d2 there is the following exchange between him and Menexenus: "Well, I say that the good is beautiful; don't you think so too? – I certainly do." And he uses this to license replacing "beautiful" with "good" in the sequel.[32] In the *Laches* 192cd there is a similar conflation of "beautiful" with "good," and so also elsewhere, e.g., *Crito* 47c9–10, *Charmides* 160e6–12, *Euthyphro* 7c12–d2, *Gorgias* 459d1–2, *Republic* VI 493b8–c1, VII 520c5–6. These passages suggest that Socrates is identifying the notions of "beautiful" and "good," or supposing that what is beautiful coincides with what is good. I suspect the latter is the better way to put it, for if the above suggestion is right, the underlying claim is that what is commendable is good for the agent, and what is good for the agent is commendable. This is a substantive claim, for which the *Republic* and the *Gorgias* supply argument.

But in the other dialogues mentioned (except perhaps the *Charmides*) it is an unargued assumption. And it can be seen operating in the *Hippias Major*: in 304e2–3 Socrates makes the apparently extreme statement that as long as one remains ignorant of the beautiful, one would be better off dead.[33] The statement is quite a bit less extreme if we bear in mind that Socrates supposes knowledge of the beautiful to be connected to, if not the same as, knowledge of the good.

---

[30] Woodruff (1982), Waterfield (1987), and elsewhere.
[31] See Dodds (1959) 249–50, Adkins (1960) 163–64, Dover (1974) 69–73, Taylor (1976) 165–66, Woodruff (1982) 109–11, Stokes (1986) 42, 458 n. 13.
[32] See Irwin (1977b) 57, Irwin (1995) 46.   [33] Cf. Friedländer (1958/69) II 115.

So however we translate it, and whatever unexamined assumptions lie behind the affinity, the background question of the *Hippias Major* is at least a close cousin of that of the *Gorgias*: which things, and which people, are good, praiseworthy, commendable, admirable, "beautiful"?

In this dialogue the question is not less concrete than its parallels in the *Laches, Charmides,* and *Euthyphro,* but it is less concentrated: there, there is a single application or coherent set of applications of the term in question which the sought-for definition would clarify; here, the preamble provides about a dozen occurrences of cognates, any of which might be made the target of the attempted definition.

2.2.7. Lysis

The question that looks most like a definition question here occurs, as already noted (§ 1.1) in 212ab: "When someone loves someone, which becomes the lover of which . . .?"; Socrates understands this as the question, "what is the lover?" or, better, "what is the friend?"

The question is raised against a background of puzzles promulgated by Socrates himself: to the extent that they can be lumped together, the lump has to do with the question "how should one treat someone one loves?" (see, e.g., 204e–205a, 206bc, 207d–210e). Hippothales loves Lysis (although there is no indication that Lysis is even aware of this), and tries to ingratiate himself with Lysis (cf. 205b–d); Socrates' own approach is more in the parental style, in that he refuses to gratify Lysis (cf. 210e2–5), but this he takes to conflict with the initial idea (expressed in 207d5–e7) that loving someone involves promoting that person's happiness by granting his wishes. In the face of this conflict, Socrates wants to go back to fundamentals: he expresses ignorance as to how one person becomes[34] loved of another (212a5–6), and that leads to his question.

So the concrete questions on which the presumed definition would have a bearing are questions about the individuals Hippothales, Lysis, and Socrates: are they in fact friends, or not?

2.2.8. Republic *I*

Lastly, in *Republic* I, we encounter Cephalus, pleasant[35] but moribund, who, as he goes to meet his reward or otherwise (see 330d–331b), is given

---

[34] γίγνεται (212a5). This makes the question a trifle ambiguous, since it could be translated "turns out to be": it need not refer to winning friends, but just to the conditions under which one person turns out to be, or is as a matter of fact, a friend of another.

[35] According to Gifford (2001) 52–80, the appearance of pleasantness and justice is a sham.

to reflection on the extent to which he has met the demands of "justice" or "right" (see the frequent use of δίκη and cognates in his speech: 330d8, e1, e5, e6, 331a1, a4). His wealth[36] has been a great comfort, since it has enabled him to stay free of debt and deception (331b1–5). From this Socrates first (331c1–3) extracts an account of justice – justice is "truthfulness . . . and giving back what one has received from someone" – and then (c3–d3) argues for its inadequacy. Here the purported definition for justice has not come on the scene as an answer to the question "what is justice?" but the explicit question is the only thing missing. There is an explicit background question, "what good is being wealthy?" and the question implicitly raised by that is whether Cephalus is, in fact, just.

2.2.9. The importance of definition

The question of definition is always raised in the attempt to answer some other question of a more or less immediate nature. The Theory of Forms is going to come in as a response to difficulties that arise in the attempt to define things. This can lend itself to distortion: for some, it means that the Theory of Forms is of minor importance.[37] This is a mistake. The problem of defining justice (say) is subordinate to the question whether Cephalus is a just man only in the sense that questions of the latter sort are what provoke the former. The way in which they do that, in Socrates' estimation,[38] is that the immediate questions cannot be answered without the definition of justice. And the Theory of Forms, in Plato's estimation, is required if there is to be anything to define. So it is hardly of minor importance.

But we are still at the stage of defining things. So let us now ask: *why* does Socrates think we need these definitions if we are to answer the question how we ought to live?

2.3. THE INTELLECTUALIST ASSUMPTION

It is not easy to say whether learning to fight in heavy armor, or to make the worse argument appear the stronger (Aristotle's formulation of Protagoras' profession: *Rhetoric* B 24. 1402ª24–26),[39] will help bring on excellence.

---

[36] Which must have been fairly substantial: cf. Lysias, *Against Eratosthenes* 19 for an inventory of goods most of which must have been part of Cephalus' estate. See Dover (1968b) 29–30, Nails (2002) 84.

[37] Cf. treatments of the Theory such as that of Woodbridge (1929) or Randall (1970) (cf. esp. 188–200).

[38] Anyway, in Plato; but so also Aristotle (§ 1.2) and Xenophon (cf. *Memorabilia* I 1.16, IV 6.1).

[39] The phrase is attached to other sophists by Cicero, *Brutus* VIII 30. It is used in connection with Socrates: in the indictment against him as quoted by him in *Apology* 19b5–6 (cf. 18b8–c1: but not

Socrates thinks we need a definition to pronounce on these questions. He is sometimes fairly explicit about the kind of assumption he may be making here. In its strongest form, it is the following, which I shall call the "Intellectualist Assumption":[40]

> (IA) To know that . . . F —, one must be able to say what the F, or
> Fness, is.

For example: to know whether Euthyphro's prosecution of his father is a pious thing to do, one must be able to say what the pious, or piety, is; to know whether excellence can be taught, one must be able to say what excellence is.

This assumption is too strong. It is, for one thing, simply false: we can tell which things on the table are books without being able to say what a book is, at least in the sense of being able to give a definition that would satisfy Substitutivity, (S) in § 2.1 above; even the *Oxford English Dictionary*, *s.v.* "book," in the course of over six columns of defining, fails to provide anything like that. And our ability to tell is not confined to cases in which we are dealing with straightforwardly perceptible items[41] like books; we are also able unhesitatingly to identify central cases of courage and central cases in which this is lacking. And if this doesn't count as knowledge, it is difficult to see why.[42] We also know perfectly well that courage (as opposed to rashness) is in general a good thing. We possess a good deal of pretheoretical knowledge about anything for which we have concepts; that is at least a part of what it is to have the concepts.

---

in the version of the indictment given by Xenophon, *Memorabilia* I 1.1; cf. Xenophon, *Apology* 10 and Diogenes Laertius II 40, Long [1964], 73.20–22, Marcovich [1999] I 119.18–120.1), and in Aristophanes' *Clouds* 882–884, 893–894, to which Socrates refers in Plato's *Apology* (19b: but he does not say, *pace* Cope and Sandys [1877] II 321, that Aristophanes was "its original author"). See Grote (1846/56) (1899/1900 ed.) VIII 362–64.

[40] It is part of what is widely referred to in the literature as the "Socratic fallacy," after Geach (1966) 371 saw it in the *Euthyphro*. Woodruff (1987) 79 (cf. Woodruff [1982] 140) refers to (IA) as the "principle of the *priority of definition*"; so also Nehamas (1986) 277 n. 6 = (1999) 51 n. 5, 290, Benson (1990) 19, Prior (1998) 98; Brickhouse and Smith (2000): "the *Priority of Definitional Knowledge*"; so also Benson (2000) 112 and *passim*.

Where I see (IA), Dreyfus (1990) (esp. 10–15) sees the source of what he calls cognitivism. Matson and Leite (1991) demur, but they (146) opt for the (to me quite improbable) suggestion that Socrates wanted to show that definitions are "*impossible*" (their italics). McDonough (1991) also protests against Dreyfus's claims, but he appeals mainly to the *Statesman* (303–305).

[41] As Prior (1998) 104 seems to imply.

[42] Prior (1998) (see esp. 107–9) beefs up the requirements for (Platonic) knowledge by making (IA) one of them. I do not see that he provides any real independent motivation for this; it is certainly no argument for it that Aristotle accepted it or something like it. And the fact that someone who claims knowledge can be expected "to provide some rational explanation of the fact known" (107) doesn't mean that such a person must do any defining. Prior (103–4) says that it does, but see text below.

There are actually two stages of error built into (IA), as we can see if we consider the fact that someone who makes a claim of the form "*x* is *F* " may, particularly if the claim is somewhat borderline (as is, e.g., Euthyphro's), justly be asked to explain why we should suppose the claim true. First, (IA) assumes that any such explanation must ultimately be based on a definition: a direct answer to the question "what is *F*ness?" But, in fact, there are lots of theories that do not take that form at all, e.g., Rawls's theory in *A Theory of Justice*.[43] So it is perfectly possible to undertake the justification of a questionable claim of the form "*x* is *F* " without basing that justification on a definition for *F*ness. But, second, it is perfectly possible to undertake a justification of a claim of that sort without having any theory of *F*ness at all. I take it we do this all the time. Such pretheoretical justifications may point the way toward a theory of *F*ness, but they do not in any clear sense presuppose such a theory.

But the problem is not just that the Intellectualist Assumption is false; more disastrously, it cannot be true if Socrates' task of defining is to be successfully performed, for that depends on our knowing things in advance. For example, the easiest way to see that the attempt to define "book" as "a written narrative"[44] must fail is to reflect that the book one is holding is a dictionary, and so not a narrative at all; and this requires one to know that what one is holding is a book, without yet (presumably) being able to say what a book is. Suppose you and I encountered a word quite new to both of us, say, "decacuminate," and neither of us has the faintest notion whether this, that, or the other is decacuminated or not. A discussion between us of the question "what is decacumination?" is foredoomed to failure.[45] If the Intellectualist Assumption were correct, that would be the predicament we would be in when we tried to say what courage is: if we did not already know, we would know nothing whatever about courage or things courageous; we would have only the word in common, as we do with "decacuminate." A search for a definition would never succeed unless one of the participants was already in a position to give it.

There is a weaker, and consequently less implausible, version of the assumption that comes of replacing "be able to say" in it by "know":

(IA_1) To know that . . . *F* —, one must know what the *F*, or *F*ness, is.

---

[43] See Rawls (1971) 51 = (1999) 44: "A theory of justice is subject to the same rules of method as other theories. Definitions and analyses of meaning do not have a special place: definition is but one device used in setting up the general structure of theory."

[44] A definition that, as I seem to recall, appeared in an older edition of *Webster's New Collegiate Dictionary*.

[45] Unless one of us recalled his or her Latin: *cacumen* means "top," as in the top of a tree. In the *Meno*, Socrates is going to resort to something rather like this strategy.

The original assumption, (IA), can be seen as a composite of this and a principle of expressibility:[46]

(PE) One can always say what one knows.

One natural response to the composite (IA) is that its fault lies in its second component, (PE):[47] I may not be able to *say* what a book is, especially if what is required is the philosopher's format for a definition, but my ability to tell a book from a bell or a candle shows, one might say, that I *know* what a book is.

In fact, this way of rendering (IA$_1$) plausible seems to me dangerously unclear. What is not clear is the nature of the knowledge that is attributed to me. If it is of the sort sometimes referred to as "tacit" knowledge,[48] (IA$_1$) may turn out to be true because it is trivial. For this sort of knowledge seems simply to *consist* in my ability to tell books from bells and candles. Saying that I know what a book is, on this line, is only redescribing my discriminatory capacities, registering the fact that sometimes or often I can tell that . . . book —: that this is a book, that that is not a book, that books generally weigh more than individual pieces of paper, that, at least before the computer age, books were required for education, etc.

But surely any defender of (IA$_1$) would want more out of it than that. It sounds like a substantive claim: in particular, it sounds as if it is supposed to *explain* one's ability to tell that . . . book —, instead of simply saying that to have that ability one must have that ability. But then it is no longer clear whether it is true. And, unfortunately, I know no way of making it true without making it trivial.

We can break (IA$_1$) down further. The sentences for which ". . . *F* —" stands in may have all sorts of different structures; two in particular crop up in our texts. Most commonly "*F*" is in predicate position: the question is whether this action is pious, or that man is temperate. But sometimes it figures, syntactically transformed, as the subject term: the question is whether excellence can be taught, or whether justice is any good to the person who has it, and these questions require definitions of excellence and justice, respectively. We have, then, predicate versions and subject versions of (IA$_1$).[49]

---

[46] See here Sesonske (1963) 3–4 (Sesonske and Fleming [1965] 84–85); Benson (1990) 20 n. 2, (2000) 114, calls this "the verbalization requirement."

[47] Benson (1990) 29 n. 20 says this; see also Benson (2000) 114.

[48] And vigorously defended by the Chomskians. See Fodor (1968), esp. 638, for a formulation of the idea.

[49] See also Beversluis (1987) 211–12 = Benson (1992) 107–8, Nehamas (1986) 277–80 with 280 n. 10 = (1999) 28–30 with 51 n. 9, Benson (1990) 20 (in n. 2), Prior (1998) 100.

How many of these claims does Socrates adopt?[50] In the dialogues here counted as Socratic, all of them; we'll shortly be looking at the texts. That leads to a problem: it is a consequence of (IA) that we cannot know that this, that, or the other action is courageous without being able to say what courage is. But we need to know things of this kind if we are ever to say what courage is. And Socrates himself will be found accepting examples of that kind in the course of attempting to find out what courage is. So, on the face of it, his procedures stand in contradiction to his principles.

Socrates, at least before the *Meno*, shows no awareness of this fact; the *Meno*, however, makes a great deal of it. That is going to be of importance for my story; as I see it, the *Meno* rejects (IA_1). But from the present vantage-point, it is worth remarking that the conflict between (IA_1) and Socrates' practice of evaluating proposed *definientia* is masked. For outright claims of knowledge about the matters he discusses in his quest for definitions are virtually nonexistent.[51] At *Apology* 29b6–7 Socrates, having said that he doesn't know much about matters in Hades, adds:[52] "but that to do injustice and to disobey one's superior, whether god or man, I know is bad and shameful." And that's about it.[53] That isn't much, and besides, first, it is not in the context of definition-hunting, and second, Socrates says nothing to indicate his commitment to (IA) or (IA_1) in the *Apology*.

---

[50] According to Vlastos (1985) 23–26 (expanded in Vlastos [1990] and again in Vlastos [1994] 67–86), not all of them, and according to Beversluis (1987), none at all. This is in part because Vlastos has adopted a chronological hypothesis according to which the *Lysis* and *Hippias Major* are transitional between the Socratic dialogues and the middle dialogues and *Republic* I 354a12–c3 has been "tacked on at the end of Book I" (Vlastos [1985] 26 n. 65; cf. [1990] 15 n. 31 = [1994] 81 n. 41: see n. 76 below), and Beversluis follows him. (Contrast Beversluis [1974] 334ab.) But mainly it has to do with the fact that Vlastos is prepared to see two senses of "know," in one of which (IA) is acceptable and in the other of which it is not.

The chronological consideration is, for my purposes, largely irrelevant. My question has to do with the emergence of the Theory of Forms, and according to both these authors, the *Lysis* and *Hippias Major* precede the dialogues in which that happens. So the views Socrates espouses in these dialogues are part of the background for that emergence, and among those views, according to Vlastos (1985) 23 n. 54 (cf. [1990] 3 = [1994] 71) and Beversluis (1987) 221 n. 4, is (IA_1).

[51] See here Vlastos (1985) 6–11 = Vlastos (1994) 43–48. Matson and Leite (1991) 151 import the verb "know" into contexts in which it does not in fact occur.

[52] This passage, to which Irwin (1977b) 58 called attention, has gained a certain notoriety since Vlastos (1985) 7, 11 = Vlastos (1994) 43–44, 48 placed so much weight on it; see Irwin (1995) 28–29, 358 n. 37.

[53] There is an exhaustive list of Socrates' claims to know things in the *Apology* in Reeve (1989) 54–55. Most of them require a certain amount of work to bring them into conflict with (IA_1): e.g., *Apology* 37b5–8 implies, for each of several alternatives to the death penalty (alternatives such as going into exile), that he knows it is bad (Brickhouse and Smith [1994] 127 list this as a case of Socrates professing "actually to *know* things of moral importance"; cf. also Brickhouse and Smith [2000] 103). And we may well suppose that 21d (along with other passages listed by Reeve [1989] 54), although it doesn't say so outright, implies that Socrates does not know what badness is. If we accept these implications, Socrates is in conflict with (IA_1).

Still, the difficulty is only a little below the surface in dialogues in which (IA) or (IA$_1$) are in play. If the analyses below are correct, those dialogues are *Euthyphro, Hippias Major, Republic* I, *Laches, Protagoras, Charmides,* and *Lysis.*

Then consider, for example, the following passages in which definition hunting is at stake. At *Euthyphro* 6d6–7, Socrates suggests that he and Euthyphro would agree that there are many pious things. In the *Hippias Major,* Socrates gets Hippias to agree that there are beautiful mares, lyres, and pots (288c–289a). In *Republic* I 350cd, Socrates explains how he managed to get Thrasymachus to accept that "the just {man} has become manifest to us as being good and wise" (c10–11). In *Laches* 191de, Socrates explains to Laches why his answer to the defining question about courage was too narrow: it included only those who are courageous in war, but not those who are courageous amid dangers at sea, in the face of disease, poverty, and so on,

> SOC: . . . for I dare say, Laches, there are some courageous {people} even in such {matters}.
> LACH: And very {courageous}, Socrates.
> SOC: Then all these {people} are courageous. (191e1–4)

And Laches of course agrees. Similar claims are made in every one of these dialogues.

But none of them is made with the verb "know" attached. So the contradiction between (IA$_1$) and what Socrates is saying is not a formal contradiction; we don't have Socrates saying anything like:

(IA$_1$C) We can't know whether these people are courageous without knowing what courage is, and

(¬KC) we don't know what courage is, but

(Kc)   we do know that these people are courageous.

That would give us a formal contradiction. The most Socrates will say is not (Kc), but

(c) these people are courageous,

and from that with (IA$_1$C) and (¬KC) no contradiction can be derived.

Still, if I unhesitatingly state (c), there is something distinctly odd about my going on "but, of course, I don't know that." And Socrates and Laches *are* unhesitatingly stating (c). Although no one ever does this in a Socratic dialogue (or even in the *Meno*), a clever interlocutor might perfectly well have responded to Socrates' efforts to gather premises for his refutations by saying: but look, Socrates, by your own lights, you can't know that these men are courageous. So what right do you have to say that they are?

If Socrates were John Rawls, he might think of (c) as a "considered moral judgment," to be kept going as long as is feasible, but in principle capable of being turned off, if the theory ultimately fails to confirm it.[54] Frankly, I cannot imagine what it would be like to give up the belief that there are people at sea who are courageous, or the belief that a person who risks his life to save someone who has fallen overboard is courageous, and so I cannot fathom why anyone would want to deny knowing these things. So, although I find this strategy quite implausible in these cases, it is there if anyone wants it. I'm going to suppose that Socrates' procedures do conflict, in the way described, with his professions. There is an interpretative principle of charity adopted by many scholars:[55] do not read a position in such a way that it involves inconsistency, if there are viable alternatives. The trouble is that here no alternatives seem to me really viable.

Various attempts have been made to read the dialogues in a way that gets around the apparent conflict between Socrates' claims and his practice.[56] The way I'm going to read them, the conflict is there, and is one of the driving forces tending toward the theory of recollection we find in the *Meno.* Attempts to make Socrates come out smelling like roses will be dealt with along the way. But a Socrates who is inconsistent on this score strikes me as more interesting[57] than these consistent ones.

Since (IA) (see n. 40) was first discerned in the *Euthyphro,* I start with that.

[54] Rawls (1971) 20 = (1999) 18: "These convictions are provisional fixed points which we presume any conception of justice must fit . . . even the judgments we take provisionally as fixed points are liable to revision."

[55] Explicitly stated by Brickhouse and Smith (2000) 5: "Other things being equal, the interpretation that provides a more interesting or more plausible view is preferable." Such a principle plainly underlies a great deal of the work of Vlastos, not simply in the area under discussion, but elsewhere as well: see, e.g., Vlastos (1965).

[56] Santas (1972) 140–41, Santas (1979) 69–70, 116–17, Burnyeat (1977b) 386–87, Irwin (1977b) 40–41, Teloh (1981) 20–21, Woodruff (1982) 139–40, Prior (1998), etc.: we can allow ourselves true beliefs to the effect that this or that action is courageous without having knowledge, for which a definition is required. Vlastos (1985), (1990) = (1994): there are different senses of "know." Beversluis (1987), Brickhouse and Smith (1994) 55–60, and, less exhaustively, (2000) 113–17: no Socratic dialogue maintains (IA).

[57] Cf. Brickhouse and Smith's formulation of the principle of charity, n. 55 above.

2.3.1. Euthyphro

The passages in the *Euthyphro* bearing on the question of Socrates' acceptance of (IA) do not *plainly* bear on it.[58] Here they are.[59]

Euthyphro tells us that his relatives are angry with him (4d9–e8):

{4d9} EUTH: . . . for {they say} it is impious for a son to prosecute his father for murder – {they say this} knowing badly, Socrates, how the divine stands concerning the pious and the impious.[60]

{e4} SOC: But, Euthyphro, you, then, by Zeus, think you know so accurately concerning things divine how they stand and things pious and impious that, since things have happened as you say, you are not afraid that in trying your father you are in turn doing an impious thing?

Let us consider carefully what each of Euthyphro and Socrates is here saying.

The participial phrase "knowing badly how the divine stands" uses a "circumstantial participle," and these are fairly vague.[61] One common way of reading them is as causal, and then Euthyphro's speech could have been translated "for {they say} it is impious for a son to prosecute his father for murder, since they know badly, Socrates, how the divine stands concerning the pious and the impious." Or, again:[62] "for {they say} it is impious for a son to prosecute his father for murder, which shows that they know badly, Socrates, how the divine stands concerning the pious and the impious." Either of these translations makes things more precise than they are in the Greek; the translation given above tries to maintain the vagueness.

Given the vagueness, all that Euthyphro outright says is that his relatives say what they do in a state of not knowing about the pious (assuming, that is, that "knowing badly" is not knowing). But plainly these are not supposed to be two independent facts about them: their saying what they do is connected with their ignorance. And then the alternative translations

---

[58] Geach (1966) 371 may have christened (IA) "the Socratic fallacy" in a paper on the *Euthyphro*, but Robinson (1953) 51 also saw it there (in both cases, at 6e, discussed a little below). These are primary targets of Santas (1972) (see 127–29), and I at least agree that the *Euthyphro* cannot, without argument, be taken as employing (IA).

[59] My treatment of these passages owes a lot to Benson (1990) 28–37.

[60] Grube's translation, reprinted in Cooper (1997) 4, reads: "For, they say, it is impious for a son to prosecute his father for murder. But their ideas of the divine attitude to piety and impiety are wrong, Socrates." This fails to include Euthyphro's reference to the state of his relatives' knowledge, and that, for my purposes is what is important.

[61] Smyth (1956) 457 § 2060: "The circumstantial participle expresses simply circumstance or manner in general. It may imply various other relations, such as *time, manner, means, cause, purpose, concession, condition*, etc. But it is often impossible to assign a participle exclusively to any one of these relations (which are purely logical), nor can all the delicate relations of the participle be set forth in systematic form."

[62] This is the way it is translated in Fowler (1914) 15 and Jowett (1953) I 312.

pretty clearly capture what the connection must be: he is attributing his relatives' saying those things to their lack of knowledge: if his relatives knew "how the divine stands concerning the pious and the impious," they wouldn't say that it was impious for a son to prosecute his father for murder.

As Socrates hears Euthyphro, Euthyphro is saying that he must suppose that, in contrast to his relatives, he does know how the divine stands concerning the pious and impious, since he is about to prosecute his father but is not afraid that this is impious.

We are shortly to see good reason to read the ponderous phrase "knowing how the divine stands concerning the pious and the impious" as simply "knowing what the pious is"; let us anticipate that. And let us abbreviate "prosecuting one's father for murder" as "p." Then Euthyphro's claim is an instance of:

(E) x thinks that p is impious $\rightarrow$ x does not know what the pious is,

and Socrates' an instance of:

(S) x is not afraid that p is impious $\rightarrow$ x at least thinks he knows what the pious is.

What is the relationship between these claims and (IA)?

Now (E) is logically equivalent to its contraposition:

(E′) x knows what the pious is $\rightarrow$ x does not think that p is impious,

and it is impossible to believe that Euthyphro is not committed to this; one of the above paraphrases was precisely to the effect that if Euthyphro's relatives had the requisite knowledge, they wouldn't say what they do say.

Again, Euthyphro is plainly presupposing that p is not impious; we can eliminate some of the build-up of negations if we take him to be supposing that p is simply pious, and that he is committed to (E′) because he supposes:

(E″) x knows what the pious is $\rightarrow$ x knows that p is pious.

Notice how little this differs from what Euthyphro outright says: according to (E″), if Euthyphro's relatives did know what the pious is, they'd know that p is pious, whereas what Euthyphro says is that they say that p isn't pious because they don't know what the pious is.

Now consider (S). Its antecedent is "x is not afraid that p is impious"; we can replace that, in the spirit of reducing negations and making the claims as comparable as possible, with "x thinks he knows that p is pious." That turns (S) into:

(S') x thinks he knows that p is pious → x thinks he knows what the pious is.

Sentential contexts containing words like "think" and "know" present astonishingly difficult logical problems, but an extremely natural presupposition that would support (S') is:

(S'') x knows that p is pious → x knows what the pious is.

And it is also natural to suppose that, in this context, this is a presupposition shared by Socrates and Euthyphro.

That puts (E) and (S) in forms that enable us to compare them with (IA) and (IA$_I$). For this purpose, we may replace (IA$_I$) with the conditional it clearly entails:

(IA') x knows . . . F — → x knows what the F is.

And then it is immediately clear that (S'') is an instance of (IA'), and that (E'') is not, but of its converse:

(IA'c) x knows what the F is → x knows . . . F —.

Euthyphro has committed himself to the claim that knowledge of what the pious is is a *sufficient* condition for knowing that p is pious, and Socrates went from that to the claim that knowledge of what the pious is is a *necessary* condition for knowing that p is pious; the former is an instantiation of (IA'c), and the latter of (IA').

So (E) and (S) are not equivalent, and I take it the important difference between them is what has emerged in (E'') and (S''). Still, fairly plainly (E) suggests (S) to Socrates. So he could merely be going along with what he hears Euthyphro saying, and not claiming (S) on his own at all.[63] But he can only be doing that if he is paying no attention to the difference between (E'') and (S''). The importance of this is that it blocks a strategy[64] that might have got Socrates out of commitment to (IA), as we shall see.

Does it make sense to suppose that Socrates is paying no attention to the difference between (E'') and (S'')? Surely it does. Although what Euthyphro says logically commits him at most to (E''), as Socrates hears him the two go together: Euthyphro's relatives think what they do about p in a state of ignorance, and knowing that p is in fact pious requires the elimination of that ignorance, that is, knowing what the pious is.

So it is possible that Socrates is only going along with what he takes Euthyphro to be suggesting. But consider 5cd, which takes us a step farther.

---

[63] So Matson and Leite (1991) 149–50.　　[64] That of Brickhouse and Smith (1994) 47–49; see below.

Socrates has pointed out that he himself is being tried on a charge part of which could be construed as impiety, and so he needs to learn from Euthyphro; he says (5c8–d5):

> {5c8} So now, by Zeus, tell me what you just now affirmed you clearly know: what sort of thing do you say the reverent and the irreverent are,[65] both concerning murder and concerning the other {matters}?
> {d1} Or isn't the pious the same as itself in every action, and the impious, again, the contrary of the pious in its entirety, but like itself and everything whatever that is to be impious having, with respect to its impiety, some one idea?

The reference in 5c8–9 to Euthyphro's having "just now" affirmed that he clearly knew something is to 4de, just quoted. There the phrase was "knowing how the divine stands concerning the pious and the impious"; here it is "knowing what (sort of thing)" the pious is: this is where it becomes plain that our substitution of "knowing what the pious is" for "knowing how the divine stands concerning the pious" was allowable.

And we have one other thing in addition: Socrates pretty clearly presupposes in 5c8–9 that, if Euthyphro knows what the pious is, he can say what it is: this is an instance of (PE), and that gives us all of (IA).

Consider now 6de; Euthyphro has just made a stab at saying what the pious is; Socrates' response to it is (6d6–e7):

> {6d6} SOC: . . . But, Euthyphro, many other things you would say are pious as well.
> EUTH: For they too are {pious}.
> {d9} SOC: Then do you remember that I did not direct you to teach me some one or two of the many pious things, but that form itself by which all the pious things are pious?
> {d11/e} For you said, I think,[66] that it is by one idea that the impious things are impious and the pious things pious; or don't you recall?
> EUTH: I certainly do.
> {e2} SOC: Then teach me this idea, what it is, so that looking to it and using it as a standard, whatever is such as it is among the things either you or anyone else does, I shall say is pious, and whatever is not such, I shall say {is} not.

For now consider only what Socrates wants to do with the correct answer to the question "what is the pious?"; that this is what he is after is assured by the fact that when at d11–e1 he reminds Euthyphro of what he had said,

---

[65] 5c9 ποῖόν τι τὸ εὐσεβὲς φῂς εἶναι: on the terms ὅσιον and εὐσεβές see Walker (1984) 64–65.

[66] The reference is to Euthyphro's assent at 5d6, but there he had only conceded that there is one "idea" for all cases of piety, and one for all cases of impiety; nothing was said to the effect that it was "by" this one idea that pious things are pious.

the reference is to Euthyphro's positive response to the question at 5d1–5. Socrates wants to use the definition to determine which actions are pious and which aren't. And this is Socrates himself talking: he is no longer (if he ever was) just going along with what he took Euthyphro to be assuming. But, it will be said,[67] all that Socrates here says is that if he had the right answer to the question "what is the pious?" he could use it to determine whether various actions were pious. That only makes the knowledge what the pious is a sufficient condition for knowing which actions are pious, not a necessary one, and (IA), construed as (IA′), makes it a necessary condition.

That's true. So if we were to charge Socrates with subscribing to (IA), he might duck the charge by saying: at 4de, I was merely making explicit an assumption I took Euthyphro to be making, to the effect that he was in a position to tell that prosecuting his father under these circumstances was not impious on the basis of knowing what the pious is. At 6de, on the other hand, I was endorsing a different assumption, namely, that knowing what the pious is will enable you to tell which actions are pious and which aren't.

What this shows is that, if Socrates is prepared to draw this distinction, he can get off the hook. But we've already seen that what he said in 4de presupposed that that distinction wasn't in play. It was *Socrates* who made knowing what the pious is a necessary condition for knowing that p is not impious, whereas *Euthyphro* had only committed himself to its being a sufficient condition: if his relatives *had* known what the pious was, they wouldn't have supposed p to be impious.

So it looks as if Socrates is committed to an instance of (IA). And there is another smoking gun at 15c–e where Socrates proposes starting over on the question "what the pious is" (15c11–12), since (he says, d2–3) Euthyphro knows the answer if anyone does. He justifies this claim with (d4–e1):

For if you did not clearly know the pious and the impious, it would not ever have been possible for you to try to prosecute your father, an old man, on behalf of a servant, for murder, but you would have been in fear of the gods for taking the risk, lest you should be acting not rightly, and ashamed before men; but as things are I know that you think you know the pious and what isn't clearly.

Here "knowing the pious" and "knowing what the pious is" are clearly interchangeable, and Socrates is saying that if Euthyphro didn't think he knew what the pious was he would never have undertaken to prosecute his

---

[67] Brickhouse and Smith (1994) 49 say it; cf. Brickhouse and Smith (2000) 116–17. This makes it sound as if the converse of (IA), or of (IA₁), were weaker and therefore more defensible than (IA) or (IA₁) itself. It would be distracting to go into this now, but surely it isn't so (and, I take it, Brickhouse and Smith [1994] 61–64 are in agreement).

father. And that must be because then he wouldn't have known that doing that wasn't impious: the knowledge of what's pious and what isn't requires knowing what the pious and the impious are.[68] And Socrates is still plainly presupposing that, if Euthyphro knows what the pious is, he can say what it is.

2.3.2. Hippias Major

According to Socrates, the questions he puts to Hippias actually stem from someone else.[69] Here is how the defining question makes its entrance (286c5–d2):

Recently, someone threw me into puzzlement when I was censuring some things in certain discourses as ugly, and praising others as beautiful, by asking, quite insolently indeed, something like this: I say, Socrates, how do *you* know which are beautiful or ugly? For come, would you be able to say what the beautiful is?

The suggestion is certainly clear that Socrates' profession to distinguish the beautiful passages from the ugly must be based on his being able to say what the beautiful is: on his having an articulate definition for "beautiful."[70]

[68] I am with Benson (1990) 36–37 n. 33, (2000) 126 n. 57 in failing to understand the claim of Vlastos (1985) 23 n. 54 (not in Vlastos [1994]) and Beversluis (1987) 215 (= Benson [1992] 112) that this passage only commits Socrates to the idea that knowing what the pious is is sufficient for knowing that *p* is not impious. Brickhouse and Smith (1994) 48 cite this passage, which they paraphrase as follows: "Socrates says that Euthyphro would not have prosecuted his own father if he did not regard himself as knowing what the holy is." They explain it as follows (but the italics are mine): "Socrates is challenging Euthyphro to show what puts Euthyphro in the position of being able to judge cases *like* this one. Nothing Socrates says rules out that Euthyphro has some special and specific knowledge pertinent to *this* one case." But if Euthyphro did have "some special and specific knowledge" to the effect that prosecuting his father under the current circumstances was not a case of unholiness or impiety, he would not have had to "regard himself as knowing what the holy is" in order to go ahead with it: this is flatly in contradiction with their own paraphrase.

[69] In Tarrant (1928) xiii, 44 *ad* 286c, and 87 *ad* 304d this device becomes a count against the authenticity of the dialogue. See Woodruff (1982) 43–44 n. 47.

[70] So also Ross (1951) 16. Santas (1972) 136–37 tries to soften the force of the passage so that it only makes Socrates' interlocutor suggest that a definition would (perhaps) help him "support his praise of certain parts of speeches as beautiful" (137). This seems to me inadequate to the passage quoted: the interlocutor is making an inference from what he hears Socrates doing, not offering him help.

Brickhouse and Smith (1994) 46–47 here apply their main device for getting Socrates off the hook: they say that Socrates is only counting the possession of a definition as a prerequisite for setting oneself up as an expert in the area; it is perfectly possible, on their account, for someone who has no definition to know that various *specific* judgments about whether something is, say, beautiful, are correct. Their favored examples of how this might be so are divination (39) and divine authority (52; see also 189–201). And they lump the passage just quoted under this heading. But it hardly appears as if Socrates' anonymous interlocutor is there leaving room for any such option: Socrates has, by his own account, been describing perfectly *specific* passages as ugly and other passages as beautiful, and the interlocutor is pretty strongly suggesting that if Socrates is in a position to say that *these* passages are beautiful and *those* ugly, Socrates must have an answer to the question "what is the beautiful?"

That suggestion is supported later in the dialogue. At 298b11, Socrates' importunate interlocutor is identified as "the son of Sophroniscus," i.e., as Socrates himself; there Socrates says that this person would no more allow him to get away with certain evasive tactics recommended by Hippias than he allows Socrates to say "things I do not know as if I knew them" (298c1–2).[71] Presumably this refers back to 286cd, just quoted: the interlocutor there was catching Socrates saying things he did not know as if he knew them. Then Socrates is being taken to have claimed knowledge: knowledge of which passages are beautiful, in the first instance, but then his inability to say what the beautiful is is supposed to show that he does not know what it is, and hence does not know which passages are beautiful.

Finally, at 304cd, Socrates speaks of his interlocutor as a close relative, who lives in the same house, and subjects him to refutation when he brings home the wisdom of such people as Hippias. Socrates says (304d4–e3, italics added):[72]

accordingly, when I go home, to my own house, and he hears me saying these things, he asks if I am not ashamed, daring to talk about beautiful practices when it has been shown so plainly, when I've been refuted concerning the beautiful, that I don't even know what this itself is. And yet, he says, *how will you know who has performed a discourse beautifully or not, or any other action, when you are ignorant of the beautiful?* And while you are so disposed, do you think it is better for you to live than to be dead?[73]

The first of these passages (286cd) seems to be employing the full-scale, composite Intellectualist Assumption. The third (304de) only gives us (IA₁),[74] but there is nothing to suggest that Socrates, in either of his personae, would distinguish (IA₁) from (IA): indeed, the second passage (298bc) suggests precisely the opposite.[75]

---

[71] Brickhouse and Smith (1994) do not cite this passage.

[72] This passage is not mentioned in either Santas (1972) or Santas (1979).

[73] I don't understand how Brickhouse and Smith (1994) 46–47 propose to take this passage. They want to write it off as hyperbole, and there is indeed hyperbole there, but not where they see it: it is in the claim that those who cannot say what the beautiful is are better off dead, not in the claim that those who cannot say what the beautiful is can't tell whether someone has performed a discourse beautifully.

[74] It might give us a little more, if Vlastos (1985) 25 is right about 304e2–3, taking it to imply that not knowing what τὸ καλόν would disqualify Socrates from *being* καλός: so we should have in the *Hippias Major* the very strong assumption underlying the *Charmides* (§ 2.3.6).
    Nehamas (1986) 288 n. 30 = (1999) 53 n. 29 objects that "Most people, according to Plato, are ignorant of the definition of the virtues, yet the life they lead in the *Republic* is not only preferable to death, but as good a life as a human being can live." This does not seem to me to cut much ice one way or the other.

[75] Nehamas (1986) 287 tries to water down the first and third passages: "The emphasis is not on the recognition of individual instances of the fine. On the contrary, it seems to me, the questioner seems

2.3.3. Republic *I*

At the end of *Republic* I, we find a statement of (IA₁) with the term to be defined in subject position. Socrates sums up the unsatisfactory course of the preceding dialogue as follows (*Republic* I 354b1–c3):[76]

just as gluttons snatch at everything as it is served to taste it before they have properly enjoyed the one before, so I seem to myself {to have acted}: before finding the first thing we inquired about, the just, what it {b5} is, I let go of that and pushed on to inquiring about whether it is vice and ignorance, or wisdom and excellence; and later, when there fell on us the account that injustice was more profitable than justice, I did not restrain myself from turning from this to that, so that now it has turned out for me, as a result of the discussion, that I {c} know nothing. For when I don't know what the just is, I shall hardly know whether it is in fact an excellence or not, and whether he who has it is not happy or happy.[77]

to ask whether Socrates can tell *in general* what is and isn't fine without knowing what the fine is. Alternatively, the questioner suggests that Socrates cannot defend his praise and fault-finding (ἐπαινοῦντα . . . ψέγοντα) and cannot justify his discoursing (διαλέγεσθαι) on the subject without knowing the definition." But, at least in the first passage, Socrates has been discussing "parts of some speeches" (the translation in Woodruff [1982] 7, cited by Nehamas; translated above as "some things in certain discourses"), calling some foul and others fine (above "ugly" and "beautiful"). The interlocutor sees that as presupposing that Socrates can, in general, tell the difference, and that in turn as presupposing that he can define the fine (beautiful). So we are back to requiring a definition to "recognize individual instances of the fine."

[76] This passage is connected by most commentators, whether or not they think of book I as a separate Socratic dialogue, with what I am calling the "Intellectualist Assumption"; Guthrie is an exception (the passage is simply dropped from his paraphrase: Guthrie [1975] 442, 443), but cf. Adam (1902) I 61, Shorey (1930/35) 107 n. *d*, Friedländer (1958/69) II 65, White (1979) 72–73 (also White [1976] 11–12). Santas (1972) 129 n. mentions the passage but seems to feel that since Socrates had earlier argued for the claim that justice was an excellence, there is no need to take it seriously. In fact, the tone seems to me precisely the opposite: the disclaimer at the end of the book undermines that earlier argument (see White [1979] 72–73 on this).

Vlastos (1985) 26 n. 65 claims that the passage is a later addition to *Republic* I; he says: " tacked on to the end of Book I, this cannot belong to the composition which precedes it, for what it says (if I don't know what justice is I cannot know if it is a virtue) implicitly contradicts {351a5–6}, where 'no one could not know that injustice is ignorance,' and so, by implication, no one could not know that justice is knowledge and therefore (350b5) virtue." Vlastos condemns the whole last paragraph (354a12–c3), without suggesting how the book might have originally ended. This seems to me pretty desperate. Anyway, philosophers, even very great ones, do contradict themselves; I am inclined to think that Plato is doing that here.

Anyway, *who* tacked this passage on to the end of *Republic* I? Vlastos does not say, but if it was Plato himself, in revising the dialogue to make it fit with books II–X, say, then Plato is still contradicting himself. Not only that, what he makes Socrates say (that he cannot define justice, and so can't know whether it is a virtue or makes its possessor happy) is going to be contradicted by what Socrates is about to do in books II–X: he is going to define justice and use the definition to show that the just man is happy. So we shall have to say that the passage was added by Plato at a point at which he was unable to remember what he had said in book I and was unable to anticipate what the main plot of the rest of the *Republic* was going to be. Alternatively, we could say that someone other than Plato added it. But there is not the slightest manuscript authority for this.

[77] The crucial last sentence, 354c1–3, reads: ὁπότε γὰρ τὸ δίκαιον μὴ οἶδα ὅ ἐστιν, σχολῇ εἴσομαι εἴτε ἀρετή τις οὖσα τυγχάνει εἴτε καὶ οὔ, καὶ πότερον ὁ ἔχων αὐτὸ οὐκ εὐδαίμων ἐστὶν ἢ εὐδαίμων.

No doubt Socrates goes too far when he says that he knows nothing after all this talk: at the very most he can only mean that he does not know anything about justice.[78] But this does nothing to distinguish justice from any other candidate for the Intellectualist Assumption: if they had been discussing the weather, and found themselves unable to define "weather," Socrates would presumably have said he knew nothing about the weather: whether it was good or bad, etc.[79] And similarly, there are in this speech of Socrates' only two examples given of what he does not know about justice: whether it is an excellence, and whether there is any advantage in having it; but there is nothing to differentiate these from any of the other things one might want to know about justice: in the absence of a definition, one would know none of them.[80]

But it is possible to work up a doubt here. Consider this instance of (IA₁), put in conditional form, to which Socrates has just committed himself:

(IA₁j) x knows that justice is an excellence → x knows what justice is.

Socrates makes this particular case of (IA₁) explicit because at 348c Thrasymachus denied that justice is an excellence and asserted that injustice is an excellence. Socrates there took pains to draw out what this involves: it means that unjust people are good (ἀγαθοί, 348d3–4) and that injustice is καλόν: "praiseworthy" or "admirable."

Proposition (IA₁j) is a case of (IA₁) in which the term to be defined appears in subject position in the antecedent. Such cases are rare: we shall find only one parallel to *Republic* I's recognition of a subject version of (IA) in the dialogues that are uncontroversially Socratic, in the *Laches*, and that, as we shall see, is a case that just might be rewritten as a predicate version of (IA). On the other hand, at the beginning of the *Meno* (71b), we find a

---

[78] Nehamas (1986) 290 = (1999) 34–35 wants to limit what he does not know to the features of justice that he goes on to list, which had been subjects of argument between himself and Thrasymachus. But Socrates *does* say that he knows nothing, and nothing in what he says suggests the limitation that Nehamas sees there.

[79] Nehamas (1986) 290: "Socrates's insistence on the priority of definition {(IA)} is therefore very narrowly circumscribed. First, it seems to concern primarily the virtues and not every thing or item." Well, the virtues are what the early dialogues are about. But I do not see anything to suggest that the assumption is *confined* to the virtues. Aristotle does indeed limit Socrates' interest to the virtues. But what could motivate limiting his assumptions about definitions to only the definitions he is interested in?

[80] Brickhouse and Smith (1994) 58–60 handle this passage by proposing two different senses of "knowledge" (60 n. 41): "In our view, there is a sense of 'knowledge' in which Socrates does deny the possibility of any knowledge without knowledge of the definition." I see no motivation for this other than that of saving Socrates' consistency, and, as I have already suggested, I am prepared to give that up.

subject version of (IA₁) quite strongly put, but this, on my own reading as well, is not a Socratic dialogue.

Claims quite like the one (IA₁j) puts beyond our knowing in the absence of definition are in fact used in other Socratic dialogues in the course of rejecting proposed definitions – and so are used in the absence of definition. Temperance (*Charmides* 159c1, d8, etc.) and courage (*Laches* 192c5–6, etc.) are unconditionally and predefinitionally classed among τῶν καλῶν – the things that are "praiseworthy."

And that suggests that perhaps we should limit the Intellectualist Assumption in the Socratic dialogues other than *Republic* I. Perhaps Plato's Socrates there was prepared to allow for predefinitional knowledge of claims *about* courage and temperance, but none for claims that apply those terms to "individuals": this person, that action.

But, as far as I can tell, the idea dies there. I know of no way to distinguish the two sorts of claims that Socrates would here have to be distinguishing that leads anywhere.[81] Elsewhere, Plato becomes much exercised over claims that have abstract entities as subjects: he becomes worried about the interrelationships among forms. But that does not seem to have much to do with the present question, and nothing in the way of a distinction seems to tie in with the concerns or attitudes of the Socratic dialogues. It does not sound like Socrates to suggest that we might be able to tell courage was admirable because that is part of the meaning of "courage," and then hope for a full definition of "courage" to emerge as the account of its meaning that has this and all other analytic truths about courage as logical consequences. It sounds more like Socrates, as we shall shortly see in connection with the *Charmides*, to suggest that a person who has a certain virtue can introspect and come up with truths about it. But even where Socrates makes such noises, namely, in the *Charmides* and not (at least not very loudly) elsewhere, what he seems to expect is that a person should just be able to come up with an entire definition by looking within. And when Charmides tries it, he goes wrong. Perhaps we are to take that as suggesting that temperance is not to be found in him, but what *shows* that his definition is wrong is an argument based on the premise that temperance is praiseworthy, and that premise is not claimed to rest on introspection (or on anything at all).

---

[81] Vlastos (1985) 26 n. 65 (not in Vlastos [1994]), Nehamas (1986) 277–79 = (1999) 28–29, Beversluis (1987) 211–12 = Benson (1992) 108, Benson (1990) 20 in n. 2, and Brickhouse and Smith (1994) 53 all point out the difference, but do not say what difference it makes. Vlastos (1990) 8 = (1994) 78 makes a good deal of the distinction, and insists that the elenctic dialogues are completely free of the subject version of (IA₁) (as he had in Vlastos [1985] 26 n. 65). But this requires him to treat *Republic* I 354a–c as a later addition, and he says nothing whatever about *Laches* 189e.

So there is nothing here to suggest that introspection on the part of the virtuous will yield predefinitional knowledge about the virtues.

Lastly, in the *Meno*, which clearly proclaims a subject version of (IA₁), Socrates employs "virtue is a good thing" (87d) as a premise that may aid in the quest for definition. There he gives an account of its status that does not make it something known in advance. It will be best, I think, to understand the firm statement of the Intellectualist Assumption in the *Meno* as a formulation of something Plato takes to have been characteristic of Socrates as he has portrayed him, which gives rise to problems of just the sort we have raised with it; the *Meno* is then an attempt to cope with those problems.

2.3.4. Laches

In *Republic* I, Socrates espouses a subject version of (IA₁). The *Laches* provides us with a parallel to that: not as blatantly, perhaps, but clearly enough. It gives us a subject version version of (IA₁), and the principle of expressibility (PE) that turns (IA₁) into (IA) as well.

At its conclusion (see 200c), Laches disqualifies himself and Nicias as candidate advisors to Lysimachus and Melesias on how to inculcate courage, or excellence generally, in their sons. He does not outright state the grounds for this disqualification. But in 199e–200a he gloats over Nicias' inability to define courage, and in 200ab Nicias counters by reminding Laches that he had done no better. Nicias goes on to suggest that a session with his son's music tutor Damon (see 180cd), whom Socrates had mentioned a little way back (197d) as the source for one of Nicias' claims, would enable him to clean up his act and explain things to Laches. It is then that Laches recommends to Lysimachus and Melesias that they not look to himself and Nicias as advisors in the matter of educating their children.

He nominates Socrates in their place, presumably on the ground that Socrates either has up his sleeve, or at least is in a better position to get, a definition. Socrates promptly (200e–201a) points out that they have all ended up in the same boat, in puzzlement (ἐν ἀπορίᾳ), and declines the nomination: since he has been unable, along with the others, to define courage, he would be no better an advisor on how to acquire it than they.

The idea that inability to define something disqualifies one as an advisor on that subject is firmly rooted in Laches' earlier admissions in the dialogue.

At 186a–187b, Socrates had recommended approaching the problem of instilling excellence by listing people who have taught it. He then forsook this quite un-Socrates-like procedure in favor of defining. The listing of teachers may be all to the good, he says (189e1–190c7):[82]

SOC: But I think the following sort of inquiry leads to the same thing, and, I dare say, would somewhat more get first things first {σχεδὸν δέ τι καὶ μᾶλλον ἐξ ἀρχῆς εἴη ἄν}. For if we happen to know about anything that, when it becomes present to something {παραγενόμενόν τῳ},[83] it makes that to which it becomes present better, {e5} and, in addition, we can make it become present to that, it is clear that we know this itself, about which we might become advisors as to how one might get it most easily and in the best way.[84]

Perhaps you do not understand what I am saying, but you will understand more easily in the following way. {190} If we happen to know that sight, becoming present to the eyes, makes those {eyes} to which it is present better, and, in addition, we can make it become present to the eyes, it is clear that we know sight itself, what it is,[85] about which we might become advisors as to how one might get it most easily and in the best way. For if we don't know this itself, what sight is, or what hearing is, we can hardly become worthwhile advisors and doctors either about eyes or about ears as to the way in which {b} one might best {κάλλιστ'} get sight or hearing.

LACH: You say what is true, Socrates.

SOC: And aren't these two {viz. Lysimachus and Melesias} now calling on us for advice as to the way in which excellence, {b5} by becoming present to their sons' souls, can make them better?

LACH: Certainly.

---

[82] It is not clear to me what happened to Santas's interpretation of this passage between Santas (1968/69) and Santas (1972). In the former (181 in Vlastos [1971]) he wrote: "If fighting in armor and similar pursuits are intended to develop courage, their worth cannot be estimated before it is known what courage is." In the latter, he only deals with the *Laches* in connection with Socrates' alleged "rejecting of examples" (see 129, 131), and not in connection with the general assumption (IA).

[83] The Greek, and the rather stodgy translation, are here for future reference: the terminology for the relation between what will later be called a "form" and its instances will be discussed below.

[84] 189e6–7: δῆλον ὅτι αὐτό γε ἴσμεν τοῦτο οὗ πέρι σύμβουλοι ἂν γενοίμεθα ὡς ἄν τις αὐτὸ ῥᾷστα καὶ ἄριστ' ἂν κτήσαιτο. Not, as in Jowett (1953) I 84 (= Hamilton and Cairns [1961] 133) "clearly, we must know how that about which we are advising may be best and most easily obtained," but as above (so Sprague [1973] 30 = Cooper [1997] 674: "clearly we know the very thing about which we should be consulting as to how one might obtain it most easily and best"; also Lamb [1924] 41, Croiset [1921] 105, etc.). The translation "clearly we know what it is" (Lane [1987] 98) captures the spirit but not the letter. The requirement is that we know the thing itself about which we are to give advice, and the immediate sequel (190a3–4) explains "knowing the thing itself" as knowing what it is.

[85] 190a3–4 δῆλον ὅτι ὄψιν γε ἴσμεν αὐτὴν ὅτι ποτ' ἔστιν: this locution is idiomatic Greek; it is not, of course, idiomatic English. The frequency of its occurrence is connected with the tendency on the part of Plato and Aristotle to equate knowing a thing with knowing what it is: notice the transition here between 189e6–7 and 190a3–4.

SOC: Then oughtn't it to belong to us to know what excellence is? For if we don't know at all what excellence actually is,[86] in what way could {c} we become advisors for anyone as to how he might best {κάλλιστα} get it?

LACH: In no way, it seems to me, Socrates.[87]

SOC: We say, then, Laches, that we know what it is.

LACH: We do say that.

SOC: And for that as to which we know {what it is}, we can also, no doubt, say what it is.

LACH: How could it not be so?

Once more, the version of (IA₁) that we have here is limited.

First, what demands our knowing what sight or excellence is, is a package: we must have this knowledge if we (a) know that sight (excellence) improves its possessor and (b) can make sight (excellence) "become present to" eyes (people). And it is this package that makes us worthwhile advisors on how to get sight (excellence).

It is not clear whether the knowledge of what sight or excellence is affects both parts of the package equally, or only the whole package. It may be that it is not so much the knowledge that sight or excellence improves its possessor (makes it better) that requires knowing what it is, but only the knowledge that doing this or that will impart sight or excellence. This would certainly make it easier for us to allow ourselves to employ, a little later (192c), "courage is admirable" as a premise in the refutation of a candidate definition.

Second, the definition would mainly be needed to support knowledge claims to the effect that if you do or say so-and-so to someone he will become virtuous, and in such claims the term "virtuous" (or "excellent") figures in predicate position, which weakens the parallel with *Republic* I.

But neither of these points does much to weaken the force of the passage.

The second one does not because it is too hair-splitting: knowing that if you do or say so-and-so to someone that person will become virtuous *is* knowing something about virtue, whatever the syntax of the sentence,

---

[86] 190b8–9 εἰ γάρ που μηδ' ἀρετὴν εἰδεῖμεν τὸ παράπαν ὅτι ποτε τυγχάνει ὄν: incorrectly translated by Sprague (1973) 30 = Cooper (1997) 675 as "if we are not absolutely certain what it is." Negative constructions with τὸ παράπαν translate as "not *at all*" (LSJ *s.v.* παράπαν): see the translations of Croiset (1921) 106, Lamb (1924) 43, Jowett (1953) I 85 = Hamilton and Cairns (1961) 133. Sprague correctly says ([1973] 30 n. 32) that the position Socrates takes here is that "taken at the beginning of *Meno* 70aff.," but that too is to the effect that if we don't know *at all* what excellence is we can't say anything about it.

[87] Brickhouse and Smith (1994) 56–57 cite 190b7–c2, and say that it only commits Socrates to saying that lack of a definition makes it impossible for one to claim expertise; that still leaves it possible for divine intervention to allow one to know particular cases. But then it would be possible for divine intervention to give one the knowledge how to acquire excellence. And then what Socrates and Laches are agreeing on here is simply false.

in a way that simply knowing that Achilles is courageous is not knowing something about courage.

The first point certainly locks into the subsequent dialogue nicely. But nothing whatever is done by way of motivating the distinction it demands. It might be better to say that Plato's Socrates was here thinking, vaguely, that perhaps some slight exception could be made for claims to the effect that this or that virtue was a good thing, with no real idea how to go about making the exception, and Plato or Plato's Socrates realized by the time he got to *Republic* I that there was no stopping short of the full generality of the Intellectualist Assumption. He might have been driven to this by facing up to the consistency of extreme amoralism or antimoralism as we find it in Thrasymachus, who is prepared to deny that justice is an excellence (348c5–10), to call unjust people good (ἀγαθοί, d3–6), and to speak of injustice as an excellence (e2–4), or in Callicles, who will not allow that justice is admirable (καλόν) except by convention (*Gorgias* 482d and ff.). Once these challenges are clearly in view, it is no longer possible to accept such claims as "courage is admirable" without argument.[88] The resulting predicament, that one cannot even know that justice or temperance or whatever is a virtue without having its definition, while one cannot hope for a definition without presupposing that justice or temperance is a virtue, might then have provoked the response in the *Meno*, according to which we can hope to make some headway with something less than knowledge, namely, true belief.

This may be right, but it is quite speculative. Anyway, it isn't necessary. The chief point is that any restriction Socrates might have wished for in the Intellectualist Assumption is unmotivated by anything he says, and nothing in what he says shows any awareness that restrictions are needed in the first place. He is plainly committed to the claim that we must know what excellence is if we are going to be able to give advice about it. Just as plainly, he is supposing that being able to give advice about it requires knowing the truth of certain claims about it. In the present context, the instance of (IA$_1$) that underlies the dialogue is:

(IA$_1$e) To know that excellence can (or need not) be inculcated through learning to fight in heavy armor, one must know what excellence is.

---

[88] At *Charmides* 175a–176a, there is some slight sense that the premise "temperance is admirable" (see κάλλιστον, 175a11) has been challenged, but this is not serious: Socrates would prefer to give up the definition.

The remaining thing to be noted in this passage is that it explicitly gives us (PE) in 190c6–7.

As the dialogue goes on, the topic is narrowed from "excellence" to "courage" (190cd), and the present admissions are transferred to that topic: Laches supposes that he knows, and is able to say, what courage is. Of course, he turns out to be unable to say what courage is. After three failed attempts, he expresses consternation (194a7–b4):

And yet I'm unaccustomed to such discussions {τῶν τοιούτων λόγων}; but still, a certain lust for victory has gripped me in consequence of what's been said, and I am truly vexed if I am in this way unable to say what I conceive {ἃ νοῶ μὴ οἷός τ' εἰμὶ εἰπεῖν}. For while I certainly seem to myself to conceive about courage what it is, I don't know how it has escaped me just now, so that I can't put it together in speech {μὴ συλλαβεῖν τῷ λόγῳ} and say what it is.

Laches is teetering on the brink of giving up the Principle of Expressibility. But he doesn't actually even state it, much less give it up. To all appearances, he actually doesn't know what courage is.

In short, we have here not just (IA₁) in a subject version, namely (IA₁e), but (PE), and so (IA).

But the fact that (IA₁e) is in a subject version is fairly trivial: "knowing that excellence can be inculcated through learning to fight in heavy armor" could as easily have been written as "knowing that someone can be made excellent through learning to fight in heavy armor."

2.3.5. Protagoras

Protagoras 360e–361d is sometimes[89] cited as adopting, amplifying, or explaining *Laches* 189e ff. In fact, the passage in the *Laches* is the more explicit one: in the *Protagoras*, Socrates does not outright state a version of the Intellectualist Assumption, but rather the converse of a subject version of (IA₁). Socrates says he would like to know (360e8–361a3)

what excellence itself[90] is. For I know that when this became clear, that about which I and you have each strung out a long discourse, I saying that excellence is not teachable, you that it is teachable, would become especially manifest.

---

[89] E.g., Friedländer (1958/69) II 42, Guthrie (1975) 132, Sprague (1973) 30 n. 32; cf. also Taylor (1976) 212–13, who speaks as if (IA) were stated in this passage.

[90] Adopting, without much conviction or enthusiasm, the punctuation τί ποτ' ἐστὶν αὐτό ἡ ἀρετή (from Adam and Adam [1893] 73), instead of τί ποτ' ἐστὶν αὐτό, ἡ ἀρετή (Burnet [1900/1907], Croiset and Bodin [1923a] 85, Lamb [1924] 254). For parallels to αὐτὸ + fem., see *Cratylus* 411d8 and *Theaetetus* 146e9–10 (Adam and Adam [1893] 192).

This tells us that the definition would be sufficient to resolve the question, not that it is necessary for that (and see also the wording of 361c5–6). But certainly the overall suggestion of the passage is that, in the absence of the definition, we shall only continue to fall into confusion of the sort we have just seen, and that makes the definition a necessary condition for clarity: (IA₁) is, we might say, unstated but only just unstated.

2.3.6. Charmides

The closest parallel to the *Laches* is the *Charmides*, which gives us (IA), with (PE) explicit, and something more as well.

At the end of the dialogue, after all attempts to define temperance have failed, Charmides is urged to see whether he has this virtue. He responds (176a6–8):

> But by Zeus, Socrates, I don't know whether I have it or don't have it; for how could I know, where you two {viz., Socrates and Critias} cannot find out what it is, as you say?[91]

Just as Laches' disclaimer was based on earlier admissions made to Socrates, so here we have an echo of an earlier passage. The initial question was whether Charmides had temperance, and Socrates in 158de had suggested that he and Charmides jointly undertake to answer it. The undertaking is the rest of the dialogue, and Socrates focuses it on the definition question as follows (158e6–159a10):

> Then, I said, the inquiry about this {viz., whether Charmides has temperance} seems to me best undertaken in this way: it is clear that, if temperance is present to you {εἴ σοι πάρεστιν σωφροσύνη}, {159} you are able to form some belief about it {τι περὶ αὐτῆς δοξάζειν}. For it is necessary that, being present in you, if it is present in you {ἐνοῦσαν αὐτήν, εἴπερ ἔνεστιν}, it offer some awareness {αἴσθησίν τινα παρέχειν}, on the basis of which you will have some belief {δόξα} about it, as to what temperance is and what sort of thing. Or don't you think so?
> {a5} I do think so, he said.
> Then, I said, since you know how to speak Greek, you can also, no doubt, tell us this itself that you think {οἴει}, how it appears to you {ὅτι σοι φαίνεται}?
> Perhaps, he said.
> Then, so that we may divine whether it is present in you or not, I {a10} said, tell us what you say temperance is, according to your belief.

---

[91] Tuckey (1951) 94–95 (adapting Schirlitz [1897]), because he thinks that Charmides has a definition (I am not clear as to what it is), introduces a tortured explanation for Charmides' profession of ignorance.

Socrates here (159a9–10) urges Charmides to define temperance so that they will be able to tell whether Charmides has it, and Charmides later (176ab) takes the failure to arrive at a definition to carry with it the impossibility of telling whether he has it.[92] This is either (IA) or (IA₁). And in 159a6–7 we are virtually given the principle of expressibility that turns the one into the other.[93]

We are, it is true, only virtually given it. But if Socrates wanted to stick with what he here says while denying (PE), he would have to say that, while one can always say what one *believes* (see δοξάζειν 159a1, δόξα a2, a10), *thinks* (οἴει a6), or what *appears* to one (ὅτι σοι φαίνεται a7), one cannot always say what one *knows*. It is difficult to think how this differentiation could be made.

Alternatively, one might choose to underline Socrates' "no doubt" (δήπου, 159a7) and Charmides' "perhaps" (ἴσως, a8), and deny that either of them is committed to what is here said. But I'd say that any doubt conveyed by these words is attached not so much to (IA) or (PE) as to the whole train of thought and where it is leading. At any rate, the claim that one can say what one believes is paralleled as late as the *Theaetetus* (206de). And there is indeed something dubious about the train of thought here in the *Charmides*.

For there is more track to be covered by the train, already laid in 158e7–159a5 (above), to which Socrates adverts after Charmides' first unsuccessful attempt to define "temperance" (160d5–e1):

---

[92] Santas (1972) 137–38 takes the later passage to express Charmides' deference to his elders, Socrates and Critias: if they cannot say what temperance is, he can hardly be expected to say whether he is temperate. This seems to me inadequate. Charmides has already given reasons of deference for refusing to answer the question whether he is temperate (in 158cd). It is no longer just a question of general deference, but a question of deference specifically in view of the fact that Socrates and Critias are unable to define temperance. Then Charmides' deference could be expressed as follows: "If even you august elders are unable to say what temperance is, how could anyone as callow as I be in a position to say that I am temperate?" But if this is to be coherent, there must be some connection between defining temperance and saying whether one has it. (Suppose Critias and Socrates had come up with a good definition. Then Charmides' deference would no longer have been in place: he could have pursued the question whether he was temperate by asking whether he fit the definition.) Then we are back where we were: definitions are required in order to answer such questions as "is Charmides temperate?"
   As to the earlier passage, Santas simply denies that it gives us (IA). True. It does not say: "in order to tell whether you have temperance, we *must* define it, and could not tell otherwise." It says: "in order to tell whether you have temperance, *let's* define it." But taken together with the later passage, that is surely enough.

[93] This passage gives Croiset the odd idea that we are merely, in this dialogue, seeking a definition that captures ordinary usage, and not a "truly philosophical definition" (*une définition vraiment philosophique*: Croiset [1921] 60–61). But the relevance of Charmides' knowledge of Greek is not that it gives him knowledge of what σωφροσύνη means, but that it enables him to say what he thinks that virtue is, and what he thinks it is is something he arrives at (as we shall see) by introspection. Conceivably, here I am in agreement with Findlay (1974) 92.

Then, Charmides, I said, put your mind more to it, look into yourself, think what sort of person temperance, which is present to you, makes you, and what sort of thing it is to make you like that: reckon all these things together, and say again, well and courageously, what it appears to you to be.

Until now, we have been confronting merely the suggestion that, in order to know anything involving *F* or *F*ness, one must know what *F*ness is. But these two passages are suggesting something even stronger: that in order to *be F* (where "*F*" is a virtue-word), one must know what *F*ness is. Perhaps this is put too strongly: Socrates is really only insisting that, if Charmides is temperate, he must be in a position to find out what temperance is: not that he already knows what it is, but that he can come to know what it is merely by thinking about it. But let us for a moment think about the stronger formulation.

It is a natural consequence of some of Socrates' favorite ideas. One of those (whether or not he fully espoused it) is that virtue is knowledge. It is not clear what this means, but it surely carries with it the weaker claim that

(1) One who is virtuous knows which actions and people are virtuous and which are not.

And it would be surprising to find Socrates (before the *Meno*, at any rate) denying this. But the Intellectualist Assumption, in the form (IA₁), gives us:

(2) One who knows which actions and people are virtuous knows what virtue is,

and that, with (1), entails:

∴ (3) One who is virtuous knows what virtue is.

But this conflicts with some other things Socrates says, as long as we take seriously Phaedo's claim (*Phaedo* 118a16–17; cf. *Letter* VII 324e1–2) that Socrates' virtue was preeminent; for now it follows from that that he knows what virtue is – but he keeps saying that he does not.

The trouble here is still a trouble if we back up to the weaker formulation, according to which someone who has virtue is in a position to tell, just by thinking about it, what virtue is. For if that is so, and Socrates was indeed virtuous, all that stood between him and knowing what virtue is was thinking about it. But surely he, if anyone, did enough thinking about such things. So if he was virtuous, he must have known what virtue is. But that is what he kept saying he didn't know.

This is not an inconsistency on Socrates' part, and no interlocutor could have fazed him by producing the above argument: it is not he, after all, who claims that he is virtuous, but others, such as Plato. But then it is an inconsistency for Plato: he cannot both accept everything he makes Socrates say and continue to extol Socrates' excellence.

Socrates proclaims his unknowing, in Platonic dialogues,[94] in *Apology* 21b3–7, d2–7, 29b4–6, *Charmides* 165b8–c1, 166d1–2, 175b2–4, *Euthyphro* 6b2–3, 15c11–12, *Gorgias* 506a3–4, 509a5, *Laches* 186d8–e2, 200e2–5, *Lysis* 212a5–6 (and at 216c4–6, he doesn't even know what his own question *means*), *Protagoras* 348c6–7, *Republic* I 337e4–5, 354b9–c3, and no doubt, elsewhere.[95] This is an impressive, even extravagant, inventory of ignorance. Yet the temptation has always been strong to regard it as sham, part of "Socrates' habitual dissimulation" (ἡ εἰωθυῖα εἰρωνεία Σωκράτους, *Republic* I 337a4–5: "irony" is not a good translation here),[96] as Thrasymachus calls it. He goes on to say to Socrates (a5–7, and cf. e1–3), "I knew this, and was saying to these people earlier, that you would not be willing to reply, and would dissemble, and do anything rather than reply if anyone asked you anything." The closest parallel to this seems to be in Xenophon. In *Memorabilia* IV 4.9, Hippias declines to give his account of the just[97] until Socrates has come up with one of his own, "for it is enough that you laugh down the others, questioning and refuting them all, while you yourself are not willing to offer an account {λόγον} or state your mind on anything to anyone." But, Socrates says (*Charmides* 165b5–6), Critias is behaving as if Socrates had professed knowledge about the subjects of his questions, and Critias, despite this disclaimer, immediately talks as if he thought Socrates did know what temperance is (cf. 166c3–4). In the *Apology* Socrates says quite generally (23a3–5): "every time, those who are present think me to be knowledgeable {σοφόν, "wise"} in those matters in which I refute another."

In this picture, many of those who encountered Socrates thought his alleged unknowing was a mask, and behind it Socrates either knew or

---

[94] In Xenophon, Socrates does not profess ignorance, although he does talk as if he is unable to teach: see *Memorabilia* I 2.3, 8, IV 4.5; but contrast I 6.14. Morrison (1987) 20 n. 8 sees in this last "a typical Xenophontic subtlety. Socrates describes what he would do *if* he could teach, but the whole thing remains hypothetical: he never affirms that he can." But what Socrates says is: "if I have anything good, I teach {it to my friends}" (ἐάν τι ἔχω ἀγαθόν, διδάσκω), and he goes on to describe reading books of ancient wisdom with his friends, "and if we see anything good, we take it away with us" (καὶ ἄν τι ὁρῶμεν ἀγαθὸν ἐκλεγόμεθα). This does not sound to me purely hypothetical. The profession of ignorance is also ascribed to Socrates by Aeschines: see fr. 11C Dittmar (1912).

[95] The catalogue is not intended to be complete. There is an overlapping catalogue in Brickhouse and Smith (1994) 3 n. 1 = 30 n. 2 = 178 n. 4.

[96] Cf. Dover (1980) 168 *ad* 216e4, Dover (1968a) 157 *ad* 449 εἴρων, Vlastos (1985) 4 n. 8, Vlastos (1987) esp. 80–81 = Vlastos (1991) 24–25.

[97] Perhaps the fact that the subject is the same, justice, in *Republic* I and at this point in the *Memorabilia*, is ominous, and this is a little too close a parallel to be taken for evidence about the historical Socrates.

thought he did. The picture has been shared by many since,[98] and it certainly saves Plato's conception of Socrates from inconsistency. It is a tedious way to do it. The inconsistency resulted from a complex set of philosophical assumptions about knowledge, excellence, and defining, and rather than looking more closely at those assumptions to see what can be done to loosen them up to make things right, this solution tells us that Socrates is simply lying. Of course, that it is philosophically unexciting does not mean that it is wrong, or that it is not Plato's, and perhaps there are reasons for Socrates' lying that make this line of thought a little less boring.[99] But we are going to encounter a response to the problem in the *Meno*, or so I think, that is supposed to preserve the possibility of Socrates' ignorance by weakening the assumptions. So it would at any rate be premature to take the easy way out now.

I am primarily concerned here to pin the Intellectualist Assumption on (Plato's) Socrates, and I take it that what has so far been said shows that to be pretty well entrenched in Plato's portrait. The further development in the *Charmides* that leads to our contradiction is the view there expressed that the possessor of a virtue must be in a position to define it. This Super-Intellectualist Assumption is considerably less well entrenched, and if the tone of hesitation in 159a had gone on to find a focus, it might well have been on this. We have seen one way in which the view might be made a consequence of other Socratic ideas, but the argument, (1)–(3) above, is not one Socrates gives.

There is another that he might have used. Later in the *Charmides* (164a1–4, and cf. d2–3), Socrates and Critias both find it unthinkable that someone could have temperance without knowing that he did. So someone who has it knows that he does, and that, with the Intellectualist Assumption, entails that he can define temperance. This, again, is not an argument Socrates uses. But we find an echo of it in the *Lysis*.

2.3.7. Lysis

The *Lysis* provides the only parallel for the idea that the possessor of a virtue must be able to define it,[100] and that parallel is quite weak. At the end of the

---

[98] See Gulley (1968) 62–74. Vlastos (1971) 12–15, esp. 14 (reprint of Vlastos [1957]) makes it sound as if Socrates in the *Euthyphro* is holding back from saying what piety is for educational reasons. This was not the view in Vlastos (1956a) xxx–xxxi, and Vlastos (1985) 3–5 is different again.

[99] For Vlastos (1957), these have to do with the need for the interlocutor to come to the answer himself. For Strauss and the Straussians (cf. Strauss [1964] 83, 84, 85), they apparently have to do with the limitations of everyone's intelligence except for Socrates and Straussians.

[100] Unless Vlastos is right about *Hippias Major* 304e2–3 (see n. 74).

dialogue, we find Socrates saying (223b4–8): "Well, Lysis and Menexenus, we have turned out ridiculous {καταγέλαστοι}, I, an old man, and you. For these people will say, when they go away, that we think we are friends {φίλοι}[101] of each other[102] – for I place myself among you – but we have not yet turned out to be able to find out what the friend is." It is not immediately obvious, but this gives us an instance of (IA_1), or even of (IA).

Suppose we are Socrates, Lysis, and Menexenus.

The audience is supposed to see an absurdity in our thinking we are friends without knowing what the friend is, or without being able to define the friend. It is not that this is itself a contradiction: according to the audience,

(1) we think we are friends of each other; and
(2) we do not know what a friend is,

so plainly the audience does not take (1) to contradict (2). Rather, the truth of (2) means that we *only* think we are friends of each other. We think that we are friends, but (2) is taken by the audience to show either that we aren't really friends of each other, or that we don't know, and hence shouldn't be saying, that we are friends of each other.[103]

If the latter, weaker, interpretation is correct, what it gives us is merely an instance of (IA_1):

(IA_1f) To know that we are friends of each other we must know what the friend is.

(Alternatively, it gives us an instance of [IA] with "we must be able to define 'friend'" replacing "we must know what the friend is.")

The stronger interpretation is the one that parallels the idea we encountered in *Charmides*, that having a virtue requires knowing that one has it. For under the stronger interpretation, we would have in addition to (IA_1f) the claim that we cannot be friends of each other without knowing that we

---

[101] Translated "lovers" above; the present context makes "friends" far more natural, and I am not concerned with the particular content of the *Lysis* at this point. But there is a serious problem here, and more than the claim that φίλος is ambiguous is required to clear it up.

[102] Not, as in Lombardo's translation in Cooper (1997) 707, "that we are friends of one another": ὡς οἰόμεθα ἡμεῖς ἀλλήλων φίλοι εἶναι, but "that we *think* we are . . ." (The same omission occurs in the citation of the passage in Vlastos [1990] 2 = [1994] 68.)

[103] Nehamas (1986) 289 = (1999) 34: the passage "implies at most that if some people are, or take themselves to be, friends then they are more likely than others to know what friendship is – or at least that they should be able to learn what it is once they apply themselves to that task." This does not seem to be enough to justify the claim that we are "ridiculous" or "laughable" (καταγέλαστοι, 223b4–5) for not having found the definition of "friend" while still thinking of ourselves as friends.

are, and so that (2) shows that we are not really friends of each other. It is not clear from this passage alone which interpretation should be adopted.

But, like other cases we have looked at, this closing passage recalls an earlier one, and that earlier passage at least suggests that the stronger interpretation is correct. In 211de, Socrates declares himself strongly attached to friendship, and goes on to say to Menexenus (211e8–212a7):

So, seeing you and Lysis, I am amazed, and envy you both, that while so young you can get this possession readily and easily: you, Menexenus, have got him as a friend so easily and firmly, and he you; while I am so far from the possession that I don't even know in what way one person becomes a friend of another, but just this I want to ask you, inasmuch as you are experienced.

Since Menexenus is a friend, Socrates expects him to be in a better position than most to answer his questions about friendship. And the closing words of this passage also provide the closest parallel to the assumption with which Socrates supports his idea in the *Charmides*: the assumption that temperance is subject to something like introspection (*Charmides* 159a1–3, 160d5–6).

The parallel is not strong enough to allow us to claim outright that Socrates is assuming that the possessor of a virtue must be able to define it. But the idea is not very far off.[104] By the same token, it is interesting that Socrates' interlocutors in these dialogues are usually themselves instances or alleged instances of the virtue about which Socrates asks.[105] In addition to Charmides, Lysis, and Menexenus, there are Laches, Nicias, Euthyphro, Cephalus, even Hippias: each a candidate for the label his dialogue tries to define. Ion is a rhapsode; he is the one to ask when the question is "what does a rhapsode do?"; so also Gorgias and Protagoras have definition questions or near-definition questions asked of them that pertain to qualities or skills they allegedly possess or can impart. Of course, this is no accident. It does not require the presupposition that the possessor of a virtue or skill or quality must be able to define it, but that is one step away: all we have to add to (IA$_1$) or (IA) is that the possessor of a virtue or skill must know he possesses it.

Still, that is a further step, waiting to be taken. Socrates is in enough trouble without it; the Intellectualist Assumption by itself ensures that. For, of course, in refuting various proposed definitions, he is going to have

---

[104] Irwin (1977b) 294 n. 4 *ad* 3: "*Lys.* 212a4–7, 223b4–8 suggests that we cannot be friends unless we know how one person becomes a friend to another or know what a friend is." Nehamas (1986) 289 n. 31 = (1999) 53 n. 30: this view "does not have to be accepted."

[105] Cf. Santas (1968/69) in Vlastos (1971) 178–79; Sprague (1973) 65 n. 23.

to make use of various claims about the things being defined, and, under the Intellectualist Assumption, it is difficult to see how he can be entitled to make those claims.

2.3.8. *The alleged ambiguity of "know"*

We shall have to live with that inconsistency, unless we resort to another device: that of finding an ambiguity in "know," so that while Socrates is claiming that, in the absence of a definition, he can't know that something or someone is temperate (or whatever) in a strong sense of "know," he can know that something or someone is temperate in a weaker one.[106] The chief problem with this device is that it sounds as it stands completely ad hoc. It is not that Socrates (or Plato) anywhere distinguishes the two sorts of knowledge in question. A fortiori, the distinction is not available to any of Socrates' interlocutors. Euthyphro is in no position to say to Socrates that he may not know what piety is, and so may not know in the strong sense that his father's action was impious or his own pious, but he certainly does know in some less stringent sense that these things are so.

Then, if the distinction is available to Socrates, we shall have to suppose that he is being pretty unfair to his interlocutors in not making it available to them. There is no reason to make Socrates a paragon of virtue; perhaps he is unfair to his interlocutors on occasion. But then we are presented with a choice between supposing that he has a very important distinction up his sleeve about which he never says a word, and supposing that there is an inconsistency between his pronouncements and his procedures.

Let's see what happens if we operate on the latter supposition.

---

[106] This is Vlastos's strategy: see n. 50, esp. Vlastos (1985) 25–26, (1990) 5–6 = (1994) 74–75. The intricate details of Vlastos's distinction are not what concern me; rather, I am doubtful of the strategy in general. Vlastos develops his distinction in another connection (see Vlastos [1985] 11 = [1994] 48), and then applies the distinction to (IA). Brickhouse and Smith (1994) 30–45 (also Brickhouse and Smith [2000] 99–13) opt for a similar distinction, but do not apply it to (IA), which they try to defuse by an examination of the texts one by one ([1994] 45–60, [2000] 113–19).

CHAPTER 3

Fixing the topic

Sometimes Socrates introduces a topic for discussion or definition by asking whether his interlocutor agrees that there is a topic there to discuss: e.g., "is there such a thing as justice?" (*Protagoras* 330c1–2, *Hippias Major* 287c4–5). Later, these existential admissions will be seen as admissions of the existence of forms.

Precisely because they carry that weight in the doctrinal dialogues, unitarians have seen them as importing that theory into the Socratic dialogues,[1] whereas I see them as merely ways of isolating the subject to be discussed.

3.1. EXISTENCE, UNITY, CAUSALITY, AND PLATONISM

Suppose you and I are standing beside the pool watching the swimmers and discussing swimming strokes. Suppose the following dialogue takes place:

I: Well, there's the Australian Crawl.
YOU: Oh, and what's that?
I: It's when you thrash about like this, and . . . {there follows an explanation, more or less, of this stroke}; like what that fellow over there is doing.
YOU: Talk about thrashing about! There's also the Butterfly Stroke, you know.
I: No, how does that go?

Suppose we are overheard by two more people, who whisper to each other as follows:

HE: Did you hear? They're Platonists!
SHE: I know; isn't it awful? But perhaps they're only immanentists, which wouldn't be so bad.

---

[1] Shorey is ambivalent: cf. Shorey (1903) 29 and 31 (he thinks the *Protagoras* does not mention "the [Platonic] ideas," but still wants to allow its existential claims some connection with the theory: see esp. nn. 185, 195), Shorey (1933) 497 *ad Protagoras* 330cd. Cherniss (1944) 213–16 nn. 127–28 is less so. Allen (1970) *passim* (cf. esp. 105–66) gives us an entire "earlier theory of forms" (see Allen [1971] for a summary of the main features).

These two people strike me as mad. No less mad are the other two people who overhear us from the other side, and say:

HIM: Did you hear? They're Platonists!
HER: I know; isn't it wonderful? They have transcended the nominalism that threatens the fabric of our society.

It is one thing to list the swimming strokes, another to do metaphysics. This is so even if one lists the swimming strokes, as we did, using "there is," the so-called "Existential Prefix."

You and I have mentioned two swimming strokes, and those in the pool are doing no other strokes, but there are three of them. So two of them must be doing one and the same stroke. We might agree that two of the swimmers were, despite appearances, really performing one and the same swimming stroke, the butterfly: one of them, say, is doing it quite badly.

Here He and She would be in great pain, while Him and Her are in raptures.

Again: we do not, in fact, refer to swimmers as "Australian crawlers" and "butterfly strokers" (at least, I do not). But we could, and the practice would be perfectly intelligible: someone would be an Australian crawler because he was doing the Australian Crawl, or a butterfly stroker by virtue of swimming the Butterfly Stroke.

In all of this, nothing has been said about the structure of the really real, and the only depth is in the water. But Him and Her are thinking: they have conceded the Existence, and then the Unity, of each of the Strokes; now they have gone on to admit their Priority: they have realized that the Strokes are a precondition for the intelligibility of the world of changing strokers, and that one can only become a stroker by swimming a Stroke. I am saying: nonsense.

We are about to consider passages in which Socrates makes claims involving existence and unity, and says that people control themselves because they have temperance. Is he doing metaphysics, or something else? Something else, I think, mostly what we should call "ethics," his approach to which centrally involves defining things like virtues. This of course requires that there be things like virtues to define, just as listing the swimming strokes requires that there be swimming strokes to list. It does not require consideration of the Ontological Status of things like virtues, any more than the other requires consideration of the Ontological Status of swimming strokes.

This is so even if we concede that Socrates "considers the crux of all ethical problems to be the possibility of the objective existence of norms which can be known in their essential nature."[2] The major drawback to conceding this is that we may not know what we are conceding. Obviously Socrates thinks that the claim that Euthyphro is doing something pious, or that Charmides is a temperate man, is, if true at all, just plain true, objectively true; he is not a relativist, subjectivist, nihilist, or whatever. And if that is all we are being asked to concede, we should concede it. But if it means that there is an entity called a "norm," "over and above" the actions and people to be judged or doing the judging[3] – well, that is another question, and we need not go into it yet. Socrates does not go into it yet. He will, in the doctrinal dialogues.

The question is not about what Plato believed when he wrote the Socratic dialogues. It is about what he does in those dialogues: what is involved in the arguments of those dialogues. In particular, I am not saying: the Socrates of these dialogues would not have conceded the existence of forms, of which things here below are merely pale reflections. If the Socrates of these dialogues is the historical Socrates, and Aristotle is right about the historical Socrates, he would have made no such concession. He might well have wondered what someone who asked for such a concession was on about: he might have supposed that such questions were merely irrelevant to what he himself was after, namely how he ought to live. At any rate, there is no discussion of such questions in the Socratic dialogues.

Would Socrates instead have insisted on a theory of "immanent characters"?[4] I have no idea whether he would have understood any better than I do what immanent characters are.[5] Once again: there is no discussion of these questions in the Socratic dialogues.

But if we reject the idea that Aristotle's Socrates speaks in those dialogues and instead think of the Socrates of those dialogues as Plato's mouthpiece, then he might perfectly well have espoused the Theory of Forms: after all, that is exactly what Plato is eventually going to make him do. But it doesn't come up in the Socratic dialogues, where he neither espouses that theory nor distances himself from it.

When, in the doctrinal dialogues, he finally espouses it, he is going to offer the Argument from Relativity (§ 1.2) in support of it. That argument begins by affirming the existence of something and then investing the affirmation with metaphysical significance. Let us look at some cases in the

---

[2] Cherniss (1944) 214 n. 128.
[3] Which, in fact, is what Cherniss meant; see also Allen (1970) 105 n. 2, which cites Cherniss's note.
[4] See Ross (1951) 21, 228–30, Guthrie (1975) 114–21.
[5] So far, I am perhaps in agreement with Allen (1970) 135 with n. 2.

Socratic dialogues in which the existence of something is affirmed without
the subsequent apparatus that turns the affirmation into metaphysics.

3.2. EXISTENCE CLAIMS IN THE SOCRATIC DIALOGUES

The claims considered here are ones that are naturally translated or paraphrased using the English Existential Prefix "there is such a thing as" and a
few close cousins (such as "you call something folly" in *Protagoras* 332a4).
Thus narrowly construed there are not a great many existential claims in
the Socratic dialogues.[6] Fairly obviously, a lot of the things people say about
this and that presuppose the existence of this and that, and would be rendered unintelligible if the person speaking added "but, of course, there's
no such thing as this or that." But I shall be mostly considering explicit
existence claims.

3.2.1. Protagoras

There is a batch of them in the *Protagoras*.

I begin with 330b–e, here presented in full: although for the moment
my only concern is with the existence claims made in c1–2 and d2–5,
understanding their force requires understanding their context. Socrates is
pushing Protagoras over the relationship between the "parts" of excellence,
that is, the "virtues"; Protagoras has just assented to the view that they
are different from each other, a view that Socrates paraphrases as follows
(330b3–6): "no other of the parts of excellence is such as knowledge {is}
{οἷον ἐπιστήμη}, nor such as justice {is}, nor such as courage {is}, nor
such as temperance {is}, nor such as piety {is}." He begins his first challenge
to this as follows (330b6–e2):

> Come then, I said, let us inquire in common what sort {of thing, ποῖόν τι} each
> of these is. First, as follows: is justice a certain thing, or no thing {ἡ δικαιοσύνη
> πρᾶγμά τί ἐστιν ἢ οὐδὲν πρᾶγμα}? It seems to me {it is a certain thing}; what
> about you?
> To me too, he said.
> {c2} Well then, if someone asked me, and you, "Protagoras, Socrates, tell me:
> this thing you just named, justice, is this itself just, or unjust {τοῦτο τὸ πρᾶγμα
> ὃ ὠνομάσατε ἄρτι, ἡ δικαιοσύνη, αὐτὸ τοῦτο δίκαιόν ἐστιν ἢ ἄδικον}?" I
> should reply to him that it is just; what would your vote be? The same as mine, or
> different?

---

[6] Despite the impression one gets from commentators, e.g., Adam and Adam (1893) 132 *ad* 330c;
Cherniss (1944) 214 n. 128; Allen (1970) 105. Cherniss and Allen construe the notion of an existence
claim very broadly indeed.

The same, he said.

{c7} So justice is such as to be just {ἔστιν ἄρα τοιοῦτον ἡ δικαιοσύνη οἷον δίκαιον εἶναι}, I should be saying in reply to this questioner; and so {would} you too?

Yes, he said.

{d1} Then if, after that, he asked, "Then do you people say that piety is something, as well {οὐκοῦν καὶ ὁσιότητά τινά φατε εἶναι}?" we should say it was, I think.

Yes, he said.

{d3} "Then you are saying that this too is a certain thing {οὐκοῦν φατε καὶ τοῦτο πρᾶγμά τι εἶναι}?" – we'd say so, wouldn't we?

He also agreed to this.

{d5} "Do you say that this thing itself is of a nature such as to be impious, or such as {to be} pious {πότερον δὲ τοῦτο αὐτὸ τὸ πρᾶγμά φατε τοιοῦτον πεφυκέναι οἷον ἀνόσιον εἶναι ἢ οἷον ὅσιον}?" I, for one, should be annoyed at the question, I said, and I'd say, "Don't commit sacrilege, fellow; something else could hardly be pious, if piety itself isn't to be pious {σχολῆ μεντἂν τι ἄλλο ὅσιον εἴη, εἰ μὴ αὐτή γε ἡ ὁσιότης ὅσιον ἔσται}."

What about you? Wouldn't you reply that way?

Certainly, he said.

The remainder of Socrates' argument against Protagoras' original admission turns on drawing from it, together with the above, the conclusion (331a7–b1): "So piety is not such as to be {a} just thing, nor justice such as {to be} pious, but such as to be not pious; and piety is such as {to be} not just – but therefore unjust, and the other {viz., justice} impious." This both interlocutors find absurd.

The question here is not as to the strength or weakness of the overall argument,[7] but as to its metaphysical depth or shallowness. And we are not at this point going to go all the way to the bottom: in c2–d1 and d5–e2 Socrates gets Protagoras to concede that justice and piety are both pious and just; such "self-predications" will require consideration in connection with Socrates' techniques for rejecting definitions, and we shall return to this passage in that connection. Here only the existential admissions of 330c1–2 and d2–5 are in question.

When Protagoras allows unhesitatingly that justice and piety are "things" (πράγματα)[8] what is he so sure about? A point that cannot be dismissed[9] is that it is Protagoras who is the interlocutor here, and not, say, Simmias;

---

[7] On which there are various opinions: see, e.g., Adam and Adam (1893) 133 *ad* 331a, Gallop (1961), Savan (1964), Weingartner (1973) 67–80, Guthrie (1975) 222–26, Taylor (1976) 109–20.

[8] Most of the time, the word "thing" appears in translations (as in the one just below of *Protagoras* 324d7) where the Greek simply has an adjective used as a noun. But here we have the word πρᾶγμα; see below.

[9] As it is by Allen, who sees Socrates and Protagoras here discussing Forms (see, e.g., Allen (1970) 91–100, 105–6, 123, 135). His explanation (Allen [1971] 330; cf. Allen (1970) 109–10): "Protagoras can

we are dealing with a person whom we would expect not to be sympathetic to the claims Plato will eventually make on behalf of the Theory of Forms. So Protagoras can hardly be unhesitatingly conceding the existence of a realm of entities "over and above" the people and actions that are pious and just.[10]

In fact, what Protagoras is here unhesitatingly conceding is something he had himself said outright earlier on. In the course of his declamation on the early state of mankind and the teachability of virtue (320c8–328d2), he begins his response to Socrates' objection (319d–320b) that the sons of good men are not always themselves good by saying (324d7–325a4):[11]

Think of it as follows: is there or is there not some one {thing} of which all the citizens must partake, if there is to be a city-state {πότερον ἔστιν τι ἓν ἢ οὐκ ἔστιν οὗ ἀναγκαῖον πάντας τοὺς πολίτας μετέχειν, εἴπερ μέλλει πόλις εἶναι}? . . . If there is, and this one {thing} is not carpentry or metalwork or pottery but justice and temperance and being pious, and, in sum, I call this one {thing} itself {ἓν αὐτό} a man's excellence – if this is that of which it is necessary for all to partake {μετέχειν}, and with this {it is necessary} for every man to act, whatever else he wants to learn and to do.

The assertion that there is such a thing as justice is here wrapped up in Protagorean cotton-wool: it is in the antecedent of an ornate conditional. But Protagoras plainly expects us to concede the truth of this antecedent: there is some one thing, justice, and citizens must partake of this itself. "Is Protagoras here expounding the . . . doctrine of Forms?"[12] Of course not, despite the presence of the Existential Prefix, the emphasis on justice being "one {thing}" (ἕν, 324d7, e3), the intensifier "itself" (αὐτό), and the talk of partaking.

There is no reason to ascribe to Protagoras an "ontology of abstract entities." But neither is there reason to ascribe to him a view to the effect that piety and justice are "reducible" to just and pious people. Within this dialogue, there is no reason whatever to ascribe to him any view at all on

hardly have meant to embrace an ontology of abstract entities; his agreement is more likely to be prompted by the uses of language: all of us who are not cynics or otherwise disreputable believe, after all, that there is such a thing as justice." But then "an ontology of abstract entities" is not required by the argument of the *Protagoras*: all that is needed is what "all of us who are not cynics or otherwise disreputable" believe in any case. Contrast Lacey (1971) 30, 31; Guthrie (1975) 223. Weingartner (1973) 70–72 thinks that the theory of forms is to be found "in an inchoate way" in this passage.

10   Penner (1973) 49–60, Devereux (1977b) 3: he is conceding the existence of states or dispositions of the soul. Perhaps; but in Teloh (1981) 34–42 this is elevated into an account of the "ontological status" of all the virtues in all the Socratic dialogues, and this generalization seems hasty.

11   The relevance of this was pointed out by Peck (1962) 173.

12   Peck (1962) 173, where it is a rhetorical question expecting the answer "No."

the matter. Even outside the dialogue, the material pertaining to Protagoras suggests that he would not have adopted the Theory of Forms if he had ever thought about it, but nothing suggests that he ever did think about it.

Socrates is a different story: in other dialogues, the Theory of Forms is going to be put into his mouth. But within the *Protagoras*, if Socrates has any theories about forms, he does not say so, and they have no visible bearing on this or any other argument. This is the point at which the irrelevance of Socrates' or Plato's beliefs becomes clearest. Socrates is trying to refute Protagoras using Protagoras' own admissions. He expects Protagoras to recognize that he has been refuted. So Protagoras must be in a position to understand his own admissions.[13] When he concedes that there is such a thing as justice, he does not concede anything about Forms, since he knows nothing about them. So Forms are irrelevant to the argument.

Then what *is* Socrates asking Protagoras when he says "is justice a certain *thing* {πρᾶγμα}?" The noun "thing," πρᾶγμα, is used frequently throughout this passage (330c1 *bis*, 330c4, 330d4, 330d5, 331a8, 332a5); perhaps it is doing some real work.

It certainly has nothing particular to do with the Theory of Forms: it is used of forms, e.g., in the phrase αὐτὰ τὰ πράγματα, "the things themselves," at *Phaedo* 66e1–2, but then, it is used of anything: e.g., of the thing that has the form by contrast with the form at *Phaedo* 103b3. Its root meaning, from the verb πράττειν, "to do," is "thing done, deed, act," but by Plato's time it had been generalized away from the verb. Consider some examples within the *Protagoras* itself. The dialogue opens between Socrates and an anonymous companion, to whom Socrates (309b) says that he had just been spending time with the handsome Alcibiades, but without paying much attention to him; the anonymous friend says: "how could such a thing {πρᾶγμα} have happened {γεγονὸς εἴη}?" (c1–2). This fits the word's derivation from the verb nicely. But the next occurrence of the word occurs when Socrates reports himself as saying to Hippocrates (who has come to him to get an introduction to Protagoras) that if he entrusts his soul to a sophist without knowing what a sophist is, he won't know whether he is entrusting his soul "to a good or a bad thing {πράγματι}"

---

[13] Klosko (1983) 370 says of arguments that admit of more than one reconstruction in Platonic dialogues: "The most important limitation is that the commentator cannot introduce material into some proof that takes him beyond the point of view of Socrates' interlocutor." I doubt that this is acceptable in general: see below on the *Hippias Major*. But something like it is surely right here: if Socrates' argument is in fact to refute Protagoras, and Protagoras is to recognize that it does refute him, he must be in a position to understand the admissions he makes.

(312c1–4). There is no apparent tie with the verbal origin of the word at all. And this is typical.[14]

In the course of his speech, Protagoras had implicitly allowed that there were such things as justice, temperance, and being pious; he wrapped those up under the label "excellence" (324d–325b). A little later, he says that it is no wonder the sons of good men many times turn out bad, "if I was speaking the truth in the foregoing: that no one can be unpracticed in this thing {τούτου τοῦ πράγματος}, excellence, if there is to be a city-state" (326e7–327a2), and just a little later he refers to justice as "this thing" (τούτου τοῦ πράγματος, 327c7; cf. 352d3.)

All this might well be true to the historical Protagoras. Sextus Empiricus tells us (*Adversus Mathematicos* VII 60–61):[15] "In starting off the *Throws*[16] he declaims: of all things {the} measure is man: of {things} that are that they are, and of {things} that are not that they are not." "Things" here is χρήματα, not πράγματα; but when Plato cites this famous fragment in *Cratylus* 385e6–386a1, he immediately (386a1–3) paraphrases it using πράγματα.[17] And Diogenes Laertius tells us (IX 51):[18] "He was also the first to say that there are two arguments {λόγους} opposing each other concerning every thing {πραγμάτου}." A use of this type occurs in the mouth of Hippias in the *Protagoras*: in 337d3–4 he speaks of the assembled sophists as knowing the nature of things (τὴν . . . φύσιν τῶν πραγμάτων).

The word πρᾶγμα, then, cannot bear much weight: Socrates is just asking Protagoras if the plain implications of these portions of his speech are ones he would own up to explicitly, and Protagoras is saying he would.

But it might carry some weight. Toward the end, Socrates reverts to our passage, 330d–331b, and rehearses it; he says (349a8–b5, b6–c2):

The question, I think, was this: wisdom, temperance, courage, justice, and piety, are these, which are five names, {names} for one thing {πρᾶγμα}, or for each of the names is there some peculiar being and thing {τις ἴδιος οὐσία καὶ πρᾶγμα} underlying, each having a capacity {δύναμιν} of its own . . .? You said {that they} were not names for one {thing}, but each of these names was allotted to a peculiar thing {ἰδίῳ πράγματι}, and all these were parts of excellence.

---

[14] The word is used of the "doing" of philosophy, e.g., in *Euthydemus* 304a1, e7, 305a6, 7, 8, 305c3, 307b8; but right in the middle of this it occurs in the phrase "says a thing {πρᾶγμα} that borders on intelligence" (306c8–d1; for the translation, see Gifford [1905] 73). The entry *s.v.* πρᾶγμα in des Places (1964) 433–34 is helpful in sorting out the six hundred or so occurrences listed in Brandwood (1976) 774–75.

[15] DK 80B1 (II 263.2–5).

[16] Plato, *Theaetetus* 161c4 "starting off *Truth*." See Guthrie (1969) 183 n. 1.

[17] But πράγματα is replaced by ἕκαστα in the corresponding passage in the *Theaetetus*, 152a6.

[18] Long (1964) II 464.13–14, Marcovich (1999) I 667.15–16 = DK 80B6a (II 266). This is immediately followed by a citation of fr. 1.

There was in fact no explicit talk of names in 330–331, but the opposition in this passage between "name" and "thing (named)" is common in Plato. It is at its clearest in the *Cratylus*, where the question is how names are appropriate to the things they name; the word πράγματα is there the word for the things as opposed to the names (see, e.g., 387d4, 388b10, 390e1, 391b1, 393d4, 401c5, etc.).

Once again there is a possible connection with the historical Protagoras. In discussing the correctness of names in the *Cratylus* Socrates and Hermogenes early on reject the subjectivism they interpret Protagoras' book as espousing (385e–386e); this leads them to the idea that correctness of names consists in the names getting the objective reality of things right. In 391bc, Socrates ironically suggests investigating the correctness of names by learning from Callias, Hermogenes' brother, what Callias had learned about this matter from Protagoras, and Hermogenes contemptuously rejects the suggestion. It sounds a little as if Protagoras did have something to say about the correctness of names,[19] and as if Socrates is attacking it in the *Cratylus*. The position might have been (to reconstruct it simply from these pages): words differ from Greeks to foreigners, and even among the Greeks (385de); since things *are* to each person as they *seem* to each person, as the names differ, so do the things (πράγματα; 385e–386a). Then Protagoras' response about the names "wisdom," "temperance," etc., as paraphrased in *Protagoras* 349a–c is simply a special case of this general line.

Protagoras promulgated the idea that for each thing (πρᾶγμα) there are two opposing arguments, but we have nothing from Protagoras himself illustrating this claim. There is, however, a curious document commonly referred to as *Twofold Arguments*[20] that does illustrate it, and there are reasons to suppose it was written under the influence of Protagoras:[21] the fact that Diogenes tells us that Protagoras was the first to make this claim, and some reasonably close parallels between *Twofold Arguments* I and *Protagoras* 334a–c. Each of its first four chapters begins by saying that there are twofold arguments concerning something: the good and the bad (I), the beautiful and the ugly (II), just and unjust (III), and true and false (IV); the first set of arguments in each case is to the effect that the two contraries (my word, not that of the twofold arguer) are identical, and the second to the effect

---

[19] A matter of some controversy: see, for speculations based on very slender evidence, Classen (1959) (repr. 1976) 218–26; more conservatively, Kerferd (1981) 68–69, Guthrie (1969) 205.

[20] DK 90, II 405–16. Translation in Sprague (1972) 270–93.

[21] See Gulley (1968) 30–31, Guthrie (1969) 316, Robinson (1979) 34–73. It is not, of course, *by* Protagoras, as it mentions the Spartan victory in the Peloponnesian war, and is in Doric. It might even postdate the Platonic writings we are considering.

that they are distinct. In I 11, III 13, and IV 6,[22] there is a formula attached to the thesis of the second argument set: the two contraries are "different, just as in the name, so also in the thing" (διαφέρον ὥσπερ καὶ τὤνυμα, οὕτω καὶ τὸ πρᾶγμα).[23]

In Plato's *Euthydemus* we again encounter the opposition between word and thing (πρᾶγμα): here it is the centerpiece of an argument to the effect that one cannot say anything false and two people cannot contradict each other (283e–286b: see πρᾶγμα in 283e9, 284d1, d5, 286a5, 7, b2, 4, 5). In 286c2–3 Socrates ascribes this argument to "Protagoras and those around him" (οἱ ἀμφὶ Πρωταγόραν).

So if there is any weight attached to Socrates' use of πρᾶγμα in *Protagoras* 330–331, it must be just this: Protagoras has used the *words* "justice," "temperance," etc., in the course of his speech. Does he take it that as these words differ, so do the things (πράγματα) for which they are words? And, if the clues listed are to be relied on, Socrates is here using Protagoras' own language to formulate his questions.

There remain three final passages from the *Protagoras* involving existential claims.

In 332a4–6 we read:

> You call something folly {ἀφροσύνην τι καλεῖς}?
> He said {so}.
> To this thing {τούτῳ τῷ πράγματι} wisdom is entirely opposite?
> It seems to me, he said.

The second passage is less than a page later (332c3–9):

> Well, there is something beautiful {ἔστιν τι καλόν}?
> He agreed.
> Is there any opposite to this except the ugly?
> There is not.
> Next, there is something good {ἔστιν τι ἀγαθόν}?
> There is.
> Is there any opposite to this except the bad?
> There is not. Next, there is something high in sound?
> He said there was.
> Is there any opposite to this except for the low?
> There is not.

---

[22] DK II 406.22 ff., 411.11, 412.11 resp.; cf. the occurrences of πρᾶγμα II 412.25, 415.16, 416.7, .9, .20.

[23] This contrast was a sophistic commonplace, found also in Euripides, *Helen* 601 and, with ἔργον instead of πρᾶγμα, *Phoenissae* 499–502, *Orestes* 454–455, *Trojan Women* 1255, *Hippolytus* 500–502, *Alcestis* 339, *Iphigenia in Aulis* 128: see Nestle (1940) 438–39, Heinimann (1945) 46–56, Robinson (1979) 154–55, Mastronarde (1994) 288–91.

Then, I said, to each one among the opposites, there is only one opposite, and not many?

He agreed.

In the first of these passages, Socrates establishes that folly is the opposite of wisdom. In the intervening lines (332a6–c3), he presents an argument whose conclusion is that folly is the opposite of temperance. The "Socratic induction" in the latter of the two passages quoted then is taken to establish the (very dubious) principle that any quality that has an opposite has only one opposite. After a review of these results (332d1–333a1), Socrates points out that they contradict the claim that wisdom and temperance are distinct (333a1–b4), and concludes that they are one (333b4–5).

The existential claims here serve merely to fix the topic on which comment is to be made. Theorizing as to the status of qualities-with-opposites plays no role whatever in the refutation of Protagoras, and the possession of that sort of theory would have been of no use to Protagoras in avoiding refutation. He might have avoided refutation had he had a good example in which a quality with an opposite has more than one. The Theory of Forms makes it no easier or harder to find such examples. Or, perhaps, he would have done well to argue that "folly" is ambiguous, and taken one way, has wisdom for its opposite, but taken the other way, its opposite is temperance. Here again, the Theory of Forms is no use at all: platonists have been known to argue that their platonic objects (whether forms, universals, or whatever) function as the senses of words, but, even if they are right about that, it is just as hard for a platonist as for the rest of us to detect actual ambiguity.

The final existential claim from the *Protagoras* (358d5–7) raises no new issues.

3.2.2. Charmides

In the *Charmides*, Critias is led to concede that there is more to being temperate than just doing good things (Critias' definition at 163e): that can take place without one knowing it, but one cannot, he and Socrates think, be temperate without knowing it (164a). So he tries saying that temperance more or less (σχεδόν) consists in knowing oneself (τὸ γιγνώσκειν ἑαυτόν, 164d3–4); this is gradually brought around to the point where temperance is a knowledge of itself as well as of other knowledges (166e5–6). Throughout, Socrates is performing "inductions": that is, looking for parallels, other sorts of knowledge (ἐπιστῆμαι, "sciences" in many translations) that are not, or are not exclusively, knowledges of something distinct from themselves. In listing candidates he does not always employ anything that translates as the Existential Prefix, but this is one of the cases in which he might as well have. He says, e.g., "medicine is knowledge of the healthy" (165c8) and "calculation is {knowledge} of the even and the odd" (166a5–6). To the latter he adds "where the odd and even are different from calculation itself" (a9–10). Another case (b1–3):

And again, weighing is weighing of the heavier and lighter weight, but the heavy and light are different from weighing itself?

Finally he does use the Existential Prefix. In 167c7–10 he says:

Think whether it seems to you that there is any sight that is not sight of the things of which the others are sights, but is sight of itself and of the other sights as well . . .

He goes on to ask a series of questions of the same form: does Critias think that "there is any of the senses that . . . ," or that "there is any desire that . . . ," or that "there is any love of that sort" (167d7–8, e1, e7–8), and ends with "but we are saying that there is some *knowledge* of that sort" (168a6).

These latter passages show that Socrates was committed throughout his previous parallel seeking to the existence of medicine, calculation, the odd, the even, the heavy, the light, and so on. But he says nothing at all about what such commitments involve: for all we would know, if we had only the *Charmides* left, it might have been the work of a nominalist.

The inductions and other clarifications just considered from the *Protagoras* and *Charmides* are typical of the Socratic dialogues, and it would be dreary to go over many more. But there is one further passage that we must look at.

3.2.3. Hippias Major

As we have noted (§ 2.2.6), in the initial conversation, Hippias uses the word καλόν, "beautiful," and its cognates with great freedom; so Socrates is led to ask Hippias what the beautiful is. He presents this question, in the mouth of his anonymous importunate interlocutor, in 286cd, but apparently feels the need to explain it some before turning it over to Hippias. He employs an induction in which many[24] have seen metaphysics. He imagines his interlocutor confronting Hippias directly (287b5–d3):

---

[24] E.g., Tarrant (1928) lx–lxi, 46–47 *ad* 287cd; Shorey (1933) 92; Moreau (1941); Allen (1970) 121 (Allen [1971] 329).

SOC: . . . For if you presented that speech you mentioned, the one about the beautiful practices, to him, he'd listen, and when you'd finished speaking, he'd not ask about anything else before {asking about} the beautiful – for this is sort of a habit {of his} – and he'd say,

{c1} "My Eleian friend, isn't it by justice that the just are just?"

Hippias, reply as if he were asking {you}.

{c3} HIPP: I shall reply that {it is} by justice.

SOC: "Then this is something, justice?"

HIPP: Certainly.

{c5} SOC: "Then are the wise wise by wisdom, and all good {things} good by the good?"

HIPP: How else?

{c6} SOC: "{That is,} by these {things}, which *are* something? Hardly by {things} that are not?"

HIPP: But of course, by {things} that are.

{c8} SOC: "Then aren't all beautiful {things} beautiful by the beautiful as well?"

{d1} HIPP: Yes, by the beautiful.

SOC: "By this, which is something?"

HIPP: It is {something}; what does he expect?

{d2} SOC: He will say, "Say then, friend, what is this, the beautiful?"

Now there is a great deal that Hippias does not understand, and he will frequently agree without knowing what he is agreeing to. So it will not quite do to say: since Hippias is assenting so readily, it can hardly be the Theory of Forms he is assenting to. That line had some strength in connection with Protagoras because Protagoras was portrayed as fairly intelligent: for example, he manages to catch Socrates in a fallacy at one point (*Protagoras* 350c–351d). But for sheer density, there are few interlocutors in the dialogues to rival Hippias.[25] So there is no reason to suppose that Hippias is clear about what he is admitting in the passage quoted.[26]

One of the things that Hippias does not understand although he thinks he does is Socrates' question "what is the beautiful?" But Socrates is going to point that out quite explicitly. What is important is what the dialogue says Hippias fails to understand, not some secret doctrine Plato has concealed in this text for the intelligent reader to discover. The refutations reveal Hippias' confusions, if not to him, to us. But they do so explicitly.

We can put the question this way. In the *Symposium*, it is said that the beautiful is (210e6–211a5):

---

[25] Beversluis (2000) 94, regrettably, ducks the task of defending the Hippias of the *Hippias Major*.

[26] Hence my dissent from Klosko's rule (cf. n. 13 above).

in the first place, always in being, and neither {ever} coming-to-be nor passing-away, neither waxing nor waning, and next, not beautiful in one way but ugly in another, nor {beautiful} sometimes and not others, nor beautiful relative to one thing and ugly relative to another, nor beautiful in one place and ugly in another: that is, being beautiful for some but ugly for others.

In the *Hippias Major*, when Hippias acknowledges that there is such a thing as the beautiful, he does not understand what he is acknowledging. This is gradually brought home to him. Is it brought home to him that he has acknowledged the existence of something that exists forever and is absolutely beautiful, that is, not beautiful relative to any thing, or time, or observer?

Almost, but not quite, and here close doesn't count.[27] So far we have only conceded the existence of the beautiful, and no one can suppose that this concession by itself lets in the super-beautiful described in the *Symposium*. All that Socrates needs is a concession that there is something to be defined, as subject for his "what is it?" question.[28]

In the final analysis, it will emerge that the construction of the super-beautiful could be done as an exercise by the reader who is looking into the implications of the refutations of the definitions offered here. But it remains true that construction of the super-beautiful is carried out in the *Symposium*, not in the *Hippias Major*. If the *Hippias Major* leaves the construction as an exercise for the reader, the *Symposium* is the answer book. But there is no hint in the *Hippias Major* that this is what is going on. So, again, it is best to leave metaphysics until it actually happens.[29]

Then, if it isn't supposed to be metaphysics, what *is* the function of the claim (287d1–2) that the beautiful exists? It is the third or fourth existential admission in this passage: we had similar concessions about justice (287c4–5) and wisdom and the good (c6–8), and now we apply the inductive generalization to the target case: the beautiful also exists, and must exist if it is by the beautiful that beautiful things are beautiful. And there is in fact something that is getting pretty close to metaphysics there: a view roughly to the effect that if it is by x that things are F, x must exist.

So there is something more in our passage from the *Hippias Major* than just the concession that justice, wisdom, and the beautiful are there to be talked about: there is also the claim that it is by justice that just people

---

[27] Cf. Grube (1927) 272–73; Woodruff (1978) 103–9; Woodruff (1982) 45 n. 56, 163–64.

[28] Tarrant (1928) 46 *ad* 287c: "There is here a suggestion of metaphysical existence." I fail to see any such suggestion, and here concur with Woodruff (1982) 163–64.

[29] So I am even inclined against as moderate a position as that of Malcolm (1968); see Woodruff (1978), Woodruff (1982) 45 n. 56, 163–64.

are just, by wisdom that wise people are wise, and by the beautiful that beautiful things are beautiful.[30] This is of great importance, and will not be ignored, but, like the "self-predications" in the *Protagoras*, it is best taken up after we have had a look at Socrates' reasons for dissatisfaction with various definitions. In any case, the function of the claim that there is something called "the beautiful," in this context, is plainly simply to motivate asking about it: if we concede that the beautiful is available as a topic for conversation, we can go on to ask what it is. And that, of course, is precisely what happens in 287d2–3.

---

[30] Woodruff (1982) 45 n. 57 notes that the cases are arguably not parallel, but nothing comes of this.

CHAPTER 4

Socrates' requirements: substitutivity

Socrates' requests for definitions get no answers that pass his tests, and there are a lot of attempts.[1] The Theory of Forms comes of investing the existence assumptions just considered with metaphysical significance, using a generalization of a pattern of argument that originates as an argument against definitions Socrates rejects. The generalized pattern is the Argument from Relativity (§ 1.2).

We are going to get at this by constructing a theory of definition for Socrates.

4.1. A SOCRATIC THEORY OF DEFINITION: PRELIMINARY

The theory is not supposed to be Socrates' (or Plato's) own.[2] Rather, it is derived in the following way. When Socrates rejects definitions he uses certain arguments against them. We ask: what would an answer have to be like in order not to fall to that argument? We identify the assumption, and ask what general claim it might most naturally be taken to instantiate. The assumptions in question are not ones that require reference to any special entities that figure as the objects of these definitions.[3]

This procedure will result in three main conditions of adequacy for a definition:

the Substitutivity Requirement: its *definiens* must be substitutable *salva veritate* for its *definiendum*;

---

[1] The list given in Santas (1979) 98–100 has thirty-one, about what I get.
[2] Cf. Robinson (1953) 52 = Vlastos (1971) 113–14; Smith (1998) 146.
[3] Allen (1970) 68 (and *passim*, also in Allen [1971]): "Forms play a regulative role in the dialectic: . . . they determine the kinds of answer that are acceptable, and . . . unacceptable in Socrates' search for definition." But the hypothesis of a form to which Socrates has access is irrelevant to the logic of his argument. If his arguments work, they do so because his premises are true and his conclusions follow from them. These premises are either ones he states or ones close by what he states, and the question of validity has nothing to do with forms.

the Paradigm Requirement: its *definiens* must give a paradigm or standard by comparison with which cases of its *definiendum* may be determined;

and

the Explanatory Requirement: its *definiens* must explain the application of its *definiendum*.

This and the next few chapters lay out these requirements and tie them to Socrates.

The requirements are taken up one by one; there is a respect in which this is artificial, as can be most easily seen by a preliminary reading of *Euthyphro* 6de:

{6d9} SOC: Then do you remember that I did not direct you to teach me this, some one or two of the many pious things, but that form itself by which all the pious things are pious? For you said, I think, that it is by one idea that the impious things are impious and the pious things pious; or don't you recall?
EUTH: I certainly do.
{e4} SOC: Then teach me this idea, what it is, so that looking to it and using it as {an} example, whatever is such as it is among the things either you or anyone else does, I shall say is pious, and whatever is not such, I shall say {is} not.

The first of Socrates' two speeches here presses the Substitutivity Requirement. But it also speaks in d11 of "that form *by which* all the pious things are pious," so we shall be coming back to it when we take up the Explanatory Requirement. And the second speech is consequent on the first: it is part of the same request that Socrates is asking for an *example* – a standard or paradigm (παράδειγμα: see e6).

And yet it is not at all obvious that the three requirements *can* be jointly satisfied. So even if Socrates talks as if there is a single package, it is best to take things out of that package one by one. I start with the Substitutivity Requirement.

4.2. THE SUBSTITUTIVITY REQUIREMENT

Substitutivity was introduced earlier as something Aristotle required of definitions; we are now going to incorporate it as one of the requirements placed on definitions by the theory of definition we are constructing for Socrates, the Substitutivity Requirement:

(SR) $w =_{df} abc \rightarrow (\ldots w - \leftrightarrow \ldots abc -)$.

In principle, the sentential context on "w," the filling in "$\ldots w -$," could be anything, of any degree of complexity; in practice, definitions are usually refuted using contexts of one of two types: "*w*" appears as predicate, or, after transformation into "*w*-ness" or "the *w*," as subject. With "*w*" as predicate, (SR) turns into the requirement that a *definiens* supply necessary and sufficient conditions for the application of its *definiendum*; with "*w*" used to form the subject, it turns into a principle I shall call "Leibniz's Law" (see § 4.4).

4.3. NECESSARY AND SUFFICIENT CONDITIONS

The requirement of necessity and sufficiency is what you get when (SR) is confined to cases in which "*w*" appears as predicate:

(NecSuf) $w =_{df} abc \rightarrow (x$ is $w \leftrightarrow x$ is $abc)$.

Another way to put (NecSuf) is: an alleged definition can be overthrown by counterexamples. Counterexamples can either be cases that satisfy the alleged *definiens* but not the *definiendum*, or cases that satisfy the *definiendum* but not the alleged *definiens*. Cases of the first type show that the *definiens* is not a necessary condition for the application of the *definiendum*; cases of the second, that it is not a sufficient condition.

We can break this up into two separate requirements:

(Nec) $w =_{df} abc \rightarrow (x$ is $w \rightarrow x$ is $abc)$
(Suf) $w =_{df} abc \rightarrow (x$ is $abc \rightarrow x$ is $w)$.

4.3.1. Laches

Socrates sets the frame for the rest of the dialogue in 190de. The background question about bravery or courage is how we can bring it about that it "comes-to-be-present" in the young: training them to fight in heavy armor is the suggestion on the table. To answer that question, Socrates says, we must first say what bravery is; he asks Laches to start.

4.3.1.1. 190e–192b
Laches responds with (190e5–6): "if someone should be willing, remaining in the order of battle, to defend himself against the enemy, then, be assured, he'd be courageous." Laches only says: if someone stands his ground, he's brave – standing one's ground is a sufficient condition for someone's counting as courageous. But in the context it is supposed to answer the question "what is courage?" And Socrates will in fact attack it for lack of necessity.

So we must treat it as a definition:

(D_1C) x is courageous $=_{df}$ x stands his ground.

There are a couple of conventions that first appear here but will figure in our subsequent discussion of definitions.

First, within the definition dialogues, the various attempts at definition will be numbered according to their occurrence in the dialogue: (D_1C) is the first definition for "courageous" in the *Laches*, and is so numbered. There is room for disagreement as to where one definition is given up and another is launched. My own approach will be fairly atomistic: almost any alteration in a definition I'll take to turn it into a new one.

Second, the definitions in these dialogues are sometimes phrased by the interlocutors using the adjectives: "courageous," "temperate," "beautiful," and sometimes using the corresponding abstract nouns: "courage," "temperance," "beauty." I think that little turns on this, but, to keep track of it, I've used capital letters in labeling definitions in which the adjective is used and lower-case letters in labeling those in which the abstract noun is used. (The practice comes from logicians' use of capital letters for predicate letters and lower-case letters for singular constants.) Hence the first definition, above, is labeled "(D_1C)," since it is formulated with "courageous"; the next one, which reverts to "courage" will be "(D_2c)."

Definition (D_1C), then, tells us that the courageous person is to be identified with the one who stands his ground. Socrates concedes that such a person would be courageous (191a); he concedes sufficiency. But he lists cases of courageous retreat (191a–c).[4] He was not just asking about some courageous men in some circumstances, but about courageous men in various circumstances; he lists some (191c–e), and says (191e4–7, 9–11):

Then all these {people} are courageous, but some show courage in pleasures, some in pains, some in desires, some in fears; while others {show} cowardice in these very same {things} . . . I was asking: what is each of these? Try again to say, first, for courage, what it is that is the same in all these cases.

Laches does not quite understand (see 191e), but the rest of us do. Socrates wants an answer "*abc*" to his question that satisfies not just

(SufC) x is *abc* $\rightarrow$ x is courageous,

---

[4] It is an interesting point, noted by Nichols (1987) 254 n. 25, that Laches had himself earlier (181ab) praised Socrates' behavior (the implication is that he showed courage) during the retreat, in which both were present, from Delium. Alcibiades is made to comment (*Symposium* 221a7–b1) on how much more self-possessed (ἔμφρων: for the translation, cf. Dover [1980] 174) Socrates was than Laches.

so that *abc* is a sufficient condition for the application of "courageous," which, he concedes, Laches' answer was, but also

(NecC) x is courageous $\rightarrow$ x is *abc*,

so that *abc* gives a necessary condition for the application of "courageous." And the upshot of Socrates' counterexample was, of course, precisely to the effect that the conditional

(Nec$_1$C) x is courageous $\rightarrow$ x stands his ground

fails.

His attempt to clarify the matter for Laches brings out the same point. He gives an example of a successful definition: quickness (τάχος, 192a1; ταχυτής, a10, b2), which we display in all sorts of activities, can be defined as "the capacity {δύναμις} that performs many {things} in a little time," which covers not just one or another of these activities, but all of them (192ab).

4.3.1.2. *192b–d*
Socrates now says (192b5–8): "Then you try too, Laches, to say what capacity courage is, the same in pleasure and in pain and in all the {things} for which we were just saying it exists, that is then called courage?" Laches' response is this (192b9–c1): "Then it seems to me to be a sort of perseverance of the soul, if one must state concerning courage[5] that which naturally pervades all {διὰ πάντων . . . πεφυκὸς}." The phrase "of the soul" is dropped in the sequel; let us then docket, as Laches' second attempt to define "courage":

(D$_2$c) courage $=_{df}$ perseverance.

Socrates (192c3–5) announces that he will show that not all perseverance counts as courage, in fact, that not all perseverance even seems to Laches to count as courage. He is done with that by 192d10, where he presents a revision of (D$_2$c). In our terms, we may take him to be showing that (D$_2$c) fails (SufC), and must be revised to be passed on that score.

But there is a difference, not just in the *definientia* between (D$_1$C) and (D$_2$c), but in the *definienda* themselves: (D$_1$C) defines "courageous" and (D$_2$c) defines "courage." In a way, this is immaterial, for both are answers

---

[5] Badham, according to Burnet (1903), bracketed περὶ ἀνδρείας, and Burnet, Croiset (1921) 109, and Lamb (1924) 50 follow him; the word order is certainly weird, but otherwise it hardly makes a difference.

to the question "what is courage?" (see 190d8, e3, 192b5–8).[6] But Socrates' refutation of (D₂c) remains on the level of the abstract noun "courage." And that means that the refutation does not directly take the form of showing that (D₂c) fails (SufC), since that is stated in terms of the adjective "courageous."

Rather, Socrates' refutation looks like this. He first extracts the claim that courage is among the things that are "beautiful" (τῶν . . . καλῶν πραγμάτων, 192c5–7) – let us say here "praiseworthy." He then[7] adduces the case of perseverance accompanied by folly (ἡ μετ' ἀφροσύνης, *sc.* καρτερία), which he gets Laches to admit is "harmful and injurious" (d1–3). He gets the concession that something harmful and injurious is not praiseworthy (d4–6). And so, he concludes, perseverance accompanied by folly is not praiseworthy (d7–9). The argument, then, is this (the first premise instantiates an important type of assumption; I'll call it a "Virtue Assumption"):

(VAc) Courage is praiseworthy.	P
(1) Foolish perseverance is harmful.	P
(2) What is harmful is not praiseworthy.	P
∴ (3) Foolish perseverance is not praiseworthy.	(1),(2)
∴ (4) Foolish perseverance is not courage.	(3),(VAc)
(5) Foolish perseverance is perseverance.	P
∴ (6) Some perseverance is not courage.	(4),(5)

Line (6) tells us that perseverance is not sufficient for courage, and it can easily be taken one step further to bring it to bear on (SufC), since it fairly directly entails

(7) Some who persevere are not courageous.

But "fairly directly" is not quite "directly": to get from (6) to (7) we should have to build some bridge principles that will take us from talk at the level of abstract nouns to talk in terms of the corresponding adjectives, verbs, concrete nouns, etc.

Such bridge principles are pertinent here. For (D₁C) fails, according to Socrates, because it does not characterize all of those who are courageous (191c8–e2), all those who possess courage (191e4–7), and (D₂c) is expressly

---

[6] I may here be in slight disagreement with Stokes (1986) 71–72, 76.

[7] 192c8–10 deals with endurance accompanied by intelligence (ἡ . . . μετὰ φρονήσεως καρτερία), which Socrates concedes is praiseworthy; this comes back after we have eliminated just "endurance" as too general, but plays no logical role in that elimination.

fashioned in order to remedy that defect (191e9–11, 192b5–8). So (D₂c) must be read as having as a consequence

(8) x is courageous $\leftrightarrow$ x perseveres,

and then (6) should also be read as having (7) as a consequence. But, even if (7) and (8) are not immediate consequences of (6) and (D₂c), they are, I take it, obvious consequences: predication relations between f and g will be mirrored in parallel relations between Fs and Gs.

Alternatively, we could restate (SufC) for the abstract case; instead of taking the definition as having the form "courageous =df *abc*," and writing the requirement of sufficiency as:

(SufC) x is *abc* $\rightarrow$ x is courageous,

we might take the definition as having the form "courage =df *F*ness," and write:

(Sufc) x is *F*ness $\rightarrow$ x is courage.

Here the variable "x" has to be taken as instantiated using abstract nouns or noun phrases like "foolish perseverance": if the definition "courage =df perseverance" were correct, it would have to be so that all perseverance, even foolish perseverance, was courage.

I do not think that there is any material difference, at this point, between these two ways of doing the job. But the present argument lends itself to treatment better in terms of (Sufc) than in terms of (SufC): its conclusion is that perseverance does not satisfy (Sufc).

Consider now the premises of the argument as it stands, starting with the less interesting ones.

Premise (5) is as uninteresting as can be; it is a tautology, there only for formal completeness and not represented by anything in the text.

Premises (1) and (2) are presumably just to be accepted as brute fact. A diligent interlocutor might have asked Socrates to define "folly," "perseverance," "harm," etc. before granting these premises, but let us allow them with only one further comment: Socrates will, in the sequel, unhesitatingly count cases of simple ignorance as cases of folly (ἀφροσύνη), and, in parallel, cases of simple knowledge as cases of intelligence (φρόνησις).

Finally, the Virtue Assumption (VAc) is parallel to others we shall encounter: "V is A," where "V" is a word for some alleged virtue or excellence and "A" is one or another of "admirable," "praiseworthy" (καλόν), or "good" (ἀγαθόν). This type of assumption goes unchallenged until the end of *Republic* I, where Socrates professes ignorance, in the absence of a definition for "justice," as to whether justice is really a virtue or not. Fairly clearly, he is taking it that if some character trait *is* a virtue or an excellence, it is commendable. The substantive aspect of assumptions like (1) is then that V, in this case courage, is in fact a virtue, an excellence, a good thing.

The use of the Virtue Assumption (VAc) gives an additional wrinkle to this argument. The argument shows that some perseverance is not courage, and that means it fails (Sufc), as already discussed. The straightforward way of showing that would be to give a counterexample: citing one or more cases of the *definiens* that are not cases of the *definiendum*, just as the argument against (D_1C) showed that it failed to give a necessary condition by citing cases of the *definiendum* that were not case of the *definiens*. In a way, that is what Socrates does: foolish perseverance is perseverance but not courage. But, rather than presenting this as plainly true, Socrates gives us in (VAc)–(3) a subargument to *show* that foolish perseverance is not courage.

And that sets a criterion of adequacy for a definition of courage that is more specific than (Sufc) by itself: in order to satsify (Sufc), whatever defines courage must preserve (VAc).

4.3.1.3. *192d–194b*

At this point, Socrates takes the argument to show that at least "intelligent" (φρόνιμος) has to be added to the definition, and Laches tentatively buys this (192d10–12): so we try again with

(D_3c) courage $=_{df}$ intelligent perseverance (192d10–11).

(D_3c) is, like (D_2c), framed using the abstract noun "courage," but the discussion of it proceeds in terms of the adjective "courageous." It raises even fewer bridge problems than (D_2c) did.

Socrates argues that (D_3c) too fails sufficiency, and he does so simply by presenting counterexamples: when someone perseveres in investing knowing that he will make a profit, he counts as persevering intelligently but not as courageous (192e); so also a doctor who perseveres in refusing the imprecations of his patient for food or drink when he knows it would be bad for the patient (192e–193a) isn't therefore courageous.

These examples are stated by Socrates in terms of the adjective "courageous" (192e4) and verb "persevere" (e2, 193a1), so the formulation we want is (SufC). How little difference that makes is clear from the fact that Laches' phrasing in his reply to the latter example shows that he has the abstract noun "courage" in mind.[8] So there are no interesting bridge problems here, as far as I can see.

The counterexamples are enough to do in (D₃c): we have, then, a complete argument against the definition. But Socrates does not stop there. On the face of it, he goes on to give four more groups of counterexamples.

He first (193a) outlines a situation in which two men are on opposite sides in a battle; the one perseveres in fighting in the knowledge that others are helping him, that collectively they outnumber the opposing side, are better fighters, and fight from a better position, while the other simply perseveres anyway. The question for Laches is: which would he say is the more courageous? He (193b1) picks the latter.

This is to count – anyway, so it seems, and Socrates will go on to treat it that way – as a case in which someone who "intelligently" perseveres fails to count as courageous. That involves a transition from saying that one is more courageous than the other to saying that the one is courageous and the other is not. Nothing is done to ease this transition, and it is one of a type we shall encounter again.

But the conclusion contains a puzzle, of which Socrates is aware: it not only counts the man who "intelligently" perseveres as courageous, it also counts the one who "foolishly" perseveres as courageous. And that, it turns out, is precisely where Socrates is headed, as he says in 193b2–4.

The remaining three sorts of counterexample all have the same twist: someone with a knowledge of horsemanship (τὸν μετ᾽ ἐπιστήμης . . . ἱππικῆς, 193b5) who perseveres in a cavalry battle is less courageous than one who perseveres without that knowledge (193b); likewise for persevering with a knowledge of the use of a sling or bow and arrows as opposed to persevering without that knowledge (193bc) and for persevering with diving in wells for people who are adept at it as opposed to those who aren't (193c): the latter are in each case more courageous.

But, Socrates reminds us (193d1–5), we a moment ago agreed that foolish perseverance was "blameworthy and harmful," whereas courage was something praiseworthy; now, however, we are saying that foolish perseverance is courage (d6–8). And there is the puzzle. In all of these cases we are saying that

(9) Foolish perseverance is courage (d6–8),

---

[8] 193a2 οὐδ᾽ ὁπωστιοῦν οὐδ᾽ αὕτη: "nor {is} this, in any way at all," where the word "this" is feminine.

and that conflicts with the conclusion arrived at before on the basis of (VAc), recalled in d4–5, and (1)–(3), recalled in d1–3, that

(4) Foolish perseverance is not courage.

So we have a contradiction.

Well, one might think, fine, we wanted to show that (D_3c) was wrong, and, if we have not merely counterexamples but a contradiction, so much the better.

But that isn't the way the logic works: the contradiction is not based on (D_3c) at all. Rather, (9) is internal to the description of the last four sets of counterexamples, and (4) is a conclusion drawn in the course of refuting (D_2c): Socrates and Nicias are committed to both (9) and (4) even if they reject (as they are presumably doing) both definitions.

I do not know how to resolve this situation, and won't try.[9] For my purposes, the important thing to grasp is the negative result that the contradiction Socrates derives has no role to play in the rejection of any definitions. What we have so far is the rejection of (D_1C) and (D_3c) entirely on the basis of counterexamples, and the rejection of (D_2c) on the basis of a counterexample constructed in such a way that we can see a futher requirement placed on the definition for courage: the truth of (VAc), the Virtue Assumption for courage, must be preserved.

Proposition (9) is a byproduct of the argument against (D_3c), and, if Socrates and Laches took it seriously, they would have to go back to the argument against (D_2c). They don't even mention the possibility; the argument against (D_2c) is simply allowed to stand, and all three attempts must be counted as failures. At this point (193e–194b), Socrates and Laches express disgruntlement but decide against quitting, and Nicias is brought in to help.

4.3.1.4. *194c–e*

Nicias' entry into the definition stretch of the conversation has him complaining that Socrates and Laches are not "defining courage well" (καλῶς ὁρίζεσθαι τὴν ἀνδρείαν, 194c7–8), in that they are making no use of something he has heard Socrates saying (194c8–9): that "each of us is good in

---

[9] Cf. Stokes (1986) 84–87 for pertinent comments, but I am not sure Stokes has seen the difficulty as I do, since he does not comment on the bearing of what he refers to as Laches' "downfall" (86) on the sequence of definitions, and I am mistrustful of attempts to distinguish "two senses of *andreia*" (which Stokes thinks would help, 86, but which he is quite correctly not willing to ascribe to Plato himself).

those {matters} in which he is wise" (d1–2). Nicias concludes from this that "if the courageous {man} is good,[10] it is clear that he is wise" (d4–5).

Wisdom is at best a necessary condition for someone's being courageous (and that only under the assumption that the courageous man is good, which presumably all would grant). So the three interlocutors promptly go on to ask "which wisdom?" (ποία σοφία e3; cf. d9, e1) courage is supposed to be: not, Socrates says, the knowledge of flute playing or lyre playing (194e). In other words, if anyone had offered

(D_4C) x is courageous $=_{df}$ x is wise

as a definition, the examples of wisdom in flute playing and lyre playing would have been instant counterexamples to show that the definition fails (SufC).

Most of us find the trading between "wisdom" (σοφία 194d9, d10) and "knowledge" (ἐπιστήμη 194e8) uncomfortable, but neither Socrates nor Nicias (195a1) does, and it is difficult to see how this could be turned into a substantive point against Socrates' procedures.

4.3.1.5. 194e–199e

The final section of this dialogue is a fantastic free-for-all: Laches is shown getting the hang of Socratic technique, and joins the fray against Nicias; the rivalry between them is a beautiful piece of comedy. Regrettably, in extracting what I want from it, most of that is left behind.[11]

It all starts with Nicias' response to the question of 194e3, "which wisdom?"; Socrates rephrases this (194e8) as "knowledge of what" is courage?, and Nicias responds (194e11–195a1):

NIC: I {say it's} . . . the knowledge of {things} fearful and {things} hopeful {τὴν τῶν δεινῶν καὶ θαρραλέων ἐπιστήμην}, both in war and in all the other {cases}.

And this gives us:

(D_5c) courage $=_{df}$ the knowledge of things fearful and things hopeful.

The discussion of this freely vacillates between formulations involving "courage" and ones involving "courageous"; I've tried to some extent to keep track of this vacillation in the summary that follows, but it is a summary, and does not include every shift.

---

[10] Sprague (1973) 38 = Cooper (1997) 679 curiously mistranslates "Therefore, if a man is really courageous."

[11] A good discussion that tries to do justice to argument as well as literary value is Stokes (1986) 36–113.

Laches attacks: after an initial volley (195ab) that has no argumentative content worth speaking of, he alleges that doctors and farmers know what is fearful and what is hopeful in the case of illnesses and farming, but are not therefore courageous (195bc). If he were right, this would show that (D₅c) failed sufficiency.

But Nicias denies that doctors know what is fearful and what is hopeful *simpliciter:* a doctor may know whether the patient is going to live or die, but he doesn't know whether it is better for the patient to live or die, for example, and so doesn't know whether the signs that the patient is being cured are hopeful or fearful (195cd).

Laches goes along with that much (195d), and Nicias then asks whether Laches concurs that the knowledge of what is fearful and what is hopeful belongs to no one but the courageous man (195d). Laches' response is that at that rate the courageous would be identified with the diviners: no one could know better than they for whom it is better to live than to die (195e).

This alleged consequence of (D₅c) is plainly regarded by Laches as ridiculous; since Nicias is going to claim that it is not in fact a consequence, he apparently concurs in finding it unacceptable. No one says just what is wrong with it. But it seems to me a natural guess that what is wrong with it is that it would show that (D₅c) provides neither a necessary nor a sufficient condition for being courageous: if those who know what is hopeful and what is fearful are the diviners, then, since most courageous people are not diviners, and diviners are not universally courageous, that knowledge neither is needed for nor guarantees courage.

Nicias denies that the identification of the courageous and the diviners is a consequence of (D₅c): a diviner, he concedes, has to know what is going to happen – who is going to die and who not, etc. – but that doesn't mean he knows whether it is better or worse for things to turn out the way he knows they will (195e–196a).

After some byplay (196a–c), Socrates reminds us of the content of (D₅c) in 196d1–2: "courage is knowledge of fearful and hopeful {things}."[12] Against this, he tries animals as a counterexample: Laches at least thinks that we all take some of them (lions, etc.) to be courageous, but deny them knowledge (196e–197a).

If this were correct, we'd have cases of courage without knowledge, and (D₅c) would fail necessity. But Nicias won't concede that it is correct: he

---

[12] ἐπιστήμην . . . δεινῶν τε καὶ θαρραλέων: almost verbatim what we had at 194e11–195a1; the translation in Sprague (1973) 42 = Cooper (1997) 681, "you say that courage is knowledge of the grounds of fear and hope?" is potentially misleading (her translation at 194e–195a was simply "it {*sc.* courage} is the knowledge of the fearful and the hopeful").

cheerfully denies that lions or children who are ignorant of the dangers to be faced are courageous; he is prepared to call them "bold" (θρασέα, 197c1) but not "courageous" (197a–c).

There is more byplay (197c–e), and it is a good deal more fun than the argument. But the argument resumes with Socrates reminding Nicias that courage was at the beginning of the argument taken to be a part of virtue (198a, referring to 190cd). Among the other parts of virtue Socrates lists temperance and justice (198a8).

Socrates' attack on (D$_5$c) is as follows. The fearful is what causes fear, and this is future evil; similarly, future goods are hopeful (198bc). But the same knowledge covers what was, what is, and what will be (198c–199a). Socrates gathers all these premises together (199b). The conclusion is that courage is the knowledge of all goods and evils, past, present, and future (199b–d); so courage is not a part but the whole of virtue (199de), which contradicts the initial assumption, so we haven't found what courage is (199e).

This argument, if it worked, would be showing that (D$_5$c) fails to provide a sufficient condition for courage: the *definiens* covers things that aren't courage, such as justice and temperance.

But, just as the argument against (D$_2$c) employed an additional assumption, (VAc), and so a condition of adequacy, the preservation of the truth of that assumption, so also the argument here employs an additional assumption, to the effect that courage is a part of and not the whole of virtue. And we might suppose that this places another condition of adequacy on a satisfactory definition: that courage must be so defined as to preserve the distinction between it and justice and each of the other virtues. But, whereas (VAc) is going to find parallels in other dialogues, this assumption does not: Socrates elsewhere espouses the thesis that the virtues are one.

Much that is of interest in this argument has been left untouched: questions as to whether the various arguments prove what they are supposed to are pushed to one side; my analyses are intended only to guarantee validity, not soundness. For all that matters here is what Socrates requires of definitions. And in this dialogue, every one of the definitions fails because it fails to satisfy one of (Nec) and (Suf).

4.3.2. Charmides

There are a lot of arguments based on (NecSuf) in this very complex dialogue; the present section takes them up. Other arguments will be dealt with in subsequent sections.[13]

---

[13] All in § 4.4 under the head of "Leibniz's Law," but that of 164c–166b will also reappear in § 7.3.

4.3.2.1. 159b–160d

Charmides' first stab at defining temperance is: "temperance is doing all things in an orderly way, quietly" (159b2–3); it "is a sort of quietness {ἡσυχιότης τις}" (b5).

The latter of these two formulations makes it sound as if Charmides is only saying that temperance is a variety of quietness; the former sounds a little more like an identification. Socrates' argument is going to be directed toward showing that this definition fails (Suf), so he cannot be taking it as saying only that temperance is a variety of quietness: that would make quietness only a necessary condition for temperance. So let us make the definition:[14]

(D₁t) temperance =$_{df}$ quietness.

Socrates' refutation is of this is a bit disorderly.

At first he formulates the thesis to be refuted as "the quiet are temperate" (159b8): this already requires the stronger of Charmides' two formulations.

He gets from Charmides the premise that temperance is to be counted among the "beautiful" things (τῶν καλῶν, 159c1–2). Let us use "admirable" for a change. Then we have the Virtue Assumption:

(VAt) Temperance is admirable.

Socrates now produces a long list of cases, a Socratic induction, in which doing something quickly is more admirable than doing it quietly (159c3–160b2); he sums this up (160b3–5); Charmides gives a qualified assent (κινδυνεύει, b6); and Socrates concludes (160b7–d3):

Therefore temperance cannot be a sort of quietness, nor {can} the temperate life be quiet, from this account, since it, being temperate, has to be admirable.
{b9} For one or the other of two things: either never or very few times do the quiet actions in one's life show up for us as more admirable than the quick and energetic {ones}.
{c2} But, my friend, even if in fact the quiet {actions} that are more admirable are at most no fewer than the forceful and quick {ones}, temperance wouldn't

---

[14] For future reference, here is a list of what I am counting as the *definientia* for temperance in the *Charmides*:
(D₁t) quietness (159b)
(D₂t) modesty (160d)
(D₃t) acting on one's own things (161b)
(D₄t) doing good things (162c)
(D₅t) knowing oneself (164d)
(D₆ₐt) knowledge of itself (knowledge of knowledge, 166c)
(D₆ᵦt) knowledge of knowledge and ignorance (166e).
This is in one respect artificial, since (D₆ₐt) and (D₆ᵦt) are actually intended as elaborations of (D₅),
but the transition is difficult enough that it will be better to flag them separately.

for this {reason} be acting quietly any more than {acting} forcefully and quickly, either in walking or in speaking or in anything else, nor would the quiet life be more temperate than the not quiet {life}, {d} since in our account temperance was assumed {to be} something among the things that are admirable, and quick {things} have shown themselves no less admirable than quiet ones.

Let us simply grant Socrates that "quick" or "forceful" – let us stick to the latter – is contrary to "quiet."[15] And let us focus, as Socrates himself does, on temperate actions, ignoring temperate people.

He is taking the Virtue Assumption (VAt) to entail

(1) All temperate actions are admirable.

For this inference to work, we must allow that at least certain things that are true of temperance are therefore true of instances of temperance such as temperate actions. We can't allow all of the things true of temperance to be true of instances of temperance, since (e.g.) temperance is a virtue but lives and actions are not. To get from the abstract to the concrete we need a bridge principle, here in the form of a properly restricted conditional. We shall need this in other contexts as well: a conditional that tells us that, given a certain restriction, when Fness is G, Fs are Gs. The restriction is very hard to get straight without begging questions.[16] So I shall for the time being simply suppose we have it straight, label it "$R(G, f)$" (for "Restriction on the relation between G and f"), and adopt the hypothetical

(H) $R(G, f)$ & $Gf \rightarrow (x)(Fx \rightarrow Gx)$.[17]

Here as before, the lower-case "f" represents the abstract noun or noun phrase corresponding to the adjective or other concrete form represented by "F"; the hypothetical can be read "if the restriction on the relation between G and Fness is met, and Fness is G, any particular F will also be G."

So far, our only departure from the text is in making (H) explicit. It will help to go on, temporarily, with an argument that is not exactly the one Socrates states. Once Socrates had got (1), he might have taken his list of actions in which quickness is more admirable than quietness to show that

(a) Some quiet actions are not admirable.

---

[15] Kosman (1983) 204 thinks we can grant him this.

[16] Roughly, it has to do with things that are true of Fness by being true by the definition of "F" of any F, where being true by definition includes terms in the definition and logical consequences of the definition. But such a formulation may beg questions.

[17] If we now look back to the argument against (D₂c) in *Laches* 192cd, this gives us a way of formulating a bridge principle we might have used there.

Then he could have concluded[18]

(b) Some quiet actions are not temperate.

This would have shown that (D_1t) fails sufficiency: an action that is quiet is not therefore temperate. This would have done nothing to defeat the weaker formulation of Charmides' claim, since that only made quietness a necessary condition for temperance, but it would have defeated the stronger formulation, which identifies temperance with quietness.

But Socrates does not say that his induction establishes (a); rather, in 160d2–3 he derives:

(c) Forceful actions are no less admirable than quiet ones,

where this has to be just an existential generalization to the effect that (the numbering conforms to that in the more formal version presented below)

(4) Some forceful actions are no less admirable than some quiet ones,

which is, in fact, all the weight the induction can bear and all Socrates says he wants from it. But he takes the result of his induction, with (VAt), to defeat (D_1t). So he must be supposing that (D_1t) and (VAt) entail a Comparative Claim such as:

(CC) Quiet actions are always more admirable than forceful ones.

In order to understand this inference, let us consider what it would be ruling out.

The Virtue Assumption (VAt) tells us that temperance is admirable; its consequence (1) tells us that every temperate action is admirable. But, one might think, what is admirable about any temperate action is precisely its temperance. If we think of actions as more or less temperate and as more or less admirable, the one goes with the other. But then an action's intemperance, which is simply the contrary of its temperance, can only count against its admirability.

Now if temperance is quietness, then what is admirable about any temperate action must be its quietness, and all the above remarks carry over to quietness and its contrary, which we are taking to be forcefulness.

And so far Socrates' inference sounds solid: quietness, if that is indeed temperance, always counts in favor of an action and forcefulness always counts against it.

---

[18] By a syllogism in the second figure, Baroco. So also Kosman (1983) 204. But this is not the way it is formulated in the text: see below.

But that is not quite enough to justify Socrates' inference to (CC). For we might suppose that the temperance-intemperance scale does not give us the only dimension in which we can evaluate actions. Abstractly speaking, it could be that the degree of injustice exhibited by someone's otherwise temperate action outweighed the degree of its temperance, so that it was on balance not admirable. And, if we went that way, we might perfectly well suppose that there could be intemperate actions that were, on balance, more admirable than temperate ones, and so, if temperance is quietness, that there are forceful actions that are more admirable than quiet ones. We might imagine someone hot-headedly and intemperately striking out against a glaring injustice and setting matters right; we might not be happy about the way the thing was done, but figure that it was, on balance, an admirable thing to do. In short, we might suppose that there are situations in which the claims of temperance can be overridden by the claims of other virtue-vice pairings.

But Socrates' inference rules this out. He seems to be employing a generalized Comparative Principle something like the following:

(CP) If a certain character trait is admirable (where this means at least that actions manifesting that trait are admirable), then, given two actions, one of which manifests the trait and the other the contrary trait, the first must be more admirable than the second.

Then, if quietness were temperance, and so admirable, an action manifesting it would have to be more admirable than any action manifesting forcefulness. But, by (4), this is false; so the definition must go.

We could circumvent the use of this forbidding principle if we were prepared to give Socrates a principle to the effect that, where one action is more admirable than another, the second isn't really admirable and the first is. And we might recall, in support of this, that in discussing *Laches* 192d–194b we found Socrates moving from a formulation according to which one person was more courageous than another to a formulation in which the first was courageous and the second was not. In fact, I have no doubt that this is a Socratic way of thinking. And then the cases in which a forceful action is more admirable than a quiet one would collapse into cases in which a quiet action just isn't admirable: we would be back at the simpler version of the argument: (1), (a), ∴ (b).

But this would require us to write off Socrates' formulation of the argument in 160b–d, as quoted above, to mere verbosity: he is, in that passage, insistent that what rules out the possibility of identifying temperance with quietness is the fact that "quick {things} have shown themselves no less admirable than quiet ones" (d2–3), and there is no way of inferring from this that quiet actions are simply not admirable. So the reconstruction of the argument that appears below employs the Comparative Principle. But before we get to it, two comments are in order.

First, Socrates, when he is in the unity-of-virtues mood (see § 4.3.1.5 *ad fin.*), might well want to deny that any such thing as the overriding of the claims of one virtue by another is possible; he might concede that we can imagine it in the abstract, but, in that mood, suppose he had arguments against its being a live possibility.

Second, although we may not be entirely satisfied with the argument Socrates gives, what has been said so far suggests a fairly closely related one, and we may suppose that this really captures what, in some sense, counts in Socrates' argument. In calculating an action's position on the scale of admirability, its temperance can only be a plus; it may be (we are supposing) outweighed by other considerations, but these other considerations do not have to do with the degree of the action's temperance. What Socrates' examples can be taken as showing is that this is not true of the action's quietness. To put it in a way not available to Socrates: an action's degree of quietness or forcefulness is morally irrelevant; its degree of temperance or intemperance is not. So the definition must fail.

Our idealized version of Socrates' argument, (VAt), (1), (a), therefore (b) above, would have shown that quietness is not a sufficient condition for temperance. Socrates' actual argument purports to show the same thing, whether or not it is sound. The way it works, Socrates takes the definition to entail that any quiet action is temperate, that is, as giving a sufficient condition. Then, since any temperate action is admirable, by the Comparative Principle, it must be more admirable than any forceful action; the existence of forceful actions that are more admirable than quiet ones then shows that this is false.

This is most easily seen in a more formal version of the argument; here it is (readers uninterested in this may want to skip to the next subsection).

Let us abbreviate as follows:

t:	temperance
q:	quietness
Tx:	x is temperate (x is an action showing temperance)
Qx:	x is quiet
Fx:	x is forceful
Ax:	x is admirable
$MAxy$:	x is more admirable than y
$con(\Phi,\Psi)$:	Φ is contrary to Ψ

Then the Comparative Principle becomes:

(CP) $(\Phi)(\Psi)\{con(\Phi, \Psi) \rightarrow$
$\qquad [(x)(\Phi x \rightarrow Ax) \rightarrow (x)(y)(\Phi x \& \Psi y \rightarrow MAxy)]\}$.

We may suppose that con(Q,F), and then, instantiating (CP) and using *modus ponens*, we get:

(CC) $(x)(Qx \rightarrow Ax) \rightarrow (x)(y)(Qx \& Fy \rightarrow MAxy)$.

The hypothetical (H) has the following as an instance:

(Ht) $R(A,t) \& At \rightarrow (x)(Tx \rightarrow Ax)$,

and we may suppose that the restriction "R(A,t)" is met, so that we have:

(Ht′) $At \rightarrow (x)(Tx \rightarrow Ax)$.

The definition becomes:

(D_1t) t $=_{df}$ q,

and the sufficiency condition, a consequence of (D_1t), is:

(Suft) $Qx \rightarrow Tx$.

And, finally, the Virtue Assumption for temperance is simply:

(VAt) $A(t)$

Socrates' argument then looks like this:

(1) $Tx \rightarrow Ax$	(VAt),(Ht′)
(2) $Qx \rightarrow Ax$	(Suft),(1)
(3) $Qx \& Fy \rightarrow MAxy$	(CC),(2)
(4) $(\exists x)(\exists y)(Fx \& Qy \& \neg MAyx)$	Induction
(5) $\Phi\alpha \& Q\beta \& \neg MA\beta\alpha$	(4)×EI
(6) $F\alpha \& Q\beta \rightarrow MA\beta\alpha$	(3)
(7) $MA\beta\alpha$	(6),(5)
(8) $\neg MA\beta\alpha$	(5)
So $\neg(D_1t)$.	

Here (D_1t) is used only via (Suft) at (2), so the argument only shows that (Suft) is false; in other words, it only shows that the definition fails the Sufficiency Requirement.

4.3.2.2. *161b–162b*

In 161b–162b Socrates and Charmides take up the definition:

(D₃t) temperance =df acting on[19] one's own things (τὸ τὰ ἑαυτοῦ πράττειν, 161b6).

(For the list of definitions, see n. 14 above; (D₂t) will be considered in § 4.4.3.) This is supplied by Charmides as something he heard from someone else (161b5); Socrates identifies the source as Critias (b8), and provokes him into entering the fray.

The argument that follows presupposes that (D₃t) carries with it a definition for "intemperance" as well, which we might phrase as follows:

(D₃i) intemperance =df acting not on one's own things, but on those of others.

Socrates protests that (D₃t) "looks like a sort of riddle" (161c9); it certainly is obscure. He does not actually profess to show that it is wrong; rather he argues that on a certain literal-minded, hard-headed reading of the phrase "doing one's own things," temperance isn't *that*.

He actually gives two arguments. In the first (161d3–e5), he construes writing something down as acting on it, and then points out that the writing teacher does not merely read and write his own name, nor does he teach boys to read and write only their own names; but writing a name other than one's own is not a matter of intemperance. Abstractly put, Socrates construes "acting on something" as a generalization instantiated by any phrase of the form "*V*ing *NP*," so that, e.g., making someone else's clothes and writing someone else's name are cases of acting on someone else's things. His first argument, "A," then has the form:

(1) To write a name is to act on it.
∴ (2) To write other people's names and not one's own is to act on things of others and not on one's own.
(3) To write other people's names and not one's own is not intemperate.
∴ (4) Some cases of acting on others' things and not on of others are not cases of intemperance.

---

[19] I've translated πράττειν as "act on" rather than "do" (which is perhaps the normal translation, and is that adopted in Lamb (1927) 35–39, Jowett (1953) I 16–17) because what is needed is a verb phrase that takes direct objects such as "your own name" in the sequel. The idiom τὰ ἑαυτοῦ πράττειν simply means "to mind one's own business," but that is bound to make hash of the argument, as the attempt in Sprague (1973) 70–71 = Cooper (1997) 647–48 shows. I don't think Watt (1987b) 187–88, which uses "to do one's own job," fares much better.

This can be taken either as showing that the alleged *definiens* for "intemperance" in (D₁i) fails Sufficiency or as showing that *definiens* given in (D₃t) for "temperance" fails Necessity. The latter, technically, requires extending the argument by two steps:

> (5) Some who write other people's names and not their own are temperate.
>
> ∴ (6) Some who act on others' things and not on their own are temperate.

Once again, the question, for present purposes, is not whether the argument is a good one or not; Socrates seems to be using it to get Critias to clarify the definition that is presumed to derive from him. Rather, the question here is: how would the argument cut against the definition if it were to be understood in the rather mechanical way Socrates suggests? And the answer is plainly to be framed in terms of necessary and sufficient conditions.

Socrates' other argument against the overliteral version of (D₃t) ends up in the same ballpark as A, but involves the Virtue Assumption (VAt). In the interim between the treatment of (D₁t) and (D₃t) there has been a stretch of argument in which (VAt) was parlayed into

(VAt′) Temperance is a good {thing}.

I want to put off until later treatment of the argument in which this occurs; for now, let us simply adopt (VAt′), and allow Socrates to get from it

(VAt″) Something temperately done is well done,

which is what he employs in his second argument "B" against (D₃t). Argument B appears in 161e6–162a9, once more intended not as a conclusive refutation but as showing the need for clarification, and it looks as if it has the following structure:

> (1) A city in which each person makes his own clothes, utensils, etc. is not administered well.
>
> (2) A city administered temperately is administered well.
>
> ∴ (3) A city in which each person makes his own clothes, etc., is not one that is administered temperately.
>
> (4) If acting on one's own things were temperance, a city in which each person made his own clothes, etc., would be one that was administered well.

∴ (5) There are cases of acting on one's own things that are not cases of temperance.

Premise (2) is supposed to derive from (VAt). We can allow that.

Unfortunately, (4) looks simply false. If acting on one's own things were temperance, then a city in which each person did that would be one in which each person was temperate. And if we understand "acting on one's own things" to mean "making one's own clothes, etc.," then a city in which each person made his own clothes, etc., would be one in which each person would be temperate. And if we suppose that a city is temperate just in case each of its citizens is, we could say that that was a temperate city. But this has nothing to do with how it is administered.

Perhaps we should understand the verb οἰκεῖσθαι "to be administered" in 161e10 and 162a4–5 more vaguely so that the whole weight of the argument falls on the claim that a city in which each citizen is temperate is itself temperate: such a city would be (we might say) temperately and so well set up.

In any case, however the argument is laid out, its intended upshot is unambiguous: it is (5), which tells us that (D₃t) fails to give a sufficient condition.

There is one final stage to the argumentation against (D₃t). Critias had conceded that people who make (ποιεῖν) things of others can be temperate (162e7–163a5), but tries to stick by the denial that people who do (πράττειν) the things of others are temperate (163a10–12). This means he is taking Socrates to have argued with the tacit identification of making and doing, in the following way, "C":

(1) Making something is the same as doing something.

(2) Craftsmen make others' things and are temperate in doing it.

∴ (3) Craftsmen do others' things and are temperate in doing it.

∴ (4) Doing others' things is not the same as a lack of temperance.

This has the same upshot as A above, but employs the examples used in B.

4.3.2.3. *163e–164d*
In 163e–164b Socrates attacks

(D₄t) temperance =df doing good things.

Of course, "doing good things" is too broad, but that is an uninteresting objection, and Socrates does not go for it.[20] His objection is rather that it is

---

[20] It might, in fact, be an objection he could not have used when in the unity-of-virtues mood.

possible to perform actions which are good, or ones which are bad, without knowing it. But to act out of virtue, especially out of temperance, is to do something where one *knows* that that virtue is the source of the action. So temperance can't be just the doing of good things; the argument is simply:

> (1) One can do good things without knowing it.   P
> (2) One cannot be temperate without knowing it.   P
> ∴ (3) Temperance ≠ doing good things.   (1),(2)

Again, the failure is ¬(Suf): the doing of good things doesn't always count as temperance.[21]

At this point in the dialogue, Critias, unwilling to accept the possibility that one could be temperate and not know it (164cd), gives the new modification that is (D₅t) (164c9–d1, d2–4):

> I'd rather take back one of those things {*sc.* to which I'd previously agreed} . . . than allow that a man who is ignorant of himself is temperate. For, really, I'd almost say that this itself is temperance, knowing oneself {σχεδὸν γάρ τι ἔγωγε αὐτὸ τοῦτό φημι εἶναι σωφροσύνην, τὸ γιγνώσκειν ἑαυτόν}.

This initiates a long discussion that is the heart of this dialogue, starting off from the definition here suggested:

> (D₅t) Temperance =df knowledge of oneself.

But (D₅t) does not stay fixed; it undergoes considerable development, and I shall treat two of the elaborations as in effect new definitions (see n. 14). This makes the dialogue sound a lot more staccato than it really is; to get at the theory of definition, I shall, with regret, ignore the transitions that provide the continuity of the dialogue.[22]

4.3.2.4. 166e–169c

The most interesting transformation (D₅t) undergoes (see n. 22) is the one that leads to

> (D₆ₐt) temperance =df knowledge of itself (knowledge of knowledge)

as formulated by Critias in 166c2–3 and repeated in 166e5–6. Consider a part of the fate of this definition.

From 167b–169c, what we get is a Socratic induction aiming at establishing the generalization, stated in 169a3–4:

---

[21] Alternatively, the argument could be taken as showing that Leibniz's Law is not satisfied, since temperance requires, but doing good things does not, reflexive awareness (or something like that).

[22] But there is one important exception: the transition from (D₅t) to (D₆ₐt), for which see § 7.3.

(G) None of the things that are is of a nature to have its faculty (δύναμις) relative to itself (πρὸς ἑαυτό).

Socrates does not suppose the attempt is successful, but can find no exception to this generalization, and supposes that it forces the question how knowledge can be an exception (168a, 169ab). The induction starts off with instantiations of the generalization

(G′) There is no *F* that is not an *F* of the things of which the other *F*s are *F*s, but is an *F* of itself and the other *F*s and con*F*s.

This is illustrated with sight (167c8–d3), hearing (d4–6), the perceptions or senses generally (d7–10), desire (e1–3), wish (e4–6), love (e7–9), fear (e10–168a2), and belief (168a3–5). Socrates then stops to point out how strange knowledge must be to constitute an exception (168a6–b1).

He then begins another formulation of its peculiarity by saying (b2–3): "this knowledge is {a} knowledge of something, and has some such faculty {δύναμις} so that it is of something {τινὸς εἶναι}." There is an ambiguity here: Socrates might mean that whatever has a faculty is *of* something, or that the sort of faculty here in question is *of* something.

Socrates illustrates the notion of "faculty" with some odd cases. The larger is said to have a "faculty" such that it is "of something" (168b5–6: here English requires "than" rather than "of"), and what it is "of" ("than") is the smaller (b8); so also the double is "of" the half (c6–7), the more is of (than) the less, the heavier of (than) the lighter, and the older of (than) the younger (c9–10).

In each of these last cases, the generalization (G) or (G′) is again illustrated, but with an extra wrinkle. Here we have a characterization of the thing an *F* is "of": let us refer to it as "inv*F*" (the "inverse" of *F*), smaller for larger, etc. To rule out reflexivity Socrates uses the principle:

(Inv) *x* is *F* of *x* → *x* is inv*F* (of *x*).

So if something is larger than itself, it is also smaller than itself (168b10–c2), if it is double of itself, it is also half (c4–7), and so on (c9–d1). He formulates his principle this way (d1–3): "whatever has its own character {δύναμις} relative to itself {πρὸς ἑαυτό} will have that substance {οὐσία} relative to which {πρὸς ἥν} it was {directed}." This suggests the more extended version of (Inv)

(Inv′) $(z)[(x)(y)(Fxy \rightarrow Gy) \rightarrow (Fzz \rightarrow Gz)]$.

Socrates illustrates this principle with examples from the first group above: not larger, double, etc., but sight, hearing, etc. Hearing is of sound (168d3–4), so if hearing can hear itself, it must hear itself as having sound (d6–7); if sight sees itself, it must have color (d9–e1).

Actually, the argument aborts before reaching a conclusion, for Socrates simply concedes for the sake of argument that there can be a knowledge of knowledge (169d). But we can ask what would have happened had we allowed Socrates (G). And the answer is that we would have had the following argument to show that ($D_{6a}t$) is wrong:

(1) Knowledge cannot have its character relative to itself.   (G)
∴ (2) Knowledge cannot know itself.   (1)
∴ (3) There is no such thing as a knowledge of knowledge.   (2)
(4) There is such a thing as temperance.   P
∴ (5) Temperance is not knowledge of knowledge.   (3),(4)

Plainly what has been shown is that ($D_{6a}t$) does not give a necessary condition for a case of temperance.

4.3.3. Lysis

This dialogue discusses ὁ φίλος (sometimes τὸ φίλον). The Greek is untranslatable into English: no English word has the same range and ambiguity.[23] It is internally related to the verb φιλεῖν, which can mean "to love," "to regard with affection," "to be fond of" (doing something), "to treat with affection," "to regard with approval";[24] in this dialogue, the verb appears frequently. Then the corresponding noun phrase ὁ φίλος can in principle be taken in that many ways, multiplied by two, for it can be read as either active or passive: "the lover" or "the loved." The *Lysis*, whether deliberately or not, trades on this ambiguity.[25] Most translations represent the Greek word by the English "friend," and I can think of nothing better.

All but one[26] of the attempted definitions or quasi-definitions of "friend" fail (NecSuf), and all but one of these fail (Suf).

---

[23] See von Arnim (1914) 42–44, Bolotin (1979) 55–56 nn. 22 and 26, Robinson (1986) 65–69, Watt (1987a) 122–23.

[24] As Robinson (1986) 66 points out, φιλεῖν "does not seem ever to mean 'to like' *individual*, particular *objects*."

[25] See Bolotin (1979) 59 n. 65, Watt (1987a) 140, 153, 153–55 nn. Mackenzie (1988) 26 says: "The systematic ambiguity of φίλος, between the befriender and the befriended, is not exploited by Plato, but carefully observed (e.g. at 218d)." I think this confidence is misplaced. See, on the other side, Robinson (1986) 70–72, 79–82.

[26] 216c–220d (the "first friend") will be treated in § 8.2.4.

For an example of a failure on grounds of sufficiency, consider 212b–d: there the quasi-definition

(qD$_1$f) x is a friend of y =$_{df}$ either x loves y or y loves x,[27]

the first in the dialogue, is refuted. The argument is that there are cases of unrequited love: x may love y where y does not love, or even hates, x; Socrates and his interlocutor Menexenus prefer to say in such a case that neither is the friend of the other (212c7–d1). So that x loves y is not sufficient to guarantee that x is a friend of y. Similarly, the arguments of 212e–213b, 213bc, 214bc, 214e–215a, 215ab, and 215c–216b all fault *definientia* on grounds of insufficiency.

The solitary argument that charges a failure of necessity is that against the second quasi-definition,

(qD$_2$f) x is a friend of y =$_{df}$ x loves y and y loves x,

which emerges from the refutation of the first definition (212c7–d5). The argument is the simple claim that then there can be no friends of (lovers of) wine or friends of (lovers of) wisdom (212d5–213a4), so that there are cases of the *definiendum* that do not satisfy its alleged *definiens*.

4.3.4. Euthyphro 5c–6e

The texts here under discussion have all been translated in § 2.3.1.

Socrates first asks for a definition in 5d7 ("what do you say the pious is, and what the impious?"), but just before that, in 5c8–d5, he had done some preparatory work: he had got Euthyphro to accept that there is some characteristic, aspect, "idea" (ἰδέα, 5d4, 6e1; cf. εἶδος, 6d11),[28] present whenever an action is pious: a necessary condition for an action's counting as pious. But this "idea" is also identified as the pious in every action, so it is going to provide a sufficient condition as well: whatever action we find it in is pious.

---

[27] More accurately, the *definiendum* is: x becomes a (lover)/(loved one) of y.

[28] It is fairly common ground that the occurrences of ἰδέα in 5d4 and 6e1 and εἶδος in 6d11 are not enough by themselves to support the claim that the Theory of Forms is operating here; cf. Heidel (1902) 48 *ad* 5d: "There is here no reference to hypostatized *Ideas*; only the definitional essence is required, in the common Socratic manner." Many other scholars would go along with at least the first clause of this (e.g., Lutosławski [1897] 199–200, Guthrie [1975] 121, Vlastos [1991] 57–59, each slightly different). Allen (1970) 29 thinks that these "words are used in a special way" (and, again, many would agree, with differences: e.g., Shorey [1903] 31, Stewart [1909] 17 n. 1, von Arnim [1914] 141–42, Burnet [1924] 31, Walker [1984] 115–17, Kahn [1996] 178); I do not think so, but I think we might agree that you can't tell one way or the other just by looking at the words themselves (so also Kraut [1992a] 40 n. 32).

But Euthyphro cannot have been clear about this. He answered that the pious was doing what he was doing, namely, prosecuting the wrongdoer, and it is hard to believe that he thought this a complete list of pious actions: sacrifices and prayers are missing, and Euthyphro knows perfectly well that they would have to be included (see 14c). So he can hardly have said to himself: let's see, I've got to find a necessary condition for anything's being pious, so I'd better put together a list that includes every pious action. And he turns out (5e2–6a5, 6d2–5) to be most defensive about the sufficiency of his condition.

But it was its necessity that Socrates eventually attacked, not its sufficiency (6d6–e3), by pointing out that there are many other pious things: Euthyphro's definition fails (Nec). But it can look as if we have something more.

We might think we are being told that Euthyphro's answer is not merely not a necessary condition for an action's being pious, but not a condition at all: it is only one of the many pious actions; it is, we might think, only an *instance*, an *individual action*, while what is wanted is something *universal*, that *can apply to more than one case*. We have known almost since leaving mother's knee[29] that Socratic interlocutors give instances and then have to be led to the universal by the nose; that may seem to be happening here.

But it is not.[30] When Euthyphro first answers Socrates' question in 5de, he does not say: consider this action of mine, a case of prosecuting my father for impiety; call it "George"; this is a proper name for this historical event, like "Sicilian Vespers"; then, I claim, the pious is George. Euthyphro is talking about the *sort* of thing he is doing now, not just his now doing it: he speaks of prosecuting people for murders in the plural, and for temple robberies, and so on.

True, when Socrates returns to the argument and rehearses Euthyphro's answer (6cd), he leaves out everything but prosecuting one's father for murder. But even that does not narrow Euthyphro's characterization to the point where only one case is involved. Socrates' response is not that Euthyphro's answer is not general, but that it is not general enough.

---

[29] Anyway, since first reading, say, Shorey (1933) 110, 485, Heidel (1902) 49, 56, Grube (1935) 11, Robinson (1953) 49–50, 51, Irwin (1977b) 42 (with a list pretty much the same as Shorey's; contrast Irwin [1995] 24), Walker (1984) 74, or Rutherford (1995) 75.

[30] The first to deliver this important message was Nehamas (1975/76): see esp. 287–88 = (1999) 159–60. I am in wholehearted agreement with his main point. But it remains true that, in some sense, these interlocutors *are* all offering examples or instances rather than a full definition. They are *not* offering particulars rather than universals.

4.4. LEIBNIZ'S LAW

This refers to the principle:

(LL) $x = y \rightarrow Fx \leftrightarrow Fy$;

from which it follows that

$Fx \,\&\, \neg Fy \rightarrow x \neq y$.

The latter consequence is what makes it a weapon against preferred definitions: if courage is defined by someone as right-handedness, you can defeat him by pointing out that courage is a virtue and right-handedness is not. What the *definiendum* is a case of while the *definiens* is not (or conversely) – here "is a virtue" – is the "defeating predicate."

Plainly (LL) is closely related to (NecSuf): objections based on (NecSuf) allege that something is a case of the *definiendum* without being a case of the *definiens* (or the converse); objections based on (LL) allege that the *definiendum* is a case of something while the *definiens* is not (or the converse). In fact, the cases we shall consider in which (LL) is invoked could more or less easily be rewritten to show failure of (NecSuf).

4.4.1. Charmides *169e–175b*

There are some fairly simple cases in the *Charmides* between 169e and the end of the dialogue. The arguments are internally quite difficult but all of the same form:

(D$_{6b}$t) temperance $=_{df}$ knowledge of knowledge and of ignorance.
(1) knowledge of knowledge and of ignorance is not useful (admirable, beneficial).
(VAt′) temperance is useful (admirable, beneficial).
∴ (2) temperance $\neq$ knowledge of knowledge and knowledge of ignorance.

So stated, they look like simple applications of Leibniz's Law; the defeating predicate is "useful" or whatever. But, in fact, none of them shows that knowledge of knowledge and of ignorance is not *necessary* for temperance; they all show that it is not *sufficient*, since that knowledge is not guaranteed to be useful, although temperance is.

4.4.2. Charmides *165c–e*

In 164d4 (repeated at 165b4), as we have already noted (§ 4.3.2.3), Critias tries defining temperance as knowing oneself:

(D_5t) temperance $=_{df}$ knowledge of oneself.

Socrates begins an argument against this in 165c. There is some confusion in the passage, to which we shall return. But for the moment, let us look at what is easy about it. Socrates runs a brief "induction" intended to show that various "knowledges" or "sorts of knowledge" are each useful for something, i.e., each produces something useful (165cd). Then, since by (D_5t), temperance is a knowledge, he asks Critias (165de): what is the useful product of temperance?

It is easy to see what it would have looked like had it gone through:

(1) Temperance is a knowledge.	(D_5t)
(2) Every knowledge has a useful product.	P (induction)
(3) Temperance has a useful product.	(1),(2)
(4) Temperance has no useful product.	P
∴ (5) Temperance is not a knowledge.	(1),(3),(4), *reductio*

And this can easily be seen as employing (LL), in the form

(LLt) Temperance = knowledge of oneself → (temperance has a useful product → knowledge of oneself has a useful product),

with "has a useful product" as the defeating predicate.

It is tempting to try to relate the suggestion that temperance might have a useful product to the Virtue Assumption (VAt) that temperance is admirable, the conclusion derived from that assumption in 160e that temperance is good (§ 4.4.3), and the related assumptions that we have noted operating in the arguments of 169e–175b (§ 4.4.1). The temptation should be resisted, for, whereas those assumptions were accepted and crucial to the arguments in which they appeared, the assumption that operates in this one is (4), which moves in the opposite direction. One wonders how it would have looked had the argument gone through.

In any case, the argument does not go through: Critias in 165e–166a refuses to allow the generalization at (2), pointing to arithmetic and geometry as cases of knowledge where there is no useful product, and Socrates concedes that he is right. It is consequently a little difficult to see what advance has been made. At most what has been put on the table is the question that charts the direction of the rest of the dialogue, for, when

Socrates asked his question about useful products, he was supposing that these useful products were in some sense what the knowledge was a knowledge *of*, its *objects*, and they were to be distinct from the knowledge itself. It emerges in 166ab that Socrates has not given up the claim that knowledge must have objects that are distinct from the knowledges themselves: accordingly, he redirects his questioning to ask about the object of the knowledge that is temperance.[31]

4.4.3. Charmides *160d–161b*

Charmides' second stab at temperance, purportedly (see 160d5–e3) based on introspection, is: "it seems to me to make a man ashamed and bashful, and modesty {seems to me} to be just what temperance is" (160e4–5: εἶναι ὅπερ αἰδὼς ἡ σωφροσύνη). This gives us:

(D₂t) Temperance $=_{df}$ modesty.

Its refutation might have been of the same sort as that of his first definition: Socrates would need only to point out that there are cases of modesty that are not good, and so not instances of temperance. The argument might then have been this (the numbers are those of the corresponding lines of fuller version that follows, to facilitate comparison):

(2) Temperance is (always) good.   P
(5) Modesty is good in some circumstances, not good in
    others.   P
(6) Temperance $\neq$ modesty.   (2),(5),(LL)

Socrates is not quite so straightforward, but still, this argument, A, is embedded in the more complex one he offers, B below, so it is worth noticing two things.

First, to get from (2) and (5) to (6), we need (LL). The defeating predicate is "is (always) good."

Second, A could be rewritten to show that "modesty," like "quietness," as a *definiens* for "temperance," fails (Suf): there are cases of modesty that are not cases of temperance. This will also be true of the more complex version. This is due to the nature of the defeating predicate. If, instead, we had had "is a virtue characteristic of Socrates" in (2) and "is not a virtue characteristic of Socrates" in (5), such rewriting would have been considerably harder,[32]

---

[31] Once again (see n. 22), § 7.3 deals with the sequel.

[32] These premises would, of course, still entail that there are cases of modesty that are not cases of temperance.

and clearly pointless. The reason for sticking to the (LL) reading is that that is the way Socrates himself puts it: there is something true of modesty that is not true of temperance, and so they must be different. The defeating predicate here, however, is a bit of a monster.

Socrates reports his refutation of Charmides' second definition as follows (160e6–161b2):

> Well, I said, didn't you just agree that temperance is {an} admirable {thing}?[33]
> Certainly, he said.
> {e9} Then {οὐκοῦν} the temperate are also good men?
> Yes.
> {e11} Could what does not make {men} good be good?[34]
> No indeed.
> {e13} Not only therefore {is temperance an} admirable {thing}, but it is also {a} good {thing}.
> {161} It seems to me.
> Well then, I said, don't you believe Homer to have spoken admirably when he said that modesty is not good to be present to a man in need?[35]
> I certainly do, he said.
> {a6} Therefore, it seems, modesty is not {a} good {thing} and {a} good {thing}.
> It appears.
> {a8} While temperance is {a} good {thing}, if it makes those to whom it is present good and not bad.
> And yet it seems to me that matters stand exactly as you say.
> {a11} Therefore temperance cannot be modesty, if the one is in fact {a} good {thing}, while modesty {is} no more {a} good than {a} bad {thing}.

We can certainly see A above embedded in this text, but there is more.

---

[33] 160e6–7 καλόν . . . τὴν σωφροσύνην εἶναι: on the use of the neuter with a non-neuter subject here and in 159d8, 11, 160e13, 161a6, etc., see the discussion of *Hippias Major* 287e4 below. It signals a general truth: temperance is, in general, admirable.

[34] 160e11 ἆρ' οὖν ἂν εἴη ἀγαθὸν ὃ μὴ ἀγαθοὺς ἀπεργάζεται; This question has no point; the text could well be corrupt, as a comparison with 161a8–9 suggests. According to the apparatus in Burnet (1900/1907) III, Schanz supposed there was a lacuna after εἴη, and Goldbacher proposed an emendation: ἀγαθούς<, καὶ μὴ ἀγαθόν, ὃ ἀγαθοὺς> ἀπεργάζεται, "and what makes men good be not good?" This is a lot of emending, and the first half of the question remains irrelevant. (But Irwin [1977b] 295 n. 13 accepts this emendation; this note does not appear in Irwin [1995].) Schanz's hypothesis of a lacuna does not do much to fix the problem, either. The simplest thing would be to move μὴ back to before ἀγαθόν: "could what makes men good be not good?" but there is no warrant for this other than sense (the reconstruction of the argument in Irwin [1977b] 49 and Irwin [1995] 359 n. 14 paraphrases e11 as if this were what it said, and there is no real alternative). See comments immediately below.

[35] *Odyssey* XVII 347, also cited in *Laches* 201b2–3. Cf. the very similar line in Hesiod, *Works and Days* 317.

To begin with, Socrates derives premise (2) of that argument from the Virtue Assumption that temperance is admirable, (VAt), and the derivation is curious: it is supposed to follow from (VAt) that

(1′) Temperate men are good men.[36]

(Here and below, " ′ " signals that the line in question will undergo some revision before it appears in the final version.) And then (1′), via a principle having something to do with what makes people good or not (160e6–13), is supposed to yield:

(2′) Temperance is good.

The first inference, from (VAt) to (1′), requires a principle to the effect that, when a character trait is admirable, its possessors are, inasmuch as they are possessors of that trait, good. Perhaps it would help to say: the trait wouldn't be admirable if it didn't make its possessors count as good; perhaps, though, the circle is too small for this to carry any weight. In any case, this inference does not play much of a role in the story to come, so I shall just adopt the principle and move on. For the moment, we may state the principle as follows:

(P1′) If a character trait is admirable, it makes those who have it so far forth good.

This is not too difficult, but the second inference is another story.

There is a difficulty over fixing the principle that governs this second inference. In 160e11, where the inference is being made, Socrates asks "could what does not make men good be good?" and gets the answer "no," but that does not justify the inference; the word "not" is in the wrong place. What he should be asking is "could what makes men good not be good?" i.e., "could what makes men good fail to be good?"; a negative answer to this would give us what we need, the principle that what makes men good must itself be good. That this is the principle Socrates thinks of himself as employing is clear from his repetition of the inference in 161a8–9: "temperance is {a} good {thing}, if it makes those to whom it is present good and not bad." We can reconstruct the argument on the basis of 161a: I imagine something

---

[36] It seems to me a bit mysterious. Irwin (1977b) 49 lays the argument out without recording the fact that Socrates purports to conclude (1′) from (VAt). In Irwin (1995) 359 n. 14 he says (I have rewritten Irwin's labels to conform to mine): "Socrates does not say that he is arguing from (VAt) to (1′), but if he is not, (VAt) plays no role at all in the argument, and (1′) is left without support that it needs." But: (a) the particle οὐκοῦν in 160e9 looks inferential (see Denniston [1934] 434–35 for a catalogue of Plato's uses of this particle; none of the alternatives fits this passage very well), and (b) I'm not really convinced that (1′) needs support.

has gone wrong with the text in 160e11, and the simplest fix is simply repositioning the negation in 160e11 so that it says what 161a does (see n. 34).

Then Socrates is arguing from the conclusion that temperate men are good to the further conclusion that it is itself good via the principle that what makes men good must itself be good. Plainly he is taking it that, when he says that temperate men are good, this means that temperance makes them good. He need not have any very sophisticated view about the sort of "causality" involved in temperance making people good in his back pocket; the background thought need only be that when temperate people are said to be good, it is because of their temperance that they are said to be good: that is what "makes" them good, i.e., inasmuch as they are temperate they count as good people.

But it is tempting to see a connection between the principle that what makes men good is itself good and our hypothetical:

(H) $R(G, f)$ & $Gf \rightarrow (x)(Fx \rightarrow Gx)$.

It looks as if the present principle could be an instance of the converse of that, with "good" instead of "praiseworthy/admirable" replacing "G." So perhaps (H) should be beefed up to the thesis:

(T) $R(G, f) \rightarrow [Gf \leftrightarrow (x)(Fx \rightarrow Gx)]$.

The need for the restriction "$R(G, f)$," whatever that restriction finally amounts to, is even clearer here. Suppose that, by some cosmic coincidence, all temperate people were red-headed; we should not want it to follow that temperance was red-headed.

If we consider this example in detail, we may begin to see what sort of restriction is needed. The relevant portion of (T), stated without the restriction, is

(T′) $(x)(Fx \rightarrow Gx) \rightarrow Gf$;

this would enable the inference from "all temperate people are red-headed" to "temperance is red-headed." In order to get the premise for this inference, we have had to suppose that it is by a "cosmic coincidence" that all temperate people are red-headed. But in the intended application of the principle to enable the inference to (2), "temperance is good," the relation between temperance and good people is not one of coincidence at all: temperate people don't just happen all to be good people; rather, their being temperate is what makes them count as good. So what we need for the antecedent of (T′) is not just the generalization "$(x)(Fx \rightarrow Gx)$," but something stronger, something like "*x*'s being *F* makes *x* count as *G*," or "*x*'s being *F* accounts for the fact that *x* is *G*," or "whatever is *F* is *eo ipso G*."

Matters are hardly fully clear here, but I shall write, instead of (T'),

(T") $(x)(Fx \Rightarrow Gx) \rightarrow Gf$,

where "$\Rightarrow$" represents the still somewhat foggy relationship in question. We shall come back to this when we consider the explanatory role of definitions two chapters below.

There is a further peculiarity about Socrates' argument against Charmides' second definition: he does not state premise (5) of A, but says, rather, "modesty is both not good and good." It is easy enough to see in this a condensed version of the claim that modesty is good in some circumstances and not in others. But Socrates' phrasing of the matter will take on importance when we begin to reflect on the metaphysics of the matter, so we had better not paint it out of the picture.

But then leaving it in creates another complication. The principles we have just been adopting so far only warrant concluding: "temperance is good." The fact that Socrates is prepared to say "modesty is both not good and good" shows that "temperance is good" is not enough to justify the conclusion that temperance is not modesty: temperance might be good and not good as well, like modesty. When Socrates says in 161a8–9 "temperance is a good thing, if it makes those to whom it is present good and not bad," he shows that he wants something stronger: temperance is good and not not good. It is easy enough to supply him with this, by strengthening our principles: instead of the principle that what makes men good must itself be good, we can adopt one to the effect that what makes men good must itself be good and not not good. This peculiar locution is to be understood as saying that the trait in question is good every time.

We get, then, this, "B":

(VAt)	Temperance is admirable.	P
(P1)	If a character trait is admirable, it makes those who have it so far forth good and not not good.	P
(1)	Temperance makes men good and not not good.	(VAt),(P1)
(P2)	What makes men good and not not good must itself be good and not not good.	P
(2)	Temperance is good and not not good.	(1),(P2)
(3)	Modesty is not good for a man in need.	P
(4)	Modesty is often good.	P
(5)	Modesty is both good and not good.	(3),(4)
(6)	Temperance $\neq$ modesty.	(2),(5) × (LL)

Here (P2) is in fact an instance of (T″), but in the argument as Socrates actually states it, however, it simply functions as a premise: Socrates does not himself infer it from anything else.

Of course, B as it stands is offensive to the ear of anyone who has ever dealt with formal logic: (5) sounds like a contradiction, and the apparent double negations in (P1), (1), (P2), and (2) cry out for elimination. What has to be kept in mind is that (5) is not a contradiction, because it really means something like "modesty is sometimes good and sometimes not," and for the same reason the apparent double negations are not real double negations.

Well, then, why not rewrite those lines accordingly, to make Socrates an honest logician?

Because he isn't a logician at all. And, more importantly, when we turn all this into metaphysics, the claim that ordinary things are both *F* and not *F* whereas the form the *F* is just plain *F* and not also not *F* will inherit the same odd logical features we see at work here: the first half of this claim is not a contradiction and the second does not employ double negation. That those features are shared between these two very different contexts is no accident.

CHAPTER 5

Socrates' requirements: paradigms

At *Euthyphro* 6e (§ 5.4) Socrates says explicitly that he wants his interlocutor to give him something he can use as an "example," an "exemplar," a "standard," or a "paradigm" (all possible translations for παράδειγμα) in determining whether the term for which he is seeking a definition applies. This term has frequently been seen as introducing Forms in the *Euthyphro*.[1]

I shall refer to the requirement there being deployed as the "Paradigm Requirement." It is a little dicier than Substitutivity was. As a first approximation, it might be stated as:

(PR) The $F =_{df}$ the $G \rightarrow$ the G is a paradigm for Fs.

We need to know what is involved in something's being a paradigm or standard for Fs. We shall first stop over the term παράδειγμα (§ 5.1).

Socrates says very little by way of explaining what he means by a paradigm in the *Euthyphro* passage. Anticipating the discussion below: he means he wants an example that can be used as an exemplar, a standard, against which he can hold up putative cases of piety and determine by comparison whether they really are cases of piety.

If I have something of this sort, a standard, for use in determining whether something is (say) a meter long, what I have is something that is a meter long,[2] that I can hold up against something else to see if it too is a meter long. Socrates plainly commits himself to this much in the *Euthyphro* passage. Elsewhere he is fairly often to be found saying or implying that the virtues for which he seeks definitions are "self-predicative": piety is itself pious, and so on (see § 5.2). It is natural to connect these two points: self-predication is involved in unpacking the notion of a paradigm.

Frequently the occurrences of self-predications and the Paradigm Requirement are associated with the question of a *definiens* performing a certain explanatory role: in some texts self-predication, the Paradigm

---

[1] See n. 14 below.   [2] *Pace* Wittgenstein (1953) § 50.

Requirement, and the Explanatory Requirement are inseparable parts of the picture. In the *Euthyphro* the introduction of the Paradigm Requirement is not directly associated with the Explanatory Requirement. This is not to say that the Explanatory Requirement is simply missing: it looms in the immediate background. But in stating the Paradigm Requirement in 6e, and in applying it in 6e–8a, Socrates does not appeal to the Explanatory Requirement. This gives us the opportunity to examine the Paradigm Requirement, with its associated self-predications, on its own.

This is possible because there are two sources for self-predications: one is a set of presuppositions about explanations, but the other is in the form of the definition question itself, and does not require consideration of explanations; it flows from the fact that Socrates frequently requests definitions by asking "what is the *F*?" where "the *F*" – a "generically abstract noun phrase" – is a type of noun phrase that lends itself to self-predication (see § 5.3).

After more detailed explanations of these terms, §§ 5.4–5.5 deal with some texts.

5.1. Παραδείγματα: SOME EXAMPLES

The term παράδειγμα actually means "example," as in *Apology* 23b1. But it is especially used of examples that function as exemplars. For example, in *Euthydemus* 278e–282d, Socrates engages in a staged dialogue with Cleinias in which he endeavors to teach Cleinias the value of knowledge. Before he does this, he explains its point to Euthydemus and Dionysodorus: he wants *them* to urge Cleinias to care for wisdom and virtue. In 278d3–5 he offers to show them the sort of thing he means; he does that, and then says (282d5–8):

Such is my example {παράδειγμα}, Dionysodorus and Euthydemus, of what I want discourses of exhortation to be like,[3] perhaps amateurish and put at some length; but whichever of you wants, give an exhibition for us doing this same thing with art.

Between *Meno* 75b and 77a, Socrates offers sample definitions (for "color" and "shape"); in 77a9–b1 and later in 79a10 he refers to to these definitions as παραδείγματα, "samples" or "models," that Meno is supposed to follow in providing a definition for "excellence."

---

[3] d5–6 οἴων ἐπιθυμῶ τῶν προτρεπτικῶν λόγων εἶναι: the MSS have οἶον for οἴων, which is an emendation due to Routh; see Gifford (1905) 27 who adds, "Cobet cuts the knot by omitting the whole clause."

In the doctrinal dialogues, a Form is sometimes referred to as a παράδειγμα,[4] as in *Republic* VI 500e3, where we hear of the "divine model" of the city-state, VII 540a9, where the Form of the Good is to be used as a παράδειγμα for the ordering of the city-state, and *Timaeus* 28a7 and *passim*[5] where the demiurge looks to an eternal model in fashioning the world.

The Eleatic Stranger, in the *Statesman*, undertakes to define παράδειγμα. He gives an example (277e–278c): when children are confused about the occurrence of letters in complicated syllables, we bring them back to the occurrences of those same letters in simpler syllables, where they already recognize the letters; then they can use these simpler syllables as παραδείγματα, as "models." So, he says, we get a "model" where we have the same thing occurring in two different contexts and can use our correct judgment about the one case to form a correct one about the other (278c2–6).

Applied to a Form (and the Eleatic Stranger is not there doing that), this might mean that the Form of, say, the beautiful is itself self-evidently beautiful, and those who are familiar with this object can use it to determine whether other things are beautiful. That is the way things are going to look.

But we have not yet erected the Theory of Forms. We are still constructing a theory of definition. Still, we are already facing the phenomenon of self-predication. So let us stop over that.

5.2. SELF-PREDICATION

"Self-predication"[6] arises when a term such as the *F* or *F*ness itself is said to be *F*. Here what makes a sentence self-predicative is a question of surface grammar: the term "self-predication" is not meant to tell us what a sentence of the surface form "the *F* is *F* " means, but only that the sentence has that surface form.[7]

---

[4] But the term is not used exclusively for Forms: cf. *Republic* VII 529d7, where the multicolored παραδείγματα in the heavens are the planets and stars or perhaps constellations (Vlastos [1980] 6, 22 n. 15; Bulmer-Thomas [1984] 108–9), III 409b1, c7, d2, where people are said to have or lack παραδείγματα, "models" of the good man and of the bad man in their souls, and VI 484c8, where those who lack knowledge of the Forms are said not to have a clear παράδειγμα in their souls. Even in the *Timaeus*, where almost all the uses of the term apply it to the Form of the Living Thing (see n. 5), in 24a3 something like the translation "analogue" is required.

[5] *Timaeus* 28a7, b2, 28c6 speak of the unchangeable standard as opposed to the changeable one; thereafter, παράδειγμα is used of the eternal living being (29b4, 31a4, 37c8, 38b8, c1, 39e7, 48e5, 49a1).

[6] The term was coined by Vlastos (1954) 324 = Allen (1965) 236 = Vlastos (1995) 170.

[7] In this I follow Malcolm (1991) 1.

It is easy enough to characterize in a rough and ready way how noun phrases such as "the *F* " work. Consider a case outside of Plato, where no accusation of metaphysics can be made. Euripides' Hecuba asks (*Hecuba* 592–602):[8]

>   . . . is it not strange, if . . .
> 595   . . . always
>   the base {man is} nothing else but bad,
>   while the noble {man is} noble, and {is} not corrupted in nature
>   by misfortune, but is always good?
>   Then do the parents make the difference, or the upbringings?
> 600   No doubt being well brought up offers
>   instruction in {the} noble; and if one understands this properly,
>   he knows also the despicable {τὸ γ' αἰσχρόν},
>   understanding it by the yardstick of the admirable.

This was written when Plato was about four years old.[9]

Hecuba uses the generically abstract noun phrases "the base {man}" (ὁ πονηρός, 596) and "the noble {man}" (ὁ ἐσθλός, 597). She uses the latter in the (sub-)sentence

(1) The noble {man} is always noble {ὁ δ' ἐσθλὸς ἐσθλός}.

This is, by definition, a case of self-predication. And, since the variation between "base" and "bad" in 596 looks merely stylistic, we may take it that there is another self-predication in that line as well.

Pretty clearly, the use of the generically abstract noun phrases here is simply a device for generalization: Hecuba means to be saying of all noble men that they are always noble; (1) translates as

(1′) All noble men are always noble.

And when she talks in 600–601 of "instruction in {the} noble" she is presumably talking about instruction as to which things are noble. At any rate, she is plainly not saying of some abstraction named "the noble" that being well brought up involves acquaintance with it, any more than in 597 she was saying of an abstraction named "the noble man" that that abstraction is always noble. She is not doing metaphysics.

So some sentences containing generic abstracts are naturally taken as equivalent to universal generalizations.

The argument against Euthyphro's second attempt to define piety, in *Euthyphro* 6e–8a (§ 5.5 below), invokes a standard, and that is where

---

[8] Text as in Diggle (1984) 366, except that Diggle follows Sakorraphos in deleting 599–602.
[9] Lucas (1970) 419a. This won't be true of 599–602 if those lines are an interpolation.

self-predication sets in: whatever Euthyphro supplies by way of defining the pious has to be pious every time, and under no circumstances impious. There is a logical difference between that and what Hecuba has to say.

Part of the difference is that Hecuba's generalization was presumably an empirical one where Socrates' claim is not. The claim that underlies Socrates' argument, which we shall register as a Self-Predication about the pious,

> (SPp) The pious is through and through pious, i.e., pious and under no circumstances impious,

is not something Socrates has arrived at through lifelong traffic with pious people and actions. It is not open to refutation by counterexample. It is not, in fact, arrived at by generalization at all, even if it should turn out to have the logical form of a universal generalization.

That (SPp) is not arrived at by generalization fits with the idea that "the pious" refers to a standard. The meter bar in Paris isn't something that was just *found* to be a meter long; on every occasion of its application it is taken to be a meter long *in advance*. This doesn't mean that that bar can never be anything but a meter long, for there are variations in temperature, etc., which would allow for expansion or contraction of the bar, and they must be ruled out, or it is no longer usable as a standard. But, once we have determined that none of those conditions obtains, we have something that we can use as a standard, and we don't find out that it is a meter long by measuring it: we find out that the proper conditions obtain, take it as a meter long, and measure other things with it.

If I am to use some answer, "*abc*," to the question "what is the pious?" as a standard for determining which actions are pious and which are not *on every occasion*, which is what Socrates' strictures (6de, where he presses the Substitutivity Requirement against Euthyphro's first answer) have demanded, then *abc* must be pious on every one of those occasions.

But it is important to be clear that the fact that (SPp) is not an empirical claim does not yet make "the pious" simply a singular term: (SPp) could still have the logical form of a universal generalization even if it is not arrived at by generalization. That is, there is not yet reason to think that it refers to a singular abstraction, the standard pious thing, and characterizes that as once and for all pious. For the picture presented by the meter bar is not the whole picture. Consider the following entry from a dictionary of physics:[10]

---

[10] Pitt (1977) 242 (with slight editing). This definition has been superseded by one in terms of the wave-length of light, but it will serve to make my point.

meter. Symbol: m. The Standard International unit of length, defined as
1,650,763.73 wave-lengths in vacuum of the radiation corresponding to the transition between the levels $2p_{10}$ and $5d_5$ of the krypton-86 atom.

We need not (fortunately) understand this definition to see a relevant point
in it. Abbreviate the whole phrase following "defined as" to "*n* wave-lengths
of radiation." What we have here is a standard, but, as it were, a movable
standard. To determine whether or not you've got a meter's worth of string,
get out a krypton-86 atom and . . . compare your piece of string with *n*
wave-lengths of radiation. The point is that the standard is, unlike the
meter bar, not numerically single. It's still a standard.

Suppose now we could describe a pious action, a repeatable one, but one
such that on every occasion it counted as pious (its piety can't be overridden
by any considerations at all): *abc.* That would be a paradigm of piety. And
then comparison of any other action with it would show that other action
as either less pious than *abc* or just as pious as *abc.* And so we'd have a
standard. But it, too, would be a movable standard: repeatable, and not
numerically single.

What we have so far is this: where we look for a paradigm for *F*s, we
look for something, possibly repeatable, that possesses in a paradigmatic
way, indefeasibly, the features that make something an *F*. So the work of
(PR) can be taken over by the "Self-Predication Requirement":

(SPR) The $F =_{df}$ the $G \rightarrow$ the G is under all circumstances F and
    under no circumstances con$F$.

But then the requirement that a definition set a standard or give a
paradigm can be seen working in passages in which the word "standard"
(παράδειγμα) does not itself appear. (SPR) is going to disqualify Euthyphro's second definition, but we shall find the same pattern of objection,
without the use of the term "standard," in the *Hippias Major.*

5.3. GENERICALLY ABSTRACT NOUN PHRASES

Consider Hilaire Belloc's couplet:[11]

(1) The llama is a hairy sort of woolly fleecy goat,
    with an indolent expression and an undulating throat.

---

[11] The example, and many of the points made in the following discussion, come from Wisdom (1969)
    42–47.

The noun phrase "the llama" is an instance of a type; let us call phrases of this type *generically abstract noun phrases* or just *generic abstracts*. They differ in their behavior from simple abstract nouns. Consider the difference between talking in terms of "llamahood" and talking in terms of "the llama." Substituting "llamahood" for "the llama" in Belloc's couplet yields even worse nonsense than the original:

(2) Llamahood is a hairy sort of woolly fleecy goat,
 with an indolent expression and an undulating throat.

The absurdity here is logical: llamahood is not the sort of thing that can be described as any kind of goat, for it is the property instantiated by llamas (if it is anything at all), and properties can't – logically can't – be goats.

Similarly, if we employ the generic abstract "the triangular," what it is natural to say using it is not the same as what it would be natural to say using the abstract noun "triangularity."

(3) The triangular has three sides

would be acceptable, but not

(4) Triangularity has three sides.

Triangularity has no shape, it *is* a shape that some table-tops have; these table-tops have three sides, and that is because the triangular has three sides.

 Generic abstracts are much more common in Greek than they are in English: Hecuba used a few, and they are rampant in Plato. It is commonly said that such an abstract noun phrase is in at least one of its senses simply equivalent to the corresponding abstract noun.[12] The preceding discussion should make us suspicious about this.[13] And suspicion here pays off. If we bear in mind the distinction in logical behavior we have just looked at, we can see a source for some of the self-predications we are about to encounter: namely, the use of generic abstracts together with the requirement that a definition give necessary and sufficient conditions for its *definiendum*.

---

[12] E.g., Ryle (1939) 142–43 = Allen (1965) 111–12, Allen (1960) 150 n. 8 = Allen (1965) 46 n. 1, Ackrill (1981) 27, Walker (1984) 74.

[13] See also Webster (1952/53) 22–24, cited by Bluck (1955) 175–76 and Vlastos (1956b) 93–94 (Allen [1965] 290–91). Webster (24) says the generically abstract noun phrase can signify "a standard member of a class (and therefore very nearly the quality by virtue of which it is a member of the class)." But a standard member of a class just is not, not even very nearly, the quality by virtue of which it is a member of the class (except in the somewhat special case of a standard member of the class of qualities by virtue of which things are members of classes).

In the *Hippias Major*, Socrates' question is: "what is the beautiful?" It expects an answer in the form

(Db) The beautiful is *abc*,

where "*abc*" is the *definiens*: anything that is beautiful is also *abc*, and conversely. Then, trivially, it follows from (Db) that the beautiful is beautiful. This inference is dependent on the fact that Socrates' question and (Db) are phrased using the expression "the beautiful" rather than with the word "beauty." If we designate the object of the definitional quest using such a noun phrase, it is natural to suppose that that object is self-predicational.

This will carry us for some distance, but not all the way. For self-predication is not confined to generic abstracts: it will also appear with abstract nouns such as "beauty." There a little more work is called for; it will mostly have to wait for the next chapter.

Often, we've noted, "the *F* is *G*" simply amounts to "all *F*s are *G*s." But if we consider the force with which (SPR) invests the self-predication "the beautiful is beautiful," we can see that this will not work. For (SPR) turns that into:

(SPb) The beautiful is always beautiful and never ugly.

It will turn out that, according to Socrates and his interlocutors, ordinary beautiful things can also be ugly, so (SPb) does not translate as "all beautiful things are always beautiful and never ugly."

The source of such assumptions as (SPb) is, at least partly, simply the logical form of statements employing generic abstracts when these are taken to answer the question "what is the *F*?" Let us suppose that (1) is to be taken as a definition for *the llama* by genus (*goat*) and differentiae (*hairy, woolly, fleecy, with an indolent expression and an undulating throat*). Then it must be intended to characterize the llama qua llama: the features it lists are to be understood as part and parcel of something's being a llama; it tells us, to use Aristotelian jargon, *what it is to be a llama*. Features that belong to non-llamas are permitted, because there are of course other goats besides llamas, and other woolly things, and so on, but features that would count *against* something's being a llama are not permitted. And that is the force of the exclusionary clause in (SPb): "and never ugly." The implicit force of (SPb) is

(SPb') The beautiful is, qua beautiful, always beautiful and never ugly.

That shows us how we might avoid the supposition that there is some one entity named "the beautiful": for (SPb′) looks as if it could be paraphrased as:

> (Eb′) Everything beautiful, is, qua beautiful, always beautiful and never ugly.

We simply have to be careful where we give the temporal quantifiers wide scope: (Eb′) comes through as acceptable as long as we don't take it as saying of every beautiful thing that it never was or will be ugly, but as saying that always, a beautiful thing is, qua beautiful, never ugly. And then it comes through, not as just acceptable, but as a tautology.

In fact, I think this goes a long way toward explaining Socrates' unquestioning employment of self-predications like (SPb) and (SPp): as we shall see, he frequently doesn't even make them explicit, but they are needed to make some of his arguments work. And to the extent that they are explicit, I imagine, they sounded tautologous.

It's time to get back to the texts: here we deal with two in the *Euthyphro* in which the Paradigm requirement is relatively easily isolated; we shall encounter more later in which that requirement is entangled with others.

5.4. *EUTHYPHRO* 6E

As we've already seen (§ 4.3.4), Socrates rejects Euthyphro's first definition as insufficiently general, as failing (Nec); he wants the one form or idea by which all pious things are pious. He explains this, introducing the Paradigm Requirement (6e4–7):

Then teach me this idea itself, what it is, so that looking to it and using it as {a} paradigm,[14] whatever is such as it is among the things either you or anyone else does, I shall say is pious, and whatever is not such, I shall say {is} not.

The definition being rejected – the pious consists in actions such as Euthyphro's own, prosecuting those who have committed injustice, whether the wrongdoer is one's father or not (5de) – was one Euthyphro had defended against what he saw as the most likely attack, coming from

---

[14] The occurrence of this word is no signal that we are talking in terms of the Theory of Forms, although it has been so taken: see, e.g., Burnet (1924) 37, Allen (1970) 29, Hare (1981) 15. Heidel (1902) 55 *ad* 6e: "Here the notion is only a norm serviceable as as test to insure correct thinking." This remark is directly concerned with the "looking to" idiom in this passage, but it is plain from the rest of Heidel's note that he is not prepared to lean on παράδειγμα to see Forms in the *Euthyphro*. See also Walker (1984) 72–73.

his relatives: that it can hardly be pious to prosecute one's *father*. He had said (5e5–6a4):

these same men in fact believe that Zeus is the best and most just of the gods, and they agree that he tied up his own father because he had devoured his sons in injustice, and that that father had in turn castrated his own father for other reasons of that sort; but they are angry with me because I am prosecuting my father for his injustice.

Euthyphro has here cited an example (or two) with which to compare his own case, and is saying that the comparison shows his action to be pious.

When Socrates asks for something he can use as a "paradigm" or "example" of piety, he is saying that Euthyphro's example is inadequate because it does not cover all the cases; what he wants is an all-purpose example.[15]

If this is the right way to read the text, we are a far cry from the Theory of Forms.

In any case, it is clear from Socrates' brief explanation in the "so that" clause in 6e5–7 that the example, paradigm, or standard for which he is looking is expected to have the feature or features that make pious actions pious: it is, say, F; then any action that is F (that "is such as it is") will be pious.

So we have the Paradigm Requirement for the pious:

(PRp) The pious $=_{df}$ the G → the G is a paradigm for pious things,

and we have this in addition about what constitutes a paradigm for pious things:

(Pp) The G is a paradigm for pious things → (Gx → x is pious).

But we can hardly turn (Pp) into a biconditional: plainly not just any action that is G will do as the standard to which to look. What more is required? Socrates does not address this general problem. But he addresses an instance of it. Euthyphro's next attempt to define "pious" fails the Paradigm Requirement, and that illustrates the point.

5.5. *EUTHYPHRO* 6E–8A

Euthyphro's second shot at the pious is (6e11–7a1): "Well then, the beloved to the gods is pious, the not beloved impious." We may register Euthyphro's starting point as the package

---

[15] See here Ausland (2002) 55–56 with n. 41, and Young (2002) 82–83.

(D₂p′) The pious =_df the beloved to the gods, and
         the impious =_df the not beloved to the gods.

Socrates responds to this (7a2–3):

Very nicely {put}, Euthyphro, and you have now answered in the way that I was
asking that you answer.

Socrates must be referring to his statement of what he was asking for in
6e4–7. But he is also contrasting this answer with Euthyphro's first attempt,
(D₁p). That answer failed (Nec). So Socrates must also be conceding that,
at least on the face of it, (D₂p′) satisfies (Nec).[16] And the objection he raises
does not, in fact, turn on (Nec), or, for that matter, on (Suf).

He starts in on this objection with a reminder (7a7–10):

Come, then, let's look at what we are saying. The {a8} god-loved {thing} and
the god-loved man are pious, while the god-hated {thing}{a9} and the god-hated
{man} are impious; and the pious is not the same as but the most contrary to the
impious; isn't that so?[17]

This is all, according to a7, supposed to be "what we are saying"; Socrates
is not yet asking for any new concessions from Euthyphro.

Then, first, the formulations that appear in a7–9, namely:

(D₂p) The pious =_df the god-loved (τὸ θεοφιλές), and
        the impious =_df the god-hated (τὸ θεομισές),

which also figure in the argument to come, are to be understood as merely
abbreviations of the clauses in (D₂p′); Socrates' restatement of the definition
is not a mere repetition, but I cannot see that the revisions are of any
importance.

And second, the formulation that appears as a9–10, "the pious is not the
same as but the most contrary to the impious," can only be reverting to
5d1–5:

Or isn't the pious the same as itself in every action, and the impious, again, the
contrary of the pious in its entirety {τοῦ μὲν ὁσίου πάντος ἐναντίον}, but like
itself and everything whatever that is to be impious having, with respect to its
impiety, some one idea?

This is going to be a premise on which the refutation of (D₂p) turns.

---

[16] So Allen (1970) 29 = Allen (1984) 31–32.
[17] Hermann's emendation, οὐχ οὕτως <εἴρηται>; (reported in the apparatus *ad loc.* in Duke et al.
[1995] 10) would make this question read "hasn't that been said?" That emendation is tempting.

At this point Socrates appeals to something else already espoused by Euthyphro (7b2–4): "Then, Euthyphro, that the gods fall into factions, and differ with each other, and there is hatred among them toward each each other, wasn't this also said?" Euthyphro agrees that it was said; it was said, in fact, in 5e–6c (see esp. 6bc). This is also going to be a premise in the refutation of (D₂p). So it is important to notice that Socrates does not accept this premise, except out of ironic deference to Euthyphro (see 6ab), and he apparently alludes to this dissent of his, quite vaguely, in the course of the argument (at 7d9–10, quoted just below).

Socrates now takes up the question (7b6–7): "And . . . difference about *what {things}* makes for hatred and outbursts of rage?"[18]

In its context, this refers to differences, hatred, and so on, among the gods; Socrates approaches this question by asking first what differences make for hatred among humans. He puts it to Euthyphro, who agrees, that, when it comes to questions as to whether things are more or fewer, larger or smaller, heavier or lighter, where we have ways of settling our differences by counting, measuring, and weighing, respectively, that doesn't happen (7bc), but when it comes to questions as to whether something is just or unjust, admirable or despicable, good or bad, it does (7cd).

No doubt Socrates' motivation in seeking definitions for such terms as *just* and *admirable* (καλόν) is at least partly, if not mostly, that those definitions, by providing standards, will put such terms on the same plane of decidability as *more, larger,* and *heavier,*[19] but he does not outright say that here.[20] All he does here is make an inference from the fact that humans disagree about which things are just, admirable, or good, and the inference sets up the objection he is trying to raise (7d9–e5):

SOC: But what of the gods, Euthyphro? Isn't it so that if in fact they differ, they must differ because of these same {things}?
EUTH: {It's a} great necessity.
{e1} SOC: And, my nobly born Euthyphro, on your account, among the gods some think some {things} just, and others {think} other {things just}, and admirable and despicable and good and bad; for, I suppose, they would not fall into factions with each other if they did not differ about these {things}; not so?
EUTH: What you say is right.

Nothing much justifies the step from what humans disagree about to what the gods disagree about, and I shall simply skip it.

---

[18] On ἔχθραν δὲ καὶ ὀργάς, see Heidel (1902) 57 and Walker (1984) 76.
[19] So Burnet (1924) 37–38, 39 (*ad* d1), followed by Allen (1970) 33, Walker (1984) 81, and others.
[20] He comes closer to saying it in *Protagoras* 356a–357b, as does the Eleatic Stranger in *Statesman* 283c–285c.

We have, by whatever means, now got Euthyphro saying that the gods disagree about which things are just, admirable, or good. Abbreviate this list to "good" alone. We might then register Euthyphro as accepting

(1′) Some of the gods think some things good that others think bad.

But by the time we get to 8a12, we'll find Socrates stating as a conclusion from previous admissions "*whatever* is god-loved is also god-hated," and the previous admissions have to include the present one. Rather than accuse Socrates of switching quantifiers, which would be an unimportant mistake compared to the one that really matters, I propose to give Socrates the universal quantifier right back here, and have him getting Euthyphro to own up to:

(1) Whatever some gods think good others think bad.

In fact, it looks as if the switch from (1′) to (1) begins to take place in 7e10–8a3 (see below).

In any case, we must keep in mind that Euthyphro's admission, whether (1′) or (1), is his alone: it depends on a premise that Socrates rejects, to the effect that the gods disagree, and his rejection of that premise would carry (1) with it; 7d9–10, "if in fact they differ" (εἴπερ τι διαφέρονται) gently reminds us of that.[21]

Socrates moves on from (1) to what the gods love and what they hate (7e6–9):

SOC: Then isn't it so that the very things that each faction thinks {to be} admirable, good, and just, it will love, and what {it thinks to be} the contraries of these it will hate?
EUTH: Certainly.

This next step is another premise, taken as obvious, I should think, to both parties:

(2) What gods think good they love, and what they think bad they hate.

Indeed, I should suppose that this depends on a more general premise to the effect that for gods or anybody else loving something is bound up with thinking it good and hating it with thinking it bad, but we have no need to pursue the argument to that level of generality.

Socrates' next move sounds like a simple rephrasing of what we've already got (7e10–8a3):

---

[21] So Heidel (1902) 59, Burnet (1924) 39 *ad* d8.

SOC: But, you say, the same {things} that some think just, others {think} unjust, disputing about which they fall into factions and make war with each other; isn't it so?

EUTH: {It's} so.

But there is an ambiguity in 7e10–8a1, "the same {things} that some think just, others {think} unjust": does this mean that for *all* of the things that some think just, others think those same things unjust, or only that for *some* of the things that some think just, others think those same things unjust? Well, the present claim is not supposed to be a *new* concession: Socrates begins his speech: "But, you say," and that has to be appealing to 7de. So it looks as if the beefing up that gets from (1′) to (1) might be starting to set in here. I'll suppose that: 7e–8a, then, has Euthyphro conceding (1).

Socrates now brings us to a step away from the clincher (8a4–9):

SOC: Therefore, the same {things}, it seems, are hated and loved by the gods, and they must be both god-hated and god-loved.

EUTH: It seems.

{a7} SOC: And therefore the same {things} must be both pious and impious, Euthyphro, on this account.

EUTH: It may be so.

To get the inference implicit in Socrates' speech at in 8a4–5 to go, we need the apparently uncontroversial definition:

(Dgl) The god-loved $=_{df}$ what is loved by the gods, and
      the god-hated $=_{df}$ what is hated by the gods.

But, however uncontroversial (Dgl) may be, the argument surrounding it is a bit more difficult. For we have to be in a position to apply (2) to (1) to get:

(4) All the same things are loved and hated by the gods.

And that doesn't strictly follow: just as we slid without warning from (1′) to (1), we are now sliding from talk about what *some of* the gods think good and others bad, in (1), to talk about what *the* gods love and *the* gods hate, in (4). In other words, there has been a further step, unannounced, after (1), which we could register as

(3) All the things the gods think good, the gods think bad.   (1)

This really won't go: (3) doesn't follow from (1). But perhaps we can be charitable here, and let Socrates off with a nonfelonious charge of vagueness, taking it that "the gods think that *S*" can be so where only some of them think that *S*. Once again, if I am right, the really important difficulty does not lie here.

Then we're allowing Socrates to get to (3), and from there on to

∴ (4) All the same things are loved and hated by the gods.   (3),(2)
∴ (5) All the same things are both god-loved and god-hated. (4),(Dgl)
∴ (6) All the same things are both pious and impious.   (5),(D$_2$p)

Two additional points about the argument so far are noteworthy.

First, it makes use of Substitutivity at (6), in the step Socrates takes at 8a7–8. It is not that the Paradigm Requirement replaces the Substitutivity Requirement.

Second, the argument is not complete at this point: it is not that Socrates professes to see a contradiction in (6).[22] The argument would, in fact, be irredeemably awful if that were the way it was supposed to go, for then we would be unable to let Socrates off when he routes the argument through the implicit (3): it would then be very important that "some gods" is not tantamount to "the gods," for there is plainly no contradiction in (1), and if there is a contradiction in (6) it would have to be imported by (3).

This can be seen more clearly as follows. If "pious" can be replaced by "god-loved" and "impious" by "god-hated," as (D$_2$p) tells us, and if we want to keep (Dgl) uncontroversial, then "pious" can be replaced by "loved by the gods" and "impious" by "hated by the gods." But then it becomes crucial what we take to be the truth conditions for "*x* is loved by the gods" and "*x* is hated by the gods." For Euthyphro is conceding at 8a4–5 that "the same things . . . are hated and loved by the gods," i.e., (4), and he is conceding that as following ultimately from his admission at (1). Now if (6) is to be contradictory, then, given (D$_2$p) and (Dgl), the contradiction must be already there in (4). But then, since (1) is contradiction-free, it must be in the implicit step (3). But it is Socrates himself who brings that in, by going from (1) to (4). Then there is no contradiction in Euthyphro's position, and no reason for him to give up on (D$_2$p) or on (D$_2$p′).

I take it that the best thing to say is that Socrates is not supposing that (6) is contradictory.

Finally, Socrates delivers the clincher (8a10–12):

---

[22] *Pace* Benson (2000) 48 (in 49 n. 57 he cites Candlish [1983] and Weiss [1986] 444 n. 8 for the opposite view).

Then you did not answer what I asked, Amazing Fellow. For I wasn't {a11} asking
for that which is, while it is the same {thing}, in fact both pious and {a12} impious;
but whatever is god-loved is also god-hated, as it seems.

This needs unpacking.

The first thing to notice is that Socrates makes no suggestion to the
effect that (6) is contradictory; his complaint appears to be another one
altogether.

The second thing to notice is that the formulation in a12 is, as we noted
in advance, a universal generalization: "*whatever* is god-loved is also god-
hated." This is (5), and signals the need for something as strong as (1) for a
starting point.

Now just what is Socrates' complaint?

He says he wasn't asking for that which is both pious and impious; what
he finds wrong with Euthyphro's nominee for the pious is that it is not *just*
pious: it is both pious and impious.

It is not, once more, that he thinks it contradictory for the same thing to
be both pious and impious; he seems quite cheerfully to be allowing that
in a11–12. That should come as no surprise. We have already found him
(at *Charmides* 161a6) saying that modesty is good and not good without
hearing any contradiction in it, and we shall find him, in the *Hippias Major*,
perfectly prepared to have something both beautiful and ugly.

Rather, Socrates' express complaint is that he was not asking for what
is both pious and impious. His question was: what is the pious? He must,
then, be supposing that (6) entails

(7) The pious is both pious and impious,

and that *that* is what is wrong with (D_2p). What is wrong with (7) has pretty
much got to be that it says that the pious is both pious *and impious*. Then
what is specified as the pious in the answer to Socrates' question "what is the
pious?" must be something *purely pious*, i.e., pious and not also impious; it
looks as if the claim that underlies his argument is a Self-Predication about
the pious:

(SPp) The pious is through and through pious, i.e., pious and under
      no circumstances impious.

And that, at last, gives us a contradiction: between itself and (7).

To see just what (SPp) is contributing to the picture, let's consider what
Hecuba might have said on behalf of (D_2p) if we had simply stopped

at (7), without invoking (SPp). She might have said: there's nothing wrong with (7), Socrates, under your assumption that it is not contradictory for something to be both pious and impious. As I employ statements of the form "the *F* is . . . ," they translate into universally quantified claims of the form "every *F* is . . . ." Then (D₂p), as I read it, translates into the equivalence:

(E₂p) *x* is pious ↔ *x* is god-loved, and
       x is impious ↔ *x* is god-hated,

and (7) into

(7′) *x* is pious → *x* is both pious and impious,

and if we put these two together we get

(5′) *x* is god-loved → *x* is both god-loved and god-hated,

which is just a thinly disguised version of (5), or a fairly direct consequence of (5). Where's the contradiction?

Socrates has a reply to this. He might say: look, Hecuba, you're forgetting the point we made in discussing llamas, namely, that a statement of the form "the *F* is . . ." when made in response to a request for a definition has to be more than a generalization; it has to characterize *F*s qua *F*s: it has to tell us, to use the phrase Aristotle will employ some years from now, what it is to be an *F*, what being an *F* consists in. So your translation of (D₂p) into (E₂p) fails to get the full force of (D₂p), which has to license the conditionals:

(C₂p) *x* is pious → *x* is, qua pious, god-loved, and
       x is impious → *x* is, qua impious, god-hated.

And then the failure of your strategy is obvious: for we surely cannot allow

(7″) *x* is pious → *x* is, qua pious, both pious and impious.

And the force of (SPp) is simply to insist that we cannot allow (7″): when we talk of the pious in the context of answering the question "what is the pious?" we must give in response only what is indelibly, through and through, pious. You may recall, my nobly born Hecuba, that at one point we were paraphrasing assumptions such as (SPp) in the form

(SPp') The pious is, qua pious, through and through pious, i.e., pious and under no circumstances impious.

And that rules out (7"): what (D₂p) gives in answer to the question "what is the pious?" is something that is not indelibly pious, as (7") shows.

I think that is the best that can be done for Socrates' attack on (D₂p). It is not enough. For Hecuba might say: who says I'm committed to (7")? I'm not. For (7) only follows from (D₂p) with the help of (1), the claim that the gods disagree and whatever some think are good things others think are bad. You don't yourself accept that; Euthyphro does, but even he is not going to go for the idea that the things some gods think good are, qua pious, ones that others think bad: the truth of (1), if it is true, is an accidental truth, and not enough to support an inference to (7").

Alternatively put: (6), given its background in (1), just says that "pious" and "impious" have, given (D₂p), the same extension; we haven't shown that all the same things are, qua pious, both pious and impious. If we derive (7) from (6), (7) does not have the force of (7"), and nobody is committed to the latter. But what (SPp') rules out is only (7"), and not (7) read Hecuba's way, i.e., as (7').

In the (relatively) real world of Socrates and Euthyphro, where none of this sophistication is in play, we have a formal contradiction between (SPp) and (7). And that looks like what they take to be the case against (D₂p). Our comments about the use of generically abstract noun phrases were not available to them. However feeble Euthyphro's intellect was, he was presumably capable of telling what looked like a contradiction when he saw it. The fact that in this particular case the contradiction is ultimately only apparent was not something either he or Socrates was at this point in a position to see.

And, furthermore, since the argument depends on (1) and Socrates does not accept (1), although Euthyphro does, the argument is at best an ad hominem argument against Euthyphro's espousing (D₂p). That is not of much importance, especially since the next definition, (D₃p), is designed to be a revision of (D₂p) that renders (1) irrelevant. And the argument against (D₃p) is of major importance.

It is time to turn to that argument. For we've been ignoring the background in the *Euthyphro* against which the Paradigm Requirement was introduced. Just before introducing it in 6e, Socrates had said that he wanted "that form itself by which all the pious things are pious" (6d10–11: ἐκεῖνο αὐτὸ τὸ εἶδος ᾧ πάντα τὰ ὅσια ὅσιά ἐστιν, and cf. d11–e1). Here "by which" translates the dative pronoun ᾧ (d11). Such datives are, in the Greek grammar trade, called "instrumental datives"; alternative translations for these two datives might be "because of which" and "because of one idea."

At the beginning of this chapter, I said that although the Explanatory Requirement was not directly connected with the Paradigm Requirement when the latter was introduced, it was in the immediate background; this is why. So we must look at the Explanatory Requirement.

CHAPTER 6

Socrates' requirements: explanations

Socrates expects satisfactory definitions to do some sort of explanatory job. At the most elementary level, this job is that of what I shall call "explaining content." I'll start by explaining the content of that phrase, and then, after yet another look at *Euthyphro* 6de, turn to one passage in which a definition is failed because it does not explain content: *Euthyphro* 9d–11b.

6.1. EXPLAINING CONTENT

Consider the following dialogue schema:

Q$_1$: What's that?
A$_1$: It's an F.
Q$_2$: Why is it an F?
A$_2$: Because it is H, and $F =_{df}$ the H.

At a minimum, Socrates expects someone with a proper definition for courage, piety, or whatever, to be able to use it in the way A does here.

Consider Q$_2$. It is vague: it may have different forces in different contexts.

It might be that Q is not a native speaker of English, A knows this, and uses "G" to define "F" on this occasion because he knows that the words that compose "G" are English words known to Q. He might define "F" quite differently for another speaker. If Socrates were only requiring this much of definitions, it would just be a question of explaining the content of a term in a way that would make the use of the term comprehensible to a given audience.

Plainly Socrates wants more: he expects the correct definition to explain the content of the term on every occasion in which explanation is demanded.

Suppose then that the phrase "an F" involves a word unfamiliar to Q: A$_1$ might be "It's an apteryx," perhaps, or "It's a case of floccinaucinihilipil-ification." Q$_2$ would then more naturally be "What does that mean?" than

"Why?" but the latter is imaginable. If Q is a novice birdwatcher, and A_1 is to the effect that that's a golden-crowned kinglet, Q might, being unfamiliar with golden-crowned kinglets, but up on ruby-crowned kinglets, ask, at Q_2, why it's one rather than the other. Here Q is asking what makes it count as a golden-crowned kinglet, and A_2 might be "Well, it's a golden-crowned kinglet, and not a ruby-crowned kinglet, because it has a prominent orange crown patch bordered in yellow and black rather than a nearly invisible red crown patch bordered in grayish olive," pointing to the birds, and the pictures and descriptions in his Field Guide.

This is what I mean by "explaining content," and it is very close to, if not spot on, what Socrates wants. It tells us what makes this bird count as a golden-crowned kinglet: *why* it is that, i.e., why anyone would *say* it is that.

Abbreviating "because" to "bec," we may state the Explanatory Requirement as:

(ER) the $F =_{df}$ the $G \rightarrow (Fx \rightarrow Fx$ bec $Gx)$

and, at any rate at the outset, we understand "because" in terms of explaining content.

The word "cause" often enters the picture at this point, but we should be cautious. We all know that, as Aristotle uses the word "cause" (αἰτία or αἴτιον), it covers a lot more ground than the English word in contemporary usage does. It can be used wherever the word "because" can be used. But this can be confusing. It would be very odd, looking at the dialogue about birds, to say that A_2 is telling Q what caused this to be a golden-crowned kinglet or saying what is the cause of this being a golden-crowned kinglet. We are going to find Socrates talking that way in various places, especially after the Theory of Forms has been launched into orbit, but also before that: in various passages discussed in the next chapter. But we should be suspicious of this move.

We won't encounter it in this chapter. We're going to be looking at an argument in which the word "cause" plays no role, although the word "because" does.

Socrates' demand that a definition explain content descends from the Intellectualist Assumption and from the roots of his definitional questions in the affairs of daily life. He thinks that the only way one can know whether something is F is by having its definition. So he thinks that the standard pattern for assuring oneself that something is an F is by going through the Q–A dialogue schema with oneself: by having an explanation of the content of "F."

This places restrictions on the terms that appear in the *definiens* "*G*": they must be the sort of thing that could be used to justify the application of "*F*" to a person who was in doubt. So there is now an asymmetry that we didn't need to think about in dealing with simple Substitutivity; the "because" relation is asymmetrical:

(Abec) p bec $q \rightarrow \neg(q$ bec $p)$.

And this makes for a difficulty.

Observe, for starters, that any statement of the form "*p* bec *p*" is incompatible with (Abec), since, plugged into (Abec), it will yield its own negation, "$\neg(p$ bec $p)$."

Suppose now we have:

(D*F*) the $F =_{df}$ the G.

The Explanatory Requirement tells us that "this is G" must be usable as an explanation as to what makes this count as an *F*: that, at least on occasion,

(1) *Fx* bec *Gx*

be acceptable. But then plainly

(2) *Gx* bec *Fx*

cannot be acceptable on the same occasions: the order of explanation is wrong. But two substitutions using (D*F*) in (1) gets us to (2). And this affects both ends of the "because" relation; a single substitution using (D*F*) gets us from (1) to

(1′) *Fx* bec *Fx*,

while another single substitution using (D*F*) gets us from (2) to

(2′) *Gx* bec *Gx*,

and either of (1′) or (2′) is incompatible with (Abec).

So when we are dealing with the Explanatory Requirement we shall have to be cautious about Substitutivity: we can't freely substitute definitional equivalents in "because" contexts. And then the difficulty is going to be that Socrates' argument against (D₃p), as he states it, employs Substitutivity in "because" contexts.

Well, one might think, maybe he doesn't accept (Abec). But, as we shall see, he does, and the argument depends on this as well.

6.2. EUTHYPHRO 6DE

We found Socrates reminding Euthyphro that Socrates had asked for "that form itself by which {ᾧ} all pious things are pious," and that Euthyphro had conceded that it was "by one idea {μιᾷ ἰδέᾳ} that the impious things are impious and the pious things pious" (6d9–11). Now in fact Socrates had not asked for precisely the former, and Euthyphro had not conceded precisely the latter: all that had been said was that the pious was "the same as itself in every action" and that everything impious had, "with respect to its impiety {κατὰ τὴν ἀνοσιότητα}, some one idea" (5d1–5).

This is easily explained, if Socrates' talk of that "by which" all pious actions are pious is really nothing more than talk of that self-same thing, the pious, that is in every pious action. And the latter, we said, just amounted to saying that, when the pious has been correctly identified, we shall have something that is present in all and only the pious actions: that the correct *definiens* will give us necessary and sufficient conditions for the application of "pious."

Once again, this is all we can get out of the passage provided we are willing to suppose that Euthyphro has a chance of understanding what is going on. If Socrates is in fact importing heavier requirements, a theory of some sort about causality, he should at least say so. He does not.

But *can* the talk of that "by which" all pious actions are pious be construed so anemically? Well, why not? We are speaking of what we shall find in all and only pious actions, by which they count as pious actions. It is not that there must be some entity that *makes* them, *causes them to be* pious. They are pious. How come? That is, what feature of them are we pointing to when we say they are pious? In other words, what is the content of the term "pious"?

That this anemic interpretation of the explanatory requirement will suffice for the *Euthyphro* is borne out by a passage in which the requirement is wielded to great effect. Let us turn to that.

6.3. EUTHYPHRO 9D–11B

Euthyphro tried defining the pious as what is beloved to the gods, and that went down the drain, since the gods disagree (§ 5.5). That suggests revising the definition so that unanimity is a part of it (9c3, 9); Socrates makes that suggestion (9d1–4):

But then, do we now make this correction in your account: what *all* the gods hate is impious, and what {they *all*} love pious . . .?

and Euthyphro accepts it (9e1–3). This is, plainly enough, the conjunctive package

(D$_3$p$_1$) The pious =$_{df}$ what all the gods love, and
        the impious =$_{df}$ what all the gods hate.

There is going to be some variation in the formulation: this is "(D$_3$p), version 1" or "(D$_3$p$_1$)."

The argument with which we are to deal can be taken as treating sentences containing "the pious" as simple universal quantifications. So (D$_3$p) can be read as saying:

(D$_3$p$_2$) x is pious =$_{df}$ all the gods love x, and
        x is impious =$_{df}$ all the gods hate x.

Socrates begins the refutation[1] of this definition with the question (10a1–3):

SOC: . . . Consider the following: is it so that the pious is-loved by the gods because it is pious, or is it pious because it is-loved {by the gods}?
EUTH: I don't know what you are saying, Socrates.

Euthyphro does not understand (10a4). Let us imagine that we do: Socrates is invoking the Explanatory Requirement, according to which if the pious is definable as that which is loved by all the gods, something that is pious is so because it is loved by the gods, and not the other way around. So when Euthyphro concedes, shortly below, that the pious is loved by the gods because it is pious, he is going to be in trouble, at least prima facie.

Socrates tries to clarify his question with inductions having to do with verb forms. The first is short and straightforward, and Socrates goes on immediately to apply it to the target verb, "love" (10a5–8, 10–11):

{a5} SOC: Then I shall try to put it more clearly. We speak of something carried and {something} carrying, and {something} led and {something} leading, and {something} seen and {something} seeing, and in all such cases you understand that they are different from each other and how {they are} different?

{a10} SOC: So also there is something loved and, different from it, the loving {thing}?

We here distinguish, for an indeterminately large class of verbs V, the agent doing the Ving from the object Ved. "Ved" represents the past participle of the verb, construed as an adjective describing the object. As this applies to the target verb "love" (a10–12), it requires us to distinguish the thing loved from what does the loving. Socrates does not make explicit the application

---

[1] The argument has received extensive treatment in the literature; I have benefited the most from Cohen (1971).

to the *definiens* of (D₃p₁), "what all the gods love," but, plainly enough, there we are to distinguish all the gods from that which all the gods love; the latter is entitled to the label "loved." We are then going to ask what entitles it to this label.

The next induction is supposed to help Euthyphro, and the rest of us, get the force of Socrates' question whether the pious is loved by the gods because it is pious or pious because it is loved by the gods. Whatever it does for Euthyphro, it doesn't do much for most of the rest of us, particularly those who, unlike Euthyphro, do not speak Greek: it turns on a feature of the passive voice in Greek that is not paralleled in the English passive. In Greek the passive of a verb such as ὁρᾶν, "see," is a single word formed from the stem of the verb and a verb ending: in this case ὁρᾶσθαι, "be-seen." English passives are formed by adding the past participle of the verb to the auxiliary verb "to be": "be seen." But this has a parallel in Greek: it is possible to add the Greek passive participle as a predicate adjective to the verb εἶναι, "be," to get the phrase ὁρώμενον εἶναι, "be seen." This "periphrastic passive" is different from the true passive, although it is indistinguishable from it in straightforward English translation.

What Socrates does in this passage plays on the difference he sees between the true passive and the periphrastic passive: e.g., between the passive ὁρᾶται (10b7), the single word meaning "is-seen," and the periphrastic passive, ὁρώμενόν ἐστι (10b7), two words meaning "is seen." Translators resort to various devices to make English of the passage; most do so only by sacrificing the structure of the Greek. I shall err in the opposite direction: I do not pretend that the following is acceptable English. I have translated the passive of the verb *V* as "is-*Ved*," the passive participle as "{a thing} *Ved*" (or, where the definite article is present, as "the {thing} *Ved*"), and consequently the periphrastic passive as "is {a thing} *Ved*." The result is somewhat unsightly (10b1–11):

SOC: Then tell me: is the {thing} carried {a thing} carried because it is-carried, or because of something else?

EUTH: No, it's because of that.

{b4} SOC: And the {thing} led {is so} because it is-led, and the {thing} seen because it is-seen?

EUTH: Certainly.

{b7} SOC: So it isn't that it is {a thing} seen, and because of that it is-seen, but on the contrary it is-seen, and because of that it is {a thing}{b9} seen; nor is it that it is {a thing} led, and because of that it is-led, {b10} but it is-led, and because of that it is {a thing} led; nor is it that it is-carried {b11} because it is {a thing} carried, but it is {a thing} carried because it is-carried.

Those are the cases for Socrates' induction; his next step will be to state the generalization to which it allegedly leads. Let's stop and look at the cases.

The pseudo-English makes it hard to get the drift of these examples. Things seem to me clearer with an example that is not a translation of any of those Socrates gives but parallel to them.

Consider an import, such as a foreign car. Why is it called an "import"? Because, we might pedantically say (and Socrates is certainly here being pedantic), it is imported. But then, why do we speak of it as "imported"? Because someone imported it. So we have here an explanatory hierarchy: the bottom of the ladder is the claim that someone imported x, and it is because of the truth of that claim that x counts as imported, and hence as an import. It sounds strange to run this the other way: to say that someone imports x because x is imported, or that x is imported because it is an import.

There is one major difference between this example and those Socrates introduces: Socrates makes no appeal to the active voice at all. We might have expected him to bring the active voice in, since (D_3p_1) is phrased in terms of the active voice, but the fact is that from here to the end of the argument the active voice is altogether absent.[2] He has, as we shall see, tacitly replaced (D_3p_1) with

(D_3p_3) the pious $=_{df}$ the {thing} loved by all the gods

and (D_3p_2) with

(D_3p_4) x is pious $=_{df}$ x is {a thing} loved by all the gods.

So all Socrates really needs, in terms of my example, is the "because" claim

(Bi) if x is an import, then x is an import because x is imported, and
     not: x is imported because x is an import

or, in terms of his own examples

(Bc) if x is {a thing} carried, then x is {a thing} carried because x
     is-carried, and
     not: x is-carried because x is {a thing} carried,

and so on.

In Socrates' statement of his examples, in 10b1–11, he infers the truth of the second, negative, clause of (Bc) from the truth of the first clause, and

---

[2] Except for the "dummy" verbs Socrates uses in framing his Inductive Conclusion: see below.

likewise with the other verbs; he is, then, employing the asymmetry of the "because" relation, (Abec).

The "because" in use here is the one that figured in the Explanatory Requirement, and that is what this argument turns on. It is not that we have here anything that looks much like "causality" or "agency." What makes this car an import is the fact that it is imported. "Makes" in that sentence does not involve agency or causality as we would understand it. True, what makes it so that something is imported is someone's importing it, and there is an agent here, namely, the importer, but he is a red herring: what we've got is merely an allegedly more basic unpacking of the original fact, that this car is an import. We are (boringly) explaining content. And precisely parallel things are to be said about (Bc): what entitles a thing to the label "carried" is that it is-carried; that's what "*x* is {a thing} carried" amounts to.

Socrates' statement of the generalization he wants his induction to establish reads as follows (10b11–c5):

SOC: . . . So is it clear what I mean to say, Euthyphro? I mean this: that if something comes-to-be, or is-affected somehow, it is not because it is {a thing} coming-to-be that it comes-to-be, but because it comes-to-be, it is {a thing} coming-to-be, nor is it because it is {a thing} affected that it is-affected, but because it is-affected, it is {a thing} affected. Or don't you agree with this?

What Socrates is doing here is using the verbs "to come-to-be" (γίγνεσθαι) and "to be-affected" (πάσχειν) as I have used the expression "to be-*V*ed" in the preceding: Socrates employs those verbs as dummy verbs, standing in for an unspecified range of verbs such as "to be-carried," "to be-led," "to be-seen." His Inductive Conclusion is, in my terms:

(IC) If *x* is {a thing} *V*ed, it is not because it is {a thing} *V*ed that it is-*V*ed, but it is {a thing} *V*ed because it is-*V*ed.

Socrates now applies (IC) to the target case, "being-loved." We get (10c7–13):

SOC: Then too, isn't the {thing} loved either something coming-to-be or something affected by something?
EUTH: Certainly.
{c10} SOC: And so this will work just as the previous cases did: it is not because it is {a thing} loved that it is-loved by those by whom it is-loved, but because it is-loved that {it is a thing} loved?
EUTH: A necessity.

In my terms, c7–9 tells us that "love" is a legitimate instantiation of "*V*," and c10–13 states the instantiation; we get the "because" statement:

> (ICl) if *x* is {a thing} loved, then *x* is {a thing} loved because it
> is-loved, and
> not: *x* is-loved because it is {a thing} loved.

Socrates then extracts the crucial concession from Euthyphro (10d1–11):

> SOC: Then what do we say about the pious, Euthyphro? Isn't it so that it is-loved by all the gods, on your account?
> EUTH: Yes.
> {d4} SOC: Because of the fact that it is pious, or because of something else?
> EUTH: No, it's because of that.
> {d6} SOC: So because it is pious, it is-loved, but it is not because it is-loved that it is pious?
> EUTH: It seems.
> {d9} SOC: But now it is because it is-loved that <the god-loved> is {a thing} loved, {a thing} god-loved.[3]
> EUTH: How not?

The adjective "god-loved" (θεοφιλές) in 10d10 makes its appearance in this argument for the first time here;[4] it is going to be with us for the rest of the argument, so perhaps its introduction should get some attention.

Here and in the sequel, "*x* is god-loved" is, like "*x* is {a thing} loved," not a passive construction, but something more like a periphrastic passive; hence the translation above, "{a thing} god-loved." In fact, as Socrates introduces it, it is a replacement for "{a thing} loved": presumably this itself is an abbreviation of "{a thing} loved by all the gods" (φιλούμενον ὑπὸ θεῶν πάντων).

---

[3] 10d10: I have here, following Heidel (1902) 71, 101 (so also Fowler [1914] 38) adopted an emendation due to Bast (early 1800s), καὶ θεοφιλὲς <τὸ θεοφιλὲς>; without it, the sentence would translate: "But now it is because it is-loved that it is {a thing} loved, {a thing} god-loved," where "it" refers back to "the pious," understood as the subject of the preceding sentence.

    Burnet (1924) 49 *ad loc.* says: "Bast's reading καὶ θεοφιλὲς <τὸ θεοφιλὲς>, which I formerly adopted with all recent editors, spoils the argument by making τὸ θεοφιλὲς {the god-loved} the subject instead of τὸ ὅσιον {the pious}." But this seems to me quite wrong. Socrates is here citing the result of his induction as applied to the target case of {a thing} loved by all the gods, and that formula has been shortened to "the god-loved." Given the way the substitutions are going to work in 10e11–11a3, where the definition is treated as enabling the replacement of "pious" with "god-loved," it is really immaterial whether Socrates employs "the pious is god-loved because it is-loved by all the gods" or "the god-loved is god-loved because it is-loved by all the gods;" either will get the same results. But the latter is a more accurate formulation of the Inductive Conclusion than the former.

[4] It had appeared in the preceding argument in 7a.

In the sequel, from 10d12 on, "god-loved" will be used as a replacement for the *definiens* of (D_3p).[5] If it is both that and a replacement for "{a thing} loved by all the gods," what has happened, unannounced, is that (D_3p_1) has been replaced by

(D_3p_3) the pious =$_{df}$ the {thing} loved by all the gods,

as was anticipated, and then (D_3p_3) in turn has been displaced by

(D_3p_5) the pious =$_{df}$ the god-loved,

which has as a shadow

(D_3p_6) x is pious =$_{df}$ x is god-loved,

just as (D_3p_3) was shadowed by (D_3p_4).

Under the assumption that these moves have been made, the argument hangs together; otherwise, there is chaos. For it is a fact that everything from here on is phrased either in terms of the passive "is-loved by all the gods" or using the adjective "god-loved," and Socrates is going to lean on the explanatory relations between these two terms, and between them and the term "pious."

This brings with it a small dividend: we shall not, from here on, have to distinguish true passives from periphrastic passives in translating the text, so, at least in translating, we can drop the supplement "{a thing}"; we can just speak of "the god-loved." But I'll stick with the hyphenated "is-loved" to represent the Greek passive, and in laying out the arguments to come we shall often have to revert to the distinction between the passive and the periphrastic passive.

Euthyphro has just (10d4–8) conceded two things:

(EC1) what is pious is-loved {by all the gods} because it is pious,

and

(EC2) what is pious is not pious because it is-loved {by all the gods}.

But (EC2) follows from (EC1) by the asymmetry of the "because" relation, (Abec). So we may think of the package containing (EC1) and (EC2) as a single Concession, (EC1/2).

In 10d9–11, Euthyphro makes another concession, but this is not a new one (if n. 3 is correct): it is simply the instantiation of Socrates' Inductive Conclusion, stated in 10c10–13 and registered earlier as

---

[5] And this is the way it was used in 7a, where Socrates had abbreviated the *definiens* in (D_2p), "the beloved to the gods," to "god-loved."

(ICl) if *x* is {a thing} loved, then *x* is {a thing} loved because it
is-loved,
and not: *x* is-loved because it is {a thing} loved,

with two slight differences: the gods are mentioned (via the adjective "god-
loved") in this formulation, and the negative consequent in (ICl) is not
stated explicitly. If we restore the negative consequent, make the reference
to the gods explicit by replacing the term "{a thing} loved" by "god-loved,"
and break the result into a conjunction of two conditionals (rather than a
single conditional with two consequents), we get:

(ICgl1) if *x* is god-loved, then *x* is god-loved because it is-loved, and
(ICgl2) if *x* is god-loved, then not: *x* is-loved because it is god-loved.

Again, the asymmetry of "because" guarantees the second given the first.

The Concession (EC1/2) answers the question asked by Socrates and
not understood by Euthyphro back in 10a1–4. If we have our eye on the
Explanatory Requirement, we can see that Euthyphro's Concession sets
him up for an attack based on that: if the definition were correct, what is
pious would be so because it is loved by the the gods.

It is plainly Euthyphro's Concession that gets him in trouble. So it is
quite important to see that his Concession does not follow from anything
in the preceding at all. It is a free admission. No generalization at which
Socrates has arrived by induction entails it or even strongly suggests it. The
previous generalizations have not forced it on us; they have at most clarified
the question of 10a1–3. Socrates was asking: is the fact that an action is pious
to be explained on the basis of the fact that the gods love it, or is their love,
their approval, based on the (logically) antecedent fact that it is pious? And
Euthyphro has jumped for the latter alternative.

It is an interesting question whether Euthyphro's Concession could be
motivated. I am inclined to think it could be,[6] but that would do nothing
to clarify the Explanatory Requirement.

Socrates now says(10d12/13):

Then the god-loved is not pious, Euthyphro, nor is the pious god-loved, as you
say, but this is other than that.

---

[6] The view that what makes an act right is that God commands it is sometimes characterized as "theistic
voluntarism," and it is not obvious that it is the orthodox view: Thomas Aquinas, e.g., is supposed
to have rejected it (see Lisska [1996] 112–15). Grube (1935) = (1980) 152–53 seems to think that "we"
would find theistic voluntarism "not . . . unnatural," but it has some fairly unnatural consequences:
e.g., that God could make Hitler's extermination of the Jews right simply by an act of his will. Theistic
voluntarism (or whatever one wishes to call it) can be made more sophisticated so as to avoid this
sort of objection: see Adams (1973); for a discussion with further references to the literature, see Berg
(1991) 525–29.

He is here announcing that Euthyphro's definition has been undone. So, first, when he says "this is other than that," he means that the god-loved is not the pious, and so he must at least be eliding some definite articles; he must be saying: "the god-loved is not {the} pious, nor is the pious {the} god-loved." And, second, he is now taking Euthyphro's definition to be (D_3p_5).

Euthyphro, of course, is not ready to concede that his definition has been undone; the dialogue continues (10e1–5):

> EUTH: How so, Socrates?
> {e2} SOC: Because we are agreed that the pious is-loved because it is pious, but it is not because it is-loved that it is pious – not so?
> EUTH: Yes.

Socrates here adverts to (EC1/2), and we can easily reconstruct an argument from just that much.

Suppose Euthyphro were right, and the pious were the god-loved, and suppose that there is at least one pious action. The Explanatory Requirement tells us that this action must be pious because it is god-loved. But (EC2) was that anything that is pious is not so because it is god-loved. So we have a contradiction, and (D_3p) (in whatever form) has to go.

Socrates' argument is more complicated; having reminded Euthyphro of (EC1/2), in "we are agreed that . . ." just above, he continues (10e6–9):

> SOC: And that the god-loved is, because it is-loved by the gods, by this being-loved itself, god-loved, but it is not because it is god-loved that it is-loved.
> EUTH: What you say is true.

This is the instantiation of Socrates' Inductive Conclusion, (ICgl1/2). Socrates goes on (10e10–11a4):

> But, my dear Euthyphro, if the {e11} god-loved and the pious were the same, then:
> if the pious {11a1} {thing} were-loved because of its being pious, the god-loved {thing} would also be-loved because of its being {a} god-loved {thing}; and
> if {a2} the god-loved {thing} were {a} god-loved {thing} because of its being-loved by the gods, {a3} the pious would be pious because of its being-loved;
> but as it is, you see that {a4} the opposite holds, so that the two are entirely different from each other.

Here he invokes (D_3p_6) in 10e10–11, uses it in 10e11–11a1 to substitute "god-loved" for "pious" in (EC1), and uses it again in 11a1–2 to substitute "pious" for "god-loved" in (ICgl1). The results of these substitutions are false, assuming again that there is at least one pious action: what falsifies the first is (ICgl2), and what falsifies the second is (EC2). Socrates says this in (11a4–6):

For the one is such as to-be-loved, because it is-loved, and the other is-loved because it is such as to-be-loved.

The god-loved is that because it is-loved: this is (ICgl1), from which (ICgl2) follows; the pious is-loved because it is pious: this is (EC1), from which (EC2) follows.

And finally, Socrates redescribes his conclusion (11a6–b1):

And perhaps, Euthyphro, when you were asked what the pious is, you did not want to make its substance {οὐσία}[7] clear to me, but to state an affect {πάθος} of it: {to state} that the pious has this affect, that it is loved by all the gods; but what it is, you have not yet said.

What we have had up to this point is argument that involves only explaining content: by virtue of what does an action count as "pious"? It can't be because it is approved by all the gods, if its piety is the reason the gods approve it, for then it must be antecedently pious, and consequently approved by the gods; that leaves us with the question we started with: what constitutes its piety? Socrates' way of summing this situation up involves some new terminology: it may be that being loved by all the gods is an affect (πάθος, 11a8–b1) of the pious, but that is not its substance (οὐσία, a7–8): that is not what it is (b1). This terminology will eventually have ontological significance. Here there is no reason to ascribe to it any but logical significance: the substance of something is what it is; affects of it are not what it is.

But, now, what of Socrates' argument in 10e–11a? He has employed a rule to the effect that if G is the *definiens* for F, "G" and "F" are intersubstitutable in "because" contexts:

(SB) the $F =_{df}$ the $G \rightarrow [(p$ bec $Fx \rightarrow p$ bec $Gx)$ & $(Gx$ bec $q \rightarrow Fx$ bec $q)]$.

This is, however, open to question, as we have already seen.

---

[7] The term "substance" is a standard translation for οὐσία in Aristotle. The word is one that means "being"; it is used in *Hippias Major* 301b6, e4 to mean being in general, the totality of being, and in the same passage at 301b8 and 302c5 it is used as it is here, to mean the being of something specific: so also *Meno* 72b1 and perhaps *Charmides* 168d2. In *Protagoras* 349b4 the phrase τις ἴδιος οὐσία appears just to mean "some unique being," i.e., "some unique thing" (so Guthrie in Cooper [1997] 779). Elsewhere in the early dialogues it has its common colloquial sense of "that which is one's own, one's substance, property" (LSJ *s.v.*): *Crito* 44c5, 53b2, *Gorgias* 472b6, 486c1. From the *Phaedo* on, the word is increasingly important in connection with ontological questions; Silverman (2002) 7–8 perhaps overestimates its importance in earlier dialogues.

"*G*" may, we might note, be coextensive with "*F*" without being inter-substitutable in "because" contexts. Suppose all and only the pious people are red-headed. Still, they pray to the gods, not because they are red-headed, but because they are pious. So being red-headed is merely an accidental concomitant of being pious.

But there is worse. The Explanatory Requirement is this:

(ER) the $F =_{df}$ the $G \rightarrow (Fx \rightarrow Fx$ bec $Gx)$.

And substitution using the antecedent results turns the consequent into "$Fx \rightarrow Fx$ bec Fx," which, because of the asymmetry of "because," entails that nothing is F.

I conclude that Socrates would have been better off to stick with the simple argument we constructed for him when we paused in the middle of 10e. There may well be suitable restrictions on substitutivity that would allow his more complex argument to work, but they are not going to be easy to work out.

Still, whatever difficulties we may find in Socrates' argument, they are in fact marginal to the Explanatory Requirement: whether or not substitutivity fails for "because" contexts, Socrates is requiring that a *definiens* be capable of explaining the application of its *definiendum* in the sense of explaining the content of that *definiendum*.

CHAPTER 7

Socrates' requirements: explaining by paradigms

The Paradigm Requirement and the Explanatory Requirement are ultimately fused, and that fusion brings in some extra baggage. The anemic interpretation of the Explanatory Requirement may be all that is needed for the use to which it is put in the *Euthyphro*, but that is not true of all the passages in which we encounter it.

In the early dialogues, Socrates occasionally imports a presupposition about what can explain something's being F to the effect that what makes things F must itself be F; it makes things F by transmitting its Fness to them. This is the beginning of a theory of causality. Let us[1] call any theory that employs this presupposition a "Transmission Theory" of Causality. The cause, whatever it is, is a "transmitting cause" of other things' being F.

The Theory of Forms is going to incorporate a Transmission Theory of Causality: the Form, the F, will make things F by transmitting its own being F to those things. The Theory of Forms is not unique in this: Aristotle will also advocate a Transmission Theory of Causality, especially in the domain of biology (ἄνθρωπος ἄνθρωπον γεννᾷ: it takes a human being to generate a human being), without Plato's Theory of Forms (Aristotle does, of course, have *a* theory of forms). So accepting a Transmission Theory does not commit one to Plato's Theory of Forms.

In Aristotle,[2] we may distinguish between two grades of Transmission Theory: a Strong one and a Weak one. The Strong one has it that, if x is F because of y, y is more F than x is,[3] the Weak one just that if x is F because

---

[1] See Lloyd (1976) 146; also Mourelatos (1984) 1. For a reservation, see Sedley (1998) 123–24.
[2] On Aristotle's theory in general, see Mourelatos (1984), Makin (1990/91).
[3] See *Posterior Analytics* A 2. 72ª27–30, *Metaphysics* α 1. 993ᵇ24–26.

of *y*, then *y* is *F*, too.[4] The Theory of Forms is a super-Strong Transmission Theory.

Transmission Theories have a heritage that antedates Plato, in the principle that like comes from like. The most important case[5] is, perhaps, Anaxagoras, for whom the fact that something is *F* is explained by the presence in it of something that is *F*. If this is not to lead to infinite regress, it must be that the something *F* that explains why something else is *F* is itself purely *F*,[6] although, on Anaxagoras' theory, there can be no question of our ever extracting anything that is purely *F*.[7] Plato's Academy apparently took a lively interest in Anaxagoras' theory: Eudoxus, it seems, even tried to revive it as an alternative to Plato's Theory of Forms.[8]

Suppose we inject a Transmission Theory into the anemic idea that the pious is what makes things count as pious: suppose we assume that whatever it is that makes things count as pious must itself be pious. Then the idea is not anemic any more. Some of it can be made to look fairly wan: if we remind ourselves of the behavior of the generic abstract "the pious," we can see part of the result of our injection as merely repeating the triviality that the pious is pious. But that is not all there is to it: we are now saying that there is something that is itself pious that makes Euthyphro's action count as pious. And this is stronger stuff. In particular, it would work where we abandon the generic abstract "the pious" in favor of the abstract noun "piety": if it is the presence of piety in an action that makes it count as pious, then piety must itself be pious.

The sort of Transmission Theory we are dealing with has the following elements:

(TT1) It is the *F* (or *F*ness) because of which anything counts as F.
(TT2) Whatever it is because of which anything counts as *F* is itself *F*.
∴ (TT3) The *F* (or *F*ness) is itself *F*.

I'm calling this a Transmission Theory of Causality, but I still want to keep the term "cause" at bay until Socrates himself uses it: hence phrasing in

---

[4] See e.g., *De Anima* B 5. 417^{a}17–21, *Physics* Θ 5. 257^{b}9–10, *De Generatione Animalium* B 1. 734^{a}29–32, *Metaphysics* Z 9. 1034^{a}21–30, Θ 8. 1049^{b}23–27.

[5] It has been alleged also for Xenophanes and for Alcmaeon (Barnes [1979] = [1982] 88–89, 118–19).

[6] See Teloh (1975) 16, Furley (1976) 80–83 = (1989) 62–65, Teloh (1981) 42. See DK 59B10 (II 37.6–7; but Schofield (1980) 135–43 argues that this is not quotation from Anaxagoras: I am not convinced), with its context (DK II 37.7–9); DK 59B6 (II 35.15–16), 11 (II 37.12–14), 12 (II 37.22–23): these latter texts come from Simplicius, Diels (1882/95) I 164.27–28, 23–24, 156.16–17, resp.

[7] See Dancy (1991) 5–9.   [8] This is the subject of Dancy (1991), Study I.

terms of "that because of which anything counts as *F* " rather than "the cause of something's being *F*."

Did we not have all these things in the *Euthyphro*? The pious was certainly what made things count as pious, and it was itself pious. But what grounded the latter claim was not (TT2): the reason the pious turned out to be itself pious was that it was to function as a *paradigm* or *standard* with reference to which one could determine which things were pious.

Still, although (TT2) did not play any role in the argument of the *Euthyphro*, it would not be surprising if it had, for it is present in other early dialogues.[9] And what is surprising is that it is consistently treated, not as a piece of abstract metaphysics, but as something to which anyone on the street would agree. Anyway, that's how it looks in the *Protagoras*.

7.1. *PROTAGORAS* 330–331, 332–333

We've already quoted *Protagoras* 330b–e in § 3.2.1, to consider its existential claims. The view under attack is, we recall, that no "part" of excellence (justice, piety, courage, etc.) is like any other (330b3–6). The first attack on it begins, in 330b6–e2, with Socrates getting from Protagoras two sets of concessions: first, that there are such things as justice and piety, and second, that justice is just and piety pious.

The latter concessions are self-predications,[10] and they employ, not generic abstracts, but abstract nouns. Nothing whatever is said to motivate the first of them: Protagoras allows without hesitation that justice is just (330c7–d1). But, when Socrates asks whether piety is pious, he gives an argument for a positive response: nothing else would be pious if piety weren't pious (d7–e1). Protagoras' unhesitating assent must signal the fact that these claims are regarded as intuitive.

The argument based on these concessions peters out in 332a4, and Socrates tries a new one; the core argument on which this turns is (see 332e–333b):

(1) Folly (ἀφροσύνη) is contrary to temperance (σωφροσύνη).
(2) Folly is contrary to wisdom (σοφία).
(3) One thing has only one contrary.
∴ (4) Temperance is the same as wisdom.

---

[9] Teloh (1981) 42 says that "Plato never explicitly asserts" the transmission theory, and (43) that "Plato is unconsciously influenced by" it. This is false.

[10] Savan (1964) 133 denies that "piety is pious" as it appears in the *Protagoras* is a self-predication, but he means something more than I do. See Vlastos (1954) 337–38 with n. 33 = Allen (1965) 249 with n. 3 = Vlastos (1995) 180–81 with n. 33.

For our purposes, the interesting thing is what Socrates says along the way to getting from (1) to (3)(332b1–c2):

{People} are temperate with temperance . . . the things that are done foolishly are done with folly, those {done} temperately with temperance . . . if something is done with strength, it is done strongly, and if something {is done} with weakness, weakly . . . and if something {is done} accompanied by quickness, quickly, and if it {is done} accompanied by slowness, slowly . . . and so if something is done in the same way, it is done by the same, and if something {is done} in a contrary way, {it is done} by the contrary.[II]

Socrates does not put things together in the following way, but we can. Let Fness be one of the virtues here under discussion. It is by Fness that F people and actions are F. And if Fness were not itself F, nothing else could be. This is not, as it stands, (TT2), but it is entailed by (TT1) and (TT2), and it is natural to suppose that they stand in back of it. Anyway, Socrates is more explicit elsewhere.

7.2. CHARMIDES 160D–161B

In Socrates' argument against Charmides' definition of temperance as modesty (160d–161b: § 4.4.3), one of the premises was:

(P2) What makes men good and not not good must itself be good and not not good.

This derives directly from the text: an instance of it is explicit in 161a8–9, "While temperance is {a} good {thing}, if it makes those to whom it is present good and not bad," and the more general premise "what makes men good is good" would be explicit in 160e11 if the text were not corrupt. We have here, then, an instance of (TT2).

7.3. CHARMIDES 164C–166B

In *Charmides* 163e–164b (§ 4.3.2.3), Critias was made to give up on the definition of temperance as doing good things, because then one could be temperate without knowing it; he then supplied a new definition (164c9–d1, d2–4):

I'd rather take back one of those things {sc. to which I'd previously agreed} . . . than allow that a man who is ignorant of himself is temperate. For, really, I'd almost say that this itself is temperance, knowing oneself {τὸ γιγνώσκειν ἑαυτόν}.

[II] Formulations with ὑπό also occur in d4, 7 (*bis*), e2–3, e3–4 (*bis*), e4.

This gives us

(D_5t) temperance $=_{df}$ knowledge of oneself.

We are here going to consider only the first argument against the definition of temperance as knowing oneself, which leads to its replacement by

(D_{6a}t) temperance $=_{df}$ knowledge of itself (knowledge of knowledge).

Socrates begins (165c4–7) by claiming that if temperance is knowing something (γιγνώσκειν . . . τι), it is *a* knowledge and is *of* something (ἐπιστήμη τις . . . καὶ τινός); he illustrates the "*of* something" clause with medical {knowledge or art} (ἰατρική), which is knowledge *of* the healthy (c8–9).

So far, he seems to be headed toward the question: what is it that temperance is a knowledge *of*, if it is knowledge of oneself? This seems a silly question, since the answer is built into the question: it is knowledge *of oneself.*

But, before Socrates gets to that question, he seems to veer off: he goes on to say about medicine that it is useful or beneficial (χρησιμή) for us because it produces (ἀπεργάζεται) health (165c10–d3). He adds another example: housebuilding (οἰκοδομική), the knowledge how to housebuild (οἰκοδομεῖν), produces houses (d4–6).

Socrates now says to Critias: since you say temperance is knowledge of oneself, you must answer the question: "Critias, what admirable work, worthy of the name, does temperance, which is a knowledge of oneself, produce for us?" (165d6–e2).

Is this the question we were expecting, or has Socrates indeed veered off? The examples Socrates produces to motivate the question are not quite parallel: medicine is the knowledge of health, and produces health; housebuilding is the knowledge how to housebuild, and produces houses. Possibly Socrates would say that the knowledge how to housebuild really is the knowledge of houses, so the two examples are parallel: the object of the knowledge is the product. If this is the way he is thinking, the question "what does temperance produce?" may actually be the question "what is temperance the knowledge of?" I shall assume that this is right.

But, in fact, although any knowledge has to have an object, it need not produce anything. Critias sees the latter point, and replies adequately in 165e–166a: look at arithmetic and geometry; there's no product there.

So Socrates reverts to the first point (166a3–7):

but I can show you this: what each of these knowledges is a knowledge *of*, which is in fact different from the knowledge itself. E.g., arithmetic is {knowledge} of the even and the odd, of how they relate in plurality with themselves and with each other,[12]

and goes on to emphasize that the odd and even are different from arithmetic (a9–11). He makes a similar point about the art of weighing (166b1–4). He then says (b5–6): "Say, then: of what is temperance also a knowledge, which is in fact different from temperance itself?" Critias' reply that temperance alone is knowledge of itself as well as other knowledges (166bc) is going to short-circuit the argument. Instead of going on, let us ask where things would have gone if Critias had said what Socrates was apparently pushing him toward saying: there is no other object, full stop.

There are two possible ways of taking the resulting argument.

(1) One employs (LL): there is a feature of every knowledge, viz., its possession of an object distinct from it, that temperance does not have; so temperance is none of the knowledges, and a fortiori not a knowledge of oneself. The defeating predicate is "has an object distinct from itself," which applies to every case of knowledge, but not to temperance; so temperance is different from every case of knowledge, and so, in particular, from knowledge of oneself.

(2) The other: temperance, construed as knowledge of oneself, is incoherent, for every knowledge has an object distinct from itself, but knowledge of oneself would not have an object distinct from itself: so there can be no such thing, and a fortiori, temperance is not such a thing.

The trouble is that it is not clear what grounds Socrates' apparent suspicion that temperance has no distinct object. Both of our two ways of reading what Socrates is up to seem to founder on the obvious reply to the question "what is the object of temperance?" noted above: oneself, according to this definition.

If line (1) were the correct interpretation of Socrates' argument, he would have to be saying: it's just obvious to everyone that temperance isn't the knowledge of something distinct from itself. I cannot imagine why he would think that. He is perfectly ready in the *Laches* to countenance the idea that courage is knowledge of something, so he is hardly in a position to take it as obvious that temperance is not a knowledge of anything, and then it is impossible to see why it shouldn't be a knowledge of something different from itself.

---

[12] See here *Gorgias* 451a7–c5, de Strycker (1950) 49–54.

The alternative is to suppose that it is not taken as predefinitionally obvious that temperance, if it is a sort of knowledge, is a knowledge of nothing different from itself, but, rather, that this conclusion is derived from the definition of temperance as knowledge of oneself. This leads us to to line (2). Our question is: what rules out the idea that temperance, defined as knowledge of oneself, has oneself as its distinct object? It must be that, if oneself is the object of knowledge of oneself, its object is not really a *distinct* object. And this is unambiguously borne out by Critias' reply in 166bc, that temperance is different in precisely this respect, that it is the object of *itself*, and by Socrates' subsequently (in 166e–167b, to which we shall return) taking it that this reply is relevant. Socrates and Critias are thinking along line (2).[13]

But it is hard to see how this could be so: surely, if I know myself, that knowledge is not identical with *me*.

There is, conceivably, some sort of confusion over the reflexive pronoun: knowledge of oneself is collapsed into knowledge of self.[14] The distance here is greater in Greek than in English: a change of gender is required, so this is not a very promising explanation. But there is another explanation for the transition. The virtues and other character traits considered in the Socratic dialogues are characteristically conceived as "self-predicative": if a certain trait makes a man *F* it is itself *F* (there was an example at *Charmides* 160d–161b). We are now discussing that character trait that makes a man a knower of himself. Then this must be a knowledge of itself. Critias himself says this, a little later in the dialogue (169d9–e5):

> For if someone has knowledge that knows itself, he must be such as that which he has; just as whenever someone has swiftness, he is swift, and whenever {he has} beauty, {he is} beautiful, and whenever {he has} knowledge, {he is} one who knows, and whenever someone has knowledge that knows itself, he will be one who knows himself.

And that is what both Socrates and Critias are assuming in 165–166.[15]

If Socrates doesn't buy Critias' claim, he is dissembling. For the course of argument he pursues against (D_5t) requires that assumption. We had

---

[13] So there really is a transition from "knowledge of oneself" to "knowledge of itself," *pace* Witte (1970) 110 n. 58 and perhaps Dyson (1974) 103–6.

[14] See also von Arnim (1914) 110–11, where the move is a fallacy; Tuckey (1951) 33–37, 107–8, where it is a fallacy but with a point; Wellman (1964) 111, where it is not a fallacy.

[15] Santas (1973) 119 n. 1 finds Critias' reasoning "preposterous," and thinks Socrates is not committed to it. But he is: in 166b–167a, he takes the task of refuting the definition of temperance as knowledge of oneself to be that of attacking the idea that there is such a thing as knowledge of itself, just as much as Critias takes the task of defending the former to be that of defending the latter.

Socrates asking, in 166b5–6: "Say, then: of what is temperance also a knowl-edge, which is in fact different from temperance itself?" And to this Critias replies in 166b7–9 that this is what is different about temperance (b9–c3): "all the other knowledges are of something else, not of themselves, while this alone is knowledge of the other knowledges and of itself." He accuses Socrates of trying for an eristic refutation without taking what he, Critias, is saying seriously, and Socrates mollifies him (166c–e). Then Socrates returns to the definition in question with this (166e4–167a1, a5–8):

SOC: So, I said, say how you want to put it about temperance.
CRIT: So I say, he said, that it alone, among the other knowledges, is knowledge of itself and of the other knowledges as well.
SOC: Then, I said, it would also be knowledge of non-knowledge, if {it is knowledge} also of knowledge?
CRIT: Certainly, he said.
{167} SOC: Therefore the temperate {man} alone knows himself . . .; and this is being temperate and knowing oneself, knowing what one knows and what one does not know. Is this what you are saying?

And the dialogue continues with examination of the question whether this sort of knowledge is possible, under the assumption that if it is not, the definition must fail.

That train of thought, if it is cogent, requires that (D_5t) entail $(D_{6a}t)$; if that entailment fails, the question whether a knowledge that knows itself is possible is not relevant, and (D_5t) stands unquestioned, for there is no objection whatever raised against (D_5t) in isolation from $(D_{6a}t)$. So if we say that Socrates is not himself committed to the transition, we must say that Socrates has no objection whatever to (D_5t). It can't be that (D_5t) is left unrefuted because it is the one Plato wants us to accept, for then the dialogue from (D_5t) on is simply irrelevant. So the argument of the dialogue must turn on what we quoted Critias as making explicit in 169de: what qualifies someone as a knower of himself is possession of a knowledge that knows itself. We have an application of a Transmission Theory.

To be more precise, what Critias there says is not an instance of (TT2); it is, rather:

Whoever has knowledge of itself is one who knows himself,

which is of the form "whoever has *F*ness is *F*," a converse of (TT2). But the other examples he offers (swiftness and beauty) show that he is prepared to accept

(TT2sk) That which makes someone a knower of himself must be a
knower of itself,

which is an instance of (TT2), and then, by (TT1),

(TT1sk) It is self-knowledge that makes someone count as a knower of
himself,

so

(TT3sk) Self-knowledge must be a knower of itself.

7.4. HIPPIAS MAJOR

In 286c Socrates introduces the anonymous interlocutor (Socrates' alter ego)
who allegedly bedevils him, and will, through Socrates, bedevil Hippias off
and on for the rest of the dialogue (see § 2.3.2). It will be useful to have a
label for this person; I'll call him "Anonymous."

Let's first review Anonymous's putting of the question to Socrates and
Socrates' turning it over to Hippias, and then turn to Hippias' first three
tries at an answer; these attempts labor under considerable misapprehension
on his part, but the refutations of these ill-conceived answers are of some
importance, since they involve all three of the Substitutivity Requirement,
the Paradigm Requirement understood in terms of Self-Predication, and
the Explanatory Requirement.

7.4.1. Hippias Major *286c–287e*

Socrates tells us (286c5–d2):

Recently, someone threw me into puzzlement when I was censuring some things
in certain discourses as ugly, and praising others as beautiful, by asking, quite
insolently indeed, something like this: "I say, Socrates, how do *you* know {d}
which are beautiful or ugly? For come, would you be able to say what the beautiful
{τὸ καλόν} is?"

Here the sought-for item is "the beautiful"; when Socrates rephrases the
question in 286d7–e1 it is "the beautiful itself" (αὐτὸ τὸ καλόν, e8):
the reflexive generic abstract "the beautiful itself" is supposed to refer to the
beautiful just by itself, in contrast with anything else.

It may help to get hold of this to translate it into the metalanguage:
asking for the beautiful itself is a matter of isolating the term "beautiful"
from a context such as "this is a beautiful speech" and asking what the word

"beautiful," all on its own, contributes to that context. And this is what Socrates is doing.

Before Socrates finally turns the question over to Hippias he has Anonymous clarify it; we looked at this passage (287b5–d3) in connection with existence claims (§ 3.2.3). Anonymous there gives us a Socratic Induction, based on three cases: justice (δικαιοσύνη), wisdom (σοφία), and the good (τὸ ἀγαθόν). He uses these three terms and the fourth, "the beautiful" (τὸ καλόν), as if there were no difference between them as far as his present argument is concerned.

He derives two generalizations from these cases. Under the supposition that the phrases "by justice" and "by the good" can be rephrased as "because of justice" and "because of the good," the first generalization can be written as a "because" claim (where "becof" abbreviates "because of"):

(B) $Fx \rightarrow$ (Fx becof the F).

And the second generalization (most explicit in 287c6–7) is an existential claim:

(E) Fx becof the $F \rightarrow$ there is such a thing as the F.

It is the latter, (E), that is instantiated to get the motivating claim, in d1–2,

(Eb) There is such a thing as the beautiful

that guarantees a subject for discussion, about which we can ask "so, then, what is it?" But to get (Eb) from (E) requires a step of *modus ponens*, the input for which comes from the instantiation of (B) for "beautiful" in c8–d1, which may be written as:

(Bb) x is beautiful $\rightarrow$ (x is beautiful becof the beautiful).

The constraint this places on the answer to the question "what is the beautiful?" is plain enough: the answer to that question must give us something about which it makes sense to say: it's because something is *that* that it counts as beautiful. In other words,

(ERb) The beautiful $=_{df}$ the $G \rightarrow$
       [x is beautiful $\rightarrow$ (x is beautiful bec Gx)],

which is the Explanatory Requirement applied to "beautiful."

7.4.2. Hippias Major *287e–289d*

Anonymous's framing of the question for Socrates and the immediate sequel read as follows (287d2–e1):

> SOC: "Tell me, then, sir," he'll say, "what is this, the beautiful? {τί ἐστι τοῦτο τὸ καλόν;}"
> {d4} HIPP: Doesn't he who asks this want to learn what is {a} beautiful {thing} {τί ἐστι καλόν}?
> {d6} SOC: I think not, Hippias, but what is the beautiful {ὅτι ἐστὶ τὸ καλόν}.
> {d7} HIPP: And how does this differ from that?
> SOC: In no way, you think?
> HIPP: Yes, it differs in no way.
> {d10} SOC: Well, {it's} clear that you know more beautifully. But nevertheless, {my} good {man}, consider: for he's asking you not what is {a} beautiful {thing}, but what is the beautiful {ἐρωτᾷ γάρ σε οὐ τί ἐστι καλόν, ἀλλ' ὅτι ἐστὶ τὸ καλόν}.

I find it extremely difficult to see how Socrates' "explanation" in d10– e1 can have helped, since it merely repeats the question and insists on its difference from the one Hippias had proposed. Still, Hippias acts as if it helped; he responds (287e2–4):

> I understand, {my} good {man}, and I'll say in reply to him what the beautiful is, and I shall never be refuted. For know well, Socrates, if one must speak the truth, {a} beautiful girl is {a} beautiful {thing} {ἔστι . . . παρθένος καλὴ καλόν}.

It is hardly clear that Hippias has managed to understand, despite his assurance. The statement he utters in 287e3–4,

> (H1) {A} beautiful girl is {a} beautiful {thing},

is really an answer to his question, "what is a beautiful thing?" and not to Socrates' question "what is the beautiful?" and that is borne out by the sequel.

But Hippias came up with (H1) as a response to Socrates' question, so Socrates will understand it as an attempt at a definition; we may write it as:

> (D₁b) The beautiful =df a beautiful girl.

That is more than a little sad; for one thing, it is obviously circular. Yet absolutely nothing in the dialogue is said about this. We must be charitable on this score, and see what Socrates thinks is really at stake.

But before we actually go on with Socrates, we should notice[16] that the grammar of Hippias' utterance (H1) is a little unusual: its predicate adjective "beautiful" does not agree in gender with its subject; hence the translation "{a} beautiful girl is {a} beautiful {thing}." This device is only slightly unusual. Here is the explanation given in Kühner and Gerth (1898/1904) I 58:[17]

If the subject is not conceived as a determinate object {*ein bestimmter Gegenstand*}, but as a general concept {*allgemeiner Begriff*} (as a thing or essence {*ein Ding oder Wesen*}), then the predicate adjective will refer to the subject, without regard to its gender or number, in the neuter singular.

Hippias, then, is not saying *this* beautiful girl, say, Helen, is something beautiful, but a beautiful girl – any one you like – is something beautiful. The translation above, "{a} beautiful girl is {a} beautiful {thing},"[18] is an inadequate attempt to get at the force of the Greek, and in the sequel I shall continue with this device: "{a} beautiful {thing}" signals that we have the neuter adjective, in disagreement with one or another non-neuter subject.

So even here, Hippias has not committed a type mistake, that of listing an individual where he should be talking about something that possesses generality. His answer is supposed to be general.[19] So we must read (D₁b) as making a general claim:

(D₁b₁) x is beautiful $=_{df}$ x is a beautiful girl.

Of course, no matter how we read (D₁b), it is far from general enough. All Socrates has to do is point out, as he did with Euthyphro, that the definition doesn't cover all the cases: being a beautiful girl is not a necessary condition for being beautiful.

But that is not exactly what he does. Instead he adverts to Anonymous again (288a7–b4):

SOC: . . . He'll question me somewhat as follows: "Come now, Socrates, reply to me: all these {things} that you say are beautiful – if *what* is the beautiful

---

[16] With Kapp (1959) 130–31 and Woodruff (1982) 50–51 n. 63.

[17] Or see Smyth (1956) 276–77 (§ 1048).

[18] I concur with Woodruff (1982) 50–51 n. 63 in rejecting the alternative translation offered by Nehamas (1975/76) 299–301 = (1999) 168–69 "being a beautiful girl is (to be) beautiful," but perhaps not for the reasons Woodruff gives; he concedes that this "is a possible reading of the Greek," but I do not. Particularly where we are asking whether the text is dealing with universals as opposed to particulars (as is true in the case of all three of us: Nehamas, Woodruff, and myself), we must be careful not to inflate it. The subject of Hippias' sentence is "{a} beautiful girl," not "being a beautiful girl," just as the term of comparison in Sophocles' *Antigone* 332–333 is "man," and not "being human" as Nehamas would have it (300 = 168).

[19] *Pace* Tarrant (1928) 47 *ad* 287d and *ad* 287e, Soreth (1953) 17.

itself, would these be beautiful?" Am I to say to him that if {a} beautiful girl
is {a} beautiful {thing}, {it} is {that} because of which {δι' ὅ} these would be
beautiful?[20]

{b1} HIPP: Then do you think he'll still try to refute you {and say} that what
you speak of is not beautiful, or, if he should try, that he won't turn out to be
ridiculous?

{b4} SOC: Well, that he'll try, I know well.

Let's start with the interchange in 288b1–4, and then return to Anonymous's
questions in a8–11.

It looked before as if Hippias really had not seen what Socrates was
after, and was only issuing the statement (H1) and not the definition (D₁b);
288b1–2 confirms this: Hippias expects Anonymous to be unable to refute
his claim, and doing that would be supporting the claim "that what you
speak of is not beautiful,"[21] i.e.,

(¬H1) A beautiful girl is not beautiful.

And if we read what Socrates says in b4 literally, he is saying that Anonymous
will undertake to do precisely that.

This is pushing the text too hard; after all, Socrates is construing Hippias
as having offered (D₁b), whatever Hippias' intentions may have been, and
it will be best to take him as saying that Anonymous will try to refute (D₁b),
not (H1).

If we look back at the questions asked in 288a8–11, it looks as if Anonymous is preparing to object that (D₁b) fails to explain the application of
the term "beautiful."

He first (a8–9) wants Socrates to consider "all these {things} that you
say are beautiful." As a matter of fact, neither Socrates nor Hippias has pronounced anything beautiful, except for Hippias' beautiful girl, for about a
page; the last things characterized as beautiful by anybody were the "practices" (ἐπιτηδεύματα) with which Hippias' demonstration speech is concerned (in 287b7), and the last things Socrates had reported himself as
characterizing as beautiful were parts of speeches (in 286c7). It is perfectly
clear that none of these things is a beautiful girl, and pointing that out

---

[20] 288a10–11 ἔστι δι' ὅ ταῦτ' ἂν εἴη καλά: so the MSS and Burnet (1900/1907) III. Schanz proposed
ἔστι τι δι' ὅ ταῦτ' ἂν εἴη καλά; this might make some difference to the commitments of the passage,
which would then read: "Shall I say to him that if {a} beautiful girl is {a} beautiful {thing}, there is
something because of which these would be beautiful?" Anyway, so Woodruff (1982) 167–68 thinks
(he does not adopt this emendation). But I doubt it would make any difference, and, in any case,
the resulting sense is pretty foggy.
[21] Hippias, like Euthyphro in *Euthyphro* 5e–6a and 6d, is intent on defending the sufficiency of his
answers.

would show that (D_1b) does not provide a necessary condition. Nobody does.

Rather, Anonymous asks, with reference to all the things Socrates is prepared to say are beautiful (288a8–9): "if *what* is the beautiful itself, would these be beautiful?"

This has to be another way of phrasing the question "what is the beautiful?" and is plainly supposed to be giving us a condition that must be satisfied by a successful answer. We could put the condition as follows:

(Cb1) The beautiful $=_{df}$ the $G \to$ all these things (which are in fact beautiful) are beautiful.

But there are two ways (at least) of reading this.

In one, it merely repeats the requirement that a definition give a necessary condition:

(Necb) The beautiful $=_{df}$ the $G \to$ (x is beautiful $\to$ x is G),

so that the objection toward which Anonymous is headed is that "all these things (which are in fact beautiful)" includes a lot of things that aren't G (aren't beautiful girls).

In the other way of reading (Cb1) what is demanded is that a successful *definiens* explain the application of its *definiendum*:

(ER1) The beautiful $=_{df}$ the $G \to$ (x is beautiful because x is G).

And what Anonymous goes on to say makes it clear that it is this second reading that he is after. For he asks the question "if *what* is the beautiful itself, would these be beautiful?" in 288a8–9 in the context of supposing that Hippias has tried to answer it with (D_1b), and he immediately (288a9–11) paraphrases this answer as: "if {a} beautiful girl is {a} beautiful {thing}, {it} is {that} because of which {δι᾽ ὅ} these would be beautiful."

It is quite clear that (D_1b) is going to fail (Necb), given that there are beautiful speeches and practices, and clear that it will a fortiori fail (ER1): a beautiful speech isn't beautiful because it's a beautiful girl. The only question is which direction Anonymous is trying to take.

Still, it is clear that there is an interrelationship of Substitutivity and the Explanatory Requirement: to meet the latter, a *definiens* must already at least meet half of the former, (Nec); if we have a candidate *definiens*

(D_1f) $Fx =_{df} Gx$

and y is an F but not a G, then y isn't an F because it is a G.

And, although it is not relevant in the present context, the other half of Substitutivity must also be met. For if being G explains why anything is F, then if something is G it must be F; so "G" must provide a sufficient condition for something's being F.

Socrates now goes on to tell us what Anonymous is going to say to him if he tries to use Hippias' answer to the question "what is the beautiful?" and it certainly sounds at first as if he is going to conclude that (D_1b) fails to provide a necessary condition (288b8–c11):

> SOC: "How sweet you are, Socrates," he'll say. "But isn't {a} beautiful mare {a} beautiful {thing}, which even the god praised in the oracle?" What are we going to say, Hippias?
> {c1/2} Are we not to say that the mare, anyway the one that's beautiful, is {a} beautiful {thing}?
> {c2/3} For how could we dare to deny {that}, and say that the beautiful is not beautiful?
> {c4} HIPP: You're speaking the truth, Socrates, since surely the god also said it rightly; for there are very fine mares among us.
> {c6} SOC: "Well," he'll surely say, "what of {a} beautiful lyre {λύρα καλή}? Isn't {it a} beautiful {thing} {καλόν}?" What are we to say, Hippias?
> HIPP: Yes.
> {c9} SOC: Then next that {fellow} will say this, judging from his manner, for I know {it} pretty well, "Best {of men}, what of {a} beautiful pot {χύτρα καλή}? Isn't {it a} beautiful {thing} {καλόν} then?"

At this Hippias waxes indignant (288d), but Socrates leans on the point, and states his own view. He describes what he takes to be a well-made pot, and concludes (288d9–e2):

> if he is asking about that sort of pot, we must agree that it is beautiful.
> {e1/2} For how could we say that {it}, being {a} beautiful {thing}, is not {a} beautiful {thing}? {πῶς γὰρ ἂν φαῖμεν καλὸν ὂν μὴ καλὸν εἶναι;}

And Hippias concedes that we couldn't.

We now have quite an accumulation of cases that show (D_1b) faulty in that it fails to give a necessary condition for something's being beautiful. And Anonymous has now said in connection with two of them that we cannot say that what is beautiful is not beautiful (288c2–3, e1–2). In the first of these cases, he uses a generically abstract noun phrase to do it: we can't say that "the beautiful is not beautiful"; in the second, he seems to be saying that, since a beautiful pot (χύτρα καλή) is, by stipulation, {a} beautiful {thing}, we can't very well say it isn't beautiful. So, we might suppose, the same will go for a beautiful girl: Anonymous cannot be going for (¬H1). And certainly Anonymous's insistence that we cannot say that what is beautiful is not beautiful fits with the idea that he is headed for the objection that (D₁b) fails to give a necessary condition.

But Hippias' response to Socrates' insistence that we must go along with Anonymous and grant that a beautiful pot is {a} beautiful {thing} leads the discussion in an unexpected direction. We read (288e4–289d2):

{288e4/5} SOC: "Then," he'll say, "isn't {a} beautiful pot also {a} beautiful {thing}?" Reply.

{e6/7} HIPP: Well, but it is, Socrates, as you say, I think; this utensil also, when beautifully made, is {a} beautiful {thing},[22] but on the whole this[23] is not worth judging as being beautiful relative to {a} horse and {a} girl and all the other beautiful {things}.

{289a1/2} SOC: Quite; I understand, Hippias, that it's then required to say in response to the one who is asking these {things} the following: Man, are you ignorant that the {saying} of Heraclitus holds good, that
{a3/4} the most beautiful of apes {is} ugly compared with the class of men,[24]
{a4/5} and the most beautiful of pots ugly compared with the class of girls, as Hippias the wise says.
{a6} Not so, Hippias?
HIPP: Socrates, you've certainly replied correctly.

{a8/9} SOC: Then listen. For know well that next he'll say: "What, Socrates? If one compares the class of girls with the class of gods, won't just the same {thing} happen to it as {happened} to the {class} of pots when compared with that of girls? Or didn't Heraclitus, whom you've brought in, also say this very {thing}, that the wisest of men shows himself an ape in wisdom, beauty, and all the other {things} relative to a god?
{b6/7} Are we going to agree, Hippias, that the most beautiful girl is ugly relative to the class of gods?
HIPP: Who could speak against *this*, Socrates?

{c1/2} SOC: Then if we agree on this, he'll laugh and say: "Socrates, do you remember what you were asked?" "I {remember}," I'll say, "that {I was asked} what is the beautiful itself."

---

[22] 288e6 καλόν: this time the subject is neuter, so there is no failure of agreement, but presumably καλόν has the same force it has had throughout.

[23] 288e7 τὸ ὅλον τοῦτο: Tarrant (1928) 51 takes this as a single phrase: "τὸ ὅλον τοῦτο, collective – 'all this class of thing'." LSJ tell us *s.v.* ὅλος I 4 that τὸ ὅλον can be used to mean "wholly, entirely," but cite no clear cases. Still, that way of construing it sounds better to me, and I follow Woodruff (1982) 10 in so taking it.

[24] 289a4 ἀνθρώπων γένει: ἀνθρώπων is an emendation of Bekker's for the MSS ἄλλῳ, which would make the translation "compared with another kind"; it is rejected by Woodruff (1982) 54 n. 79, quite possibly rightly. For my purposes, there is little difference, but Socrates' point is a little clearer with the emendation, so I have gone with that.

{c3/4} "Then," he'll say, "when asked for the beautiful, you give in reply, as you yourself say, what is in fact no more beautiful than ugly?" It seems so, I'll say; or what would you advise me to say, my friend?

HIPP: I {advise you to say} this; for of course he'll be saying truly that the human class {is} not beautiful relative to gods.

{c9/d} SOC: "But," he'll say, "if I had asked you from the beginning what is both beautiful and ugly, if you'd given me in reply what you just now did, wouldn't you have replied correctly?"

The rest of Socrates' speech here will carry us back to the Explanatory Requirement. But it certainly looks as if Anonymous is already saying that he has shown that (D₁b) has failed. We must consider how that might be.

The argument is:

> (R) Any beautiful girl is more beautiful than any pot but uglier than any god.
> ∴ (O) Any beautiful girl is both beautiful and ugly.
> (SPb) The beautiful cannot be both beautiful and ugly.
> ∴ (C) The beautiful cannot be any beautiful girl.

What is implicit in the text and explicit here is (SPb). There is no alternative; Socrates must be presupposing (SPb). Why might he think it true? Plainly, on the ground that the beautiful can't be ugly at all: it is just though and through beautiful. This is an instance of Self-Predication.

It is an instance that is in one respect typical: what counts in the argument is not so much the positive claim that the beautiful is beautiful as the negative claim that the beautiful is not ugly.

The argument is reminiscent of, or, better, anticipatory of, the Argument from Relativity, AR (§ 1.2.2). We can heighten the resemblance. Socrates had led up to asking Hippias what the beautiful was by getting him to concede its existence. So we have all the materials for the following argument, ar:

> (arE) There is such a thing as the beautiful.
> (arO) Any beautiful girl is also ugly.
> (arF) The beautiful cannot be ugly.
> ∴ (arC) The beautiful is not the same as any beautiful girl.

This is not quite an instance of AR: it does not establish the sweeping non-identity of the beautiful with any ordinary beautiful thing. For all the text has to tell us, the beautiful might be found among the gods. Socrates' point here is not the super-negative one that makes the beautiful an entity of another type; it is the merely negative one that the beautiful is not a beautiful girl: that this attempt to define the beautiful is a failure.

It makes the definition a failure, not on the expected ground that it fails to give a necessary condition for something's being beautiful, but on the ground that its *definiens* fails to give us something beautiful in a way that rules out ugliness. And this is actually closer to a charge of failure of Sufficiency: it turns out that something's satisfying Hippias' candidate *definiens* does not guarantee that it is beautiful in every context; in a beauty pageant featuring beautiful girls and gods, the girls are not beautiful. Of course, that same pageant can be used to illustrate the failure of Necessity: gods are not girls, but are beautiful.

But in 288e–289d down to 289d2 no appeal is actually made to Substitutivity; the argument there involves only the Paradigm Requirement, understood in terms of Self-Predication, which appears as (SPb) in the above.

Still, Socrates doesn't stop at 289d2; he makes Anonymous continue with this (289d2–5):

"But does it still seem to you that that the beautiful itself, by which all the other {things} are adorned and show themselves as beautiful when this form is added {ἐπειδὰν προσγένηται ἐκεῖνο τὸ εἶδος}, is a girl, or a horse, or a lyre?"

Something is a little different here from what we have had before: the talk in d2–3 of the form being "added" to things. This will occupy us at the beginning of the next section.

But, whatever we make of that, it is plain that Anonymous adverts in d2–4 to the requirement that a proper *definiens* for the beautiful must explain the application of the term "beautiful": the Explanatory Requirement. By itself this is no surprise, since that Requirement has been alluded to repeatedly in the course of 287d–289d. But the question now is: what is the relationship between the Explanatory Requirement and the Paradigm Requirement understood in terms of Self-Predication?

Nothing Socrates says constitutes even a very broad hint at an answer; he does not follow up on *either* the failure of (D$_1$b) to provide a necessary condition, *or* its failure to provide something because of which beautiful things are beautiful. Lines of argument appealing to the three Requirements are simply placed side by side, and only the one involving the Paradigm Requirement is carried through to the end.

But the fact that these lines of argument are placed side by side is of itself significant, and the Transmission Theory tells us how they might be related. We have already seen how Substitutivity and the Explanatory Requirement might be related. All we need to do now is bring the Paradigm Requirement, understood in terms of Self-Predication, into the picture, and we can do that simply by appealing to (TT2): whatever explains the application of "beautiful" to all and only the things that are beautiful must itself be beautiful.

7.4.3. Hippias Major *289d–291c*

Lines 289d2–5, quoted just above, told us that none of a girl, a mare, or a lyre is a plausible candidate for the form that, when added to other things, makes them beautiful. Hippias picks up on the "added to" terminology (289d 7–8), and as his next stab at telling Anonymous what the beautiful is he tries (289e2–3): "this beautiful for which he is asking is nothing other than gold." This, he says, when added to something will make something, even something ugly to start with, beautiful (e4–6). Hippias does not advert to Anonymous's term "form," εἶδος, from 289d4, but that word may have helped his confusion; for in non-technical Greek the εἶδος of a thing is its "look," and Hippias is telling us what, when added, will make something look better. So we get:

(D₂b) x is beautiful $=_{df}$ x has gold added to it.

Socrates first points out (290a–c) that Pheidias made his statue of Athena beautiful by adding ivory and stone rather than gold to it. And then he makes use of a qualification Hippias himself offers, to the effect that stone is beautiful "when it is appropriate" (290c7), to argue that, when the beautiful pot mentioned back in connection with (D₁b) has a beautiful bean soup boiling in it, a figwood ladle is more appropriate and therefore more beautiful than a golden one (290e–291a); Hippias does a lot of balking, but in the end gives in (291c4–5). These counterexamples point toward saying that the definition fails to give a necessary condition.

But once again that is not where Socrates takes us. After we get the concession that the figwood ladle is more beautiful than the golden one, phrased by Hippias as a reply for Socrates to make to Anonymous, Socrates says it's time to try out a new definition, since according to this one (291c7–8): "it looks to me as if gold will be shown up as being no more beautiful than wood of a figtree."

The train of thought is parallel to the refutation of (D₁b). We have the same three elements that composed the argument of 287–289: Socrates wields Necessity, but does not make the final blow with it; he makes an essential appeal to the assumption that the beautiful is through and through beautiful; and, in the context, we are trying to find something that will *make* things beautiful, something whose presence would explain why things are beautiful.

And, as with the refutation of (D₁b), the argument can be unified by supposing that satisfying the Explanatory Requirement in turn demands that the *definiens* give necessary and sufficient conditions and at the same time give us something that is paradigmatically, through and through, beautiful, so we must again invoke the Transmission Theory.

There are two important differences between the refutation of (D₁b) and that of (D₂b).

First, the refutation of (D₁b) showed that a beautiful girl is not paradigmatically beautiful by putting beautiful girls in different comparison classes: against apes and pots, they're beautiful, but against divinities, ugly. The refutation of (D₂b) makes gold "no more beautiful than the wood of a figtree," in fact, ugly,[25] not by a simple comparison of gold and figwood, but by comparison of the one with the other in a specific context in which the one is more appropriate than the other: figwood is more beautiful than gold for stirring hot soup. If we think of the demonstration that something is both *F* and con*F* as showing that it is only relatively *F*, then we might see the device of direct comparison as opposed to that of comparison-within-a-context as using slightly different dimensions in which the relativity is presented. We shall see other such dimensions.

The second important difference between the two refutations is in the use, starting in 290c, of appropriateness as a criterion of beauty.[26] In fact, "the appropriate" is going to become the *definiens* of (D₄b), but it is going to be up to Socrates to revive it, for Hippias is already clamoring to try out a new definition before Socrates has disposed of (D₂b) (see 291b7–8).

7.4.4. Hippias Major 291d–293c

Hippias says (291d1–3, d9–e2):

you seem to me to be seeking to reply that the beautiful {is} some such thing as will never show itself as ugly anywhere to anyone.
{d9} Then I say that it is most beautiful always, everywhere, and for every man, being wealthy, healthy, honored by the Greeks, arriving at old age, having interred

---

[25] The term "ugly," αἰσχρόν, is not applied to gold in the course of the refutation, but that, I take it, is merely an accident: the clear implication of 290c8–9, according to which what isn't appropriate is ugly, with 290d–291a, according to which the golden ladle would not be appropriate, is that in that context gold is ugly.

[26] Hippias' admissions in 290c7–d6 appear to commit him to the claim that it is both necessary and sufficient for beauty: see also Woodruff (1982) 58 n. 93; 58 n. 92 suggests that Hippias and Socrates are using "appropriate" differently in 290cd, but I see no sign of this.

his parents beautifully when they died, to be buried beautifully and magnificently by his own children.

Hippias is expressly trying to describe something that is through and through beautiful: beautiful every time.[27] I shall call his nominee "Hippias' Biography," and write it as:[28]

(D₃b) The beautiful =$_{df}$ living Hippias' Biography.

Socrates' response is of nearly the same pattern as before. Anonymous, he says, would berate him for giving this reply (292c8–d6):

"What?" he'll say, "can't you remember that I was asking what the beautiful itself is, that which, when it comes-to-be added to anything, it belongs to that {thing} to be beautiful, to a stone, to a stick, to a man, to a god, to every action and to every study?
{d3/4} "For, man, I am asking what beauty itself is, and I am no more able to make you hear than if you were a stone sitting beside me, and that a millstone, having neither ears nor brain."

It is worth noticing that Anonymous makes his question "what the beautiful itself is" (ὅτι τὸ καλὸν αὐτὸ ἠρώτων) at 292c9 and "what beauty itself is" (κάλλος ἐρωτῶ ὅτι ἐστίν) at d3–4: although the generic abstract "the beautiful" (or "the beautiful itself") is the expression primarily used, this use of the abstract noun "beauty" to replace it shows that no differentiation between the two is intended.[29]

As for the main content of Anonymous's speech, there are two familiar elements. First, there is the expectation that the correct *definiens* will somehow explain why beautiful things are beautiful: when you add it to something the thing comes out beautiful. Second, there is the requirement that, if the beautiful is *abc*, wherever *abc* is, there is beauty: wherever someone

---

[27] It is sometimes supposed that Hippias has finally, in 291d1–3, recognized the force of Socrates' question; see, e.g., Tarrant (1928) 56 *ad* 291d. She cites *Symposium* 211a, and says: "This is a more promising opening. Hippias for the first time recognizes that τὸ καλόν must be something essential and universal; but he immediately applies his own words in a partial and personal sense." But his application of those words actually shows that that is not what he meant by them. The "definition" he offers is something that, he thinks, satisfies the description in d1–3 precisely: it is a single type of event or action which, he supposes, always has qualified and always will qualify as "beautiful." It still gets nowhere near what it is about events, actions, people, or whatever, by virtue of which they qualify as "beautiful."

[28] It is a little hard to see *what* is beautiful here: are we to say that the person who lives Hippias' Biography is a beautiful person, or that it is beautiful to live Hippias' Biography, or what? I've gone for the latter, given the course of the refutation.

[29] The occurrence of the abstract noun "beauty," κάλλος, at 292d3 is one of only two in the entire dialogue (the other is in what may or may not be a quotation from Heraclitus at 289b5).

lives Hippias' Biography, it is beautiful. This is no longer Necessity, but Sufficiency.

There is nothing explicit so far about self-predication, but that comes in immediately, for Socrates continues (292d6–e8):

SOC: Then, Hippias, would you not be vexed if in fright I should in response to that say this:
{d7/e1} "But Hippias said this was the beautiful; and yet I asked him in just the way you {asked} me for what is beautiful to all and always."
{e2/3} What do you say? Wouldn't you be vexed if I said this?
HIPP: Well now, Socrates, I know quite well that what I spoke of is and will seem beautiful to all.
{e6} SOC: "And will be, as well?" he'll say; "for the beautiful, I suppose, is always beautiful."
HIPP: Certainly.
{e7} SOC: "So {it} was {beautiful}, as well?" he'll say.
HIPP: {It} was, as well.

So Anonymous and Socrates are supposing that asking for "what is beautiful for all and always" is bound up with, or, in this context, is precisely the same as, asking for what will explain why anything that enjoys the proper relationship to it is beautiful. That is our package containing Substitutivity, the Paradigm Requirement interpreted in terms of Self-Predication, and the Explanatory Requirement reinforced by the Transmission Theory.

And the refutation Anonymous was embarking on in the passage just quoted makes use of the whole package. He instantiates Hippias' Biography for cases in which it would not be beautiful, the cases, namely, of those heroes who have gods for one or another parent, so that it would be "terrible, impious, and ugly" (293b7) for them to bury their parents. This bears out the emphasis on Sufficiency just noticed: these are cases in which, if the *definiens* were satisfied, the *definiendum* would not be.

In the case of the preceding two definitions, it looked at first as if Necessity was the primary target; here it looks like Sufficiency. But, just as in those cases, Socrates veers off before quite getting there. He has Anonymous say to him (293b5–8):

"So according to your account, it seems, among the heroes, it {*sc.* living Hippias' Biography} is terrible and impious and ugly for Tantalus, for Dardanus, and for Zethus {sons of Zeus}, but beautiful for Pelops {son of the mortal Tantalus} and the others born in that way."

Hippias goes along with Anonymous (b9), who continues (293b10–c5):

"Then," he'll say, "being buried by your children once you've buried your parents seems to you to be sometimes and {c} for some people ugly, which you just now denied;[30] and it is even more impossible, it seems, for this to come-to-be and be beautiful for all, so that this, just as those preceding, the girl and the pot, has undergone the same {thing}, and even more ridiculously, it is beautiful for some but not beautiful for others.

And not yet, even to this day, Socrates, can you give in reply what's asked about the beautiful: what it is."

This, by itself, might be taken as a weird way of putting a charge of insufficiency. But taken with the preceding two failures, which Anonymous plainly wants us to do, it shows once more that the candidate for the beautiful fails because it is not through and through beautiful.

But, as with the preceding refutations, we must take note of a way in which this one is different. In the first case, the nominee failed to be indelibly beautiful because it (she) was beautiful by comparison to some things and ugly by comparison with others; in the second case, the nominee failed because it was beautiful in some contexts of use and ugly in others; in this case, it fails because it is beautiful for some people and ugly for others. We have, then, three different dimensions in which something can be relatively beautiful and relatively ugly. These different "dimensions of relativity" will figure in setting up the Theory of Forms.

7.4.5. Hippias Major *293c–294e*

The Transmission Theory of Causality underlies the first three refutations. But the next *definientia* are of a different character from the preceding, and the Transmission Theory of Causality comes into play in a different way. It is, in fact, rejected. This occurs in connection with (D_6b).

In discussing (D_2b), "the beautiful is gold," Hippias had commented that stone, too, was beautiful where it is appropriate (290c7); he had (290d5–6) even formulated the generalization that "whatever is appropriate to each thing makes it beautiful." Nothing came of that generalization back then. But in 293cd Anonymous suddenly turns helpful, and Socrates goes on to put a suggestion in his mouth (293d8–e5):

". . . consider {e} whether this sort of thing seems to you to be beautiful, which we just now had hold of in the reply where we said that gold is beautiful for those things for which it is appropriate, but not for those things for which it is not, and

---

[30] The reference is to 291d2–3, d9–e1, where Hippias' Biography was given as a case of something that would never show itself as ugly to anyone.

all other things {are beautiful} to which this is added; consider whether this itself, the appropriate, the nature of the appropriate itself, is in fact the beautiful."

And Socrates promptly turns the suggestion over to Hippias: "does the appropriate seem to you to be a beautiful {thing}?" (e7: σοὶ δ' οὖν δοκεῖ τὸ πρέπον καλόν εἶναι;). The formulation is precisely parallel to those Hippias had employed in giving his three answers:[31] it does not read "the appropriate is the beautiful," but simply "the appropriate is beautiful."[32]

Nonetheless, the definition once regimented is pretty clearly going to be, in parallel with the preceding ones:

(D₄b) The beautiful =$_{df}$ the appropriate.

But in at least one respect this definition is supposed to be different from the preceding ones:[33] Anonymous instructs Socrates to "stop giving replies of that sort, in that way" (τὰ μὲν τοιαῦτα . . . καὶ οὕτω, 293d7–8) and characterizes the previous attempts as "stupid and easily refuted" (εὐήθη καὶ εὐεξέλεγκτα, d8). This is all that is said by way of characterizing how (D₄b) is different from (D₁b)–(D₃b). One difference is plain enough, whether Socrates means to be pointing to it or not. The previous attempts were examples of beautiful things; "the appropriate" is not. It is not that "the appropriate" is at a general level while "a beautiful girl" is not: as we saw, the answer "a beautiful girl" was not intended to pick out one beautiful girl, but referred indifferently to any beautiful girl; similarly, gold was to be gold wherever it occurred, and Hippias' Biography was supposed to be something that counted as beautiful for anyone whose biography it was. The difference is not one of ontological type.[34] Still, the previous attempts were examples. Suppose Helen is a beautiful girl; if we now ask: what is it about Helen that makes her count as beautiful?, it will not do to say: it is the fact that she is a beautiful girl, and all beautiful girls are beautiful. Similarly, gold may make some things beautiful, but it is only one example of something that does that: it may have played no role in making Helen beautiful. And Hippias' Biography is in the same boat.

[31] Except that the neuter predicate "beautiful" here has a neuter subject: cf. n. 22.

[32] See Woodruff (1982) 64–65 n. 116. But I am not convinced by Woodruff (or by Nehamas [1979] 95–96 = [1999] 179) that the formula "The F is abc," used to define the F, does not make the F something that is abc.

[33] That this definition is at least a step in the right direction is borne out by Aristotle's apparently accepting the identification of τὸ καλόν and τὸ πρέπον in Topics E 5. 135ᵃ13; he does not accept τὸ πρέπον as a definition for τὸ καλόν for the peculiar reason that definitions (definientia, pace Moravcsik [1967] 130; cf. Poetics 20. 1457ᵃ23–30, Janko [1987] 128 ad 57ᵃ23, 57ᵃ26) must contain more than just a name (Topics A 5. 102ᵃ2–6), but the question whether the beautiful is the appropriate is "definitory" (ὁρικόν ᵃ5).

[34] So also Woodruff (1982) 169.

One might hope that the point that the initial *definientia* give examples and the point that they are subject to impurity are correlative points. But the *Euthyphro* seems to belie that: there the transition from (D_1p) to (D_2p) was the transition from examples to the right level of generality, but (D_2p) was rejected on grounds of impurity.

So it remains unclear what the difference is that Anonymous/Socrates sees; he is simply not forthcoming, and any attempt to characterize the difference is in some measure speculative.

Socrates' objection (he drops Anonymous for a while) to (D_4b) is not very compelling, and does not add much to our understanding of what he is looking for in a definition. He asks Hippias whether the appropriate, by its presence, makes something *show itself* as beautiful,[35] or actually *be* beautiful. Hippias responds as one would have expected him to, given that his earlier introduction of the generalization was in the context of defending his attempt to define the beautiful as gold: for gold, he had said, was something that when added to something made it show itself as beautiful (289d8, e5–6).[36] So here: the appropriate, he says, makes things show themselves as beautiful. Then, Socrates responds, the appropriate is not what we are after; we are rather looking for what it is that makes things *be* beautiful (294a6–b1).

In the course of this, Socrates says that the appropriate, on Hippias' reading, "would be a sort of deception about the beautiful" (a7): he is taking it for granted that something can show itself as beautiful without really being beautiful.[37] And a few lines later (295b6–8), he takes Hippias to have said that the appropriate "makes things show themselves as more beautiful than they are . . . and does not allow them to show themselves as they are." If that is the way Socrates is going, he is showing that something can satisfy the *definiens* without satisfying the *definiendum*: that the definition fails Sufficiency.

But the rest of what he says (294a–b6, b8–c2) permits a different reading: he says that what he is looking for is that by which all beautiful things are beautiful, whether or not they show themselves as beautiful. This goes the

---

[35] 294a2 ποιεῖ ἕκαστα φαίνεται καλὰ τούτων οἷς ἂν παρῇ: this is ambiguous between "makes each of those things to which it is severally present appear to be beautiful" and "makes each . . . be obviously beautiful." See Woodruff (1982) 54 n. 80, and, in a quite different context, Dancy (1987) 99 n. 16 to p. 64.

[36] But in 290d, after Hippias has introduced the notion of the appropriate, Socrates talks in terms of the appropriate's making things show themselves as beautiful (d2), and Hippias just in terms of its making them beautiful (d6).

[37] So here the ambiguity in the phrase translated "show itself as beautiful" would apparently be settled in favor of the reading "appear to be beautiful" (so also Woodruff [1982] 65 n. 118).

other way: there are, at least conceivably, things that satisfy the *definiendum* without satisfying the *definiens*, so the definition fails Necessity.

Nothing is done to settle which, if not both, of these two objections is the crux; instead, Hippias punts (294c3–4), telling us that "the appropriate, when it is present, makes things both be and show themselves as beautiful." It is not clear why he says this, other than to avoid refutation.[38] Socrates' response is simply to get Hippias to concede that a great many things are beautiful without showing themselves to be so: indeed, this is precisely what people argue over (294cd). So "appropriate" can't do both jobs at once; nothing can (294de).

Socrates again asks Hippias to choose between "makes things beautiful" and "makes things show themselves as beautiful"; Hippias again chooses the latter; and the whole attempt fizzles out (294e).

The objection to the definition amounts, then, to this. The appropriate, when added to something, makes it seem beautiful. But since there are things that seem beautiful without really being beautiful, and things that are beautiful without seeming beautiful, the appropriate isn't what makes things be beautiful. So it is not the beautiful.

This certainly leans heavily on the Explanatory Requirement. So does the example Socrates offers in the middle of his speech at 294ab of the sort of thing that would satisfy him when he is looking for that by which all beautiful things are beautiful (294b2–4):

just as that by which {ᾧ} all large {things} are large is that which exceeds; for by this all are large, and if they do not show themselves as {large}, but exceed, it's a necessity for them to be large.

But nothing in the passage does much to expand our understanding of that requirement, since the objection turns on Necessity and Sufficiency and this sample definition merely reiterates Sufficiency.

The question whether this example of a definition satisfies Socrates' own requirements stares us in the face here, but there doesn't seem to be much that helps us answer it. It doesn't look as if "that which exceeds" (τὸ ὑπερέχον), because of which something is large, need itself be particularly large, and if that is right, Self-Predication isn't satisfied. And perhaps, by the time Plato gets to the *Phaedo*, this has come to his attention (cf. 96c–e, 100e–101b, 102bc).[39] But this is more speculation.

---

[38] Woodruff (1982) 65 n. 118 suggests that Hippias' claim derives from his reading the ambiguous phrase φαίνεσθαι καλά as "be obviously beautiful" rather than as "appear to be beautiful." That might be.

[39] See Woodruff (1982) 65–66 n. 119.

Still, we have at last got away from examples: the candidate definitions from here on are on at least roughly the right level of generality.

7.4.6. Hippias Major *295b–296d*

In 295c2–3, Socrates has his interlocutor suggest:

(D$_5$b) x is beautiful =$_{df}$ x is useful (χρήσιμον).

He asks (295e7–9):

Then what is capable {δυνατόν} of performing each {thing}, for that which it is capable of, is also useful for that, and what is incapable is useless?

and gets an affirmative answer.[40] This amounts to an equivalence:

(1) x is useful for doing y ↔ x is capable of doing y;

perhaps the left-hand side should read "x can be used for doing y." He says, on the basis of this and (D$_5$b) (295e9–10): "Therefore capacity is beautiful, and incapacity ugly." The argument turns on this alleged consequence; it turns out that what Socrates actually wants is:

(2) Every capacity for doing anything is beautiful.

Socrates, after an aside at 295e10–a7, asks whether anyone could do what he didn't know how to do and wasn't capable of doing, and Hippias agrees one couldn't (296b3–5). The words "he didn't know how to do and" are irrelevant here,[41] and Hippias drops them from his reply, as does Socrates in restating the claim in b7–8 and c2–3; all he really wants is:

(3) x does y → x is capable of doing y.

In b5–8, he takes an instance of this:

∴ (4) x does something bad → x is capable of doing something bad

(he specifically says he wants this to cover cases where one does something bad "involuntarily"; cf. ἄκοντες b7), and says (b8–c1): "But by {a} capacity those who are capable are capable; not, I dare say, by an incapacity," to which Hippias agrees. All this amounts to is:

(5) x is capable of doing y → x has a capacity for doing y.

---

[40] This follows from nothing that precedes (but see c5–6), and it is difficult: see Woodruff (1982) 69–70 n. 134.

[41] They may have connected with the "wisdom" motif Socrates had just introduced.

Socrates reiterates (3), and adds:

(6) People do bad things

(according to him, most of the time: c3–5).

Socrates now cashes in all his chips at once (296c5–d3): "Well then, do we say that this capacity and these useful {things}, which are useful for doing something bad, are beautiful, or far from it?" The steps this compresses are obvious:

∴ (7) People are capable of doing bad things   (6),(3)
∴ (8) People have a capacity for doing bad things   (7),(5)
   (C1) The capacity for doing bad things is not beautiful
∴ (C2) Some capacity is not beautiful   (C1) × EG

Conclusion (C2) contradicts (2).

The argument, so described, is like a stick figure; we can fill it in some. Socrates has tried construing "beauty," or perhaps "nobility," as a disposition or state of the man who is called "noble." He will continue to construe it that way in subsequent arguments. This argument is merely to the effect that it cannot be just any old state or disposition: it must at least be a disposition toward doing *good* things.

There are two points (at least) of extreme fuzziness in the argument as it is laid out in the steps from (D_5b) to (C2) above: first, it is unclear how (2) is supposed to follow from (D_5b) and (1), and second, it is not clear what justifies (C1). These may be connected unclarities.

Socrates is arguing that the disposition we identify with nobility must at least be a disposition to do good things. We have seen assumptions like this at work elsewhere. A general principle,

(T) $R(G,f) \rightarrow [Gf \leftrightarrow (x)(Fx \rightarrow Gx)]$,

was introduced (§ 4.4.3) as possibly standing in back of these assumptions. If we imagine that the relevant restriction in the antecedent of this conditional has been identified and satisfied, we are left with the biconditional

(T bic) $Gf \leftrightarrow (x)(Fx \rightarrow Gx)$.

Suppose we appeal to (T bic), taking f to be the disposition to do things that are F.

Reading our principle from left to right, we have as an instance of it one we have already encountered nearly explicitly in the *Laches* and *Charmides*: if a disposition is admirable ("beautiful"), the actions that display it will also be admirable. The argument above, at step (8), has uncovered a disposition (capacity) for doing bad things; if this disposition were admirable, everything displaying it – every bad action – would be admirable. This is false, so the capacity for doing bad things is not beautiful: that gives us (C1).

Consider now the steps that lead to (2). It is clear from (1) that Socrates is understanding (D_5b) as having the force:

(D_5b') x is beautiful $=_{df}$ x is useful for doing something or other.

This, with (1), will give him

(1a) x is beautiful $\leftrightarrow$ x is capable of doing something (or other)

and so

(1b) x is capable of doing something $\rightarrow$ x is beautiful.

And presumably, if the definition were correct, and the claim recorded in (1) also has something like definitional status, we could read "x is beautiful" in (1b) as "x is *eo ipso* beautiful."

But, reading (T bic) from right to left, we have

(Trl) $(x)(Fx \rightarrow Gx) \rightarrow G(f),$

so, for anything that is capable of doing anything at all, we can derive the claim that the capacity possessed by that thing is beautiful; that is, we can derive (2) (assuming that every capacity is reflected in something that has it).

The argument, so fleshed out, is rather complex. To put it all together in one place:

(T bic) $G(f) \leftrightarrow (x)(Fx \rightarrow Gx)$
(D_5b) x is beautiful $=_{df}$ x is useful, i.e.,   S
(D_5b') x is beautiful $=_{df}$ x is useful for doing
     something.
(1) x is useful for doing y $\leftrightarrow$ x is capable of doing y.   P
(1a) x is beautiful $\leftrightarrow$ x is capable of doing something. $(D_5b),(1)$
(1b) x is capable of doing something $\rightarrow$ x is beautiful. (1a)
∴ (2) Every capacity for doing anything is beautiful.   (1a),(T bic)
(3) x does y $\rightarrow$ x is capable of doing y.   P
∴ (4) x does something bad $\rightarrow$ x is capable of doing   (3)
     something bad.

(5) x is capable of doing y → x has a capacity for   P
    doing y.
(6) People do bad things.   P
∴ (7) People are capable of doing bad things.   (6),(3)
∴ (8) People have a capacity for doing bad things.   (7),(5)
(9) The capacity for doing bad things is beautiful →   (T)
    everything bad is beautiful.
(10) ¬ (Everything bad is beautiful).   P
∴ (C1) ¬ (The capacity for doing bad things is   (10),(9)
    beautiful).
∴ (C2) Some capacity is not beautiful.   (C1)

But (C2) contradicts (2).

We have encountered arguments of this general pattern before, and the pattern is easier to cope with than the gory details: the definition of "beautiful" as "capable" fails to capture the positive evaluation that goes with "beautiful."

7.4.7. Hippias Major 296d–297d

Hippias suggests the obvious revision of the preceding definition to avoid the objection: perhaps the capable and useful without qualification can't be identified with the beautiful, but (296d4–5) the capable of and useful for good things will do the job. Accordingly, Socrates formulates what Hippias and he had really been trying to say as the thesis (d8–e1): "that the useful and the capable of making-or-doing something good is the beautiful." "Making-or-doing" translates the single word ποιῆσαι, whose range of sense is broad enough to cover at least that much; we'll shortly see reason for supposing that here "making" is what is primarily at stake.

Plainly, the effect of this move is to restore the positive evaluative component carried by the term "beautiful."

We start, then, from

($D_{6a}b$) The beautiful $=_{df}$ what is capable of making-or-doing some
    good.

But Socrates immediately replaces this as the dialogue continues (296e1–6):

SOC: But this, of course, is {the} beneficial {ὠφέλιμον}. Or isn't it?
HIPP: Certainly.

{e2} SOC: Then in this way also the beautiful bodies, the beautiful customs, wisdom, and all the others we were just speaking of are beautiful: because {they are} beneficial.

HIPP: It's clear.

{e5} SOC: Therefore the beneficial seems to us to be the beautiful, Hippias.

HIPP: In every way, Socrates.

When Socrates says, in 296e1–2, "but this, of course, is the beneficial," he means to be referring to the *definiens* of (D_{6a}b); he makes this explicit just below, in 296e7. So we may ascribe to Socrates a definition for "beneficial":

(Dbn) The beneficial $=_{df}$ that which makes-or-does good.

This enables the shift from (D_{6a}b) to

(D_{6b}b) The beautiful $=_{df}$ the beneficial,

and the subsequent argument takes this as its target. That argument is rather difficult.

It begins with this (296e7–297a1):

SOC: And yet the beneficial is that which makes-or-does good.

HIPP: So it is.

{e8} SOC: And that which makes-or-does is none other than the cause {τὸ αἴτιον}, isn't it?

HIPP: That's so.

{297} SOC: Therefore the beautiful is cause of the good.

HIPP: So it is.

Here Socrates states (Dbn) in e7, and then identifies that which makes or does something with the cause of that something (296e8–9). That looks like a definition of "cause":

(Dc) The cause of $x =_{df}$ that which makes-or-does x.

He then concludes from (Dbn), (D_{6b}b), and (Dc) (e9–297a1):

∴ (L1) The beautiful is the cause of the good.

His use of the definite article in these lines is erratic: there was none for "good" in the formulation of (Dbn) in 296e7, but there is one for "good" in the formulation of (L1) in e9. But, if the argument for (L1) is to be valid, "good" in (Dbn) must mean the same as "the good" in (L1).

The next step is this (297a2–b2):

SOC: And yet the cause, Hippias, and that of which the cause is cause, are different {ἄλλο}; for I dare say the cause can't be cause of {a} cause. Look at it this way; didn't the cause show itself as doing-or-making?

HIPP: Certainly.

{a5} SOC: Then it's none other than that which comes-to-be {τὸ γιγνόμενον} that is made-or-done by that which makes or does, but not that which makes-or-does?

HIPP: This is so.

{a7} SOC: Then that which comes-to-be is one {thing}, that which makes-or-does another?

HIPP: Yes.

{a8} SOC: Therefore the cause is not cause of {a} cause, but of what comes-to-be by {the cause} itself.

HIPP: Certainly.

In 297a2–3, Socrates states (as the sequel shows) a conclusion he wants to draw:

(L3a) The cause is different from that of which it is a cause,

and, with it, in a3–4, another conclusion that seems bound up with the first:

(L3b) The cause is not cause of {a} cause.

Just from a2–4, it looks as if (L3b) is being offered as support for (L3a), but in a7–b1 he seems to draw conclusion (L3a) first and (L3b) second. So perhaps it is best to understand (L3a) and (L3b) as a package.

Socrates knows he has some explaining to do; in 297a4, he offers us, as a start on arguing for his package,

(L2) The cause of x makes or does x,

which plainly enough follows from (Dc). Socrates seems to think that the shift to talk of "making-or-doing" (ποιοῦν) clarifies matters, and he introduces more terminology that is supposed to help: he speaks of what is caused as being made or done *by* (ὑπό, first in a5 and *passim* thereafter) that which makes or does, and he refers to what is caused as "that which comes-to-be" (τὸ γιγνόμενον, a6 and *passim* thereafter). We might again see Socrates as offering definitions for these terms such as the composite

(Dcb) That which comes-to-be by y =$_{df}$ that of which x is cause.

To some extent, this is an excess of zeal. For what Socrates really wants is (297a5–6)

(P1) When y makes or does x, y is the maker or doer, x is what is made or done and comes-to-be by x, and x is different from y.

The teeth of this are in the last clause: it is from it that (L3a) follows (a7–8), and so, allegedly, does (L3b) (a8–b1).

Lemma (L3a) is easy enough. Lemma (L3b) is another matter. A lot depends on how we understand it.[42] We cannot take it to mean

(*L3b) No cause is ever a cause of another cause,

for this rules out the possibility that something that is caused might be the cause of something else; if we use the term "effect" for whatever is caused, then (*L3b) is saying that no effect is ever a cause. Not only does this seem plainly false, but, if we look ahead to the example Socrates gives us in 297b9–c1, its falsehood is made plain by that example. There Socrates will tell us that the father is not a son, nor is the son a father. Read straight, this is so outrageous even Hippias might have seen through it: every father we know of (ignoring cloning) is also a son.

Two other options present themselves. We might take (L3b) as saying:

(L3b′) In any particular causal transaction, the cause is not the cause of the cause in that transaction.[43]

This simply says: in a cause-effect sequence, the cause is not the effect. Or, again, we might take (L3b) as saying:

(L3b″) The cause of something is not *eo ipso* the cause of a cause.

The latter is to be understood as saying: the characterization of something as a cause does not entail that its effect is also a cause.

Let us put these options in terms of the example we shall encounter in 297b9–c1. If we construe (L3b) along the lines of (L3b′), it says: in any particular case in which a father has a son, the father is not the son. In the manner of (L3b″), it says: a father has a son, but that by itself does not entail that the son is himself a father.

---

[42] What I say here differs, mostly in vocabulary, from Woodruff (1982) 75 n. 142. Other differences emerge below.

[43] Woodruff (1982) 75 n. 142 rules this out as an interpretation of 297a3–4 ("for I dare say the cause can't be cause of {a} cause"): "Most translators supply a definite article with the predicate: 'I don't suppose the cause would be a cause of *the* cause' (understand: 'a cause of itself'). But if Plato had meant that he would have said it. It would not, in any case, have had any role in the argument." The first of these two reasons will not do: we have already seen that Plato is not consistent in this passage when it comes to the definite article. The second is only right if we exclude the possibility that the argument is fallacious.

Lemma (L3b′) may be taken as following from (P1). In fact, it does not, unless we restrict the notion of a causal transaction so that there are only two transactors: one maker and one thing that comes-to-be by its agency. But perhaps we can allow that: then it becomes relevant to point out that the maker and what comes-to-be by it are different.

Lemma (L3b″) is more difficult. Perhaps it can be made independently plausible: a father, by having a son, is not thereby siring a father; his son may or may not beget, but neither of these outcomes is determined, logically, by the father's being a father. But nothing in the argument Socrates gives lends any support to this. In particular, it is not support for it to point out that the father and the son, or the maker and what comes-to-be by its agency in general, must be *different*: in other words, (P1), as it stands, is of no use. Perhaps, then, (P1) should be understood as saying:

(P1a) When y makes x, y is the maker, x is what is made and
comes-to-be by y, and the role x plays is different from the role y plays.

Then it might be taken as following from this that something that plays the role of what comes-to-be is not *eo ipso* playing the role of a cause: that would give us (L3b″).

We are now to apply the results about causes and effects to the target case, the beautiful and the good (297b2–8):

SOC: If, therefore, the beautiful is cause of the good, the good would come-to-be by the beautiful;
{b3/4} and for this reason we are concerned for intelligence and all the other beautiful {things}, because their product, their offspring, the good, is worthy of concern,
{b6/7} and from what we are finding, it's plausible that the beautiful is in the form of a father of the good.
HIPP: Certainly; you're speaking beautifully, Socrates.

The beautiful is the cause of the good, so the good is what is made or done and comes-to-be by the beautiful. He states only the last clause, in 297b2–3:

(L4) The good comes-to-be by the beautiful.

This follows from (P1) with (L1) and (Dc); there is as yet no need for (L3a) or either version of (L3b).

The father-son example entered with the reference to the good as "the offspring" (τὸ ἔκγονον) of the beautiful in 297b5, and is expanded on in b6–7. Socrates now makes something more of it (297b9–c3):

SOC: Then do I say this also beautifully, that neither is the father {a} son, nor is the son {a} father?

HIPP: Quite beautifully.

{c1} SOC: And the cause is not {something that} comes-to-be, nor is what comes-to-be again cause?

HIPP: You speak truly.

In the translation of b9–c1 I have supplied the indefinite article, "a," and that is the weakest possible translation. But it lends itself to the misunderstanding registered in (*L3b) above. Besides, as we have already seen, Socrates is not consistent in his use of the definite article here; it could be supplied instead of the indefinite article. Either way, we still have our two options for articulating this example: along the lines of either (L3b′) or (L3b″), as saying either that where a father has a son, the two are not the same, or that a father's having a son is not thereby siring a father.

In 297c1–3 Socrates states and Hippias accepts a corollary to (L3b) that derives from rewriting (L3b) using (Dcb):

(CL3b) The cause is not what comes-to-be, and what comes-to-be is not a cause.

And comments parallel to those on (L3b) itself carry over to this: to be plausible, it must mean either that, in a particular causal sequence, the cause is not the same as the effect, or that when x causes an effect y, it does not thereby cause y itself to be a cause.

But, ultimately, the problem lies in the application Socrates wants to make of either (L3b) or (CL3b). For the dialogue continues as follows (297c3–6):

SOC: By Zeus, my good man, therefore the beautiful is not good, and the good is not beautiful; or does it seem to you that they can be, on the basis of the things already said?

HIPP: No, by Zeus, it doesn't appear to me {that they can be}.

We might think that we must here once again have recourse to Socrates' erratic deployment of the definite article, for surely the most that follows from (L3b), however understood, is

(C1) The beautiful ≠ the good.

Unfortunately, that isn't enough for what Socrates wants.

The penultimate stretch of the argument reads like this (297c7–d2):

SOC: Then does it satisfy us, and would we want to say that the beautiful is not good nor the good beautiful?

HIPP: No, by Zeus, it certainly doesn't satisfy me.

{c10} SOC: Yes, by Zeus, Hippias; it satisfies me {the} least of all the accounts we've stated.

HIPP: It looks that way.

This does not look as if it depends on (C1), but on

(C2) The beautiful is not good, and the good is not beautiful.

Whichever the conclusion is supposed to be, it is supposed to be absurd. For the whole thing ends here (297d3–9):

SOC: Therefore it's plausible to us, not as it appeared just now to be {the} most beautiful of accounts that the beneficial, that is, the useful and capable of doing or making something good, is beautiful, that it isn't like that, but, if it's possible, it's more ridiculous than those first {accounts}, in which we were thinking that the beautiful was the girl and each one of the ones stated earlier.

HIPP: It seems.

The trouble, of course, is that (C1) does not look absurd at all, and (C2), which might conceivably be seen as absurd, does not really follow from the argument. For, read flat-footedly, (L4) is telling us that

(L4a) The good is something that comes-to-be (by the beautiful), and the beautiful is a cause (of the good).

If we apply (CL3b) to this, we get, not (C2), but

(C4a) The beautiful is not the good, and the good is not the beautiful.

Offhand, it is hard to see why Socrates or Hippias would have found (C4a) absurd. If the beautiful is defined as the beneficial, and that makes it the cause of the good, of course the beautiful is different from the good. This is not what they find absurd: they find (C2) absurd. But how can (C2) be made to follow from (CL3b) and (L4a)?

Let us recall our two alternative readings of (L3b), and apply them to (CL3b). We get:

(C3a) In any particular causal transaction, the cause is not what comes-to-be, and what comes-to-be is not a cause.

This comes out true enough (the restriction to one cause and one "effect" is implicit in the phrase "what comes-to-be"), but not strong enough: the most this will give us is (C4a), which is not absurd.

Suppose we try:

(C3b) The cause is not *eo ipso* what comes-to-be, and what comes-to-be is not *eo ipso* a cause.

This can be made plausible in the same way as (L3b''). We now apply it to (L4a):

> (C4b) The beautiful is not *eo ipso* the good, and the good is not *eo ipso* the beautiful.

But this looks no more absurd than (C4a).

The definite articles in the predicates of (C4a) and (C4b) are standing in the way. They make it look as if we are dealing with two units, the beautiful and the good, and then, of course, there is no absurdity in their being distinct units. What we must do is reinterpret the entire argument, from the definitions on. Definitions (D_6ab) and (D_6bb) were not identities in the style of "The morning star = the evening star;" (D_6bb) was telling us that anything beautiful is *eo ipso* beneficial, and conversely. Then (L1) is saying that anything beautiful is the cause of some good (that is what makes it count as beautiful) and anything good is caused by something beautiful. Lemma (L4), then, is saying:

> (L4b) Anything good is something that comes-to-be (by the agency of something beautiful), and anything beautiful is a cause (of something good).

Suppose we apply (CL3b) to this. In the form (C3a), all we get is that whenever something beautiful brings about something good, the two are not the same, and there is no absurdity in that. Applying (C3b) gives us:

> (C4c) Something beautiful is not *eo ipso* good, and something good is not *eo ipso* beautiful.

If we are to see Socrates' argument as sound, we must find this absurd: we must suppose that either "*x* is good" follows directly from "*x* is beautiful," or the converse, or both.

I do not know whether we should suppose any such thing.[44] It is true that the terms καλόν, "beautiful," and ἀγαθόν, "good," are intimately related in Plato's vocabulary. But why shouldn't we say that the definition of the beautiful that makes it the cause of the good is an expression of that intimacy? We have already (in § 7.2) considered one case, at *Charmides* 160d–161b, in which Socrates wanted to get from "*x* is beautiful" to "*x* is good." He wanted to get from "temperance is admirable" ("beautiful") to "temperance is good," and to do it he invoked the premise:

---

[44] Woodruff (1982) 74 thinks we should.

(P1) If a character trait is admirable, it makes those who have it so far
    forth good,

and routed the argument through good men. What we must notice here is
that (P1) would be supported by the definition ($D_{6a}b$).

Perhaps, then, the argument against that definition should be rejected
as unsound. There is another reason for thinking that that might be so.

The argument easily lends itself to generalization: (L4b) is an instance of

(L4g) Anything F is something that comes-to-be by the agency of
    something G, and anything G is a cause of something F, and
(C3b), as we used it in deriving (C4b), really amounts to
(C3c) x's being G causes y to come-to-be F x is not eo $ipso$ F.

But we have been dealing with a theory of causality according to which

(TT2) Whatever makes things count as F is itself F.

There is a potential conflict here: if we equate "cause of" and "what makes
something count as," (TT2) is telling us that

(TT2a) Anything F is something that comes-to-be by the agency of
    something F,

and in the way that is intended, it is precisely the fact that the "cause" is F
that makes the "effect" F. But (C3c) has as an instance

(C5) x's being F causes y to be $F \rightarrow x$ is not eo $ipso$ F.

There are two possible ways out of this trap. One is to distinguish sorts
of causality, and the other is to lean even more heavily on the "eo $ipso$" rider.
Neither is very satisfactory. I think, on balance, that the argument against
($D_{6a}b$) is an experiment that failed. Either it or the Transmission Theory
has to go. But, of the two, it is going to be the Transmission Theory that
survives in the Theory of Forms. And the contradiction (C5) causes is not
just external, that is, a contradiction between (C5) and the Theory of Forms
to come; it is internal to the *Hippias Major*. From the very first, we have
been supposing that the beautiful was to be paradigmatically beautiful, and
yet the cause of other things' being beautiful.

CHAPTER 8

Explaining: presence, participation; the Lysis

To say that *x* is *F* because of the *F* or *F*ness is elliptical or incomplete: the relationship between *x* and the *F* by virtue of which *x* is *F* remains unspecified. The Socratic dialogues we are examining are quite unselfconscious about that relationship, by contrast with *Phaedo* 100cd, where we shall find Socrates using a variety of terms for the relationship between a Form and the things here below that partake of it and expressing a studious indifference about which is the right one. Back where we are, he also uses a variety of terms for the relationship between the *F* and the things that are *F*. He does not say much about this variety of terms (but see §§ 8.2.3 and 8.2.4.1). He frequently speaks of the relationship as one of *presence*: temperance *is-present-to* someone or something (παρεῖναί τινι); common variants have the virtue or character *being-added-to* (προσγίγνεσθαι) or *being in* (εἶναι ἐν or ἐνεῖναι) that which has it, or of someone or something as *partaking of* or *getting a share of* (μετέχειν) that virtue or character.[1]

Does this mean that Socrates has in these dialogues a theory of forms according to which they are *immanent* in things?[2] Well, he talks of forms, and he talks as if they were present in things. But does he have a *theory*, or is he just talking that way? *Phaedo* 100cd suggests that he might just be talking that way, without commitment as to the force of the idiom, for even there, where he definitely *does* have the Theory of Forms, he is not prepared to settle what the relationship is. In fact, he is still prepared to call it "presence" (παρουσία), where that is particularly hard to square with his Theory.

---

[1] There is a useful but incomplete list of references for such idioms in Ross (1951) 228–30. It, and the use to which Ross puts it (namely as the basis for a claim that the forms of the early dialogues are "immanent" rather than "transcendent"), are also much maligned (e.g., by Dancy [1991] 126 n. 36, with further references). There is another useful but incomplete list of references for such idioms in Fujisawa (1974) 42 (but see Dancy [1991] 126 n. 36, 127 nn. 42, 45). My discussion here does not aim at completeness.

[2] Ross (1951) 21, 230 thought so; see also Grube (1935) 9; perhaps Ostenfeld (1982) 11–21; Rowe (1984) 55.

We must be clear from the outset that all the verb phrases I've listed, and others, are ordinary Greek: they have no particular attachment to any philosophical theory. And that means that their use, by itself, is no pointer to anything by way of such a theory. This chapter makes a case for the noncommittal reading of these terms[3] in the Socratic dialogues.[4]

Since one of the major players on the terminological battlefield when we get to the Theory of Forms is "partaking" (μετέχειν), with "participating" (μεταλαμβάνειν) alongside it but a little less common, let's begin by looking at how these words enter the Socratic dialogues. Then we can turn to presence and locutions associated with that.

That will carry us into a passage in the *Lysis* (216c–221d) in the middle of which presence becomes the center of attention. Many have seen the Theory of Forms operating in this passage, so I take it up here, although only 217c–e is relevant to the question of presence.

8.1. PARTICIPATION AND PARTAKING

Protagoras, toward the beginning of his great speech, tells a tale to the effect that Prometheus stole from the gods certain arts that were necessary for human survival and gave them to humans; he says (*Protagoras* 322a3–5):

Since man partook of a divine portion {θείας μετέσχε μοίρας}, because of his kinship with the divine he alone of animals recognized gods, and put his hand to erecting altars and images of gods.

A little later, he has Hermes asking Zeus how he is to distribute justice and shame among humans (322cd): is he to hand them out only to some humans, as with the other arts, or to all? Protagoras continues (322d1–5):

"To all," Zeus said, "and let all partake {of them} {καὶ πάντες μετεχόντων}; for cities would not come-to-be, if few partook of them as of the other arts; and lay down a law from me to kill the one who is not able to partake of shame and justice as a disease to the city."

Protagoras uses the verb "to partake of" in parallel with his triple use of it in this latter sentence also in 323a3, 6, c1, 324d8, 325a3, and 5. It is plain that in that use "to partake of justice" involves becoming in some degree just. It is not so plain that, when he spoke of man partaking of a divine portion in

---

[3] So far I am in agreement with Allen (1970) 145–46: although he wants to ascribe a Theory of Transcendent Forms to the Socrates of our dialogues, he does not make it turn on the use of παρεῖναι, etc.

[4] The present chapter covers some of the same ground as Dancy (1991) 9–14, and then some.

322a3, that involved man becoming in any degree divine: the most he will say there is that man has a kinship with the divine, and it is not even clear that that kinship is due to man's partaking of the divine portion.

That partaking of something characterized in a certain way may not result in the partaker's also being characterized in that way is clear from other passages: in the *Euthydemus* Socrates says of Dionysodorus (271b8): "he too {*sc.* along with his brother Euthydemus} partakes of speeches {μετέχει δὲ καὶ οὗτος τῶν λόγων}," where this means: he joins in argumentative discussions. Pretty clearly, that doesn't, just by itself, make him characterizable by any of the terms that can be used to characterize the discussions. And the same is true when Socrates later asks Clinias (279e6–280a1): "While performing military service, with which would you more readily partake of danger and risk, a wise general or an uneducated {one}?" There is no question of Clinias or the hypothetical general becoming dangerous.

So we can anticipate a distinction we are going to find Socrates thinking about in connection with being-present-to: sometimes *x*'s partaking of something characterizable as *F* will not, and sometimes it will, carry with it *x*'s itself being *F*: sometimes partaking of something *F* will transmit being *F*, and sometimes it won't. Transmitting partaking is what is going to be of interest when we want to explain how it is that something or other is *F*. That is what is at stake when Socrates speaks of men participating in the "parts" of virtue (justice, temperance, etc.) in *Protagoras* 329e2–4, and of pleasant things as ones that partake of pleasure in 351d7–e1.

Now we can ask the big question. Was Plato thinking about the question of what transmitting participation consists in when he wrote this? Did he have a theory of causality in mind? I haven't the faintest idea. Nothing in the dialogue requires it. So nobody in the dialogue is committed to any such theory. Obviously Protagoras is not, and he is the one who introduced the verb "partake" into the discussion. But neither is Socrates, who seems simply to be following suit. A fortiori, Plato is not committed to any theory about participation by what he wrote in the *Protagoras*.

8.2. PRESENCE

Any number of passages in Plato himself illustrate the ubiquity of the verb "to be-present," παρεῖναι. Various people are at various times said to "be present," just meaning that they are here.[5] In *Phaedo* 58c–59b, Phaedo relates who was there and who wasn't at Socrates' execution, and the verb "to be

---

[5] E.g., *Lysis* 211c5–6, 215b5–6, *Laches* 188b7, *Protagoras* 317e4, and *passim*.

present" is used five times in that connection (58c8, d1, 59b7, b11, c5); but right in the middle of this *Phaedo* says (59a5–7) "quite an absurd feeling was present to me," and it just means "I had quite an absurd feeling."

So we should expect that the use of "to be-present-to" doesn't carry much theoretical weight. But there is a theoretical question raised about it in the dialogues we are considering, although it does not get an answer in those dialogues. For we shall find that Plato's characters are sometimes aware that presence can be either transmitting or nontransmitting.

8.2.1. Charmides

Charmides gets headaches (*Charmides* 155b). In 158b5–c4 Socrates says to him:

> If temperance, as Critias here says, already is-present-to you, and you are sufficiently temperate {εἰ μέν σοι ἤδη πάρεστιν . . . σωφροσύνη καὶ εἰ σώφρων ἱκανῶς}, then there is no longer any need on your part for the charm-songs of Zalmoxis or of Abaris the Hyperborean, but we can give you the drug for your head right away; but if you seem still to be lacking in this, we must sing the incantation before giving the drug. So tell me yourself: do you agree with him and say that you already partake sufficiently of temperance {ἱκανῶς ἤδη σωφροσύνης μετέχειν} or are lacking {in it}?

The opening clause equates "temperance is present to you" with "you are temperate"; the closing sentence puts "you partake of temperance" in the same bag. So these locutions by themselves carry no metaphysical weight. But further, Socrates' reference to Zalmoxis alludes to a tall story Socrates had just told. He had, he said, learned from a Thracian doctor to the king Zalmoxis that the body should not be cured without the soul (156d–157a). He goes on to say (157a3–b1):

> And, my dear fellow, he said that the soul is cured by certain charm-songs, and these charm-songs are beautiful words; from such words temperance comes-to-be-in {ἐγγίγνεσθαι} the soul, which, when it has come-to-be-in {ἐγγενομένης} and is-present-to {παρούσης} {the soul} it is easier to supply health both to the head and to the rest of the body.

It is, I take it, quite clear that Socrates is not here ascribing a theory of immanent forms to this Thracian doctor. Temperance's coming-to-be-in the soul and being-present-to the soul is just a matter of the soul's getting it and having it, and that is all that is being said in 158b5–6, where Socrates ascribes to Critias the claim that temperance is "present to" Charmides. In fact, what Critias had said, which Socrates is here paraphrasing, was just that Charmides is temperate (157d1–8).

Things are a little more loaded when Socrates opens his examination of the question "what is temperance?" by saying to Charmides (158e7–159a3):

> it is clear that, if temperance is present to you {εἴ σοι πάρεστιν σωφροσύνη} {159} you are able to form some belief about it {τι περὶ αὐτῆς δοξάζειν}. For it is necessary that, being present in you, if it is present in you {ἐνοῦσαν αὐτήν, εἴπερ ἔνεστιν}, it offer some awareness {αἴσθησίν τινα παρέχειν}, on the basis of which you will have some belief {δόξα} about it, as to what temperance is and what sort of thing.

For there is certainly a strong suggestion here that temperance is something within Charmides that he can look at with his mind's eye; it would be difficult to paraphrase what Socrates here says in terms of just Charmides' being temperate. But there is still no suggestion of a general theory to the effect that the possessors of virtues have immanent forms within them. Temperance is something that Charmides allegedly has got, and Socrates here goes on to claim that if it is something that Charmides has, he should be aware of it. This is a theory, all right, but it is not a theory about immanent forms.

Let us look at one last occurrence of the verb "to be-present-in" in the *Charmides*.[6] Charmides looks within, and proposes that temperance is quietness; that goes down the tube in the way we considered earlier (§ 4.3.2.1). In 160d5–e1, Socrates adverts to the idea that temperance, inasmuch as it is-present-to (παροῦσα, 160d7) Charmides, is introspectible, and asks Charmides to have another look within; Charmides' response to this is the claim that temperance is modesty, and we have already (§ 4.4.3) considered how that is refuted. In the course of the refutation, Socrates quotes Homer (161a2–4; also in *Laches* 201b3): "Well then, I said, don't you believe Homer to have spoken admirably when he said that modesty is not good to be-present-to a man in need?" Here it is Homer who uses the locution "to be-present-to,"[7] and Socrates' use of the same expression in 160d7 and again in 161a9 can hardly import any more than can be found in this quotation.

The same completely noncommittal reading extends to the other locutions Socrates uses for the relation of temperance to the temperate person in this dialogue: the temperate person "partakes of temperance" (σωφροσύνης

---

[6] The three occurrences in the *Hippias Major* (294a1, c4, c6) require no further comment.

[7] So also Allen (1970) 146 n. 1.

μετέχειν, 158c3–4) or "possesses" it (κέκτησαι, 158d8), it "is-in" that person (ἐνεῖναι, 159a1, a2, a9).

8.2.2. Gorgias

Perhaps the *Gorgias* shows a further stage of reflection on the "presence-to" idiom, for there Socrates generalizes it (in 497e1–3):

don't you call the good {people} good by the presence-to {them} of goods {ἀγαθῶν παρουσία}, just as {you call} those beautiful whom beauty is-present-to {κάλλος παρῇ}?

And he repeats this generalization in 498d2–3:

Don't you know that you say the good {people} are good by the presence-to {them} of goods, and {that the} bad {are bad by the presence-to them} of bad {things}?

Finally the generalization is varied a little, in 506d2–e4:

But we and all other {things} that are good are good when some excellence comes-to-be-present-to {us} {παραγενομένης, d3–4}? ... But then the excellence of each {thing}, of an implement and of a body and again of a soul and of an entire animal comes-to-be-present-to {it} {παραγίγνεται, d6–7} in the most admirable way not at random but by {an} organization and correctness and art which is given to each of them ... Then by organization the excellence of each {thing} is organized and ordered? ... Therefore a certain order which is appropriate for each {thing}, when it comes-to-be-present-in {ἐγγενόμενος, e2} each {thing}, renders each of the {things} that are good?

But it is difficult to see what metaphysical impact this generalization might have.[8] In the first of these three passages the exact form of the generalization is very foggy: is it that things are *F* by the presence of *F*s, or by the presence of *F*ness? The second passage sticks with the former reading; the third, if we read "excellence" (ἀρετή) as the abstract noun corresponding to the adjective "good" (ἀγαθός: see *Protagoras* 324d5–6, *Republic* I 352d–354a, esp. 353d11, e4–5, *Laws* VI 770c7–d2), goes toward the latter. The whole question of metaphysical import seems quite beside the point if our object is understanding what is going on in the *Gorgias*: no reading of these passages that commits Socrates to one metaphysical view over another has any bearing on the arguments in which they are embedded.[9]

---

[8] Cf. Irwin (1979) 203.   [9] So also Dodds (1959) 21 n. 1.

8.2.3. Euthydemus *300e–301a*

Amid the madcap humor of this dialogue, questions of weight get raised, but not always answered. That is true of the question(s) raised in 300e3–301c2:

> Socrates, said Dionysodorus, have you ever yet seen any beautiful thing?
>
> I certainly {have}, I said, and a great many, Dionysodorus.
>
> {301}{Ones} that are other than the beautiful, he said, or the same as the beautiful?
>
> {a2/3} And I came under the influence of extreme perplexity, and I thought I had justly suffered {it} because I had complained, but still I said {they were} other than the beautiful, although there was present-to each of them some beauty {πάρεστιν μέντοι ἑκάστῳ αὐτῶν κάλλος τι}.
>
> {a5/6} Then, he said, if {an} ox comes-to-be-present-to you, you are {an} ox, and because I am now present-to you, you are Dionysodorus?
>
> Don't even say it, I said.
>
> {a8/9} But in what way, he said, when one {thing} comes-to-be-present-to another, could the one be other? {ἀλλὰ τίνα τρόπον . . . ἑτέρου ἑτέρῳ παραγενομένου τὸ ἕτερον ἕτερον ἂν εἴη;}
>
> {b1/2} Does this perplex you, I said? And already I was trying to imitate wisdom of the men, as I desired it.
>
> How could I not be perplexed, he said, I and all other people, at what is not {so}?
>
> {b5/6} What are you saying, Dionysodorus?, I said. Is not the beautiful beautiful and the ugly ugly?
>
> If it seems so to me, he said.
>
> Then does it seem so?
>
> Certainly, he said.
>
> {b7/8} Then also the same {is} the same and the different different? For no doubt the different {is} not the same, but I think even a child would not be perplexed at this, that the different is different.

The chief question this poses is the one that Dionysodorus puts, pretty obscurely, at 301a8–9. The question arises from Socrates' saying in 301a3–4 that certain things other than the beautiful can be beautiful by some beauty's being present to them; Dionysodorus jumps on this in 301a5–6 by saying that then, if an ox were present to Socrates, he would be an ox, and since Dionysodorus himself is present, Socrates must be Dionysodorus. Socrates wants to deny these things, especially the latter. And if we now ask: what question is raised by this?, the obvious answer is: what is the difference between the cases? Why does the presence of some beauty make something beautiful and the presence of an ox not make something an ox? If Dionysodorus' question at 301a8–9 makes any sense at all (and in this dialogue that may be a big "if"), that must be the sense it makes.

It can be read that way, and the above translation was intended for that reading. Unfortunately, the Greek is a lot worse. Where I have "one {thing}," "another," "one," and "other," the Greek has the same word, "other," in all four places. This is common enough Greek: repeated occurrences of the word "ἕτερον" get the sense "one thing . . . another. . . ." And here the dialogue makes play with that feature of the Greek. "Literally" translated, his question becomes:[10] "But in what way, he said, when {an} other comes-to-be-present-to {an} other, could the other be {an} other?"

Now I take it that Dionysodorus' question was, in fact, the straightforward one. But at that point Socrates became responsible for the sophistry, and that is what he means when in 301b1–2 he introduces what he next said by talking about how much he wanted to emulate Euthydemus and Dionysodorus. Dionysodorus had asked "how could the one be other?" which meant, e.g., "how could something that is not the beautiful – something than which the beautiful is other – be beautiful?" But his actual words looked more like: "how could the other be other?" and Socrates jumped on that: he treated "the other is {an} other" as on a par with "the beautiful is beautiful" and "the ugly is ugly," as a trivial self-predication,[11] and so treats Dionysodorus' question as the ridiculous question "how can the other be other?"[12]

And then there is no prospect of any gain in understanding of the relation of presence-to here, and a fortiori none of any gain in understanding the Theory of Forms.[13] But at least there has been an intelligible question raised: what kind of presence is transmitting presence, as opposed to the presence of an ox such as Dionysodorus?

The *Lysis* treats this question in passing.

8.2.4. Lysis 216c–221d

The logic in this passage is extremely complex; I forgo detailed discussion of that here. But there are two issues about the passage that we cannot

---

[10] The only translation I know of that aims at this degree of literalness is that of Sprague (1965) 57: "But in what way, he said, can the different be different just because the different is present with the different?" (In Cooper [1997] 739 without Sprague [1965] 55–56 n. 95, which helps with the sense.) See Sprague (2000) 15.

[11] Not (*pace* Chance [1992] 181–82) an identity.

[12] This reading is opposed to those of Sprague (1962) 26–27, (1965) 55–56 n. 95, and Mohr (1984) 298; *per contra*, cf. Gifford (1905) 60 *ad* a8, b1 and Guthrie (1975) 278 n. 2.

[13] The interpretations of Sprague (1967) and Mohr (1984) import Plato's Theory of Forms, as does that of Chance (1992) 175–83; for a long list of others that do the same, see Chance (1992) 269–70 n. 112. See also Sprague (2000) 5, Kahn (2000) 93–94.

avoid. The first is that just mentioned: in the course of 217b–218c, Socrates touches on the difference between ox-presence and transmitting presence. The second is that in the course of 219b–220b he presents an argument that has seemed to many to introduce the Theory of Forms. This second point is not very tightly connected to the first, but it must be addressed.

The main question in the *Lysis* is, as we've seen: under what circumstances does x become a "lover" or "friend" – let us stick with "friend" – of y? The formulations to come I shall refer to as "quasi-definitions" for "friend"; the qualification "quasi" is especially important here, for many of the formulations, if taken for definitions, would be open to fairly obvious objections that are not in fact raised in the dialogue (e.g., circularity: see n. 14). So I shall write these using, not "$=_{df}$," but "$\leftrightarrow$" for "is equivalent to." Still, by the time we get to 221c, we find Socrates defeating one of these equivalences by imagining a possible world, distinct from the actual one, in which the equivalence does not hold. So they are being treated as very strong equivalences indeed.

Here is a quick sketch of the whole passage.

After a half-dozen failed answers,[14] Socrates, in 216cd, lays out a relatively complicated quasi-definition:

> (qD$_{7a}$f) x is a friend of y $\leftrightarrow$ x is neither good nor bad and y is good.

He then gives an illustration that leads to elaborations, presented as reformulations of (qD$_{7a}$f) that simply add further clauses. In 217ab he adds a "because"-clause, to get:

> (qD$_{7b}$f) x is a friend of y $\leftrightarrow$ x is neither good nor bad and y is good, and something bad z is present to x, and x is a friend of y because of z's presence to x.

The "because"-clause introduces the notion of presence; in the course of the discussion of this quasi-definition Socrates touches on a distinction relevant to that between ox-presence and transmitting presence; this is the first point we must consider in this passage (§ 8.2.4.1).

---

[14] The refutations show nothing that helps for present purposes, so I have not discussed them; as I count them, they define "x is a friend of y" as: (qD$_1$f) either x loves y or y loves x (212b2; refuted in 212b–d), (qD$_2$f) both x loves y and y loves x (212c7–8; refuted212de), (qD$_3$f) y loves x (212b1–2; refuted in 212e–213b), (qD$_4$f) x loves y (212b1; refuted in 213bc), (qD$_5$f) x is like y (213d–215c, with elaborations introducing the fateful term "good"), and (qD$_6$f) x is unlike y (215c–216b). Treated as definitions, the first four look circular ("love" translates φιλεῖν, cognate to φίλος, "friend").

My enumeration lays no claim to being the only one; see, e.g., Bordt (1998) 61–62, 78–79, 148–49, who glosses over (qD$_1$f), but as a consequence has to suppose that Menexenus is confused (149–50).

The other is this. In 218d–219b Socrates tacks on two further clauses in quick succession. He first adds, in 218d–219a, a "for the sake of" clause to get:

(qD$_{7c}$f) x is a friend of y ↔ x is neither good nor bad and y is good, something bad z is present to x, and x is a friend of y because of the presence of z, and something good w is related in the right sort of way to y and x is a friend of y for the sake of w.

And then in 219ab, he adds the further point that w is also a friend to x to get:

(qD$_{7d}$f) x is a friend of y ↔ x is neither good nor bad and y is good, something bad z is present to x, and x is a friend of y because of the presence of z, which is an enemy of x, and something good w is related in the right sort of way to y and x is a friend of y for the sake of w, which is a friend to x.

It is this last addition that leads to the first refutation, which operates with an infinite regress that must be halted at something called a "first friend." Many have seen a Form here: even that of the Good. I do not (§ 8.2.4.2).

8.2.4.1. 217b–218a: presence

Socrates' addition of a "because" clause to (qD$_{7a}$f) in 217ab gives us:

(qD$_{7b}$f) x is a friend of y ↔ x is neither good nor bad and y is good, and something bad z is present to x, and x is a friend of y because of z's presence to x.

It is, we are saying, because of the presence of the bad to x that x is a friend of y; but that demands a distinction, as Socrates points out in 217b6–c2:

But it's quite clear that {the neither bad nor good comes-to-be a friend of the good because of the presence of the bad} before it itself has come-to-be bad by the bad which it has {πρὶν γενέσθαι αὐτὸ κακὸν ὑπὸ τοῦ κακοῦ οὗ ἔχει}. For having come-to-be bad it would no longer desire and be {a} friend of the good; for we said it was impossible for {a} bad {thing} to be {a} friend to {a} good {one}.

Yes, impossible.

So, for (qD$_{7b}$f) to work, we must suppose that the presence of something bad to x is not such as to make x itself bad; as Socrates puts it, we are to take x "before it has itself come-to-be bad by the bad which it has" (217b6–7).

So it is that Socrates feels called upon to distinguish two varieties of presence (217c3–e1):

Examine what I say: I say that, for some things, where what is present to them is such-and-such, they themselves are such-as-that, for others, not {οἷον ἂν ᾖ τὸ παρόν, τοιαῦτά ἐστι καὶ αὐτά, ἔνια δὲ οὔ}. Just as if someone were to plaster something with some color, I suppose what was plastered on would be present to what was plastered {with it}.

Very much so.

Then is that which is plastered also therefore at that time of such a color as that which is on {it}?

{d} I don't understand, he said.

Well, {it's} like this, I said. If someone plastered your hair, which is yellow, with white lead, would it then[15] *be* white, or *seem* white?

It would seem white, he said.

{d4} And whiteness would be present to it.

Yes.

But nevertheless it wouldn't yet *be* any more white, but while whiteness is present to it it is neither at all white nor black.

True.

But when, my friend, old age brings on it this same color, then it has come-to-be such as what is present to {it}: white, {d8} by the presence to {it} of white.

{e} How else?

This, then, I am asking now: whether, where something is present to a thing, that which has it will be such as that which is present to {it}; or {is it that} if it is present to {it} in a certain way, it will be, and if not, not?

Rather the latter, he said.

That is not exactly the distinction between ox-presence and transmitting presence, but it is close. It is a distinction between two relations of presence both of which bear on the properties of that to which something is present. Ox-presence does not do this in any but the most trivial of ways: if an ox is present with, say in the same room as, you, then you are present with, in the same room as, an ox. But this entails no real difference in any of your nonrelational properties. By contrast, the nontransmitting presence to which Socrates here draws our attention may make a difference to a thing's nonrelational properties: it may change a thing's appearance, and it may, over time, change what is really true of it.

The example Socrates offers to help us grasp his distinction is that of Lysis' hair color. It is, to begin with, blond. We first plaster it with white lead; the result is that it appears white instead of blond, but it is not, according to Socrates, in fact white. But then we allow Lysis to age, and as a result of that his hair becomes in fact white. In both cases, what is present-to the hair is whiteness (λευκότης, 217d4) or white (d8), "the same

---

[15] Accepting, with Burnet, Heindorf's τότε for the ποτε of BT; Bordt (1998) 195 translates ποτε "finally" (*am Ende*), which seems unnatural to me.

color"(d7), but in the first case what we get is apparently but not really white hair, and in the second really white hair.

Socrates does not say that if we left the white lead on Lysias' hair long enough, the hair would become really white. It becomes really white with old age, but white lead has nothing to do with that. But the preceding passage (217ab) has already given us another case to which Socrates' distinction is supposed to apply: disease, a bad thing, is present to a body, and because of that the body becomes a friend to medicine. Immediately after giving that example, in 217bc, Socrates added the qualification that the thing that is neither good nor bad, in this case the body, must not itself have already become bad because of the presence of the bad thing, in this case disease. What is envisaged is at least the possibility that in the case of some things that are present initially nontransmittingly, time may effect a transmission.

It is nontransmitting presence that figures in Socrates' codicil to (qD$_{7b}$f). So we must ask: how central to this notion is the eventual transmission of a property due to a presence that is not initially transmitting? Plainly, if ox presence were included in this nontransmitting presence, eventual transmission could be no part of it: oxen could be around us all the time without in any way increasing our propensity toward being oxen. But then again, if Lysis wore white lead on his hair for forty years, although he might go gray in that time, the white lead would have nothing to do with it. So eventual transmission is only a possibility for the nontransmitting presence Socrates is after; the realization of that possibility is not built into it.[16]

When we get to the Theory of Forms, we are going to be faced with a causal relation, sometimes referred to by Plato as "presence," that requires transmission. Is Socrates alluding to that theory and that causal relation here? It has been supposed that he is.[17] He is not. The example that he uses to make the distinction is the presence of white to hair: in the one case it doesn't make the hair really white, in the other it does. It is the one that doesn't on which Socrates focuses. And he gives us no theory whatever of the causal relation in which he is not here interested, that of transmitting presence.

---

[16] Mackenzie (1988) 33 makes it a general feature of Socrates' nontransmitting causes that they are pushing toward transmission; she even refers to what I am calling "nontransmitting causality" as "imminent παρουσία" (28). I am rejecting this.

So far I am in agreement with Bolotin (1979) 150–51. But Bolotin also ascribes to Socrates an "apparent confusion of different manners of being present with differences in duration" (150) and goes to great lengths (151–57) to explain this confusion away. I see no such confusion.

[17] By Taylor (1926) 70–71, Shorey (1933) 117, Glaser (1935) 55, Crombie (1962/63) II 255–56, Levin (1971) 247; *contra*: Vlastos (1973a) 35–36, Bordt (1998) 191–92.

The presence in question in (qD$_7$bf) is nontransmitting presence: the bad thing, disease, is present to the body, but not in such a way that the body is itself bad, since in the latter case it could no longer be a friend to anything (217e–218a).

In fact, transmitting presence has not been involved anywhere in the discussion to date,[18] and, at least on the face of it, it drops out of sight after this passage.[19] So it is not entirely clear why Socrates bothers making the distinction explicit at all: he had already got the concession he needed in 217b without drawing the distinction.

Perhaps we can explain the train of thought as follows: we have in (qD$_7$bf) a clause to the effect that x is a friend of y because of something z's presence; this sort of phenomenon can be a matter of z having a feature that it transmits to x or y, but not in this case; hence it requires special mention. If that is correct, even though we are not going to receive any further enlightenment on Dionysodorus' question from the *Lysis*, we may say that transmitting presence is at least in the background of what Socrates is thinking about. Unfortunately, he doesn't tell us any more about it.

Socrates now cashes in his chips, as follows (217e4–218a2):

And so the neither bad nor good sometimes, although bad is-present, is not yet bad, but sometimes it has already come-to-be such.
Certainly.
Then whenever it is not yet bad, although bad is-present, this presence makes it desire the good; whereas the {presence} that makes it bad deprives it of the desire and at the same time the friendship of the good. For it is no longer {218} neither bad nor good, but bad; and good was not a friend to bad.[20]
So it {was} not.

That is the difference the distinction between transmitting presence and nontransmitting presence makes: if the presence of the bad is nontransmitting, (qD$_7$b) can stand. That isn't much of a difference, as far as I can see, and certainly requires nothing on the order of the Theory of Forms to back it up.

---

[18] The two occurrences of the verb παρεῖναι so far (in 211c5 and 215b5) had to do simply with people being on the scene.

[19] The verb παρεῖναι appears for the last time in the *Lysis* at 217e7; the noun παρουσία appears in 218c2, in connection with the nontransmitting presence needed in (qD$_7$bf), and then no more.

[20] 218a1–2 φίλον δὲ ἀγαθὸν κακῷ οὐκ ἦν: going by Burnet's apparatus, ἀγαθὸν κακῷ is the text of B and a correction in T (T itself has ἀγαθῶν κακῷ). Burnet, Croiset (1921) 148, and Lamb (1925) 32 adopt an emendation due to Heindorf, ἀγαθῷ κακὸν: "bad was not a friend to good"; this is what is translated by Wright (Hamilton and Cairns [1961] 161) and Lombardo (Cooper [1997] 702); Bordt (1998) 27, 195–96 translates as I have.

8.2.4.2. 219b–220b: qualms; the "first friend"

Socrates takes aim at $(qD_{7b}f)$; the result is to replace it, in 219ab, with:

> $(qD_{7d}f)$ x is a friend of y $\leftrightarrow$ x is neither good nor bad and y is good, something bad z is present to x, and x is a friend of y because of the presence of z, which is an enemy of x, and something good w is related in the right sort of way to y and x is a friend of y for the sake of w, which is a friend to x.

To understand what happens next, we should focus on just a part of this, namely its entailment that something's friend is always a friend for the sake of some (other: see below) friend.

After stating $(qD_{7d}f)$, Socrates continues with (219b5–c1):

> Well now, I said, since we've come to here, my boys, let's apply our mind lest we be deceived. For I'll let it pass that the friend has become {a} friend of the friend, and the like becomes a friend of, in fact, the like,[21] which we say is impossible; but nevertheless let's examine the following, lest what's now being said deceive us.

The charge Socrates says in b6–8 he will dismiss is apparently (n. 21) that, if the friend, x, is a friend of the friend, y, then x and y are like each other in that both are friends, whereas 214e–215a had argued that like is not a friend to like. That argument was not actually one of Socrates' more impressive ones, and it would be particularly hard to adapt it to the present case,[22] so I'll let it pass, too.

The heart of Socrates' case to the effect that "what's now being said is deceiving us" is the argument we've been waiting for; here is its opening (219c1–d2):

> The medical {art}, we say, is a friend for the sake of health.
> Yes.
> {c2} Then health is also a friend?
> Certainly.
> {c2/3} Therefore, if a friend, for the sake of something?
> Yes.
> {c3/4} Of some *friend*, then, if it is going to follow our agreement earlier.
> Certainly.

---

[21] 219b6–8 ὅτι μὲν γὰρ φίλον τοῦ φίλου τὸ φίλον γέγονεν, καὶ τοῦ ὁμοίου γε τὸ ὅμοιον φίλον γίγνεται: the relation between these two clauses is, presumably, that the latter ("the like becomes a friend of the like") is a consequence of the former ("the friend has become a friend of the friend"), but there are no inferential particles connecting the two. Translations that put a "thus" or a "therefore" in the second clause (Croiset [1921] 150 [*ainsi*], Lamb [1925] 59, Jowett [1953] I 61, Watt [1987a] 155, Lombardo in Cooper [1997] 703, Bordt [1998] 29) are, then, intruding an element of interpretation. Still, it seems to me that the interpretation is correct: see Denniston (1934) 157 on καὶ . . . γε.

[22] Cf. Watt (1987a) 155 n. 4: there may be a fallacy here.

{c4/5} Then that too will be a friend for the sake of some friend again?
Yes.
{c5/6} Then {is}n't {it a} necessity that we tire of going on[23] like that and[24] arrive at some beginning,[25] which will no longer carry us back to another friend, but will have come to that which is {a} first friend, for the sake of which all the others are friends?
{A} necessity.

When Socrates speaks in c6–7 of arriving at a "beginning" that "no longer" carries us back "to *another* friend," he makes one presupposition plain: that, as long as the series of friends goes on, it produces a new friend every time. To get that we have to add to our premises. One addition we can get from Socrates himself: when he says that the series of friends must go to ground in a first friend, for the sake of which all the others are friends, he is presupposing that the "for the sake of which" relation is transitive (219cd). Where x is a friend of y for the sake of z, and a friend of z for the sake of w, x is a friend of y for the sake of w; formally:

(Tf)   Fxy fso z & Fxz fso w → Fxy fso w.

Now if we add that, whenever x is a friend of y for the sake of z, z is not identical to y,

(NIf)   Fxy fso z → $y \neq z$,

we rule out the possibility of "loops":[26] situations in which we have, e.g.,

Fxy fso z
Fxz fso w
Fxw fso y.

Then the series of friends is a series of new friends for as long as it continues.
Socrates plainly thinks that any such series must terminate (219c5–d2), and in real life, any chain of desires or wants does come to an end in what

---

[23] 219c5–6 ἀπειπεῖν . . . ἰόντας: or "give up going on" (Lombardo, in Cooper [1997] 704); see also Bolotin [1979] 46); but the participial construction is perhaps less common with this sense (see LSJ *s.v.* ἀπεῖπον IV 3 f).

[24] 219c6: reading καὶ, with the MSS (and Bordt [1998] 209), rather than ἢ with Burnet (1900/1907) III (following Schanz).

[25] 219c6 ἐπί τινα ἀρχήν: alternatively, "at some first principle" (so Lamb [1925] 59, Jowett [1953] I 61, Lombardo in Cooper [1997] 704; Bolotin [1979] 46 has "at some beginning principle"). But that lends itself too easily to metaphysical inflation; here it simply refers to the beginning of the series of friends.

[26] We also rule out the possibility that anything is a friend of something for the sake of that thing itself: the first friend, when we get there, is not, then, a friend for the sake of itself, but just a friend, and not for the sake of anything. That is faithful to the way Socrates is going to be talking: see 220b4–5.

sets up the whole chain. As a matter of fact, the argument does not require anything that strong: Socrates need only suppose that some such series terminate. Still, as he states the argument, it sets up regresses that would be infinite if not halted,[27] and he supposes that such regresses must indeed be halted.

Consider such a halted regress. What set up the regress to begin with was the claim that something's friend is always a friend for the sake of (another) friend:

(ff) $Fxy \rightarrow (\exists w)(Fxy \, \text{fso} \, w \, \& \, Fxw)$

together with the combined apparatus of (Tf) and (NIf).[28] Nothing whatever is done to call either (Tf) or (NIf) in question; Socrates' focus is on (ff). The point at which any of these regresses comes to a stop is a point at which (ff) ceases to operate. So we must restrict (ff), and the simplest restriction would be to rule that something's friend is so for the sake of another friend only where something's friend is not its "first friend":

(rff) $Fxy \rightarrow [\neg FFxy \rightarrow (\exists w)(Fxy \, \text{fso} \, w \, \& \, Fxw)]$.

And we might then register Socrates' view that chains of friends must always terminate in a first friend as

(FF) $Fxy \rightarrow (\exists w)(^{*}Fxw \, \& \, FFxw)$

(where "$^{*}F$" represents the ancestral of "F": the relation between x and z in which there may be intermediate terms $x_1, x_2, \ldots x_i$ such that Fxx_1, $Fx_1x_2, \ldots Fx_{i-1}x_i$, Fx_iz).

But at this point the argument takes a somewhat strange turn.

We must first go back to 219b5–6, 8–c1, where Socrates had introduced the regress argument with the suggestion that we had better pay attention lest we be deceived. He explains this comment (219d2–5):

This is what I'm saying: I'm afraid that all the other {things} which we were calling friends for the sake of that, being, as it were, images of it {ὥσπερ εἴδωλα ἄττα ὄντα αὐτοῦ}, are deceiving us, and it is that first {friend} which is truly {a} friend {ἦ δ' ἐκεῖνο τὸ πρῶτον ὃ ὡς ἀληθῶς ἐστι φίλον}.[29]

---

[27] And, I imagine, it is the first such regress in Plato (so also Guthrie [1975] 149).

[28] Notice the close parallel between the regress here and that known as the "Third Man": (NIf) here plays the role of the Non-Identity assumption in the Third Man, and (ff) plays that of the combined One over Many and Self-Predication assumptions (laying the "Third Man" out as in Dancy [1991] 103).

[29] Burnet places a comma after πρῶτον, which may suggest the construction "and what is truly a friend is that first {friend}"; Kahn (1996) 287 n. 38 suggests removing the comma.

It sounds from this as if, in a chain of purported friends, all those except the first are in some way imposters (more on this in § 8.2.4.4), and it is only the first that is really a friend; that is the way things are going to go, and this is the strange turn just mentioned.

Socrates argues for his claim that the only real friend is the first one in terms of the example of a father whose son has taken hemlock; the father's overarching desire is the preservation of his son's life (219d5–220a6). The details are forbidding, but we can get by just giving the claim to Socrates, emphasizing only that the chain of "friends" is a chain of things wanted for the sake of other things: one wants one thing for the sake of another, and that for the sake of another, . . . , back to the "first friend." Each term is valued for the sake of the next, and what Socrates is now saying about it is that, in fact, at least in the context of that chain, the only thing that is really valued is the first term, the first friend.

His application of his example is as follows (220a6–b3):

Then for the friend {is there} the same account? For, with those we say are friends to us for the sake of some other[30] friend, we plainly are saying it using {the} word {"friend"},[31] whereas presumably {a} friend in reality is that itself at which all these so-called friendships terminate.[32]

Presumably that's how it is, he said.

The contrast between "using the word 'friend'" (see n. 32) and "being a friend in reality" (φίλον . . . τῷ ὄντι, b1–2) picks up Socrates' suspicion back in 219d that all the friends spoken of so far are really imposters. Those who are friends for the sake of another friend are friends in name only, "nominal friends," let us say; the first friend that terminates the chain of nominal friends is the only real friend.

Socrates is now telling us that the truth of the locution "*x* is a friend of *y* for the sake of *z*" rules out the truth of "*x* is a friend of *y*"; where before we thought we were talking about friends, we were actually only talking about

---

[30] Reading Hermann's emendation ἑτέρου for the ἑτέρῳ of the MSS, with Burnet (1900/07) III et al.

[31] 220b1 ῥήματι φαινόμεθα λέγοντες αὐτό: every translation I have consulted resorts to paraphrase at this point; most add "merely" or "only" to get "merely with the word 'friend'" (or something like that). And that has to be, at least roughly, the sense.

[32] Here in 220b2–3 Socrates speaks of "that in which all these so-called friendships terminate" (εἰς ὃ πᾶσαι αὗται αἱ λεγόμεναι φιλίαι τελευτῶσιν); in 220d8 he will speak of "that friend to us in which all the others terminate" (τὸ φίλον ἡμῖν ἐκεῖνο, εἰς ὃ ἐτελεύτα πάντα τὰ ἄλλα). Kahn (1996) 288 n. 39: "Of course the regress argument does not prove uniqueness. It is simply assumed that there is one *philon* in which all *philiai* terminate (220b2, d8)." Bordt (1998) 201–2 takes it that there may be different first friends for different people, but refers to 220a7–b3 as showing that there is to be only one to a person. I see no need for any such assumption; the first friend simply terminates a chain of friends, and nothing is said to confine us to one chain, or even one to a person.

nominal friendship:

(Nff) $Fxy \text{ fso } w \rightarrow \neg Fxy$.

This puts what Socrates says a little starkly: the antecedent contradicts the consequent. But it is close to what Socrates actually says in 220ab, and revision to avoid the contradictory sound of (Nff) (which is, since it is a conditional, not in fact contradictory) would require recasting the whole argument to date (which can be done, but is very boring).

If we now recall

(ff) $Fxy \rightarrow (\exists w)(Fxy \text{ fso } w \text{ \& } Fxw)$

and put it together with (Nff), we get the consequence that there are no friends at all.

So if we assume that there are cases in which something is a friend to something, one or the other of (Nff) or (ff) must go; Socrates here is going to stick by (Nff), and then the upshot is that in any series of "friends" the only real friend is the last one, the first friend, not now a friend for the sake of anything further. That first friend is now a counterexample to (ff), so (ff) must go.

But, in fact, it is not just that the first friend is a counterexample that dooms (ff), it is the revision in the notion of friendship according to which if y is a putative friend of x's but is so for the sake of something else w then y is not a friend of x's at all: there are *no cases at all* in which y counts as a friend for the sake of something else w. And that is precisely what Socrates concludes (220b4–7):

Then the friend in reality is not a friend for the sake of some friend.
True.
{b6} So this has been dismissed: it is not for the sake of any friend that the friend is a friend.[33]

This is really quite a drastic conclusion; in this argument, a friend is now something valued or desired, and then this conclusion amounts to saying that we never desire anything for the sake of anything else. Perhaps it makes things a bit more palatable if we put it by saying: in cases in which we putatively want something, but do so for the sake of something else, we really want, not the first something, but that for the sake of which we seemed to want the first thing.

---

[33] Mackenzie (1988) appears to have missed this passage; she says (29) that Socrates "modifies, implicitly" (ff). He does not implicitly modify it; he explicitly rejects it.

In any case, that is the fate of (qD₇df). Let us now turn to metaphysics, and ask: how many "first friends" are there? To get to a first friend, we start with a chain of nominal friends; we track these to the point at which we have a "friend" that is no longer a "friend" for the sake of anything further, and we have a first friend. For the sick man, it might be health; for the father whose son has taken hemlock, the preservation of his son's life. If the father happens to be the same person as the sick man, he has two first friends. He might have indefinitely many, depending on how many chains of nominal friends there are. There is no suggestion anywhere so far that the first friend must be a single, unique friend for each person, and a fortiori none to the effect that there is one first friend for all of humanity or for all actions of all of humanity.[34]

Drawing the conclusion that there is only one first friend depends on a famous fallacy, the exchange of quantifiers illustrated in:

$$(x)(\exists y)Fxy$$
$$\therefore (\exists y)(x)Fxy.$$

Using this we could conclude from the premise that each of us has a mother that there must have been a mother of us all. In honor of that, we might call this the "Mother of Us All" fallacy. In fact, all that the premise does is set up chains of mothers, with no first mother in sight.

Does Socrates commit a Mother of Us All fallacy in the *Lysis*? Since nothing that he says depends on there being just one first friend, or even one per person,[35] there is no reason to saddle him with that.

8.2.4.3. *220b–221d: the first friend and the good*

After dismissing (qD₇df), Socrates abruptly asks (220b7): "but then is the good {a} friend?" (ἀλλ' ἆρα τὸ ἀγαθὸν ἐστιν φίλον;). He gets an affirmative answer. So have we finally got to the Form of the Good? Some have thought so.[36] But it is not so. We are, at this point, taking it that the only real friend is that in which a chain of putative friends terminates; this is the good about which Socrates now asks. So, once again, "the good" refers whatever it is for the sake of which one has a putative friend, and there is no reason given in the argument why this has to be one thing for all chains

---

[34] I am here in agreement with Versenyi (1975) 192–94.

[35] *Pace* virtually everybody; recently, Robinson (1987) 75, Bordt (1998) 201–2. But Socrates does not say that there is only one first friend for all the actions of all people. Even Versenyi (1975) 194 wants to find a sort of single first friend: "a formal principle like well-being, self-fulfilment, the overcoming of any particular *endeia* as such."

[36] Shorey (1930) 381 n. 1 = Shorey (1980) II 5 n. 1; see also 382 = 6. See also Levin (1971) 248, 258 n. 90.

of putative friends, or even one thing for all chains of friends starting from a single person *x*.

So we are not talking about the Form of the Good,[37] at least not if we are being guided by the argument Socrates is giving us.

8.2.4.4. *The metaphysics of the* Lysis

The passage we have been considering, 216–221, contains one of the weirdest arguments in all the early dialogues.[38] But it is not as weird as some have thought: it makes no reference, covert or otherwise, to the Form of the Good.

The first friend in any particular chain of putative friends is referred to as "the good." What does this mean? Consider 219a6–b2: "What is neither bad nor good, therefore, because of the bad, the enemy, is {a} friend to the good for the sake of the good, {a} friend." In its context, "the good" does not refer to the Form of the Good; in fact, it either refers to *health*, which is the good for the sake of which the ailing body desires medicine (219a4), or is a generalization of that example, in which case, in one chain of purported friends, the real friend, the good, is health. This is not the Form of the Good; it is the concrete good that is desired in each situation.

When we get to the Theory of Forms, some features of the discussion in the *Lysis* will get recycled. Here are two.

We have already quoted Socrates characterizing the nominal friends as "images" (εἴδωλα, 219d3) of the first friend, and the force of that characterization was clear in its context: they are not really friends, but look like friends; only the first friend is a real friend. This ultimately dooms (qD$_{7d}$f) and (qD$_{7c}$f), and that, in the *Lysis*, is what Socrates is up to.

But in *Republic* VII 534c5 he is going to speak of an image (εἴδωλον) of the Form of the Good, and there and in the Cave passage it is plain that he thinks of earthly good things as images of that awesome Form. And the

---

[37] Or about the good in any sense in which it contrasts with things that are good, as Bordt (1998) 211 thinks. He distinguishes between the property of the good and things that are good, and supposes that we strive for the property, the Good, even if we are not motivated by the presence of something bad. I do not know what it could mean to say that we strive for the property the Good.

[38] Mackenzie (1988) 29–31 runs the argument on to 222c, trying to play claims that arise after 221d off against the (qD)'s (as I am calling them) of 216–221. This is puzzling, given 221d. She cites 221d1–2, which says "there appears to be some other cause of loving and being loved {φιλεῖν τε καὶ φιλεῖσθαι}," *sc.* than the bad, and says (30), "Surprisingly this proposition does not herald a renewed citation of the πρῶτον φίλον."

It is difficult to imagine what such a "citation" could look like. The first friend is the terminus of a chain of putative friends, and is the only real friend in any such chain. The question now is whether for any real friend, any such first friend, the cause of its being a friend is the bad or something else. Socrates says: something else. He is in no position to say that this something else is itself the first friend.

Form of the Good is plainly enough the ultimate goal of the philosopher's striving. So the fact that the nominal friends are characterized in the *Lysis* as images of the first friend has been taken as proof all by itself that the Form of the Good is the first friend.[39] But if that is what is involved in Socrates' argument against $(qD_{7c}f)$ and $(qD_{7d}f)$ he does nothing to signal the fact. In the *Republic* Socrates is made to rework the sort of material we are encountering in the context of a metaphysical scheme that is not mentioned or alluded to in the *Lysis*.[40]

And the same sort of point must be made concerning the notion of presence.[41] There is a distinction drawn between two kinds of presence, as we have seen, in 218c–e (§ 8.2.4.1): transmitting presence and nontransmitting presence. The former is the sort of presence that will be involved when we get to the Theory of Forms. But what is here in question is nontransmitting presence: on Socrates' account, the bad thing whose presence is the cause of friendship is present but nontransmittingly. He does not go on to say that the good thing for the sake of which there is presence is present in a transmitting way. He has other fish to fry. The idea of transmitting presence will recur in the Theory of Forms. Here it is simply material that is discarded.

The *Lysis* is hard. The Theory of Forms doesn't make it any easier.

---

[39] So Glaser (1935) 56–57, Krämer (1959) 499–501 (Krämer sees here the One of the "unwritten doctrines"); perhaps Kahn is appealing to this as well: see Kahn (1988) 545, Kahn (1996) 287–88. Vlastos (1973a) 36–37 is deflationary, as am I.

[40] My reading here is curiously close to Kahn's. He admits that one could not tell from the *Lysis* that the Form of the Good is in question, but this is part of his "proleptic" reading of the early dialogues: the *Lysis* somehow points forward to the *Republic*. And I agree with this. What I do not see is why we should suppose that to understand the *Lysis* we must see that forward pointing, or, differently put, how reading the Form of the Good back into the *Lysis* makes the *Lysis* any clearer. Kahn (1996) 290: "philosophy is the form of love in which the good is understood as wisdom. Here we have the implicit positive conclusion of the *Lysis*, which (together with the notion of the primary dear as the good and *kalon*) directly prepares for Diotima's doctrine of *erōs*. But this positive conclusion is buried under Socrates' final aporetic flourishes. In this respect the end of the *Lysis* resembles that of the *Laches* and *Charmides*, where we catch a glimpse of a positive conclusion that is then whisked out of sight by some final perversity or opacity on the part of Socrates." I am hardly the one to try to get Socrates acquitted of the charge of perversity or opacity, but it seems to me that he is a good deal less perverse or opaque on my account than he is on Kahn's.

[41] Here again Glaser (1935) 55–56 indulges in metaphysical rhapsody, faintly echoed in Kahn (1996) 286.

PART II

Between definitions and Forms

CHAPTER 9

The Meno

The *Meno* begins as a Socratic definition dialogue whose topic is "excellence" (ἀρετή). At 80d, Meno causes the dialogue to abort by asking Socrates how he can expect to find out what excellence is when he doesn't have even a clue to start with. Socrates' response and the rest of the dialogue bring in several new things.

First, Socrates propounds the Doctrine of Recollection:

(DR) What we call learning is not really that, but recollecting something we knew beforehand.

Next, Socrates is prepared to discuss, using a certain method, whether excellence is teachable even in the absence of a definition. This requires renunciation of the Intellectualist Assumption, although the dialogue opens with a firm restatement of that assumption.

The method Socrates goes on to describe is often referred to as the "Method of Hypothesis." It bears some resemblance to the method of Geometrical Analysis, on which it is based.

Finally, Socrates retreats from the claim that knowledge is a prerequisite for excellence: he suggests that true belief might be enough. This change from the stance of the Socratic dialogues is not of central concern in this book, and I shall have only a little to say about it.

Section 9.1 below discusses a background problem for the Intellectualist Assumption. Section 9.2 briefly discusses definition in the mini-Socratic dialogue. Section 9.3 deals with Meno's question at 80d, and § 9.4 with Socrates' response, the Doctrine of Recollection. Section 9.5 takes up the Method of Hypothesis.

We still have not reached the Theory of Forms, but we are closer: see §§ 9.2.1.1 and 9.6.

9.1. THE INTELLECTUALIST ASSUMPTION AND THE
SOCRATIC PARADOXES

Socrates in the Socratic dialogues espoused the Socratic paradoxes. Two of them are:

> (SP1) No one willingly (knowingly) does wrong; and
> (SP3) Virtue is knowledge.

These are closely related (see § 1.1), and if we add the Intellectualist Assumption to the mix, we get trouble. For then it will follow that being virtuous requires knowing what virtue is. And this poses a problem, if not for Socrates, then for Plato in reflecting on Socrates. For Plato put Phaedo on record as saying that Socrates was the best ("most virtuous"), wisest, and most just of the men he had known (*Phaedo* 118); if the *Seventh Letter* is in fact by Plato, he said it himself (324de). But Socrates specifically says at the outset of the *Meno* that he does not know what virtue is. So if Plato adopts the Socratic view that virtue is inseparable from the knowledge of what virtue is, he must conclude that Socrates is not virtuous.

So one assumption or another has to go; the *Meno* gives up the Intellectualist Assumption.

9.2. 70A–80D: A SOCRATIC MINI-DIALOGUE

The Socratic definition dialogues with which we have been dealing all opened with conversation that motivated the request for definition. The Socratic dialogue in the *Meno* does, too, but it is condensed. Meno opens the dialogue with the abrupt[1] question (70a1–2): "Can you tell me, Socrates, whether excellence is teachable?"[2] and Socrates responds that any Athenian would have to reply (71a5–7): "I lack knowing whether {it is} teachable or not teachable by so much that I actually don't even know at all {τὸ παράπαν} what it is." Socrates insists that this is how it is with him too (71b1–2); he reviews his situation using a subject version of (IA), stated explicitly and generally (71b2–7):

I reproach myself for not knowing about excellence at all {τὸ παράπαν}; how could I know what something is like about which I don't know what it is? Or does it seem to you possible for whoever does not know at all {τὸ παράπαν} who Meno is to know whether he is handsome {καλός} or wealthy or again well-born . . .?

---

[1] For various conjectures as to why, see, e.g., Taylor (1926) 130, Bluck (1961) 199 *ad* 70a1, Brague (1978) 54–55, Sharples (1985) 123.

[2] Or, instead of "teachable," "taught": the word is διδακτόν, and words of this type are ambiguous in this way.

The claim of total ignorance about excellence is one we have already encountered in the *Laches* (190b8–c2: § 2.3.4. above), and Meno is going to return to it in 80d (d6; cf b4).

The question "how could I know what something is like about which I don't know what it is?" (71b3–4 ὃ δὲ μὴ οἶδα τί ἐστιν, πῶς ἂν ὁποῖόν γέ τι εἰδείην;) employs language that, in Aristotle, signals a distinction between the category "what it-is" (τί ἐστι) and the category "what-it-is-like" (ποιόν), "quality."[3] The category distinction in 71b (and 86d8–e1) is between what excellence (or whatever) is and everything else about it, just as the *Euthyphro* distinguished between the "substance" (οὐσία) of the pious and any affect (πάθος) of it (11a: § 6.3); 72b1 paraphrases asking what something is as asking what it is "about its substance" (περὶ οὐσίας).[4]

9.2.1. 71e–73c: the excellences

The first stab Meno makes is a list of excellences (71e–72a): there is the excellence of a man (ἀνδρὸς ἀρετή, 71e2), that of a woman, that of a child, that of an old man, that of a free man, that of a slave, and so on.[5]

Nothing Socrates says against this definition turns on Necessity or Sufficiency: we may assume both that Meno's list is correct as far as it goes (satisfying Sufficiency) and that it goes far enough (satisfying Necessity). The same is going to be true of Meno's other efforts; Socrates' refutations do not finally turn on any of the three components of our "Socratic theory of definition," but on a requirement to which we may refer as a "Unity Requirement": see § 9.2.1.2.

9.2.1.1. The Theory of Forms?

Socrates responds to Meno's list by expressing gratitude for his good fortune: "while looking for one excellence I have found a swarm of excellences" (72a7–8). His metaphor of a "swarm" carries him to an example to clarify what he is after (72b1–c5): he imagines asking "for {the} substance of {a} bee" (μελλίτης περὶ οὐσίας, b1); bees might be many and various, but they would not differ "in being bees" (τῷ μελίττας εἶναι, b4–5), and Meno agrees that they would not differ "in that they are bees" (ᾗ μέλιτται εἰσίν, b8–9), so Socrates asks what that is "in which they do not differ but are the same" (ᾧ οὐδὲν διαφέρουσιν ἀλλὰ ταὐτόν εἰσιν, c2–3).

---

[3] See Thompson (1901) 63–65, although Thompson injects too much later baggage into the present passage.

[4] So also Allen (1984) 133. But see Napolitano Valditara (1991).

[5] Perhaps this comes from the historical Gorgias, who is mentioned in 70bc as having influenced Meno, and cf. also 71cd, 73c, which suggest that this first definition is due to Gorgias: see Aristotle, *Politics* A 13. 1260ᵃ27–28 (cf. Guthrie [1969] 253–54).

He then undertakes to persuade Meno that the excellences "all have some one form, the same, because of which they are excellences" (ἕν γέ τι εἶδος ταὐτὸν ἅπασαι ἔχουσιν δι' ὃ εἰσὶν ἀρεταί, 72c7–8). The persuasion takes some work on Socrates' part, and it makes use of the term "form" that occurred in the sentence just quoted. So, naturally, the passage as a whole raises the question: are we here getting the Theory of Forms?

Socrates begins (72de) by getting Meno to concede the parallel point for health, size, and strength; for health "the form is the same everywhere" (ταὐτὸν πανταχοῦ εἶδός ἐστιν, d8); a woman is "strong by the same form, i.e., the same strength" (e5) as a man; strength in a man or a woman "is no different relative to its being strength" (οὐδὲν διαφέρει πρὸς τὸ ἰσχὺς εἶναι ἡ ἰσχύς, e6).

No one is going to use the word "form" again until Meno himself does so at 80a5, where it certainly does not signal that he is subscribing to some background theory of forms (see § 9.2.4). Does the word signal that when Socrates uses it as we have just quoted him using it in 72c7, d8, and e5? If the question is: did Plato accept the Theory of Forms at the time of writing this dialogue?, there is no way of getting an answer. But if the question is: does the Theory of Forms play a role in the argument at this point?, the answer is easier.

Socrates offers an explanation of what he means by "by the same form" in 72e5–7: a woman is strong by the same form as a man, i.e., strength in the two cases is the same thing, if there is no difference between a man's strength and a woman's strength as far as its being strength goes. And this echoes the bee example: Socrates had spoken of that by which bees do not differ but are the same (72c2–3), and that isn't very far from paraphrasing the talk of bees not differing in being bees in terms of its being the same thing in the case of each bee that makes it count as a bee. In 72b1 he spoke of the "substance" of a bee, so he would no doubt be willing to talk of what the bees all have that makes them count as bees as one "substance" for bees. In the case of strength, we could say: what counts as strength in a man is the same thing that counts as strength in a woman; Socrates could as well have spoken of that same thing as the "substance" of strength, and he now is calling it a "form."

But he has not said anything whatever about the "ontological status" of these forms.

Consider Meno's responses to Socrates' questions in this passage. Meno doesn't make incredulous noises when Socrates introduces the terms "substance" and "form," but continues focused on the main question about bees, health, strength, and the rest. That is hardly because he knows about and accepts Socrates' Theory of Forms; there is no need for such a theory here. In saying what he does, Socrates need be going no farther than he had in the *Euthyphro*. If the Theory of Forms is not required to make sense of the *Euthyphro*, it is not required to make sense of this passage in the *Meno*.

9.2.1.2. The Unity Requirement

Even if we are not going for a Theory of Forms, we must consider how Socrates makes a case for the claim that there is just one form for excellence, whether womanly or manly.

Meno has conceded that health, size, and strength are the same in a man as in a woman, but when Socrates tries to make excellence parallel to these (73a1–3), Meno responds: that's different (a4–5). So Socrates has to argue, in 73a–c, that excellence is indeed like the other cases.

In a6–c1 he gets from Meno concessions that amount to:

> (1) No one can be good without being temperate and just, from which he takes it to follow that
> ∴ (2) No one can be good without temperance and justice.

And then we find him concluding from just this that human beings are good in the same way, i.e., that their excellence is the same (c1–5); he promptly asks what this excellence is that is the same for all men (c6–8).

Is that enough? It was not for Aristotle, who, in the face of this argument, differentiates excellence on the ground that temperance, justice, and the others are different for a woman and for a man, and commends Gorgias' enumeration of the virtues over against those who go for definitions (*Politics* A 13. 1260ᵃ20–28; cf. *Poetics* 15. 1454ᵃ22–24).

On the face of it, Socrates infers from (2):

> ∴ (3) All people need the same things in order to be good.
> ∴ (4) All people need the same things in order to possess excellence.
> ∴ (5) Excellence is the same for all people.

Aristotle is denying the inference from (2) to (3).

Meno does not raise Aristotle's objection, and the overall structure of Socrates' refutation is just this: Meno so defines excellence that it is different things for different people; it is not; so Meno's definition is wrong. This can be seen as invoking a requirement, the Unity Requirement, to the effect that:

> (UR) Where $x, y, \ldots$ are F and are no different in being F, a *definiens* for F must give the single form by virtue of which $x, y, \ldots$ are F.

The argument can be construed as instantiating (UR) either to get:

> (URg) Where a man, a woman, etc. are good and are no different in
> being good, a *definiens* for good must give the single form by
> virtue of which they are good,

or to get:

> (URe) Where the excellence of a man, the excellence of a woman, etc.,
> are excellences and are no different in being excellences, a
> *definiens* for excellence must give the single form by virtue of
> which they are excellences.

(URe) seems to be operating in 72c–73a, and (URg) in 73a–c.

The general requirement (UR) contains at least one obscure clause: we are to look for a single form for F where x, y, etc. are "no different in being F." This has been variously formulated in the text (72bc, e–73, 73c). We can get closer to the sense by asking: what kinds of cases could there be in which x and y are both F but are different in being F, or are F in different ways? Socrates does not say, but we can think of possibilities.

One kind of case might be ambiguity. Two pitchers, one of which holds water and the other of which throws baseballs, differ as far as their being pitchers goes. Meno might, then, have said that the sense in which a woman is good is different from that in which a man is good.

But that would leave some discomfort: if there really is a difference between the goodness of a man and that of a woman, it seems unlikely to be a matter of sheer ambiguity like that of "pitcher." So there might be something more subtle at stake. Consider a tall man and a tall building: these differ, we might say, in their tallness, since what counts as tallness in a man is quite different from what counts as tallness in a building. But the word "tall" is not *ambiguous* between men and buildings, for it can be given a "contextual" definition:

> (Dt) a tall Φ $=_{df}$ a Φ above the height standard for Φs;

this will cover men as well as buildings.[6]

The Unity Requirement will clearly fail to apply where "F" is ambiguous, and it may fail where "F" is contextually defined: in either case, perhaps, we cannot expect to find a single form for F.

The Unity Requirement is pretty much new to the *Meno*.[7] Dialogues already discussed, such as the *Euthyphro*, have required that the *definiens*

---

[6] See here Dancy (1975) 107–8, Dancy (1984) 168–72, 173–74.

[7] There is something like it in the complex argument of *Hippias Major* 298a–303e, which I have for reasons of space passed by. See Woodruff (1982) 77–80, Kahn (1985) 266–67, 284.

for which Socrates is seeking give a single form. But there the cash value of this requirement was simply that the *definiens* give necessary and sufficient conditions for the application of the *definiendum*. The Unity Requirement is different on two counts. First, it is here used to rule out a definition that could not have been ruled out on grounds of Necessity or Sufficiency. And, second, it makes explicit a restriction on the requirement of giving a single form for F: that requirement only kicks in where the things that are F do not differ in being F.

That means that more thought is being devoted to the requirement that the definition for a term must be *one* as opposed to many. This is still not the Theory of Forms, but it is a step closer.

9.2.2. *73c–74b: the ability to rule*

Socrates convinces Meno that "excellence" passes the test: all humans are good in the same way, i.e., they do not differ with respect to their being good, so (UR) takes hold and we must look for a single form for excellence. Meno's second try is (73c9–d1): "What else but to be able to rule men? If, indeed, you are seeking some one {thing} for all."

Socrates first objects (73d2–6) that this cannot be the excellence of a child, or that of a slave. This objection is ¬(Nec): there are cases of excellence that fall outside the *definiens*. Meno acquiesces. Socrates then says (73d6–74a10) that we must add "justly, and not unjustly" to the phrase "to be able to rule men" (d6–8). It sounds as if he is saying: if someone is able to rule unjustly, that doesn't count as excellence. This would be an objection on grounds of insufficiency: some cases of being able to rule are not cases of excellence.

But this train of thought is not really completed. Meno, in responding to Socrates' suggestion, accepts it, and adds "for justice, Socrates, is excellence" (d9–10). Socrates pounces on this: he gets Meno to concede that justice is not (simply) excellence, but *an* excellence (ἀρετή τις), and there are others, such as courage, temperance, etc. (73e–74a). He then says (74a7–10): "we've once more found many excellences when looking for one, but in another way than just now; but we're not capable of discovering the one which is through all these." He is invoking (UR) again, and in the form (URe). It is not entirely clear how he got here, but one suggestion might be: the definition as given fails (Suf), and so it can only be saved by adding to it; but adding to it piecemeal, adding "with justice," "with temperance," and so on, is going to give us a new list of excellences that do not differ in being excellences, and so (UR) applies.

It remains unclear what the status of this new list of excellences is. Perhaps the list is thought of as a new candidate for defining excellence; if so, Meno's second attempt has already been abandoned, and we are considering a new *definiens*. If, on the other hand, we are still dealing with Meno's second attempt, the list is to be conceived as having the form: being able to rule men with justice, being able to rule men with courage, being able to rule men with temperance, etc.

It makes little difference; in either case, we are to apply (UR). But this application raises the same questions we encountered in connection with the preceding *definiens*. Suppose the list is the simpler "justice, courage, temperance, etc.," conceived as a list of excellences and taken as an attempt to define excellence. If Meno doubted that the excellence of a man, of a woman, etc., were excellences that were the same in being excellences, why should he not also doubt whether courage and temperance are the same in being excellences? Here we have many excellences, and about the only thing that will show that they are the same in being excellences is a definition, itself unambiguous, for excellence. It is not clear what should lead us to suppose there *must* be such a definition.

But Meno does not pursue this line: he simply accepts the unity of this plurality. At this point, his confidence begins to run out: he confesses he cannot get the single excellence Socrates is after (74a11–b1). So Socrates offers some help, in the form of sample definitions (74b–77a), at least one of which he himself accepts. One would have thought that these would be of help to us in coming to understand what Socrates is after. But, although they somehow soften Meno up for one more attempt on excellence, they tell us nothing that I can discern about what an acceptable definition might be like.

9.2.3. 77b–79e: desire and power

Meno's last attempt to define virtue is at 77b4–5:

> (D3) virtue $=_{df}$ the desire for beautiful things together with the power to get them.

The term "beautiful" (καλός) has, especially in English, the wrong connotations, and in the sequel (from 77c1 on), Socrates replaces it by the more general term "good" (ἀγαθός). So what is really under attack is

> (D3′) virtue $=_{df}$ the desire for good things and the ability to get them.

Socrates' argument against this is curious: he first argues that the first half is superfluous, since everyone desires good things (77b–78b), and then that the second half is inadequate by itself to guarantee that the actions are virtuous (78b–79e).

The first of these two stages of the argument, which involves the Socratic paradox labeled (SP1) in § 9.1 , is quite complex, and ultimately, I believe, fails; but we must forgo its complexities here, and I shall simply grant Socrates the conclusion he wants, namely, that all we need consider is the pared-down definition

(D3'a) virtue =$_{df}$ the ability to get good things.

He attacks this in 78c–79a, and the argument is simple: for this to count as virtue, the acquisition of good things must itself be done justly, with temperance, and so on, so we are once more back to the list we rejected in the second definition (79a–c).

So we are back to (UR). And so (UR) is the weapon Socrates has been wielding in the case of each of the *definientia* in the mini-Socratic dialogue.

9.2.4. *79e–80d: perplexity*

Now we encounter perplexity (ἀπορία). Socrates puts his question "What is virtue?" again (79e), but Meno caves in: he has heard before that Socrates was perplexed and perplexed others (79e–80a; the verb is ἀπορεῖν), and confesses that he has himself now become full of perplexity (80a3–4, μεστὸν ἀπορίας γεγονέναι). He compares Socrates to an electric ray (80a): the Greek word is νάρκη, which is, in the first instance, an abstract noun meaning "numbness," and is applied to the electric ray through its numbing anything that comes in contact with it. Let us imagine that English behaves like Greek here, and "numbness" is a name for the electric ray. Then we can translate Meno as saying (80a4–6): "You even seem to me, if it is proper to joke, entirely to be most like, in form {εἶδος} as well as in other {respects}, the flat numbness of the ocean." Meno is, he says, thoroughly numbed by contact with Socrates (80ab), and while he has had a lot to say about excellence on prior occasions, he is now unable to say what it is "at all" (τὸ παράπαν, 80b4).

Socrates allows the comparison only if the ray, "numbness," is a transmitting cause of numbness (80c6–d1):

I, if numbness is itself numb, and in that way makes others numb {εἰ μὲν ἡ νάρκη αὐτὴ ναρκῶσα οὕτω καὶ τοὺς ἄλλους ποιεῖ ναρκᾶν}, am like it; if not, not. For I do not make others perplexed {ἀπορεῖν} while I myself am in the clear {εὐπορῶν}, but, more than anything, I, being myself perplexed, in that way make others perplexed.

This is philosophical joking: if the ray, "numbness," is a transmitting cause of numbness, Socrates is like it: he is a transmitting cause of perplexity. And if Plato's audience does in fact include people familiar with the Theory of Forms as it appears in the *Phaedo*, Meno's saying in 80a5 that Socrates is like the fish "numbness" "in form" is part of the joke. But here nothing comes of it.

9.3. 80DE: MENO'S PARADOX, I

In other dialogues, Meno would at this point plead another engagement and walk off. He does not: he is not as numb as he makes out. He asks a question, and Socrates says something, apparently by way of elaboration of that question, but somewhat differently put, and this has led to controversy. The exchange reads as follows (80d5–e5):

MENO: In what way, Socrates, will you look for that about which you don't at all know what it is?[8]
{d6/7} For having put before yourself which[9] of the things you don't know will you look for it?
{d7/8} Otherwise,[10] even if you run straight into it, how will you know that *this* is what you didn't know?
{80e} SOC: I understand what you want to say, Meno. Do you see how contentious an account you are bringing in,
{e2/3} that it is possible for a man to look for neither what he knows nor what he doesn't know?
{e3/4} For he could[11] not look for what he knows –

---

[8] τοῦτο ὃ μὴ οἶσθα τὸ παράπαν ὅτι ἐστίν; Alternatively: "for this {*sc.* excellence}, about which you don't at all know what it is?" Bluck (1961) 271 insists this is right, despite μὴ in d6, which he then explains by saying that the clause "about which you don't at all know what it is" is "virtually conditional." Sharples (1985) 143 follows Bluck. Neither mentions the fact that τοῦτο is neuter and ἀρετή feminine, which is not crushing (see 73a4 for what may or may not be a parallel), but certainly makes their rendering less plausible.

[9] ποῖον: the contrast between τί ἐστιν and ὁποῖόν or ποῖόν τι invoked in 71b4, 86d8–e1, 87b3, recalled at 100b4–6, was one between what something is and what things are true of it over and above what it is; there is no question of that here, *pace* Bluck (1961) 271–72. The correct translation, I think, is "which" (as in 83e11, 84a1).

[10] Cf. *Phaedrus* 237c1–2: "One must know what one's deliberation is about, otherwise necessarily one misses everything." Some translations of the *Meno* simply ignore ἤ in 80d7 (e.g., Grube [1981] 69 = Cooper [1997] 880, Allen [1984] 163); many translate it as "and" (Sharples [1985] 63, Jowett [1953] I 277, Croiset and Bodin [1923b] 249); Lamb (1924) 299 translates it as "or"; Guthrie (1956) 128 (= Hamilton and Cairns [1961] 363) has "to put it another way." On my reading, the sense is: if you haven't put something before yourself, you'll have no way of telling when you've found it. That way there is just one argument involved rather than the two that, e.g., Sharples (1985) 142 finds.

[11] So Lamb (1924) 301 translates; Guthrie (1956) 129 (= Hamilton and Cairns [1961] 363) and Sharples (1985) 63 translate "would." "Could" seems too strong for the immediate context, but the argument requires something like it: see below.

{e4/5} for he knows it, and there is no need, for such a person, for looking –
{e5} nor for what he does not know – for he doesn't even know what he is going
to look for.

Suppose we do not know at all what decacumination is. Then, according
to the difficulty Meno is raising, if we undertake an inquiry of the Socratic
type into what it is, we are doomed to failure, for we shall be unable to
tell when we have been successful: as Socrates puts the point of Meno's
argument later on, it is that "it is not possible to find what we do not know,
nor should we look for it" (86b9–c1). This is more guarded than what he
says in 80e2–3, which makes it sound as if it isn't even possible to try, but
it is the guarded position that Socrates is really after.[12]

Meno puts the difficulty in three questions that suggest an argument.[13]
The question of 80d5–6 suggests that the conclusion of the argument
will be:

(C) One cannot successfully look for something without knowing
what it is in some way or other.

The question of 80d6–7 suggests that (C) is to be derived from a premise
such as

(P2) Successfully to look for something requires putting what one is
looking for before oneself,

where "putting something before oneself" (προτίθεσθαι) is a matter of
somehow representing it to oneself.[14]

The question of 80d7–8 suggests (see n. 10 above) a reason for (P2):

(P1) If one does not put what one is looking for before oneself, one will
not recognize it when one gets to it.

If I do not somehow represent what I am looking for to myself, I shall be in
no position to find it, for finding it involves not just having it, but knowing
that one does. If I am looking for the answer to a question such as "what is
excellence?" I am able somehow to represent to myself that about which I
am asking the question "what is it?" even if only by the word "excellence,"
whose meaning I know but, by hypothesis, am unable to state. And this
is essential to the possibility of success, since it is this minimal capacity to

---

[12] See Scott (1995) 29–32.

[13] This analysis differs from others I know, most of which see two distinct arguments in Meno's speech,
e.g., Sharples (1985) 142, Ebert (1973) 172–73 (or Ebert [1974] 94; Ebert [1973] 173 even sees in the last
question echoes of Gorgias). Nothing in the sequel suggests that there are two distinct arguments.

[14] Ebert (1974) 94 n. 18 notes the usefulness of the German *sich vorstellen* in translating προθέμενος
in d7.

represent the object of my search to myself that will enable me to know when I've finally got what I'm looking for.

Then the argument is as follows. A presupposition of successfully looking for something is the ability to tell that *this* is the thing being looked for; this is (P1). That ability in turn presupposes the minimal knowledge of what is being looked for that requires an ability somehow to represent to oneself the object of one's search; that is (P2), watered down to make it plausible. And the conclusion is that without such a representational ability, one's search cannot be successful, where success involves awareness of success; and that conclusion is (C).

Socrates puts the difficulty in the form of a dilemma that would show that successfully looking for something is in general impossible. He states his conclusion in e2–3: it isn't possible (successfully: but this is the passage in which Socrates leaves out such qualifications) to look for what one knows or for what one doesn't know. The first horn of this dilemma has no parallel in Meno's formulation, and I shall (mostly: see n. 34) ignore it here.

The argument in the second and more important horn is extremely concise in Socrates' statement of it (80e5): the inquirer can't look "for what he does not know – for he doesn't even know what he is going to look for." It seems natural to flesh this out as follows:

(1) x does not know what y is.   S
(2) x is trying to get to know what y is.   S
∴. (3) x does not know what he is trying to get to know.   (1),(2)
(4) One cannot try to get to know something without
       knowing what he is trying to get to know.   P
∴. (C) It isn't possible to try to get to know what one
       doesn't know.

Here (1) and (2) simply unpack the notion of trying to define y; (3) draws a conclusion from those premises, and (4) contradicts it.

But it is possible to feel discomfort with (3) and (4), for they may appear to trade on an ambiguity: with the word "what" read as an indirect interrogative pronoun, (4) looks true and (3) false, but with "what" read as a relative pronoun, (3) looks true and (4) false.[15] At that rate, Socrates' formulation of Meno's Paradox is quite unlike Meno's own formulation of it.[16]

---

[15] See Ryle (1976) 7–8 for this "resolution of Meno's sophism."
[16] Moravcsik (1970) 57 thought the formulations were importantly different; White (1974/75) 290 with n. 4 objected.

This interpretation points to a sophism whose conclusion is that you can never, under any circumstances, try to get to know what you don't know. But that is not what is at stake. Meno is (legitimately) trading on Socrates' claim not to know *at all*[17] what excellence is, which he takes to imply that Socrates does not even have the minimal ability to represent to himself what he is after. This is what is compelling about Meno's Paradox: the situation in which Socrates has placed himself vis-à-vis questions such as "what is excellence?" leaves him in no position to recognize an answer even he trips over it.

It is better to suppose that at 80e5 Socrates is only being laconic: he means what Meno meant, that if he "doesn't know at all" what excellence is, then he doesn't know what he is going to look for. It is this to which he is going to respond by producing the Doctrine of Recollection.

9.4. 81A–86C: THE DOCTRINE OF RECOLLECTION

Socrates tells Meno that the argument for Meno's Paradox does not seem to him to be a good argument; Meno asks what is wrong with it (81a); and Socrates produces the Doctrine of Recollection. This has two parts.

Socrates ascribes the first part of (DR) to certain priests and priestesses, to Pindar, and other divine[18] poets (81ab): it is Reincarnation. By itself, it does nothing for Meno's Paradox.

Socrates does not ascribe the second part of (DR) to the priests and poets[19] (81c5–d5):

So, since the soul is immortal and has come-to-be many times, and has seen both the {things} here and those in Hades and all things {πάντα χρήματα}, there isn't anything it hasn't learned; so no wonder it can recollect, both about excellence and about other {things}, what it knew before as well {καὶ πρότερον ἠπίστατο}. {c9/d1} For since all nature is akin, and the soul has learned all things {μεμαθηκυίας τῆς ψυχῆς ἅπαντα}, nothing prevents one, once having recollected just one {thing} – which men call learning – finding out all others as well, if one is courageous and does not shrink from looking for {them};
{d4/5} for the whole of looking for and learning {something} is recollection.

Call this second aspect of the Doctrine of Recollection just "Recollection."

---

[17] See Nehamas (1985) 9–10 (= Nehamas [1999] 8–9).

[18] Or divinely inspired: see Bluck (1961) on θεῖοι in 81b1.

[19] The indirect discourse construction is discontinued after 81b6. Vlastos (1965) 161–63 = (1995) 161–63 argues that the Pythagoreans did not have Recollection, although they had Reincarnation; cf. Kahn (2001) 51.

The verb here translated "recollect," ἀναμιμνήσκεσθαι, is the passive of a verb meaning "to remind one of."[20] It will occasionally be helpful to remember this.

It is in Recollection that we get whatever it is that constitutes Socrates' reply to Meno's Paradox. Unfortunately, all Socrates says by way of direct comment on (MP) is that the argument would make us lazy (81d5–e2), which tells us nothing about where that argument goes wrong.

Let us first see what Recollection amounts to, and then come back to (MP).

9.4.1. Recollection

According to this aspect of (DR), most if not all of what we call "learning" is not really learning but recollecting. So Socrates puts it in the speech just quoted (see 81d2–3, 4–5), and so it appears consistently in the sequel (82b6–7, e4–6 with 12–13): he is not analyzing "learn" but showing that what we call "learning" is not learning at all.

Socrates does not say so but it looks as if not *all* of what we call "learning" is really recollecting. The byplay in 81e–82a, where Meno asks Socrates to teach him the truth of (DR), and Socrates alleges that Meno is trying to catch him in a contradiction, makes it sound as if Socrates is committed to denying the existence of any learning (81e4) or teaching (82a1–2) at all.[21] But what Socrates says in 81d4–5 is that "the whole of *looking for something* and learning it is recollection." Not all learning is the consequence of a search: reading the newspaper does not require asking questions, throwing out proposals, and refuting them. And it is easy enough to imagine someone just stumbling over the fact that there is an infinity of prime numbers: he happens to notice that if you multiply together all the primes up to any given prime and add one, you get a number whose smallest prime factor must be larger than any of those you started with. Anyway, Meno's Paradox does not cover all learning, but only learning that comes of looking

---

[20] LSJ suggest that the verb can, in the passive, mean "remember." But Aristotle distinguishes μνημονεύειν ("remember") from ἀναμιμνήσκεσθαι ("recall" or "recollect") in ways that make the latter sound episodic where the former is dispositional (*De Memoria* 2. 451ᵃ31–ᵇ6: cf. Bergemann [1895] 339 ff., Ross [1955a] 243 *ad* 451ᵃ18–ᵇ10, Sorabji [1972] 92). Plato may have a similar distinction: cf. *Philebus* 34a–c, and perhaps *Phaedo* 73e1–4.

[21] Calvert (1974) 147 apparently takes this passage as supporting the position that all learning is written off to Recollection. But he also cites 81d, quoted immediately below, to the same effect, and that is not what it says.

for it.[22] There remains room for learning something just by seeing its truth.[23]

In fact, if we take what Socrates says in 81c–e at face value, there *must* still be room for some learning: Socrates makes the foundation for our recollecting things in this life our having *learned* those things, indeed, *all* things, in previous lives (81c7, d1). If the soul has learned all things in previous lives, it cannot have done so every time by asking about them beforehand, since every time that occurs, Meno's Paradox applies: this would put us on an infinite regress of acts of nominal learning.

There is a difficulty. While 81c–e unambiguously commits Socrates to the idea that the soul has learned all that it knows in previous lives, in 86ab he appears to be arguing that the soul is always, "for all time" (τὸν ἀεὶ χρόνον, 86a8, 9), describable as "having learned" (μεμαθηκυῖα, 86a8).[24] Pretty clearly one of these passages has to be discounted.

The later one, 86ab, certainly gives a more satisfactory view, just because it does not require us to suppose that the soul ever really learns anything: the soul comes prefabricated with knowledge of everything. But it seems to be the weaker passage. For it still describes the soul as having learned, and then we must ask *when* it did this learning. Besides, whatever argument there is in that passage is pretty weak: taken as an argument for the conclusion that the soul can always be described as "having learned," Socrates simply begs the question. And, last, he doesn't seem to think the matter is of much importance: nothing comes of the supposed conclusion that the soul has for all time been in a state of having learned. Socrates is mainly concerned to urge on Meno the practical consequence that we should pursue our inquiries and not get hung up on Meno's Paradox.

At any rate, we have not yet arrived at 86ab: back here at 81c–e there is not the slightest hint that the soul has forever been describable as "having learned"; rather, Socrates is explicitly saying that the soul learns things in earlier lives. And that means that there must be, to salvage Socrates' position, some knowledge acquisition that is not Recollection.

This is not a distinction between the sorts of things about which knowledge can be acquired: Socrates leaves no room for such a distinction, and

---

[22] So also Moravcsik (1970) 54.

[23] I am here in partial agreement with Phillips (1948/49) (in the reprint of 1965) 79, but my distinction between learning by asking and learning by just seeing is not one between the a priori and empirical realms.

[24] Scott (1995) 16 n. 2, 34 leans on this latter passage and dismisses 81c–e.

81cd is insistent that the doctrine covers everything that is learned. Later, after he has illustrated how Recollection works in the sub-dialogue with Meno's slave, on a geometrical problem, he will say that his procedure generalizes to "every {part} of geometry,[25] and all other subjects of study {τῶν ἄλλων μαθημάτων ἁπάντων}"[26] (85e2–3). It is the same things that are now recollected that were in earlier lives learned, and those things are simply whatever there is to be known: "the truth of the things that are" (86b1).

The resulting position is not an altogether comfortable one for Socrates to be in. The priests, priestesses, and poets from whom Socrates derives Reincarnation may not have had Recollection, but they did occasionally profess to recollect things. Empedocles, from whom we have the most material on Reincarnation,[27] says:[28]

> For I have already come-to-be a boy and a girl and
> a shrub and a bird as well as a traveling jumping fish.[29]

He is here recollecting fairly low-level stuff. Empedocles would have known that he was a boy, or a girl, in pretty much the way we all know we are boys and girls. It is less clear how birds and jumping fish know that they are birds and jumping fish, or even whether they do, and totally unclear how Empedocles could ever have become aware that he was a shrub. But one supposes that something like the use of senses is involved. Similarly, Socrates' introduction of Recollection on the basis of Reincarnation speaks only of the soul "having seen all things" (81c6–7), and so having learned them (c7, d1), and so now being able to recollect them (c7–9). If this is all there is to it, the position is very shaky. Why appeal to previous lives? Why shouldn't I learn things in this life by seeing them? The trouble with Reincarnation as a basis for Recollection is that previous lives, for all Socrates here says, are too much like this one: whatever obstacles there are

---

[25] 85e2 πάσης γεωμετρίας: so translated by Sharples (1985) 79. Alternatively: "all geometry," but cf. Bluck (1961) 313 *ad* e1.

[26] Scott (1987) 352 paraphrases μαθήματα as "scientific disciplines . . . of which geometry is a paradigm example"; he apparently thinks that this restricts the scope of Recollection to "*a priori* truths" (351). But it is not so that μαθήματα are restricted to a priori disciplines (*pace* Bluck [1961] 313 *ad* e2): in *Laches* 180a2, for example, Lysimachus, speaking of fighting in armor, asks for advice "about this study" (περὶ τούτου τοῦ μαθήματος). Socrates has said nothing in the *Meno* to invest the term with any more exalted sense than that.

[27] Conveniently collected in Kirk, Raven, and Schofield (1983) 314–21.

[28] DK 31B117, I 359.1–2 = Kirk, Raven, and Schofield (1983) 319 t417.

[29] In DK 31B137 (I 367.16–20 = Kirk, Raven, and Schofield [1983] 319 t415), it sounds as if Empedocles is using Reincarnation as a reason for prohibiting animal sacrifice and meateating (so, e.g., Kirk, Raven, and Schofield [1983] 320). Given the shrub of 117, it is difficult to see what he could have eaten.

in this life to learning things, there were in those lives also. So it is hard to see how the (DR) package explains anything, and, a fortiori, hard to see how it might dispose of Meno's Paradox.

The picture of Recollection based on Reincarnation is quite misleading: as if, in a previous life, I watched them bury the treasure under the old oak tree, and now all I have to do is recall that. But what we are supposed to be able to recall, if Socrates is still on target, is the answer to the question "what is excellence?" How could I have learned this in a previous life? Not by watching people bury things under oak trees. Nor could I have learned that the side of a square double in area to a given square is the diagonal of the given square in that way, and that is the piece of mathematics that Socrates is about to use to illustrate Recollection.

What we look for, but do not find here in the *Meno*, is a sharp distinction between the conditions of life as we know it and the conditions of life in which the soul can learn things: perhaps in a discarnate state, as in the *Phaedrus* (245c–249d). But, although nothing is said that sounds like that in the *Meno*, we shall soon see that Socrates might be prepared to introduce some modifications, here in the *Meno* (see below on 85d–86a), and again in the *Phaedo*.

9.4.2. *Meno's Paradox, II*

All we have is a distinction between two ways of coming by knowledge: by learning it in the first place, and by recollecting it later, which people also call "learning," although that is not really what it is.

That, since it is all we have, has to be enough to dispose of Meno's Paradox. But a glance at that paradox shows that to apply Recollection to it requires answering a further question: does a person who has not yet recollected something know it, or not?

In 81c9 Socrates says that the soul can recollect "what it knew before"; this makes it sound as if the soul does not know it again until it has recollected it.[30] And this is the way it is in the sequel:[31] in the dialogue we are about to get between Socrates and the slave boy, the latter is characterized outright as not knowing the answer to Socrates' question, although he thinks he

---

[30] If Socrates had employed the analysis of "learning" as "coming to know" that he employs elsewhere (*Euthydemus* 277b6–7, 277e5–278a1, *Gorgias* 454c–e, *Theaetetus* 209e2–210a1) in the *Meno*, this would have given him trouble: he would have to say that most of the cases we think of as learning, i.e., as coming to know, are not really cases of coming to know, and that would involve one's first not knowing something and then knowing it without ever coming to know it. I suspect he would simply have modified the analysis of "learn" to "come to know for the first time."

[31] See Vlastos (1965) 153 n. 14 = Vlastos (1995) 155 n. 14.

does (82e5–9), and he is so characterized repeatedly (84a4–b1, b3–4, b10–11, c5, 85c2, c6–7, 86b2–3).[32] So, whatever the temptations are to speak of the boy's "latently knowing" or "tacitly knowing" in this connection, they did not get to Socrates.[33] He just has the soul formerly knowing and now not knowing, but able to recollect (see further § 9.4.3.2).

Socrates is attacking (C), the claim that one cannot try to get to know what one doesn't know.[34] He must be saying: one *can* look for what one doesn't know, *provided* it is something one used to know, so that one can recollect it. Then he appears to be accepting the argument down to (3): he appears to be conceding that *x* does not know what he is looking for: that is, that *x* is looking for *y*, and *x* does not know *y*. Then he is rejecting (4): *x* can look for something *y* where he does not know *y*, provided he used to know *y*.

What made (4) seem right, on this analysis, is that if one knew nothing whatever about *y*, one would never be able to tell when one had stumbled on it. This is now false: even though one does not know *y* now, the fact that one knew it before means that one should be able to recognize it when one encounters it again; that may be enough to remind one of what one knew.

9.4.3. 81e–86c: Recollection illustrated

Socrates has said nothing to support the claims of the Doctrine of Recollection, and as far as Reincarnation goes, he is not going to say anything on this occasion.[35] But he stages a micro-mini-Socratic dialogue with a slave boy of Meno's,[36] which he thinks shows or at least illustrates[37] the truth of Recollection.

---

[32] On 85d6–7, d9–10, see § 9.4.3.2 *ad fin.*

[33] They did get to Bluck (1961) 8–9, 272. He does not cite a text to show that this is Socrates' view of the matter; rather, he tells us what Plato "had to show": that "we have *latent* knowledge" (8–9). Socrates says nothing to indicate that he has to show this; Bluck is deducing what the text must be saying, not telling us what it in fact says. Bluck is followed by Calvert (1974) 146–47.

[34] It looks as if Socrates is accepting the argument for the claim that it is impossible to try to get to know what one knows; at least, nothing he says touches that argument. If he were prepared to say that one latently knows what one learned in previous lives, that claim would need to be reexamined.

[35] Vlastos (1965) 165–67 = (1995) 164–65: it is a matter of Plato's personal religious faith. But arguments are offered for it in the *Phaedo*, where Recollection is taken to provide some indirect support for Reincarnation (cf. 72e3–73a3, 76c–e; but contrast 77a–c).

[36] Cf. Slings (1999) 138–41.

[37] Notice Socrates' reservations about the argument in 86bc; on the scope of those reservations see Bluck (1961) 11–12, 317, Gulley (1962) 22–23, Sharples (1985) 156–57.

9.4.3.1. 82b–85b: the dialogue with Meno's slave

This is not a definition dialogue, although it is devoted to a question that can be construed as a "what is X?" question.

Socrates draws a square, presumably in the sand at their feet, with two transversals that bisect the sides of the square;[38] he supposes each side to be two feet long; the transversals then mark out lengths of one foot on the sides, and make subsequent calculations more obvious.[39] The whole then has an area of four square feet:[40] the boy works this out (82b–d). Socrates (82de) gets him to imagine another square with twice the area, namely eight square feet, and asks him how long[41] its side will be. The question is easily rewritten as a "what is X?" question: "what is the length of the side of a square double in area to a square on a side two feet long?"[42] And the slave boy's first shot is: "double the side of the given square."

Socrates refutes this by drawing a square whose side is twice that of the one he started with; this is not twice but four times the original area: sixteen square feet rather than eight (82e–83c).

So Socrates asks for another answer. He does some prompting: he makes it plain that what is wanted is a line longer than the two-foot side of the original square but shorter than the four-foot side of the quadruple square (83c–e). The slave boy comes up with: three feet (e1–2).[43] Socrates duly extends the sides of the original by a foot each to get a square whose area is nine square feet, rather than the required eight (83e).

So Socrates asks for another answer (83e11). He suggests that, in the absence of a numerical answer – the numerical answers having been exhausted (see n. 43) – the slave boy just try to point to a line that would give

---

[38] This is the traditional interpretation: cf. Bluck (1961) 294. But it is disputable: Boter (1988) argues that the lines are diagonals, and I am at least partly convinced. Sharples (1989) and Fowler (1990) defend the traditional reading, but do not completely rule out Boter's. It seems to me that nothing substantive turns on this, but see Boter (1988) 213–15.

[39] Assuming that they are there in the first place: see n. 38; cf. Bluck (1961) 294 *ad* 82c2, 299 *ad* 83b3, 302 *ad* 83e6 *ad fin.*, and Brown (1967/68) 61 = Brown (1971) 204.

[40] The Greek just has "four feet": see Bluck (1961) 295 *ad* 82c5, Sharples (1985) 150 *ad* c6.

[41] 82d8 πηλίκη τις: curiously, πηλίκος is used just three times in all of Plato: here, at 83e1, and at 85a4.

[42] It was just put in the form of a "what-is-it?" question in 82e1–2. See also Brown (1967/68) 202 with n. *: Brown originally wanted to construe 82d8 (see n. 41 above) and 83e1 as "what-is-it?" questions, but was persuaded that he could not count 83e1; he seems to think he can still count 82d8 as of the form "what-is-it?" because of 82e1–2. If he does think that, he is in error: the interrogative in 82d8 is still πηλίκη.

[43] In fact, as long as he is confined to numerical answers, this is the only one available to him: see Fowler (1987) 226–70 = Fowler (1999) 227–68. For Greek mathematicians of this period, the only number between two and four was three; and the correct numerical answer, namely $\sqrt{8} = 2 \times \sqrt{2} = 2.8284\ldots$, is not even rational, much less integral.

the desired area (e11–84a1).[44] This time, the boy just confesses he doesn't know (84a1–2).

Socrates starts again from the original square, and adds three more equal to it to get the quadruple square again; he then draws in the diagonals to form an inner square composed of four triangles each of which is half one of the four squares; the slave-boy sees that this must be double the area of each of those squares, and so that the side of a square double the area of a given square is the diagonal of the given square (84d–85b).

9.4.3.2. *82e, 84a–d, 85b–86c: Socrates' commentary*

The dialogue with the slave boy does not by itself tell us how we should see it as illustrating Recollection; Socrates tries to tell us this along the way and at the end.

After the boy's first incorrect answer, he points out to Meno and to the rest of us that the boy doesn't know the answer but thinks he does (82e). After the next, when the boy has confessed he doesn't know, Socrates points out that the boy is in a state of perplexity like Meno's own earlier one (cf. 84bc with 80ab), and he persuades Meno that this is an improvement over their initial confidence.

In 82e12–13, after the first wrong answer and before its refutation, Socrates says we are to see the boy "recollecting in order {ἀναμιμνῃσκόμενον ἐφεξῆς}, as one ought to recollect." It is foggy what "recollecting in order" refers to. The slave boy recollects the following, in this order: that the answer "four feet" (double the side of the original square) is wrong, that the answer "three feet" is wrong, and finally that the answer "the diagonal of the original square" is right. Each of these acts of Recollection requires an argument.

At the beginning of the enterprise, Socrates had asked us to attend to the question whether the slave boy was recollecting (being reminded) or learning from Socrates himself (82b6–8); in 82e4–5, he alleges that he has not been teaching the boy, since everything had been put in the form of a question; after the refutation of the second wrong answer, before the construction of the correct answer, he warns us again to watch to see that he is not teaching the boy but asking him for his beliefs (84d1–2; see also 83d1–2).

---

[44] He says "on which {line does the eight-foot area come-to-be} {ἀπὸ ποίας}? Try to tell us exactly; and if you don't want to count, at least point out on which {line} {ἀπὸ ποίας}." (1) The use of ἀπό is presumably the same as that in Euclid, e.g., II 2 (vol. I 69.4 in Heiberg/Stamatis [1969/77]): such-and-such is equal in area "to the square on the whole line" (τῷ ἀπὸ τῆς ὅλης τετραγώνῳ). (2) ποῖα just means "which": this is not the use in which it contrasts with τί ἐστι in 71b3–4, *pace* Brown (1967/68) 64 = Brown (1971) 207–8 and Bedu-Addo (1983) 236–37: see 82e5–6 (see also Sharples (1985) 151).

It is this last fact that is critical for Socrates' case: the boy never responds with something he does not believe. We read (85b8–c8):

SOC: How does it seem to you, Meno? Did he reply with any belief that is not his own?
{c} MENO: No, rather his own.
SOC: And yet he did not know, as we said a little before.
MENO: You're speaking the truth.
SOC: But these beliefs were present in him; or not?
MENO: Yes.
SOC: Therefore in one who does not know about whatever {things} he does not know true beliefs are present about the things he doesn't know?[45]
MENO: It appears.

This is difficult. The true belief at which the slave boy has arrived is that the side of a square double the area of a given square is equal to the diagonal of the given square. Socrates is telling us that some true belief was in this boy in advance. He cannot be saying that the boy believed all along that the double square has the diagonal for its side. When he says the true belief was present in the boy, either he does not take this to entail that the boy believed it, or, if he does mean that the boy believed it, he does not mean the true belief to be that the side of the double square is the diagonal.

Let us consider the second option first: the true belief that the boy has is not the belief that the side of the double square is the diagonal, but something else: that belief, or rather those beliefs, from which it follows that the side of the double square is the diagonal. If we look back at 84d–85b, we find the boy claiming or conceding the following:

(B1)   It is possible to add to the original square three squares equal to it to form a new square (84d4–8).
∴ (B2) The resulting square is four times the area of the original (d8–e2).
(B3)   There is a line from corner to opposite corner (call it the "diagonal," 85b4–5)[46] of each of the smaller squares (84e4–85a1).

---

[45] 85c6–7 τῷ οὐκ εἰδότι ἄρα περὶ ὧν ἂν μὴ εἰδῇ ἔνεισιν ἀληθεῖς δόξαι περὶ τούτων ὧν οὐκ οἶδε; Bluck (1961) 311 defends this text, not very convincingly, and gives an ungrammatical translation. Thompson (1901) 244 is more plausible. There is no good reason to doubt the text: it is, for whatever reason or for no reason, repetitive.

[46] This says "The sophists call this {a} diagonal" (καλοῦσιν δέ γε ταύτην διάμετρον οἱ σοφισταί). Brown (1967/68) 71–73 = Brown (1971) 217–19 jumps on the word "sophists" as further support for his view that the construction of the correct answer in 84de was intended by Plato to be sophistical. But, of course, the word "sophist" by itself just means "sage, wise man"; it does not automatically carry a pejorative sense, even in Plato (cf., e.g., *Cratylus* 403e4).

(B4) Each diagonal is equal to any other diagonal,[47] and they enclose a square (85a2–3; call the square the "square on the diagonal").

(B5) Each diagonal cuts off half of one of the smaller squares (a5–6).

(B6) There are four such half-squares in the square on the diagonal (a7).

(B7) There are two such half-squares in the original square (a8).

(B8) Four is double two (a8–9).

(B9) The original square is (by hypothesis) four {square} feet.

∴ (B10) The square on the diagonal is eight {square} feet (a9–b1).

∴ (B11) The side of a square double the area of a given square is the diagonal of the given square.

These are most if not all of the (relevant) true beliefs the boy has by the time he has recollected. We are supposing that he has some of these true beliefs in advance. To get to these, we must prune the above list. It should in the end include only those claims that the boy makes or grants straight off, without their being deductive consequences of previous claims: (B2), (B10), and (B11), for example, would then be crossed off. The hypothetical (B9) should also presumably go: nobody need actually believe that the original square has any particular area. The residue is to be the rock-bottom store of true beliefs on the basis of which the boy comes to recollect that the double square is the square on the diagonal.

Clearly the most that Socrates could claim is that those seven or eight (or however many remain after pruning) beliefs were beliefs the boy had, in the sense that he believed those things, before beginning the process of Recollection. But even this seems too strong: there is really no clear sense in which we can say that the boy believed, before seeing the diagram, that the diagonals of the original square and its replicas formed a new square, as

---

[47] Thompson (1901) *ad* 85a: "Euclid would have thought it necessary to prove the equality of the diagonals." And, of course, Euclid would have been right. Plainly Socrates does not want the mathematics to take up so much space that it overwhelms the main point. But for Brown (1967/68) 67 = Brown (1971) 211–12, the failure to prove the equality of the diagonals is further proof that Socrates disapproves of the whole procedure.

Brown (1967/68) 67–70 = Brown (1971) 211–15 also makes much of the occurrences of γίγνονται, "come-to-be," in 85a2–3 in which the diagonals are said to "come-to-be" equal. This shows, Brown thinks, that the construction of the correct answer in this section of the sub-dialogue (84de) is no longer focused on *being*, as was the initial stretch of the sub-dialogue (82b–84d), but has degenerated into consideration of coming-to-be. It seems he has missed the occurrences of γίγνεσθαι in 82d2 (*bis*), d3, d5, e6, 83a1, a5, b1, b5, e5, e7, and e10. The uses of γίγνεσθαι in the final stretch (84d8, e2, e3, 85a2, a3, b1, b6) are simply continuations of the preceding. There is not the slightest reason for singling out those in 85a2–3. (Bedu-Addo [1983] 238–39 notices one of the earlier occurrences, 83a5, and rejects Brown's cleavage between the initial and final stretches of the sub-dialogue.)

in (B4). Rather, he is led by Socrates' questions and diagrams to consider the claim that they do form a square, and sees immediately that this claim is true.

The slave boy's situation is fairly accurately described by Socrates' next comment (85c9-d1):

And now these beliefs have been stirred up, on the spot {ἄρτι}, as if in a dream; while if someone asks him these same things many times and in many ways, you know {οἶσθ'} that he will finally know {ἐπιστήσεται} about these {things} less accurately than no one.

There is room for error here, but one natural way of taking Socrates' claim in c9–10 that "these beliefs have been stirred up on the spot" is that the slave boy only just came to believe these things.

But whatever beliefs they were, they were "in him" all along (c4, c6); this is unavoidable: it is simply what Socrates says. At this rate, it cannot be that they were in him as things that he believed. They come from him only in the sense that, once he considers the questions they answer, he has no need of anyone else's help: he can see, by himself, the truth of the matter.

And then, despite the air of paradox about it, our first alternative was better: the boy has in him beliefs to the effect that so-and-so and such-and-such, but that does not mean that he believed that so-and-so or such-and-such. And we might as well say that about all the relevant beliefs, including (B11): the belief that the side of the double square is the diagonal was a belief in him, although he didn't believe that the side of the double square is the diagonal.

This may bring out better what Socrates meant in 82e12–13 when he predicted that the slave boy would be seen recollecting (being reminded of) things "in order." Once he has been brought to a state of self-conscious ignorance, perplexity, he is ready for the right answer. But it is essential that the questions be put to him in the right order: at the beginning of the final ascent, the boy is in no position to answer the question "what is the length of the side of the double square?" but by the end of it he can answer that question, and it is because the intervening questions, to which (B1)–(B10) are the answers, are presented to him in the right order. He would not be able to see, by himself, the truth of the matter if he did not ask himself the questions in the right order.

Somewhat similar comments are called for in connection with what Socrates says about knowledge: once the boy has had these same questions asked of him in different ways, he will know them as well as anybody (85c10–d1, just quoted). The clear implication is that he does not know them yet, but will then know them. That is precisely what Socrates says: "he will know {ἐπιστήσεται}, . . . he himself having got back the knowledge from himself" (85d3–4), and "getting back knowledge in oneself" is recollecting (d6–7). In 85d9 (cf. d12) Socrates speaks of "the knowledge which he now has." A moment ago (c10–d1) he said that the boy *will* know, after the questions have been put to him repeatedly and variously. He will repeat in 86b2–3 the claim made over and over that we do not know before we have recollected. So, *if* Socrates' position is consistent, it must be that the claim

> (K1) The boy has the knowledge that the diagonal is the side of the double square,

to which he is committed in 85d9 and d12, does not contradict

> (K2) The boy does not know that the diagonal is the side of the double square,

which he has said many times. It must be that the boy has the knowledge that S (that the diagonal is the side of the double square) without knowing that S, just as he had the belief that S without believing that S. Indeed, in d12 Socrates is prepared to say that the boy is a *knower*, although he does not know these things. The knowledge, just as the belief, is there in him.[48] It is not that there is a difference of content between the knowledge and the belief. The boy has in him the belief that the side of the double square is the diagonal in the sense that, once he is asked questions in the right order, he will be able to say, on his own, that it is; the knowledge is in him in the sense that, once he has answered these questions, put in different ways, a number of times, he will know that it is.

The knowledge in question is that the diagonal is the side of the double square; the belief in question is the same thing. One way to put it would be: what is in the boy is the truth that the diagonal is the side of the double square: that is in him, although, before today, he was not aware of it, and neither knew nor believed that the side of the double square was the

---

[48] Vlastos (1965) 153 n. 14 = (1995) 155 n. 14 says, of 85d6–7: "The received translations . . . put Plato in the position of saying that the subject already *has* the knowledge he recollects, thus flatly contradicting his earlier assurances that the boy did *not* know, and still does not know, the theorem he has discovered, but has only a true belief of it (85c2–10)." This is incautious: Vlastos seems to be committing himself to saying that Plato would deny that the boy has the knowledge, and then a reference to 85d9 or d12 shows him wrong. White (1974/75) 304 n. 27 refers to these passages, rejects Vlastos's apparent position, and says that when Socrates denies earlier that the slave boy knows he "is obviously speaking in accordance with ordinary usage." Then is he "speaking in accordance with ordinary usage" in 86b2–3? (White apparently thinks that 86b1–2 commits Socrates to the claim that the boy already knows, although that is not what it says, and is contradicted in the immediately following lines.)

diagonal. And this is the way Socrates formulates his doctrine in 86b1–2: "the truth of the things that are is always present in the soul."

In this formulation, the truth/belief/knowledge that is in the boy's soul is "always" in it: what is the force of this?

Socrates has in fact argued for the "always" in 85d–86a. He began with a disjunction (85d9–11): either the boy at some time (ποτε) acquired the knowledge that he now has or he has always had it. If he acquired it at some time, Socrates continues (d12–13),[49] it wasn't in the present life. He confirms that it was not in this life that he learned the truth of geometry under discussion in d13–e6, by a curious argument: if the boy acquired the knowledge that the diagonal is the side of the double square in this life, say by being taught it, then, since he has the same ability to recollect with regard to every other theorem of geometry and, indeed, with regard to any study whatever, he would have had to have been taught everything there is to know. So Socrates asks Meno if anyone has taught the boy everything there is to know, and Meno replies that no one has.[50]

Still, the boy has those beliefs (85e7–8); if he didn't acquire them in this life, he must have "learned" (ἐμεμαθήκει) them at another time (e9–86a1) when he was not a man (86a3–5); so, since "for all time" (τὸν πάντα χρόνον) he either is or isn't a man (a9–10), his soul "always" (τὸν ἀεὶ χρόνον) will be in a state of having learned (μεμαθηκυῖα ἔσται: a8–9).

The whole argument looks like this (using "b" for the boy's soul and "S" for the truth he possesses):

(1) Either b acquired S at some time t or b always had S.

(2) b acquired S at $t \rightarrow t$ was not in this life.

∴ (3) b acquired S at $t \rightarrow t$ was when b was not a man.

∴ (4) At any time at which b is not a man, b has S.

(5) At any time at which b is a man, b has S.

(6) At any given time, either b is a man or b is not a man.

∴ (7) b has S at all times.

A lot needs filling in.

Let us grant Socrates (2): the odd argument for it (85de) is not very good, but nothing very interesting comes of analyzing it further.

---

[49] He first says, in d12, "Then if he always had it, he was also always a knower"; but this plays no further role in the argument.

[50] It is my impression that this stretch of argument is universally ignored. The analysis in Jowett (1953) I 251 would lead one to suppose that all Socrates asked was whether anyone had taught the boy geometry, as would, e.g., Cherniss (1937) 498 = (1977) 262 n. 3: "Socrates asks (85 d–e) whether anyone had taught the slave geometry." Socrates' final question is not that, but whether anyone has taught the boy *everything*.

In 86a3–4 he goes from (2) to (3). That presupposes one of two things.

First, at any time at which the boy's soul was not in this life, that soul was not the soul of a man. This would mean that Reincarnation was effectively scrapped.[51] Nothing was said in 81a–e about whether animals were involved in Reincarnation, but the one piece of poetry Socrates cites (81b8–c4) seems to involve the souls of men being reborn as men, and that this could happen is, of course, common stuff among those who take Reincarnation seriously, including Plato himself elsewhere (*Phaedrus* 249b, *Republic* X 618a). So there were times when the boy's soul was not in this life but when it was nonetheless the soul of another man. So (a) seems pretty unlikely.

We have already (§ 9.4) seen that Reincarnation is a lousy basis for Recollection. And the outcome of the present argument may well be to scrap it as a basis for Recollection anyway. But it is odd if Socrates is just quietly assuming it away, and even odder if the way he assumes it away is by denying that the soul can be the soul of a man more than once. So perhaps the other option is preferable, as follows.

Second, any other human life will present us with the same situation we have now with the slave boy: at any given time, any human being is in a position to be reminded that the side of the double square is the diagonal, that the perpendicular bisectors of the sides of a triangle meet in a point, and so on for all of geometry, and so on for all that can be known. This comprehensiveness of what can be recollected was supposed to show us that the slave boy can't have learned his stuff in this life; it shows also that no human being can have learned his stuff in a human life.

This is a lot of arguing to be simply presupposed, but, perhaps, it is less implausible than the first option. Even if it is, it must be noted that it still requires scrapping at least part of the picture Socrates had given us under Reincarnation. There the idea was that the soul had lived enough lives that it has, over time, seen everything, and so learned everything (81c5–7). What forces us to conclude that the slave boy has not been taught that the side of the double square is the diagonal is the consideration that he is situated with regard to every truth in the same way as he is with regard to this one. It is nonsense to suppose that someone has taught him everything. So it is no good supposing that someone has taught him this random geometrical theorem. But this consideration is null and void if we have Reincarnation to work with: he could have been born indefinitely many times and have been taught everything. That, indeed, is just what

---

[51] See Sharples (1985) 147–49 on the unclarity of the *Meno* as to the origin of the knowledge that is to be recollected.

Socrates had said. He is, for reasons he has not expressed, no longer allowing that. So at least part of the picture Reincarnation gave us has been painted out.

Some of the picture might be left: we might now suppose that, although the fact of incarnation as a human being requires the soul to have all truth embedded in it already, that is not true of incarnation as something else: we might have acquired our knowledge that the side of the double square is the diagonal when we were shrubs, or jumping fish. We might even suppose that our knowledge was acquired when we were not incarnate at all: this would square with the sort of thing we get in the *Phaedo* and especially the *Phaedrus*, but it would involve even further departure from the picture we got from Socrates under Reincarnation; there nothing whatever was said or implied about the soul's ability to do things when discarnate. But still, there would be a point left for Reincarnation to make in connection with Recollection: our ability to recollect would still be dependent on the fact that our souls exist before incarnation in human form.

Lines (4) and (5) are presented together as the antecedent of a conditional (86a6–7) whose consequent is (7); (6) appears in 86a9–10 as the basis for the implication. The logic is impeccable: given (4) and (5), (6) is an instance of the Law of Excluded Middle, and (7) follows. But there are problems at both ends.

We can give Socrates (5): at any time at which the soul is incarnated as a human being, S is there in it, in the sense that the man would assent to S if it were presented to him in an orderly way. (We just ignore the period when the human being is an infant, and not yet in a position to assent to any geometry at all.)

But where does (4) come from? Socrates makes it sound as if it follows from (3), which immediately precedes it in the text. But this is partly due to the peculiar wording Socrates has for (3): he says, in 85e9–86a1, that if the boy did not acquire his stock of truths in this life, it follows that "he had them and *had learned them* in another time." Now what actually follows is just that either he had them for all time or he acquired them at some time previous to this life. If the latter alternative is correct, and the boy acquired them at some time t_1 previous to this life, it will follow that at any time t_2 between t_1 and the beginning of this life the boy's soul "had them and had learned them." But it is not true that he "had learned them" at t_1: that is *when* he learned them. So (4) does not follow, and cannot be made to follow.

But Socrates cannot get (7) without (4). So his argument cannot be made to work.

Still, its conclusion is (7): the soul is for all time in possession of its stock of truths. If Socrates accepts it, it makes Reincarnation completely irrelevant. That the slave boy's soul has been incarnated before plays no role whatever in Recollection. The most that remains is not Reincarnation but simply Incarnation: the soul has to have existed before its Incarnation in this body. It may or may not have existed in other bodies; in any case, it did not learn what it knows in other incarnations, or even when it was (if it was) discarnate, for it never learned them at all: it is forever in a state of having learned.

So Socrates has given us an unsalvageable argument for a conclusion that undermines the position he began with (in 81a ff.). At 86b1–c2 he adverts to the hortatory consideration that Meno's Paradox would make one "lazy" so that it is better to think it possible to find out what we don't know, and says he will stick to this consideration in favor of the Doctrine of Recollection no matter what; he apparently has reservations about some of the other points. Later, after referring once more to Recollection (98a), he says (98b1): "And yet I too am not speaking as one who knows, but as making a conjecture {εἰκάζων}." Regrettably, he says nothing that focuses his reservations,[52] and so there is no saying whether his reservations at this point are significantly related to mine.

9.5. 86C–100C: THE METHOD OF HYPOTHESIS AND THE TEACHABILITY OF EXCELLENCE

The remainder of the dialogue reverts to the opening question, whether excellence is teachable. That it does this is surprising: something grievous has plainly befallen the Intellectualist Assumption. But Socrates provides us with a method to apply in such circumstances; he describes the method, and then applies it. But then he rejects the results of the enterprise, and in the course of doing that, rejects (SP2).

9.5.1. 86c–e: the Intellectualist Assumption

Socrates has spent the last five pages convincing Meno that it is possible to seek out answers to "what is it?" questions. Meno has even said that

---

[52] For stabs in the dark, see Thompson (1901) 144 (he is uncertain about myths) and Brown (1967/68) 74, 76 (esp. n. 32: sophistry), revised in Brown (1971) 220, 222 but essentially the same. Bluck (1961) 318 (he doesn't think he has established immortality, reincarnation, or recollection), Gulley (1962) 22–23 (Plato is tentative about his theory of knowledge), Klein (1965) 182–83, and Sharples (1985) 156–57 are less specific, as, I think, one must be.

he is convinced (86c3). And yet the dialogue does not go on to face that question; Socrates wants to, but Meno wants to take up the initial question whether excellence is teachable (86cd). Socrates should, given everything he has said so far, protest that this is impossible. He does not. He states a strong preference for settling what excellence is first (86d3–6), but goes on (d8–e1):

I'll give in to you – for what is one to do? – so it seems we are to examine of what sort something is {ποιόν τί ἐστιν} about which we don't yet know what it is {ὅτι ἐστίν}.

The Intellectualist Assumption said that this could not be done, not just that it would be better not to do it. So (IA) has been sacrificed.

9.5.2. 86e–87b: the Method of Hypothesis

The death of (IA) has not rendered Socrates speechless. Indeed, he now thinks there is a way of handling questions as to what sort something is in the absence of an answer to the question what it is, and he now sketches that method. He says it will involve examining excellence "from a hypothesis" (ἐξ ὑποθέσεως, 86e3) to see whether it is teachable. Regrettably, he provides no second-order description of this method, but only an example (in 86e–87b), drawn from the method's source, geometry, and the example is obscure and much disputed.[53] It would do us no good to discuss it in detail here. The upshot, however the example works, is relatively clear.

The geometrical question is whether a certain area can be inscribed in a circle as a triangle (for short, just "is inscribable"); the method consists in laying down a certain hypothesis about the area. I shall summarize this hypothesis as:

(H) The area is Φ.

We may think of this as: the area is not too big; any area that is not too big can be so inscribed, although, for small areas, the resulting triangle is likely to look quite anorexic.

We are aiming, then, at a requirement to the following effect:

(R) The area is inscribable ↔ the area is Φ.

---

[53] The version I favor is that first propounded in English, apparently, in Butcher (1888) (Bluck [1961] 441 says he was anticipated "by E. F. August in his edition of Euclid's *Elements* in 1829"), and elaborated by Cook Wilson (1903), followed by Knorr (1986) 71–74 and Menn (2002) 209–11. See reviews of the literature on this problem in Bluck (1961) 441–61, Sharples (1985) 158–60.

Nothing is said in Socrates' exposition of the example as to how to determine that the area is F; the truth of the conditional "if (H), then the area
is inscribable" is plain even if we do not know how to determine that. Of
course, if the method is to produce results – to tell us whether some particular area is in fact inscribable in some particular circle as a triangle – it must
at some point get back to a hypothesis we can verify. But the application of
the method cannot presuppose that we *will* get back to such a hypothesis.

9.5.3. 87b–89c: application of the method; excellence is teachable

Socrates looks for a hypothesis on which to base the examination of
the question whether excellence is teachable; something that satisfies the
requirement

(Re) Excellence is teachable ↔ excellence is *F*.

In 87b6–c1, he nominates "knowledge" for *F*.

A glance forward to c5–6 shows that he does not intend an *identification*
of excellence and knowledge; the hypothesis is not "excellence is the same
as knowledge," but "excellence is *a* knowledge" (ἐπιστήμη τις); in more
natural English:

(H1) Excellence is a kind of knowledge.[54]

In 87c, Socrates commits himself to two claims:

(1) If excellence is not knowledge, it is not teachable; and
(2) If excellence is knowledge, it is teachable.

The second claim is not billed as an inference from anything that precedes:
there are no inferential particles in c5.[55] This is as well: it does not follow
from anything that precedes.

In any case, our hypothesis is (H1), and (1) and (2) tell us that excellence
is teachable if and only if (H1) is true, so (Re) is satisfied. The next question
is whether (H1) is true (87c11–d1). Socrates argues that it is. The argument
is unbelievably complex. This is because it is not, in fact, one argument:

---

[54] Robinson (1953) finds a number of difficulties with the idea that (H1) is the hypothesis here; he
thinks none of them decisive, and finally adopts that idea (120), but only with reluctance ("in spite
of these serious objections," 120). Stokes (1963) 297 finds the arguments "overwhelming." Robinson's
own replies to them are pretty flimsy. Many of them turn on the assumption that there can be only
one hypothesis, and that looks simply false.

[55] So also Bluck (1961) 326 *ad* c5, followed by Sharples (1985) 162 *ad* 87c1–6.

there are several arguments intertwined here. And once more, this is not the time to disentangle things; fortunately the overall outline is again clear.

Socrates proposes a new hypothesis (87d2–3):

(H2) Excellence is a good {thing}.

We have encountered claims like this before, starting in § 4.3.2.1, where Socrates employed the "Virtue Assumption," as we called it:

(VAt) Temperance is admirable.

But here "virtue" ("excellence"), the abstract noun associated with "good" (ἀγαθός: see 87d8–e1), is itself the subject instead of "temperance" or "courage," and the predicate is "good" rather than "admirable." So (H2) is a case of self-predication, and we might naturally suppose that it is here associated with a Transmission Theory of Causality. It will shortly turn out that it is.

Plainly, if Socrates could show that everything good is a case of knowledge, he could get from (H2) to the conclusion that excellence is a knowledge. That, it may seem, would be too much to show. But that is what he proposes to do in 87d4–8, and it is not the only time Socrates had tried to show it. In the *Euthydemus*, in an argument reminiscent of the present one (278e–282d), Socrates had claimed that it followed that (281e3–5):

none of the other things {*sc.* wealth, health, beauty, temperance, justice, courage, etc.: cf. 279b} is either good or bad, but . . . wisdom is good and ignorance is bad.

And that, to make a long and difficult story short, is what he sets out to do: to establish

(3) If anything is good, it is a case of knowledge.

The longer version of the story would have to take into account the fact that "good" is replaced in the argument by "beneficial" (see 87e): that is, that (3) actually occurs in the form

(3′) If anything is beneficial, it is a case of knowledge.

And the longer version would also have to take into account the fact that a great deal of the apparatus Socrates introduces along the way is never put to any use. The crucial point is that, as Socrates sees it, excellence is not merely sometimes good (beneficial) and sometimes not, as other states of a person are, but is good (beneficial) without qualification, *necessarily* good or beneficial, as he puts it in 88c5. And that is where the Transmission Theory kicks in: it is going to tell us that if anything causes other things to be good (beneficial) it must itself be good, and have no admixture of the opposite. And then Socrates takes it that the only thing that can cause a state of a person to count as good is knowledge (88b). So, given the way in which knowledge is good, namely, through and through good, as being the cause of everything else's being good, it must be that excellence, which is what (trivially) makes something good, is itself a case of knowledge. And that establishes (H1) on the basis of (H2), and we are home: excellence is teachable.

This sketch of Socrates' argument makes it look pretty poor. So I should add two things. First, a longer and fully formalized version can be constructed according to which it is valid, but still poor, since it depends on some quite implausible assumptions. And second, Socrates does not himself accept the conclusion: it emerges in the sequel that he thinks something *other* than knowledge is capable of making things good, namely, true belief.

This makes for a certain degree of disappointment. The Method of Hypothesis was introduced as a way of getting at answers to questions as to what sort of thing x is – e.g., whether excellence is teachable – without having an answer to the question what x is. And the net effect of all this is that we still do not know whether excellence is teachable.

9.6. THE METAPHYSICS OF THE MENO

The Theory of Forms does not inform the *Meno*. One might suppose that it comes in at the point at which the Transmission Theory of Causality is invoked. But it needn't, for, although the Transmission Theory of Causality is, unavoidably, a piece of metaphysics, it is not the Theory of Forms, as we've already seen.

In 88ab Socrates and Meno affirm that there are such things as temperance, justice, courage, readiness to learn, memory, magnificence. They are not described as forms, but as "{things} pertinent to the soul" (τὰ κατὰ τὴν ψυχήν, 88c6) that are in themselves neither beneficial nor harmful, but become beneficial with the addition of knowledge. Nothing is done to signal to us that they have any special ontological status.

But there are a few things that point toward the Forms.

As already noted (§ 9.2.1.2), Socrates' attacks on definitions in the *Meno* focus on the *unity* of the *definiendum*. And perhaps this goes with a tendency to think of the *definiendum* as some sort of unitary object, by contrast with its instances.

Also: we've seen Socrates referring to the object of his quest in answering a "what is X?" question as a *form* (εἶδος). By itself this is of no great significance. But once the Doctrine of Recollection is in place, it begins to be significant. For that doctrine is supposed to tell us how we can go about answering "what is X?" questions: by recollecting the answer, which we've already got, having learned it prenatally. If the exposition of the Doctrine of Recollection is to connect up with the definition dialogue with which the *Meno* opens, it must be that what is recollected is a form. So a form is going to have to be something with which we can be in prenatal contact.

Last, in the course of propounding the Doctrine of Recollection, Socrates makes a curious claim at 81c9–d4:

> For since all nature is akin, and the soul has learned all things, nothing prevents one, once having recollected just one {thing} – which men call learning – finding out all others as well, if one is courageous and does not shrink from looking for {them}.

Just what does Socrates mean to be getting out of the idea that "all nature is akin" (τῆς φύσεως ἁπάσης συγγενοῦς οὔσης) here?

The "kinship of all nature" is supposed to make it possible, once one has recollected one thing, to go on to recollect everything else. So all the things that can be recollected are akin to each other, and recollecting one thing is a model that can be followed in recollecting others. If what is recollected must be a form, perhaps what Socrates is saying is that the kinship of these forms to each other makes them susceptible to approach by a single strategy, and again, if his comment here has any bearing on the sequel, perhaps that single strategy is the Method of Hypothesis.[56]

Socrates does not say any of these things; they are, rather, conjectures based on what he does say.[57] Things will be less conjectural when we turn to the *Phaedo*. At this point, we have not been given the – or, for that matter, any – Theory of Forms. We have the word "form," the implication that it is what is to be recollected, some inconclusive and conflicting comments about when the original acquisition of knowledge took place, and a couple of educated guesses as to where Socrates might be headed. If the *Phaedo* had never been written, the views we are going to encounter in it could not have been reconstructed from the *Meno* and its predecessors.

---

[56] This owes a lot to Tigner (1970) 4.

[57] If there is any cash value at all in comments such as that in Levinson (1953) 149 n. 29: "The ideas are not here referred to as such, though they are clearly implied," it is here. But I have not seen the "clear implication" spelled out anywhere.

PART III

Platonic Forms

CHAPTER 10

Phaedo *64–66: enter the Forms*

In every dialogue apart from the *Parmenides* in which the Theory of Forms puts in an appearance, the main topic is something else. In the *Phaedo* it is immortality: the Forms are used in three arguments for the immortality of the soul. But they make a separate entrance before that.

10.1. 64C: AN EXISTENTIAL ADMISSION

Socrates defends his readiness to die beginning with the question (64c2) "do we think there is such a thing as death?" (ἡγούμεθά τι τὸν θάνατον εἶναι;). He immediately says what death is (c4–5): "the release of the soul from the body" or the "coming-to-be in separation" of soul and body (c5–8). He now argues that the philosopher, whom he portrays as ascetic, is engaging in separating his soul from his body (64c–69e).

Socrates' question at 64c2 concerns an existential claim to which Simmias' assent commits him. It is, once again, a topic-fixer: Simmias is only conceding that people sometimes die; he is not committed by his concession to the Theory of Forms. It is a clear implication of 105d9, d13–14, etc., that there is a Form for death. But it is only in retrospect that we can say: in 64c, Simmias had already acknowledged the existence of the Form, Death; that is like saying that someone who has acknowledged the existence of the number 13 has committed himself to the existence of a prime number, or to the existence of a positive root of the equation "$845 + 1183x - 96x^2 = 0$." He has, but there is no reason to suppose he knows it.

A page later, the situation is somewhat different.

10.2. 65A–66A: THE FORMS AND THE SENSES

Here Socrates is trying to persuade us that, when it comes to gaining knowledge, the body only gets in the way. The centerpiece of his case is this (65d4–66a10):

Do we say that there is something itself just {τι . . . δίκαιον αὐτό}, or nothing?
Of course we say {there is}, by Zeus.
{d7} And again something beautiful and good {καλόν . . . τι καὶ ἀγαθόν}?
How not?
{d9} Now then, have you ever seen any of such things with your eyes?
In no way, he said.
{d11/12} But have you made contact with them by any other perception among those that run through the body? And I am speaking about all: e.g., about largeness, health, strength {μεγέθους πέρι, ὑγιείας, ἰσχύος}, and, in a word, about the substance of all the others, what each in fact is;[1] is it through the body that the most true of them[2] is contemplated, or is it rather as follows: whichever of us prepares best and most accurately to think that itself about which he is considering will come nearest to knowing each thing?
Certainly.
{e7/8} Then he could do this most purely who came to each thing as much as possible with his thought itself, neither applying sight[3] in his thinking nor dragging in any other perception along with his reasoning, but, using pure thought itself by itself, tried to hunt each thing, pure, itself by itself, being detached as much as possible from eyes and ears and practically from his whole body, since it confuses the soul and does not allow it to acquire truth and intelligence when it communicates with {the body}? Isn't it this one, Simmias, if anyone, who will encounter that which is?
{66a9/10} How magnificently, said Simmias, you are speaking the truth, Socrates.

Are we getting the Theory of Forms here? Do we have anything more than we have already encountered in the Socratic dialogues?

The existence claims of 65de are nothing new; even the use of the intensive "itself" (αὐτό) is familiar from the Socratic dialogues.[4] The Theory of Forms will come in explicitly later (72 and ff.), so it would be best if we could read Simmias here as assenting to home truths and nothing stronger.[5]

---

[1] 65d13–e1 τῶν ἄλλων ἑνὶ λόγῳ ἁπάντων τῆς οὐσίας ὃ τυγχάνει ἕκαστον ὄν: for the construction, see Burnet (1911) 34, Gallop (1975) 227 n. 7, Rowe (1993) 141.

[2] 65e1–2 αὐτῶν τὸ ἀληθέστατον: see Gallop (1975) 227 n. 8, rejecting Hackforth's "the full truth of them," and Bluck's "the truth about them"; Gallop himself translates (p. 10) "their truest element," and I do not see what that is supposed to mean. Perhaps Plato is hearing ἀ-ληθής in its etymological sense of "unconcealed," and is here talking about those Forms contemplated with the greatest clarity.

[3] 65e8 τὴν ὄψιν: the reading of the MSS, restored in Duke et al. (1995) (Burnet [1900/1907] had printed τιν᾽ ὄψιν, against which see Gallop [1975] 227 n. 9).

[4] So also Wieland (1982) 133–34.

[5] This assumes that Burnet (1911) 33 *ad* 65d4, 34 *ad* d6 is wrong in treating Simmias as an adept in the theory. See below on Simmias. Generally I am in agreement with Rowe (1993) 140–41, but Rowe ignores what I shall shortly be calling the "Imperceptibility Thesis."

But we cannot quite do that; there is one thing Socrates says, to which Simmias readily assents, for which nothing before has prepared us. He asks (65d9) whether Simmias has *seen* these things, and Simmias unhesitatingly says he has not (d10). Socrates then generalizes the question (d11–12): has Simmias perceived them by means of the body at all? He plainly expects the same unhesitating assent, and does not even wait for it.

So here are the beginnings of a theory:

(TF1) The things about which Socrates has been asking "what is it?" exist; and

(TF2) The things about which Socrates has been asking "what is it?" are not perceptible.

It is (TF2) – I'll call it the "Imperceptibility Thesis" – that makes this a theory: the things about which Socrates has been asking are to be distinguished from, detached from, or even "separated" from perceptible things.[6] And it is something distinctive to the *Phaedo*, by contrast with the Socratic dialogues. The Imperceptibility Thesis is really the tip of an iceberg: it is thematic in the whole of the *Phaedo* that the senses are to be condemned. There has been nothing about this in all the dialogues to date.[7]

The new element in the *Phaedo* is the condemnation of the senses. If we look back at Aristotle's account of the development of Plato's views (§ 1.2), and suppose that Aristotle is right in what he says, we could say: this distinctive element is Plato's contribution; it is not a part, but an extension of the Socratic heritage.

I am not concerned so much with history as with logic. Aristotle's report, I bet, is correct, and the previous dialogues were in some sense truer to the historical Socrates than the *Phaedo* is; others disagree. But it is enough to say: the dialogues down to this point do not indulge in the condemnation of the senses seen here, and this squares with what Aristotle says about the development of Plato's views out of those of Socrates. Whether this is correct as history is a question on which we can, if we have to, agree to differ.

---

[6] Wieland (1982) 136 would interpret an assertion that appears to imply the existence of separate forms as picturesque language, "a mere means of illustration . . . of which one makes use if one does not wish to renounce assertions altogether" (*ein bloßes Veranschaulichungsmittel . . . dessen man sich bedient, wenn man auf Aussagen nicht überhaupt verzichten will*). It is not at all clear to me what this picturesque language is supposed to be expressing, and I do not see how to read (TF2) as a "a means of illustration" of anything whatever.

[7] Even the *Gorgias*, which is as insistent on the difference of the soul and the body as the *Phaedo*, contains no hint to the effect that the senses are to be condemned: see 523a and ff. It is interesting that the first dialogue to contain the word ὁρατόν, "visible," is the *Phaedo*.

10.3. SIMMIAS' AGREEMENT

It is surprising that Simmias assents to the Imperceptibility Thesis so readily. Perhaps it is not so surprising for the first entries on Socrates' list: it is hard to think what it could mean to say that the just and the good were perceptible to the senses. The beautiful can, arguably, be assimilated to these by the same technique Diotima describes to Socrates in the *Symposium*: if we notice the *generality* of the notion of καλόν, which covers not just visible, bodily, things, but also laws, theories, and so on, we will see that beauty cannot simply be seen, or heard, or, in general, perceived by the senses (see *Hippias Major* 298b, where, perhaps, this is being suggested; see also 298cd, where it seems to be retracted).

But one of the things that Socrates says is inaccessible to the senses is largeness (μέγεθος), and another is strength (ἰσχύς): on the face of it, these are perceptible properties of things. We could, perhaps, run a gambit parallel to that just run for beauty for these as well: among the things that count as "large" there are not just big people, or tall people (the word μέγας, "large," can when used of people bear the sense "tall," as later in the *Phaedo*, in 102b and ff.), but big noises, big questions, and so on.[8] And it is not just bodies that are strong, but currents, tastes, points, and so on.[9] But when Socrates makes the largeness (tallness) of Phaedo and Simmias a Form later on, there is not the slightest hint that he is trading off the multiplicity of contexts in which "large" (or "tall") can be used, and strength is never treated as having such a plurality of contexts.

But then largeness (tallness) is just the kind of thing Phaedo possesses and Socrates does not, and you can tell by looking that that is so.

And if that is so, putting tallness and strength in the same bag with beauty and justice, as Socrates does, shows that he is not relying on the special content of any of these terms as founding his claim that they are not perceptible by the senses: it is not just the fact that the justice of a person, or of an action, is not a visible, audible, etc. property of the person or action that makes the object to which Socrates refers as "something itself just" not visible or audible or perceptible by any other sense. For it is a parallel fact about tallness that it is not visible. But, on the face of it, the tallness of a building *is* a visible property of that building.

Then Socrates has something else up his sleeve by way of justifying the Imperceptibility Thesis. He does not at this point say what. He will: it is

---

[8] See LSJ *s.v.*   [9] Again, see LSJ *s.v.*

the Argument from Relativity. But Simmias' assent, in the absence of a statement of that argument, is surprising.

According to one standard view of the dialogue, and of Simmias and Cebes in particular (see n. 5 above), Simmias' assent is not so surprising, because he knows all about the Theory of Forms already. But, if Simmias is an adept in Platonic metaphysics, he is a very stupid one: in 73a he cannot even remember the argument for the Doctrine of Recollection, and in 85d–86e he puts forward as at least plausible a view about the soul (that it is an attunement of the body) that is incompatible with the Doctrine of Recollection (see 91e–92e), which has by that time already been proved to his satisfaction (76e–77a). Again, if he is an adept, Socrates treats him as a stupid one: Socrates is shortly (74a–c) going to find it necessary to rehearse the Argument from Relativity for the existence of Forms.[10]

Simmias and Cebes are plainly part of the Socratic circle: they are mentioned at *Crito* 45b4–5[11] among those prepared to put up money for Socrates' release or escape from prison; Xenophon (*Memorabilia* I 2. 48) mentions them among the associates of Socrates; Diogenes Laertius (II 124–25) groups them with the Socratics.

We might suppose, then, that Simmias recognizes in the references to "something just, something beautiful, and something good" the things for which Socrates is constantly seeking definitions; there is no more difficulty in conceding their existence here than there would have been in the Socratic dialogues. The claim that they are not accessible to the senses suggests more. But anyone who had got beyond the initial definitions in the definition dialogues might be prepared for this generalization, although he might not be in a position to give a general argument for it. Perhaps Simmias is being portrayed as just such a person.

With this in mind, one might try looking back to the Socratic dialogues to see if there is any material there on which Socrates might now be drawing to get the conclusion that largeness is not visible, audible, or accessible to the senses in any way.

There is one passage that suggests an argument for this conclusion: *Protagoras* 356cd. There Socrates says (c5–6): "The same largenesses (τὰ αὐτὰ μεγέθη) appear to our sight to be larger nearby, smaller far away," and he goes on (c6–7) to make parallel points for thicknesses (τὰ παχέα) and "the many" (τὰ πολλά): thicknesses close by will seem thicker, ones

---

[10] Much of what I say here is in agreement with Grube (1935) 291–94.

[11] Simmias is also mentioned at *Phaedrus* 242b3, but that only says he produced a fantastic number of λόγοι (see Hackforth [1952] 54, Rowe [1986] 164). Cebes and Simmias are both mentioned in *Letter* XIII 363a, but all that is said about them is that they appear in the *Phaedo*.

farther away thinner; a plurality of objects close by will seem to contain more objects than one farther away. Perhaps this is the sort of argument Socrates has at the back of his mind in *Phaedo* 65de.

There are two difficulties. First, *Protagoras* 356 does not sound anywhere nearly as drastic as *Phaedo* 65: Socrates does not in the *Protagoras* say anything like "so largeness is not perceptible to the senses."[12] It would be nice to have something that explicit, if the point is to be one familiar to Socrates' interlocutors. Second, we can look forward to the *Republic* to see what kind of thing Socrates will produce to support the sort of claim he makes in *Phaedo* 65de: in VII 523e–524a he claims that sight does not adequately see largeness and smallness, and he has just (523b5–7) dismissed "things that appear from far off" as support for his claim. He means, he says, that sight tells us that the same thing is at the same time both large and small, even if it is seen from close by (523c8). Presumably this is because one and the same thing will appear large relative to one thing and small relative to another.

This is the *Republic*, not the *Phaedo*; it is possible that, at the stage of the *Phaedo*, Plato has not yet distinguished the distance and the relativity cases of the same thing's being both large and small as clearly as he is going to do in the *Republic*, so that he is prepared to think of *Protagoras* 356 as feeding into his conclusion. But later in the *Phaedo* it will become plain that relativity considerations are the primary ones at work: so even if he has not distinguished them from distance cases, they must be given greater emphasis.

Can such considerations be operating as early as 65de? I suppose they must be. Socrates is then, perhaps, being portrayed as thinking that anyone who had realized that the same girl would be beautiful in one context but ugly in another would have to know that her beauty was not something that could be simply seen, like her hair color; that the fact that gold was beautiful in some contexts and not in others showed that its beauty was not something that could be simply seen, like its color; and so on. And the same consideration works as well with her size: that she is large for a woman does not make her large for a human being, or large in comparison with a building. So her largeness too is not something that can be simply seen.

But these considerations are not made explicit this early in the dialogue. And that leaves us a little in the dark still about Simmias' ready assent to the Imperceptibility Thesis.

[12] Cf. Taylor (1976) 191.

10.4. THE EASE OF FORGETTING THE DISTINCTION

The language in which the theory is couched does not always point unambiguously toward the Forms. We have just heard the Form for justice referred to as "something itself just" (65d4–5), that for beauty as "something beautiful" and that for goodness as "good" (65d7), and those for largeness, health, and strength referred to by just these abstract nouns. We shall soon be encountering the generically abstract noun phrase "the equal" as a way of referring to the Form for equality.

We can see how tricky the language can be by looking forward to 69–72 and its aftermath.

Cebes finds Socrates' defense of his complacency in the face of death satisfying except on one point: most people are not as convinced as Socrates is that the soul is immortal (69e–70a). This sets the theme for the rest of the dialogue: Socrates will undertake to prove[13] that the soul is immortal. His first attempt, standardly referred to as the "Cyclical Argument" (69e–72e), is to the effect that contraries come-to-be from contraries, so that the living come-to-be from the dead, so there must be souls waiting for birth.

The major premise of the Cyclical Argument is stated as "contraries come-to-be from their contraries" (70e1–2); this is illustrated with the beautiful and the ugly (e2–3: articles in the Greek), just and unjust (e3: articles omitted), something larger and smaller (e6–71a2), the weaker and stronger, the swifter and slower (71a3–5), something worse and better, and more just and more unjust (a6–8). In 71a9–10 the premise is repeated as "the contrary things come-to-be from contraries" (ἐξ ἐναντίων τὰ ἐναντία πράγματα, *sc.* γίγνεται).

The claim that the beautiful is contrary to the ugly, in isolation, could be read as an assertion about the Form, The Beautiful. But the question is whether it comes-to-be from its opposite, the ugly, and we shall eventually find that Forms cannot come-to-be at all. So this occurrence of "the beautiful" does not refer to a Form, and neither does "the weaker" in 71a3.

---

[13] He suggests that he and the others might "discuss" these issues: the verb is διαμυθολογῶμεν (70b6), which has "μῦθος" in its root; the latter word is sometimes contrasted with λόγος, the latter meaning something like "rational account" and the former meaning something like "story," "tale," or even "myth." See Gallop (1975) 15 and 228 n. 15. But in none of its three occurrences in Plato need διαμυθολογεῖν have anything to do with myths or stories; it need mean nothing more than "discuss." See its occurrence in Aeschylus, *Prometheus Bound* 889, cited by LSJ *s.v.*; they offer "communicate by word of mouth, express in speech" as paraphrases, and David Grene, in Grene and Lattimore (1959) I 343, translates the whole phrase γλώσσᾳ διεμυθολόγησεν "gave it tongue." In any case, the language of demonstration will be used by Socrates of what he is doing before he is done: see ἀποδεικνύναι in 77a5, b3, c2 (cf. c3 προσαποδεῖξαι), c6, d4, 87a4, c4, 88b5, and, finally, 105e8.

They must, rather, be ways of referring to *things* that are beautiful and weaker. And Socrates actually employs a word for "things," πράγματα, in 71a10.

The occurrence of πρᾶγμα does not by itself show that it is not Forms that are being discussed: the Forms were called "the things themselves" (αὐτὰ τὰ πράγματα) in 66e1–2.[14] It is rather the context together with some advance knowledge we have from later in the *Phaedo* (103a–c). There Socrates is discussing how Forms are immune from infection by their opposites. But he encounters some resistance from an anonymous interlocutor who, according to Socrates, fails to distinguish the claim that the contrary *thing* (τὸ ἐναντίον πρᾶγμα, 103b3) comes-to-be from its contrary from the claim that the contrary *itself* (αὐτὸ τὸ ἐναντίον, b4) comes-to-be from its contrary: it was the former, he says, that was being affirmed in the Cyclical Argument, but it is the latter that is being denied in 103.

So the generically abstract expression "the large" may refer to the Form, or to the things that have the Form, and confusion can result where this is not clear. Back in 64–66, the distinction is implicitly drawn: there nothing was actually said using "the large" and "the just," and nothing was said about the difference between "something just" and "largeness" on the one hand and large things and just people on the other, but there is going to have to be a difference, if the former are not available to the senses, since the latter plainly are. When we get to 70–71, where Socrates is making the claim to which the anonymous interlocutor has adverted, the distinction has yet to be brought into the open. So his confusion is not unnatural. In order to see his own way clear of it, he would have had to synthesize the claim of 70–71 with the results of 64–66, once the distinction implicit in the latter passage has been brought out as it is in 74, to which we now turn.

---

[14] See also the discussion of *Protagoras* 330b–e in § 3.2.1.

CHAPTER II

Phaedo 72–78: the Forms and Recollection

In the *Phaedo* even more than in the *Meno*, it is important to bear in mind that what we are calling "recollection" is actually a three-termed affair: it is a matter of *x*'s being reminded *by y* of *z*; the term occupying the "*y*" position acquires importance in the *Phaedo*.

II.I. 72–73: RECOLLECTION AGAIN

Socrates concludes the Cyclical Argument by saying that there really is such a thing as coming-to-life-again (ἀναβιώσκεσθαι): the living come-to-be from the dead and the souls of the dead continue to exist (72d8–10). The next argument is to have the same conclusion.

It is Cebes who sets it going by adverting to the Doctrine of Recollection, which, he says (72e2–3), Socrates has often propounded. The Theory of Forms is also presented as something often propounded by Socrates. But in the case of the Forms, we can see how the Theory is a natural extension of what Socrates had been saying in the Socratic dialogues, whereas Recollection is a drastic innovation.

As Cebes states it, it is that "learning for us is nothing but being-reminded {ἀνάμνησις}" (72e3–4). So learning isn't that for others. In the next clause (e4–5), he says that what we now recollect we must have learned at some prior time, and he adds (73a1–2) that this must have been before the soul was "in human form" (τῷ ἀνθρωπίνῳ εἴδει). By "for us," then, we can take him to mean "for us, in human form"; the others who learn without recollecting are ourselves in some other form.

But then Cebes either did not hear an exposition of the Doctrine in which Socrates went on to claim, as he did in the *Meno*, that the soul must always have had the knowledge it now recollects, or he did not understand that part of the exposition any better than we did, and dropped it in favor of the more picturesque view with which Socrates started in the *Meno*, that the soul learned its stuff earlier in its career. This view surfaces again later (76c4), but there is no trace of the view that the soul possessed its knowledge from all eternity.

Simmias, it turns out (73a4–6), is not as familiar with the Doctrine as Cebes is – anyway, he cannot remember by what arguments the Doctrine is established. Cebes and then Socrates in turn help him out.

In 73ab Cebes helps by adverting to argument with which we are familiar from the *Meno*. Cebes was not present at the meeting of Socrates and Meno's slave, so we are to suppose that he heard Socrates' exposition of this argument on another of the many occasions on which, he alleges, Socrates gave voice to it. In favor of Recollection, Cebes adverts to the success that ensues when one asks questions in the right way (73a7–9), and to the efficacy of visual aids (a10–b1).[1]

Socrates introduces his aid for Simmias by recalling the formulation of the Doctrine of Recollection as it appeared in the *Meno*: "what is called learning is being-reminded" (73b5); it is not that learning *consists* in recollecting, but that (at least much of) what we think of as learning is *not* learning, but recalling things we have forgotten. But the argument we are about to get for the doctrine here is, according to Socrates himself (73b3–4, above) different from that in the *Meno*. It is, in fact, so different that it could make for a difference in the doctrine.

One obvious difference between the account of the doctrine here and that in the *Meno* is that the argument Socrates here gives connects Recollection with the Theory of Forms. That difference is the one that is ultimately important, and it does not constitute a difference in the Doctrine of Recollection, but an expansion of it.

On the standard account of the matter,[2] hereafter the "Standard Interpretation," there is another difference. Here, it is said, we are to be shown that what we think of as learning which things are, and which are not, equal to which, is really a matter of getting those things to remind one of the equal: that is, of a Form. On this reading, Socrates is applying Recollection to situations of alleged "learning" that are very different from those in focus in the *Meno*. There the slave boy was already in possession of the various

---

[1] It isn't clear from what he says whether we should count these considerations as two aspects of a single argument or as two arguments: Bury (1906) 13 and Burnet (1911) 52 *ad* a7 opt for two, Verdenius (1958) 208 *ad* a10 (and cf. *ad* a7), Gallop (1975) 19, 228–229 n. 19, and Rowe (1993) 164 for one. It makes no difference here.

[2] See, e.g., Archer-Hind (1894) 33–34, Burnet (1911) 55–56, Taylor (1926) 187, Cornford (1935) 108, Gulley (1954) 197–200, Bluck (1955) 63, Hackforth (1955) 75–76, Gulley (1962) 31–32, Ackrill (1973) 192 = (1997) 28–29, Gallop (1975) 115, 119–21, 129, Dorter (1982) 56–57, Bostock (1986) 66–71. *Per contra*, see Scott (1987) 353–59, (1995) sec. I: I am mostly in agreement with Scott, despite Williams (2002).

concepts he would need to understand the argument; what he was doing was entering on the stage of knowing a certain geometrical truth involving those concepts, and that required recollecting. Here in the *Phaedo*, the mere possession of a concept – if this interpretation were right – would require its possessor already to have done some recollecting. This constitutes, not an expansion of the Doctrine of Recollection as we saw it in the *Meno*, but a difference in the doctrine itself.

I think this interpretation is not right, although there is a grain of truth in it. In the *Meno*, we were presented with a situation in which, we should have said, a boy learns a geometrical truth: that the side of a square double in area to a given square is the same length as the diagonal of the given square. Here in the *Phaedo* we are homing in on a situation in which a single concept, *the equal*, is at stake.

But this difference goes with the fact that Socrates is concerned in the *Phaedo* with connecting Recollection with the Theory of Forms. What was recollected in the *Meno* was: that the side of a square twice the area of a given square is the diagonal of the given square, while here in the *Phaedo* it is: the Form, the equal itself. But in one dimension, this difference is not as great as it looks. For it will emerge that recollecting the equal itself is not a prerequisite for employing the word "equal," but for saying what the equal itself is, making a claim of the form "the equal is . . .," parallel to the claim at stake in the *Meno* that the side of a certain square is . . ..

We should hope that the Standard Interpretation is wrong, for if it is correct, Cebes' reference in 73ab to experiments like that undertaken in the *Meno* is of no clear relevance, and Socrates' express intent in 73b to argue for the same view in another way is misguided.

Besides, the Standard Interpretation would make the application of the Doctrine of Recollection to the solution of Meno's Paradox impossible, for that interpretation makes no connection between the doctrine and Socrates' attempt to define things. It will emerge that there is such a connection still in the version of the doctrine we are getting in the *Phaedo*.

II.2. BEING REMINDED OF SOMETHING

Socrates' help for Simmias starts with an analysis of recollection.

II.2.I. *The Prior Knowledge Requirement*

He first gives a necessary condition (73c1–2): "I suppose we agree that if someone is to be reminded of something {τὶ ἀναμνησθήσεται}, he must have known {ἐπίστασθαι} this itself at some time earlier." Let us refer to that as the "Prior Knowledge Requirement":

(PKR) x is reminded by y of z at $t \rightarrow x$ knew z before t.

11.2.2. A sufficient condition for Recollection

Socrates next describes a situation in which, he alleges, someone will be reminded of something by something; this description is plainly supposed to give us a sufficient condition.[3] It reads (73c5–d1):

> Then do we agree on this as well, that whenever knowledge comes on {παραγίγνηται} in the following way, it is being-reminded {ἀνάμνησιν}? In what way do I mean? This. If someone having seen, heard, or got something by any other {means of} perception, not only knows {γνῷ} that, but also thinks of[4] something else, of which the knowledge is not the same but different,[5] wouldn't we justly say in this case that he had been *reminded* of that of which he had {d} got the thought?

There are several clauses involved here. We have someone x (1) *seeing* (or otherwise perceiving) something y, and in the act *knowing* y, and, because of that, (2) *thinking of* something z, where (3) knowing z is not knowing y. The second clause, that x thinks of z, stated that way, is plainly too weak. Socrates in c5–6 made the subject of his question *knowledge* coming about in a certain way, not just *thinking of* something (cf. n. 4), and we shall find in the sequel that the stronger clause is required: not just thinking of something z, but *knowing* something z. In fact, the third clause, in insisting that knowing z is not the same as knowing y, has in effect presupposed the stronger version of (2).

If these clauses are jointly satisfied, Socrates says, x will be reminded of z by y.

We shall have to include a reference to the *time* at which this takes place; then Socrates needs the following conditional, whose conjunctive

---

[3] Gosling (1965) (155; cf. 154–55) lumps the conditions together as giving "the necessary (and also, he {*sc.* Plato} seems to consider, sufficient) conditions for a case of someone's being reminded of one thing by another." But the text distinguishes these conditions: cf. 73c1–2, and then 73c5 ff. (see also Gallop [1975] 115–16). So my analysis of the structure of the argument differs from Gosling's (cf. Gosling [1965] 159, 160). In particular, the talk of likeness turns out to have a much less commanding role to play under my analysis.

[4] 73c9 ἐννοήσῃ: the word ἐννοεῖν covers a broad range, from "understand" to "form a notion of"; LSJ suggest the latter for the translation here and in the sequel. But it is clear from the present context and from the sequel that the verb is a replacement for "know": cf. esp. 74b4–6.

[5] 73c9 οὗ μὴ ἡ αὐτὴ ἐπιστήμη ἀλλ' ἄλλη: reinforcing the point of the preceding note.

antecedent is supposed to be a Sufficient Condition for Recollection (subsequent revisions will remove the "'"):

> (SCR') At t, when perceiving y, x knows y & at t, when perceiving and knowing y, x knows z & knowing $z \neq$ knowing $y \rightarrow x$ is being reminded of z by y at t.

The antecedent, the Sufficient Condition proper, breaks down into three sub-conditions or clauses: the Perceptual Knowledge Clause,

> (PKC) At t, when perceiving y, x knows y,

the Contemporaneous Knowledge Clause (which will be modified twice: hence "''"),

> (CKC'') At t, when perceiving and knowing y, x also knows z,

and the Different Knowledge Clause,

> (DKC') Knowing $z \neq$ knowing y.

The Sufficient Condition (SCR') tells us that if all these clauses are satisfied, we have a case of Recollection:

> (R) x is being reminded of z by y at t.

The Prior Knowledge Requirement carries us from (R) to:

> (C1) x knew z before t.

The conclusions Socrates is ultimately aiming for are (where x will be Simmias and z a Form, the equal itself):

> (C2) x knew z before he was born

and, consequently,

> (C3) x (or, more precisely, x's soul) existed before he was born.

Getting from (C1) to (C2) will require working on the variable "t."

I shall refer to the above argument, down to (C1), as the "Core Argument."

Immediately after Socrates' statement of (SCR'), 73cd as just quoted, Simmias requests clarification (73d2); Socrates offers examples (73d3–74a1). Knowledge of a person and of a lyre are different (73d3–5), but when a lover sees a lyre or a coat that belongs to the one he loves, he "knows" or "recognizes" (ἔγνωσαν, d8) the lyre and in thought gets "the form" or "image" (εἶδος, d9) of the one he loves: "that is being-reminded" (d9–10). "So also one who sees Simmias is often reminded of Cebes" (d10–11). Seeing a portrayed horse or lyre might also remind one of a person (e5–7). And seeing a portrait of Simmias might remind one of Simmias (e9–74a1).

Romeo sees Juliet's lyre, satisfies Socrates' conditions, and so is allegedly reminded of Juliet. In satisfying the conditions, Romeo must, in seeing the lyre, think of Juliet, and that must be a matter of his knowing her; he must, in seeing the lyre, know it; and his knowing Juliet cannot be the same as his knowing the lyre. This all sounds a bit odd. Let us consider it slowly.

11.2.2.1. The Perceptual Knowledge Clause

If we refer to the thing that does the reminding, the lyre, as the "reminder," then, according to the first of our three clauses, Romeo is supposed to see the reminder, and in seeing it, know it. We can give a sense to this: he must know it when he sees it; he must recognize it.[6] In the first instance, that just means knowing that it is Juliet's lyre.

After 73d7, the claim that the man who is reminded of something must know the reminder drops out. This is natural. If I am reminded of you by a raincoat I see and take to be yours, I am reminded of you by that raincoat whether or not it really is yours. If it is not, I only thought I recognized it. So although 73c states the condition as (PKC), all Socrates really uses in the subsequent argument is a weaker condition. But before we formulate that weaker condition, we should take a look at the other illustrations, which make it clearer what sort of condition we need.

In 73d9–10, someone, call him Romeo, is supposed to see Simmias and be reminded of Cebes. Our conditions become: Romeo perceives Simmias and knows him; he thinks of and knows Cebes; and knowing Simmias is not knowing Cebes. Socrates would have it that this is a case of Romeo's being reminded of Cebes.

What would be the force of the requirement that he know Simmias? One first supposes that it is a matter of his recognizing Simmias. But Socrates is not specific about this, and there are alternatives. Someone might perceive Simmias, whom he does not know, but he might know that this man (whoever he is) resembles Cebes, or know that this man is someone with whom he has frequently seen Cebes, or know that he is a lyre player, as is Cebes, or whatever. The essential thing is that he knows something about

---

[6] "Recognizes" would do as a translation for γνῷ in 73c8 (cf. d7; Bluck [1955] 65 so translates it). See here Lyons (1963) 179, 204 (and ch. 6 *passim*); and esp. his comments on the LSJ entry for γιγνώσκω (179 n. 2).

what he is seeing, and his awareness of this feature is what triggers his thinking of Cebes. Let us say: he knows, or recognizes, or becomes aware, that this (which he is seeing) is *F*; it is this awareness that brings Cebes to mind.

In 73e5–6, Romeo is to see a portrayed lyre and be reminded of Juliet. Again, it is not said or even implied that he must recognize the lyre there portrayed to be Juliet's.

In e6–7, he is to see Simmias portrayed and think of Cebes. Socrates does not say that he need recognize who is being portrayed, and the last case will suggest that this is not required.

In 73e9–74a1, Romeo is to see Simmias portrayed, and be reminded of Simmias himself (αὐτοῦ Σιμμίου). One of the conditions in Socrates' package is the Different Knowledge Clause. So we cannot say that here Romeo's knowledge of the thing that reminds him of Simmias is simply his recognition of the man in the portrait as Simmias, for that is just the same knowledge all over again. To get a minimum distance between what Romeo recognizes about the portrait at the reminding end, and the thought of, the "knowledge" of, Simmias at the other end, we might stop at the portrait: Romeo sees that the figure in this portrait looks *so*, and that, he recalls, is what Simmias looks like. Something like that *is* what happens when someone's portrait genuinely reminds you of the person.

Those are the cases. Eventually, we will have Simmias seeing a stick, equal to another stick, and being reminded of a Form called "the equal." To fit the description we are working with, Simmias will have to know that stick, or recognize it. In that case he will be recognizing it as a stick that is equal to another. All these cases can be covered by the general formula offered above: one knows, that is, sees, recognizes, or becomes aware, that *this* is *F*. Then this recognition triggers another thought.

Now suppose we weaken the condition in the way already mentioned, so that knowledge of the reminder is no longer required. We might formulate the result as the Perceptual Uptake Clause:

(PUC) At *t*, *x* perceives *y* and takes it to be *F*.

It is plain that using the weaker (PUC) instead of (PKC) will require modifying the other two conditions to suit. The required modifications will mostly be obvious. These modifications make matters no worse than they are already: the set of modified conditions is sufficient to guarantee recollection if the unmodified set was in the first place. In fact, the modified set is not sufficient, as we shall see, but the original set of conditions was also insufficient for the same reason.

11.2.2.2. The Contemporaneous Knowledge Clause

In our elaboration of Socrates' first example, Romeo, on seeing the lyre, was supposed to think of Juliet. But the second of our three clauses demands more: he is supposed to get some sort of current knowledge of Juliet.

One might think that this clause undergoes some weakening in what Socrates says: he repeatedly speaks, as he did in 73c8 above, of the one doing the recalling simply as "thinking of"[7] that which he recalls; in c9–d1 above, he is said to "get the thought" of what he recalls; in 73d7–8 we read that lovers who see lyres that belong to the object of their affections: "know {ἔγνωσάν} the lyre and in thought get the form {ἐν τῇ διανοίᾳ ἔλαβον τὸ εἶδος}[8] of the boy whose lyre it is." But, once again, we cannot allow Socrates to weaken his claims to that: he had said in c5–6 that he was concerned with *knowledge* coming to us in a certain sort of way, and how we come by knowledge is precisely what he has to explain.

Some of the prima facie oddity of speaking of Romeo's getting knowledge of Juliet when he sees the lyre can be dispelled. Suppose he sees the lyre, and her image comes to mind; suppose the image is a photographically correct one of Juliet. But suppose Romeo does not realize that it is Juliet whose image has come before his mind: he has, let us say, forgotten her, and cannot think who it is whose image has come before his mind. Then he is not reminded of Juliet: for him to be reminded of Juliet, he must know who it is that he is reminded of. And if we lapse into saying just that he must think of Juliet, we must remember that he cannot very well be thinking of her if he doesn't know who he is thinking of.

No doubt further thought would yield cases that show all this a bit too hard-edged. But all we need is the minimal idea that Socrates is prima facie justified in including a rider to the effect that the recollector have some current knowledge of the thing of which he is reminded, in particular, knowledge as to what or who it is of which he is reminded. So, for the sake of clarity, even if it is a trifle too hard-edged, we can make (CKC″) more explicit as follows:

(CKC′) At *t*, when perceiving and knowing *y*, *x* also thinks of *z*, which requires his knowing what *z* is.

---

[7] The verb is ἐννοεῖν: 73c8 (cf. c9), 74a6, b6, c8, d1, d9, etc. It takes sentential complements elsewhere in this passage (as at 74a6), but not here: it is not that Romeo thinks or takes note of the fact that Juliet is good at playing the lyre; he just thinks of or takes note of Juliet.

[8] 73d7: recalling the derivation of εἶδος from *εἴδω, "I see," it might easily be understood here as "visual appearance" or "image"; Bluck (1955) 66 translates the passage "form a mental image of the boy." This is perhaps all right; but his importation of mental images into 74d1 (Bluck [1955] 67) is not. Hare (1964) makes Plato's theory of knowledge too much a matter of calling up mental images (see also Hare [1965] 22–24).

But we must make one further alteration in this clause, consequent upon our relaxing (PKC) to (PUC). Here the modification is obvious; what we want is

(CKC) At t, when perceiving y and taking it to be F, x also thinks of z, which requires his knowing what z is.

11.2.2.3. *The Different Knowledge Clause*

The Sufficient Condition (SCR') includes a clause to the effect that the knowledge of z must be different from the knowledge of the reminder y. The motivation for that might just be that if I see x, think of y, and "know" both, but to know x is *eo ipso* to know y, I am not recalling anything. I am just seeing something, and knowing it. At that rate, there might be little more to the Different Knowledge Clause than the nonidentity of z and y. The examples bear that out: "a knowledge of a person and {that} of a lyre are different" (ἄλλη που ἐπιστήμη ἀνθρώπου καὶ λύρας), Socrates says (73d3–4); so lyres can remind us of people. So can raincoats (73d7). The differences here are not differences of metaphysical station or levels in a hierarchy of cognitive objects.

But perhaps there are cases in which z and y are different but so connected that knowledge of y carries with it knowledge of z. Socrates mentions such a case in 97d, in describing his reaction to his first encounter with the works of Anaxagoras and the claim that mind is the cause of all things; he says he then thought that one should explain things by appealing only to "the best, the most good" (d3–4), but also that (d4–5) "it would be necessary for this same {person} also to know the worse; for there is the same knowledge about them." This comment plays no role in the sequel; it is apparently only an aside. But it illustrates the possibility that, in some cases, even though the objects known are different, there is the same knowledge of them.[9] If one's awareness of goodness causes one to think of badness, Socrates would not necessarily count this as a case of one's being reminded of badness by goodness, for the knowledge of the one carries with it knowledge of the other.

So perhaps we should say that, for (DKC') to be satisfied, not only must the things known be different, the knowledge of the one cannot carry with it the knowledge of the other. This still does not mean that the objects known have to occupy different ranks in the hierarchy of being. In most cases, it will be enough if they are just different; in some, that will not be enough,

---

[9] So Burnet (1911) 54 *ad* 73c8; differently: Hackforth (1955) 67 n. 4, Gallop (1975) 117; cf. Ackrill (1973) 184–85 = Ackrill (1997) 21.

and we shall have to ask whether knowing the one can be disentangled from knowing the other.

When Socrates applies his conditions to show that Simmias is reminded of the equal by sticks and stones, the ontological distance is great. But that distancing is not built into the Different Knowledge Clause.

This point is of importance when we look even farther forward, beyond the *Phaedo*, into the *Republic*. For there (V 476e–479e) it turns out that a Form differs by enough of a world from its participants that we can know only the Form, not the mundane things that partake of it. This thesis is not explicit in the *Phaedo*, and the phrasing of the sufficient condition for recollection makes it clear that it is not implicit either: we *see* sticks and stones, *know* them, and eventually come to a knowledge of the equal; our knowledge of the sticks and stones is not the same as our knowledge of the equal, but it is not so different that it is not *knowledge*.

Phaedo 83ab may point toward the skepticism of the *Republic*. Socrates tells us (a1–3) that the "lovers of learning" (οἱ φιλομαθεῖς) know that the love of wisdom, philosophy (ἡ φιλοσοφία), having taken over a soul imprisoned by desires and perceptions, tries to set it free, and does so (a3–b4)

by pointing out that examination through the eyes is full of deception, and {examination} through the ears and the other perceptions {is full} of deception, and by persuading it to withdraw from these, as far as there is no necessity to use them, but, urging {the soul} to collect and gather itself into itself, and to trust nothing else but itself, whenever, itself by itself, it thinks {one of} the things that are itself by itself; and {by persuading the soul} to think that whatever it examines through other means, which is different in different {contexts} (ἐν ἄλλοις ὂν ἄλλο), is nothing true (μηδὲν . . . ἀληθές); and that this sort of thing is perceptible and visible, while what it itself sees {is} intelligible and unseen.

Whatever the soul contemplates using the senses is not true. At that rate, there can be no knowledge of such things.

Socrates cannot have this clearly in mind back where we are, in 72–76, for it conflicts with his initial formulation of the Perceptual Knowledge Clause. But perhaps he is moving toward it, and that is why the clause is weakened to the Perceptual Uptake Clause.

That weakening has an effect on the Different Knowledge Clause, just as it had on the Contemporaneous Knowledge Clause. The Different Knowledge Clause as it stands insures that, where the other conditions are satisfied, but the knowledge of the reminder carries with it knowledge of the object allegedly recalled, we shall not have to call it recollection. If we weaken (PKC) to (PUC), we shall be considering cases in which there is not necessarily any knowledge of the reminder at all. Then what we want to rule out is cases in which x's merely taking y to be F would carry with it knowledge of the object allegedly recalled: we want not to have to count these cases as cases of being reminded. The clause (DKC′) becomes:

(DKC) Taking y to be F does not carry with it knowing z.

11.2.2.4. *The argument previewed*
So the Sufficient Condition for Recollection becomes:

(SCR) At t, x perceives y and takes it to be F &
 at t, when perceiving y and taking it to be F,
 x also thinks of z, which requires him to know what z is &
 ¬(taking y to be F carries with it knowing z)
 → x is being reminded of z by y at t.

Our forecast of the structure of the argument, then, is this. Someone makes sensory contact with something, say, a stick, and is aware, or thinks he is aware, of a certain feature of it. This makes him think of something else, a Form, and he knows what it is. His awareness of the stick's being whatever he takes it to be does not carry with it knowing the Form. The conditions are satisfied, so he is being reminded of the Form by the stick. But then, by the Prior Knowledge Requirement, he must have known the Form of which he is reminded at some earlier time. That conclusion puts us on the way to showing that our souls must have existed before we were born.

This is what I am calling the "Core Argument."

We must notice that the argument has an obvious hole in it. Fiction has Isaac Newton encountering an apple and thinking of an axiom for mechanics. Suppose that were true, and that what Newton came to see was the truth of that axiom. He fits Socrates' description of a man being reminded of something, namely the axiom. Only he was not reminded of that axiom, because he never knew it until he encountered the apple.[10] We could say: Newton may satisfy Socrates' conditions, and yet not be recalling anything, simply because the Prior Knowledge Requirement need not be satisfied by someone who satisfies those conditions.

It would not help to include the satisfaction of (PKR) among the conditions that guarantee recollection, for the main question for the sake of

[10] In fact, even if he had known it before, he might not be recalling it now: cf. Aristotle, *De Memoria* 2. 451^b6–10.

which Socrates is introducing his conditions would be begged. He is arguing that, *as (SCR) shows*, certain people are reminded of the equal; *then* (PKR) kicks in to show that they must have had prior knowledge of it.

Insisting that people do acquire knowledge in the way that the mythical Newton did would be begging the question against Socrates. But nothing Socrates has said *shows* that people do not acquire knowledge in that way.

II.3. 74A: THE ANCILLARY ARGUMENT, I

In 74a, Socrates is led from the examples we have been considering to a generalization and an associated principle concerning the relationship between reminders and objects recollected (74a2–8):

> Then doesn't it follow, in accordance with all these {cases}, that recollection is sometimes from like {things}, and is sometimes from unlike {things}?
> It follows.
> But whenever someone is reminded of something from the {things} like {it}, isn't it necessary {for him} to undergo this as well: to think {ἐννοεῖν, "notice"} whether this {that reminds him} falls at all short, with respect to its likeness, of that of which he is reminded, or not?
> {It's a} necessity, he said.

We have these Likeness Principles:

(LP1) x may be reminded of z by y whether y is like z or unlike z.
(LP2) x is reminded of z by y & y is like z
$\rightarrow$ x must think or notice whether y is less than exactly like z.

The force of (LP1) must just be that we do not have to have a resemblance between the reminder and the object recollected. The force of (LP2) is somewhat obscure; we shall have to see what use Socrates wants to make of it.

The Core Argument makes no use of these principles.[11] After showing that equal sticks and stones lead Simmias to think of the equal (74a9–c10), Socrates points out that this is true whether the two are like or unlike (74c11–12), and says immediately that it makes no difference: he will be recalling the Form either way (74c13–d2). This appeals to (LP1) but forms no premise in the argument, which would be complete without appealing to either principle.[12]

---

[11] Here I disagree with Gosling (1965) 159, 160, and with Bluck (1955) 62–63, Bluck (1961) 47 and ff.

[12] Archer-Hind (1894) excises the passage running from 74c11–d3: he says that the reintroduction of talk of likeness in that passage is "worse than pointless." But he does seem to think that likeness is involved in the definition of recollection, and I cannot see that.

Socrates does have a use for them: they set up, as we shall see, an Ancillary Argument. But for now he continues with the Core Argument.

II.4. 74A–D: THE COMPLETION OF THE CORE ARGUMENT, I

In (§ 1.2) we looked at the Argument from Relativity (AR). This argument is now to be used to show that the Different Knowledge Clause is satisfied. It will contrast the equal with ordinary equal things: whereas the equal is under no circumstances unequal, ordinary equal things are under certain circumstances unequal (§ 11.4.1.3).

Socrates' way of thinking and talking about equal things is odd. In 75c10–d3 he tells us that he is discussing not just the equal, but The Beautiful itself, The Good itself, etc. It would have been less odd had he run the argument with "beautiful" instead of "equal." For prima facie if you say

(B) This statue is beautiful

you can stop there, while if you say

(E) This stick is equal

you can't: you must go on to say what the stick is equal *to*, at the very least, and presumably also in what *respect* you are claiming it to be equal to that. But here Socrates seems to be assimilating the behavior of "equal" to that of "beautiful."

But in the *Hippias Major*, "beautiful" was *not* what we might call a "stan-dalone" term. Hippias' beautiful girl was beautiful relative to an ape, but ugly relative to a goddess; hence she was both beautiful and ugly. Here Socrates is not so much assimilating "equal" to "beautiful" as assimilating "beautiful" to "equal." But then he expected, in answer to the question "what is the beautiful?" something that was beautiful, full stop. The pre-supposition of his procedure is something like this:

(Rel) Any term that applies to x, y, and z relative to p, q, and r applies to something s full stop.

Then why does Socrates switch from such things as the beautiful, the good, the just, and so on, to the equal? Here is a conjecture.

In the *Laches* (192ab), Socrates switched from the target case of courage to the easier case of quickness to illustrate how definitions should look. Equality, compared to beauty, is also an easy case. In the *Parmenides*, Plato gives two definitions for it: at 140b7–8, the equal is defined as that which has the same number of measures as that to which it is equal, and at 161d4–7, equality is said to be what is intermediate between largeness and smallness.[13] The latter can be rephrased, less puzzlingly, as:

> (DE) The equal (to something y) $=_{df}$ that which is neither larger nor smaller (than y).

Nothing will ultimately turn on the question what definition Socrates or Simmias might actually have had in mind, but it will emerge that the availability of some definition or other is essential, and (DE) will do; in fact, it ties in with other material in the *Phaedo* (e.g., 75c9).[14]

Then why "equal" and not, say, "quick," as in the *Laches*? Here is another conjecture. The word "equal" and its compounds appear fairly often in the fragments of and doxographical material relating to Archytas;[15] they also turn up in what we have pertaining to Philolaus.[16] Simmias and Cebes are portrayed as having studied with Philolaus (61d6–8, e6–7), and even if that does not mean they are Pythagoreans, it means they are familiar with things Pythagorean. Archytas is the Pythagorean whose acquaintance Plato had relatively recently made in Sicily,[17] and who may have had a great deal of influence on him. So perhaps Socrates picks "equal" supposing that it will be an example familiar to Simmias.

11.4.1. 74a–c: ideal and mundane objects

Lines 74a9–c6 read as follows:

> We say, I suppose, that there is[18] an equal {τι εἶναι ἴσον} – I don't mean a stick {equal} to a stick, or a stone to a stone, or any other of such {things}, but something else apart from all those {παρὰ ταῦτα πάντα ἕτερόν τι}, the equal itself {αὐτὸ τὸ ἴσον}; would we say there is something, or not?

---

[13] Brown (1972) 27 refers to these definitions, but his attempt (24–27) to trace these definitions back to pre-*Phaedo* times, in particular to Bryson, won't work: see Döring (1972) 158–59 and Mueller (1982) 148 on Bryson.

[14] See also Archytas DK 47B2 (I 436.8), Philolaus DK 44A13 (I 401.17, 21–22).

[15] Cf. DK 47B1 (I 433.5), B2 (436.8), B3 (437.9, 12), A17 (esp. 429.15–21), A19 *passim*, A23 (430.32), A23a (430.38; on this see Frank [1923] 378–79).

[16] See the fragment of Speusippus' *Philolaic On Pythagorean Numbers*, DK 44A13 (see I 400.24, and then 401.5, 17, 21–22 and *passim*); see also 44B6 (409.7, defended as genuine by Burkert [1972] 250–62 and Huffman [1993] 124).

[17] In *Letter* VII 324a5–6, Plato (?) says that he first went to Sicily when he was about forty years old; later in the letter (338c5–d1, 339b1, d2, 350a6) he mentions Archytas. In two passages Cicero says Plato went to Sicily in order to familiarize himself with Pythagorean views, especially those of Archytas (*De Re Publica*. i.x.16, *De Finibus* v.xxix.87; *Tusculanae Disputationes* i.xvii.39 says the same thing without mentioning Archytas). Cf. Vlastos (1988) 386–87 = (1991) 128–30 (but, in the references in 386 n. 76 = 129 n. 90, for "*Acad.*" read "*Rep.*" and for "350a–b" read "338c–d").

[18] 74a9–10: so Gallop (1975) 10 with 266 n. 5, 21; Kahn (1981b) 110 makes τι εἶναι predicative.

{b1} Surely, by Zeus, we'd say that there is, wondrously.[19]

And do we know it, what it is?

Certainly, he said.

{b4} Having got the knowledge of it from where? Wasn't it from the things we were just now speaking of: having seen sticks or stones of other such equals, we've thought of[20] that, and that is different from them? Or doesn't it show itself[21] to you as different?

{b7} But consider it in this way. Don't equal stones and sticks sometimes, although they are the same, show themselves as equal at one time, and at another {as} not {equal}?[22]

That's certainly so.

{c1} Well then, are there {times} when the equals themselves have shown themselves to you as unequal, or equality as inequality? {αὐτὰ τὰ ἴσα ἔστιν ὅτε ἄνισά σοι ἐφάνη, ἢ ἡ ἰσότης ἀνισότης;}

Never at all, Socrates.

{c4} Therefore, he said, these equals and the equal itself are not the same {οὐ ταὐτὸν ἄρα ἐστίν, ἦ δ' ὅς, ταῦτά τε τὰ ἴσα καὶ αὐτὸ τὸ ἴσον}.

In no way, it's plain to me, Socrates.

There are two issues interwoven in this passage: one has to do with Simmias' knowledge, and the other with the objects of that knowledge. The first three subsections here are concerned with the latter issue, and the next, § II.4.1.4, returns to the question of Simmias' knowledge, definitions, and recollection.

The heart of the passage is the Argument from Relativity. Socrates announces that he is going to distinguish the equal from ordinary equal things in 74b6–7, produces an argument, and concludes that he has drawn his distinction in 74c4–5. But there is an oddity in the argument: the plural "the equals themselves" in 74c1. If the argument is cogent, this plural phrase has to be a way of referring to the equal itself. I shall for now assume

---

[19] 74b1 θαυμαστῶς: if my conjecture above about the reason Socrates picks "equal" as his example were right, it might explain Simmias' otherwise somewhat overdone enthusiasm.

[20] 74b6 ἐνενοήσαμεν: here the reference to "getting the knowledge of it" immediately above in b4 reminds us that we must not read the verb ἐννοεῖν as weakly as "form a notion of."

[21] 74b7 φαίνεται: alternatively, "doesn't it appear to you to be different," which is the standard way of translating it. See discussion below.

[22] Reading, in b7–9, ἆρ' οὐ λίθοι μὲν ἴσοι καὶ ξύλα ἐνίοτε ταὐτὰ ὄντα τότε μὲν ἴσα φαίνεται, τότε δ' οὔ; (with Tarrant [1957] 125 and Verdenius [1958] 209–10). More commonly (e.g., Burnet [1900], Robin [1926] 29, and Duke et al. [1995] 115), the text is printed as ἆρ' οὐ λίθοι μὲν ἴσοι καὶ ξύλα ἐνίοτε ταὐτὰ ὄντα τῷ μὲν ἴσα φαίνεται, τῷ δ' οὔ; and translated as: "Don't equal stones and sticks sometimes, although they are the same, appear to one {person} equal, and to another not?" Both readings have support in the MSS. We have to arrive at the same sense either way: Simmias is being asked whether stones and sticks present themselves to him sometimes as equal and sometimes as unequal; the former text does this more directly, but it could be got out of the latter (the two "persons" being Simmias on one occasion and Simmias on another occasion).

that it is: see § 11.4.1.3, where I argue that the plural translation is actually incorrect.

11.4.1.1. *The equal*

In 74a9–10 and a12, Socrates asks Simmias to concede that "there is an equal"[23] or "there is something equal." In this construction, ἴσον, "equal," is grammatically an adjective: the sort of word that *could* be attached to ξύλον and λίθον, "stick" and "stone," in 74a10, but which, Socrates there says, should not be taken as carrying either of those nouns with it.

Socrates tries to explain his question in a10–12. Wherever we have a stick equal to a stick, we have "an equal" (in fact, we have two "equals"). But Socrates wants us to focus on just *equal*. Start by considering a stick (say) that is equal to another; now ignore the stick, leaving just the equal, the equal by itself, the equal itself (alternative translations for αὐτὸ τὸ ἴσον).[24]

In 64d4–8 we heard Simmias allowing that there was something itself just, something beautiful, and something good; he had even allowed that none of these things was perceptible (65d9–12), and had extended that allowance to cover a wide area (cf. 65d12–e1). And now in 74b1 we have him conceding the existence of the equal itself. So it is a bit odd that Socrates brings the question up for review in b6–7.

But the argument is not superfluous. Socrates' interlocutors in the Socratic dialogues conceded the existence of such things as the just and the beautiful as preludes to discussion. Simmias' concession that there is such a thing as death in 64c2–3, subsequently defined as the sundering of soul and body (64c4–8), was just such a concession. In 65de, he was conceding something more: something itself just and its fellows existed and were also not accessible to the senses. But there was no argument given for this additional claim.

In 74a–c it is important that Simmias be clear on the weight carried by his concessions. There is such a thing as the equal; what matters here is not how we should define it, but that it is different from ordinary equal things. For it is of this that we are to be reminded by ordinary equal things, and

---

[23] τι εἶναι ἴσον. Not: "there is such a thing as equality," as in Jowett (1953) I 426 and Fowler (1914) 257; see also Tredennick (1954) 122 = Hamilton and Cairns (1961) 57, Hackforth (1955) 68. Contrast Robin (1926) 29, Bluck (1955) 67 (with 64 n. 1), Gallop (1975) 2, Grube (1981) 112 = Cooper (1997) 64. So also αὐτὸ τὸ ἴσον (74c4–5) is not "equality itself" (Hackforth [1955] 68), "equality in the abstract" (Fowler [1914] 257), or "absolute equality" (Tredennick [1954] 122 = Hamilton and Cairns [1961] 57, Jowett [1953] I 427) or "the very thing which is the property equality" (Crombie [1962/63] II 264).

[24] See Owen (1968) 114–15 = Owen (1986) 230–31.

to show that, in order to satisfy (DKC), we must see that to know those ordinary equal things is not *eo ipso* to know the equal.

11.4.1.2. The ordinary equals

We are going to advert to Leibniz's Law: we need some defeating predicate true of any ordinary equal thing that is not true of the equal itself.

At first sight, it looks as if the defeating predicate is "— shows itself to Simmias as unequal under some conceivable circumstances": this is true of any equal stick but not of the equal.

But the reference to Simmias is irrelevant: Simmias is standing in here for anyone at all.[25] The defeating predicate is, in effect, "— shows itself to someone under some conceivable circumstances as unequal": any equal stick, stone, or whatever does this; the equal does not.

Suppose Socrates had jumped, not on "equal," but on "beautiful," to make his case. The *Hippias Major* would readily suggest some examples in which something that is in one context beautiful is in another context ugly. Things that are beautiful in the eyes of some are ugly in the eyes of others; things that are beautiful at some times are ugly at others; things that are beautiful in some respects are ugly in others; things that are beautiful in comparison with some things are ugly in comparison with others; and so on.

But Socrates goes for "equal." Take, then, any stick, equal to another. It may be equal to that other in length, but not in diameter; it may be equal now but not later; it may be equal to that stick, but not to this one; it may be equal in Simmias' eyes now, but not after he has had too much to drink; and so on. Equal sticks and stones here below are subject to various sorts of relativity; the equal, peeled away from sticks and stones and considered in isolation, is not.

11.4.1.3. "The equals themselves"

The trouble is, Socrates appears not to ask: does the equal ever strike you as unequal? but (74c1–2): "Well then, are there {occasions} when the equals themselves have shown themselves to you as unequal, or equality as inequality?" The plural "the equals themselves" is mysterious.[26]

---

[25] Mills (1957/58) 129–30, 133 n. 1, and *passim*, seems to make unduly heavy weather of the occurrence of σοι in 74c1.

[26] The Form for equal, because it is a paradigm for equal things, has been thought to be a *pair* of things; hence the plural. This goes back to Heindorf, quoted approvingly by Archer-Hind (1894) 37–38 and Verdenius (1958) 210, revived by Geach (1956) 76 = Allen (1965) 269–70, accepted by Vlastos (1956b) 90–91 = Allen (1965) 287–88 (but this is retracted in the "additional note" in Allen [1965] 291). See also Bluck (1957) 117–18, Mills (1957/58) 40–51; Bluck (1959) is a response. This certainly seems to compromise the unity of the Form.

If the argument is to differentiate the equal (itself) from equal sticks and stones via Leibniz's Law, Socrates has to be determining, from the negative answer he gets to this question, that the equal has never struck Simmias as unequal, for he immediately draws the conclusion: "therefore these equals and the equal itself are not the same." And, in fact, determining that the equal has never struck Simmias as unequal is not only what he needs to do, it is the *only* thing he needs to do: if there is any upshot to this negatively answered question beside the claim that the equal has never struck Simmias as unequal, it plays no logical role in the argument.[27]

But some have supposed that "the equals themselves" refers to entities distinct from both the equal and equal sticks: "perfect particular instances"[28] of the equal, e.g., according to Burnet,[29] the base angles of an isosceles triangle. Then there would have to be two questions in 74c1–2: one about perfect instances of the equal and the other about equality. But we must make the first of these questions somehow relevant to the argument. We must suppose that Socrates would count the equal as a "perfect particular instance" of itself: then, when Simmias responds that he has never taken (and, by implication, no one *could* ever take) such things to be unequal, it follows that he has never taken the equal to be unequal.

But why should Socrates route the argument through perfect instances of equality in general? It has been standard in Socratic definitional procedure to reject a candidate *definiens* if it led to the result that the *F* is con*F*; the parallel absurdity here would be: the equal is unequal. If Simmias has ever participated in or even just listened to Socratic definition badgering, he knows that this is an absurdity. All Socrates has to do is ask him for it.

Anyway, if Burnet's example is the sort of thing intended by talk of "perfect instances of equality,"[30] Socrates' routing of the argument through such perfect instances is disastrous. That the angles at the base of an isosceles triangle are equal requires proof (Euclid I 5): just looking at them won't tell you that they are equal.[31] And the same is true under any other specification I know of for "perfect instances of equality," short of just defining them as instances no one could under any circumstances take to be unequal. And so defined, who knows what they might be?

---

[27] Cf. Wedberg (1955) 94–97, Mills (1957/58) 128 and *passim*, Dorter (1982) 54.

[28] Ross (1951) 22; cf. 60.

[29] Burnet (1911) 56 *ad* c1; so also Cornford (1939) 70–71, Hackforth (1955) 69 n. 2, Bluck (1955) 67 n. 3, Bluck (1957) 118–19.

[30] Brown (1972) 32 takes Burnet to be talking about "things equal by definition"; but the base angles of an isosceles triangle are not equal by definition.

[31] So Ackrill (1958) 108.

For the argument to come off, the apparent plural must refer to the Form the equal itself. There is a way of explaining that.[32]

When Socrates asks Simmias in 74a9–11 whether he grants the existence of an equal, he lifts the term "equal" from the context "equal stick": he asks Simmias, in effect, whether this term has a referent, as does "stick"; he calls this purported referent "the equal itself" or "just equal." There he uses the singular; the context is singular. When he asks Simmias whether the equals themselves have ever seemed to him unequal, he has just asked again about equal sticks, but here the context is plural. We might try to represent the situation by a translation that leans on the fact that Greek adjectives, unlike English ones, take plural forms just as nouns do, making Socrates' question at 74b7–9 read: "Don't equal sticks and stones sometimes, although they are the same, show themselves as equals at one time, and at another {as} not {equals}?" And then in 74c1, he isolates "equals" and asks whether "they" have ever presented themselves as unequals. But if we stick by our former translation of the question in 74b7–9 as asking whether the equal sticks sometimes turn up equal (although the adjective is plural) and sometimes not, we shall have to do the same in 74c1, and have Socrates ask: "But has the equal itself ever presented itself as unequal?" "The equal itself" is in the plural, but the plural is there in the Greek *only* because it was there in the context from which the term "equal" was lifted, and in that context the adjective had to be plural. So, in fact, this is the correct translation.

The second clause of Socrates' question, 74c1–2, asks: "or {are there occasions when} equality {has shown itself to you} as inequality?" On the present reading, the two clauses are asking the same question in two different ways. The second way is rather foggier: its bearing on the argument is dim. We cannot contrast equal sticks with equality on the ground that equal sticks can always be seen as unequal while equality can never be seen as inequality.[33] And, although it is true that "equality" and "the equal itself" are alternative ways Socrates has for referring to the same thing, the Form, that does not fully explain the equivalence of the two clauses. For, even if "the equal itself" is equivalent to "equality," "is unequal" is not equivalent

---

[32] One version of this response is in Vlastos (1956b) 91–92 = Allen (1965) 289; a quite different one is in Owen (1968) 114–15 = Owen (1986) 230–31. I follow the latter, as do Bostock (1986) 81–83 and White (1987) 204–5. Guthrie (1975) 343 n. 5 conflates Owen's interpretation with that mentioned in n. 26.

[33] White (1987) 203 builds steps in to make the second part of c1–2 the operative one. His version of the argument would apparently start off like this: "Suppose (what is to be shown false): (1) Equality is a sensible object. Then: (2) Inequality is a sensible object (by parity of reasoning). But: (3) Any sensible equal is capable of appearing unequal." Unfortunately, I cannot see where it goes from here. But it will, allegedly, avoid ascribing Self-Predication to Plato (205–6).

to "is inequality." Socrates must be supposing that "the equal is unequal" is tantamount to "equality is inequality," but this cannot be because the two claims are piece-by-piece equivalent, and it remains unclear what precisely motivates the supposition.

The argument, then, is (ARE):

> (1) There is such a thing as the equal
> (2) Any ordinary equal thing is also sometimes unequal
> (3) The equal is never unequal
> ∴ (4) The equal ≠ any ordinary equal thing

where "sometimes" and "never" cover a great deal of ground: (2) is to be understood as "any ordinary equal is, at some time, or in some respect, or to someone, or in some circumstances, unequal," and (3) denies all this of the equal.

The difference (ARE) makes between the equal itself and any ordinary equal is so great that the two must be objects of different knowledges. And that is the instance of the Different Knowledge Clause we need.

II.4.1.4. Simmias' prior knowledge

Socrates is trying to establish the preexistence of the soul by first establishing that Simmias satisfied the tripartite Sufficient Condition for being reminded of the equal, applying the Prior Knowledge Requirement to show he had known the equal beforehand, and then specifying the moment implied in the word "beforehand" in such a way as to show that Simmias knew the equal before he was born.

Start with (SCR); instantiate y with an arbitrary equal stick named "Stanley," x with "Simmias," and z with "the equal":

> (PUCs) When he perceives Stanley, Simmias takes Stanley to be equal.
> (CKCs) When he perceives Stanley and takes it to be equal, Simmias also thinks of the equal, which requires his knowing what the equal is.
> (DKCs) Taking Stanley to be equal does not carry with it knowing the equal.

Under our assumption that his arguments have worked, what he has shown so far, using the Argument from Relativity, is (DKCs).

But then we must abandon the Standard Interpretation, for (DKCs) makes it explicit that it is not enough to know the equal that one merely be able to make claims about the equality of sticks and stones.

The stronger Sufficient Condition (the original one) is no better off on this score. For even on that reading, when Simmias perceives the stick and "knows" it, what he knows *about* it is presumably that it is equal, or unequal. And then there must be more to the knowledge of the equal than just the ability to judge one stick to be equal and another not.

That is not the end of the case against the Standard Interpretation, but let us get back to the text.

In 74b2–3, Simmias admits to having knowledge of the Form: indeed, he says, of the equal, that he knows what it is. In the immediate sequel, b4, Socrates asks how he got that knowledge; in b4–6, he suggests that Simmias got that knowledge "from" (ἐκ) equal sticks and stones, by having seen them. What is in question here is (CKCs):[34] Socrates is suggesting that what prompted Simmias to a knowledge of the equal is his having seen equal sticks and stones; they are to be the reminders, and it is to be the object recalled. This train of thought is interrupted by the presentation of the Argument from Relativity, and resumed immediately after that (74c7–10):

But still, he said, it is from *these* equals {ἀλλὰ μὴν ἐκ τούτων γ᾽, ἔφη, τῶν ἴσων}, although they are different from that equal, that you have thought of and got your knowledge of it?
What you are saying is most true, he said.

Socrates here turns toward (CKCs), but he does not exactly come around to face it: he first develops the Ancillary Argument.

Still, all the materials are there for the argument as previewed: whether Socrates says so or not, he has a complete case for the conclusion that Simmias, at the moment of judging the stick to be equal, when that prompts in him the awareness of the equal, is being reminded of the equal. The Ancillary Argument is merely frosting on the cake.

II.5. 74C–75A: THE ANCILLARY ARGUMENT, II

Simmias is reminded of the equal by the equal sticks, Socrates says (74c11–75a4, omitting Simmias' responses, all positive):

Then either where it is like them or unlike them? . . .
{c13} But it makes no difference, he said; as long as having seen one {thing}, from {d} this sight you have thought of another, whether like or unlike, he said, it necessarily comes-to-be being-reminded. . . .

---

[34] Compare the use of λαβεῖν in 74b4 with its use in formulating the sufficient condition in 73c7, d1, d7, 76a2; the use of ἐννοῆσαι in 74b6 with 73c8, 76a3; the use of ἰδεῖν in 74b5 and in 73c6, d5, d9, e5, e7, e9, 76a1.

{d4} Well then, he said, don't we undergo some such thing concerning the {equals} among the sticks and the equals of which we were just now speaking? Do they show themselves to us as equal just as the what is itself {equal} is, or do they somehow fall short of that, with respect to being such as the equal is, or not at all? . . .

{d9} Then do we agree that whenever someone who has seen something thinks: that which I am now seeing wants to be such as some other of the {things} that are, but falls short and is unable to be such as that, but is inferior, it's necessary, I suppose, for the one who thinks this, in fact, to have known before that which he says this resembles, but does so deficiently? . . .

{e6} Well then, have we too undergone this sort of thing with the equals and the equal itself, or not? . . .

{e9} Therefore, it's necessary for us to have known the equal before that {75} time at which, having first seen the equals, we thought that they all wish to be such as the equal, but are deficient. . . .

This is a departure from the Core Argument. According to that Argument, we were to find that seeing equal sticks and stones provoked in us the thought of the equal. Down to 74d3, nothing more is required. The intrusion of considerations of likeness between the equals and the equal itself is, apparently, irrelevant, and Socrates himself says precisely that in c13–d2, echoing (LP1): recollection occurs when we think of the equal, *whether or not* there is any resemblance between the equals and the equal itself (cf. 76a3–4).

But in 74d–75a, Socrates claims that, when it comes to equal sticks and stones reminding us of the equal, we not only think of the equal, we have the specific thought that the sticks are not equal in the way that the equal is, but fall short of it; that this stick wants to have the character that the equal has, but cannot quite do that; it's at best deficiently like it. And Socrates invites us to agree that anyone who, seeing an equal stick, thinks *that*, must have known the equal beforehand.

If we do agree, we have an argument from the premise

(P) When someone, e.g., Simmias, sees an equal stick, he thinks "this wants to be like the equal, but can't be"

via our agreement

(A) Anyone who sees y and thinks "y wants to be like z but can't be" must have known z beforehand

to the conclusion

(C15a) Simmias must have known the equal before seeing an equal stick and thinking it wants to be but can't be like the equal.

This is the Ancillary Argument. As it stands, it is entirely self-contained: if this is really the way it is to be taken, we can just scrap (SCR). We can't have that, so Socrates must be supposing that his premises have some basis in the preceding concessions.

The place to look for that basis is the discussion of likeness in 74a (§ 11.3). Socrates employs one of the Likeness Principles there propounded, (LP1), to the effect that someone can be reminded of something by another thing like or unlike it, when at 74c11 he asks Simmias to concede that he can be reminded of the equal whether or not it is like an equal stick. The other principle was:

(LP2) x is reminded of z by y & y is like z →
    x must think or notice whether y is less than exactly like z.

Let us take the stronger form of this:

(LP2′) x is reminded of z by y & y is like z →
    x must notice whether y is less than exactly like z.

To apply that here, we must assume that we already have the conclusion

(Rs) Simmias is being reminded by Stanley of the equal at t

as well as the assumption that any equal stick will be like, but less than exactly like, the equal:

(L) Stanley is less than exactly like the equal.

These premises guarantee that Simmias will notice that Stanley is less than exactly like the equal. This then becomes premise (P) of the Ancillary Argument.

This way (SCR) is still in play: it is used to get (Rs). The Core Argument is now supplemented: our agreement (A) in the Ancillary Argument reinforces the conclusion for which we had employed the Prior Knowledge Requirement in the Core Argument. Simmias sees an equal stick, thinks of the equal, and so on; we draw the conclusion (Rs), and put it together with (L); then (LP2) makes it follow that

(SL) Simmias thinks that Stanley is deficiently like the equal,

and (A) tells us that this means he must have known the equal before that time: (C15a).

We now have two routes to that conclusion. Both require the satisfaction of the antecedent of (SCR). In the sequel, Socrates does not distinguish these two routes. What remains to be established is that Simmias must have known the equal before he was born, and we are to derive that from (C1sa), however we get there.

11.6. 75A–76D: THE COMPLETION OF THE CORE ARGUMENT, II

Simmias has allowed that it is in sticks and stones presenting themselves to him as equal that he is led to the knowledge of the equal itself (74b4–5, c7–10, d4–9, etc.). Socrates begins by repeating this (75a). He then rephrases it so that it fits the Ancillary Argument (75ab): it is on the basis of one's perceptions that one thinks that the sticks fall short of "what the equal is" (ὃ ἔστιν ἴσον), and heads for (C2): we must have got knowledge of the equal before we began to perceive, but, since we began to perceive at birth, it must have been before birth (75bc).

To get from

> (C1e) Simmias knew the equal before he saw the equal stick that
> prompted his recollection of the equal

to

> (C2e) Simmias knew the equal before he was born

he needs some lemmas: specifically, Socrates wants first to get from (C1e) to:

> (L1e) Simmias knew the equal before he began to use his senses,

and then from there via

> (L2) Simmias began to use his senses at birth

to (C2e).

The point that it is equal sticks that remind us of the equal is differently understood by the Standard and the Alternative Interpretations. For if the Standard Interpretation is right, sticks do this as soon as we pronounce them equal (or unequal). For the Alternative Interpretation, they do this not immediately, but eventually, when we finally come to know again, as we knew before birth, what the equal is.

Socrates' move from (C1e) to (L1e) seems to speak in favor of the Standard Interpretation: we recollect as soon as we see. Let us suppose that the Standard Interpretation is correct, and see what happens.

The first point at which we see an equal stick is, then, the point at which we recollect. But this is not quite right: clearly it is not the first point at which we see an equal stick, but the first point at which we see one and are able to tell that it *is* equal, and this does not happen as soon as we open our eyes at birth. Then there is some time after we first open our eyes and before which we recollect the equal. Let us suppose that we are first able to tell that sticks are or are not equal at the age of a year; on the Standard Interpretation, that is when we are recollecting the equal. There is therefore a gap of a year in the argument: we must have known the equal before we recollect it, but we have a year's time in which to acquire that knowledge.

How does Socrates propose to rule that out? He does not say. But it is fairly clear what to supply him with. The child is to display his knowledge of the equal by discriminating equal from unequal sticks at the age of one year. The supposition that he acquired that knowledge in the course of that year is plainly absurd: anyone can see that infants do not at the age of six months come to know the equal, only to display their knowledge six months later.

But if our way of telling that the child knows the equal is his ability to discriminate between equal and unequal sticks, this is not obvious at all. For all we know, he is first able to discriminate between equal and unequal sticks at the age of six months. What is obvious is that at no point in the year can the child *say* what the equal is.

What we have to supply to Socrates is the claim that children do not at six months acquire the knowledge they recollect at one year. Shortly (in 76d1–3), Socrates will be assuming, as just as obvious as (PKR), the fact that we must have known what we recollect before we recollect it, that we must have forgotten what we recollect before we recollect it. So if the child is recollecting at the age of one year, but first acquired the knowledge then recollected at the age of six months, he must have forgotten it in between. And this too manifestly does not happen.

Suppose we supply Socrates with all that. That saves the Standard Interpretation on this point. But it also saves the Alternative Interpretation. On this Interpretation, what shows that a person has recollected is his ability to say what the equal is. Suppose he is first able to do this at the age of fifteen years. It is just as obvious that he did not acquire this ability at the age of ten and lose it in between as it is that he did not acquire the ability to discriminate equal from unequal sticks at the age of six months and lose it at nine months.

In either case, there is a question about the period before recollection takes place: why does Socrates suppose the recollector cannot, during that period, first come to know and then forget what he recollected at the end of it? And the answer that this just does not happen is as good for the one interpretation as it is for the other.

The fact is that Socrates' case here is weak, and it is so on either interpretation. An "empiricist" might say to Socrates, under the Standard Interpretation: it is the exercise of the senses that leads, at the age of a year, to the ability to differentiate between equal and unequal sticks; there is no question of anybody's recollecting anything, for all there is is a discriminatory capacity, developed postnatally. To Socrates under the Alternative Interpretation he might say: the ability to say what the equal is is one acquired by reflection on the activity of differentiating equal from unequal sticks.

In either case, what the "empiricist" is doing is denying that recollecting is taking place when Socrates says it is. And, either way, Socrates has certainly not managed to show that recollecting *is* taking place.

This particular race between the Standard and the Alternative Interpretations is a draw.

At this point the Core Argument is completed down to (C2); all that remains is to infer that we, or our souls, existed before we were born, (C3). But Socrates does not immediately do this: he stops, apparently to plug a gap in the argument as we have it so far. But he raises another question in midstream.

11.6.1. 75cd: the scope of the argument

What worries Socrates is the question whether we know, not only before birth, but from birth on. If it is the latter, we are not being reminded when perceived sticks and stones prompt us to knowledge of the equal: we just know it all along.

Socrates opens this line of thought, and immediately digresses. He makes two claims: first, that if, when we were born, we retained the knowledge we got before birth, we knew the Forms both before birth and from birth on (75c7–10), and second, that whatever claims are here to be made about our knowledge, including the claim that we acquired knowledge before we were born, apply not just to the equal, the large, and the small, but to "all the things which we put this seal, 'what {it} is'[35] both when questioning in our questions and answering in our answers" (c10–d5). Simmias assents (75d6).

Socrates refers to the Forms as "things labeled 'what {it} is' {ὃ ἔστι: see n. 35} in questions and answers"; see also 74a11–b2, where the question asked about the equal itself was whether "we know what it is" (see also

---

[35] 75d2 τοῦτο ὃ ἔστι: the reading of the MSS Burnet (1900) prints τὸ "αὐτὸ ὃ ἔστι," "what it itself is"; cf. Burnet (1911) 74–75. Gallop (1975) 23, 230 n. 28 follows the MSS, but suggests τοῦτο τὸ ὃ ἔστι; Duke et al. (1995) follow this (ascribing it to Heindorf).

75b1–2, b5–6). But the reference to the questions and answers in which this type of talk[36] occurs is plainly not just to those of the *Phaedo*. The word "what" in "what {it} is" is the indirect interrogative pronoun, and we all know where to find Socratic conversations concerning what this or that is: the definition dialogues. Socrates is here reverting to those dialogues, and reminding us that the scope of his present argument is exactly that of his quest for definitions.

11.6.2. *75d–76d: forgetting and being reminded*

Once Simmias has conceded this, Socrates reverts to the question of whether we know immediately at birth and all along or are actually recollecting (75d–76a). Simmias can't decide (76b3), so Socrates argues as follows (76b5–c5):

> Can a man who knows give an account about those things that he knows, or not?
>
> It's a great necessity, Socrates.
>
> {b8} And do all seem to you to be able to give an account about those things of which we were just now speaking?
>
> {b10} I certainly wish it were so, said Simmias; but I'm much more afraid that at this time tomorrow there may no longer be any among men who is able to do this properly.
>
> {c1} Therefore, he said, all do not seem to you to know these things, Simmias. Not at all.
>
> {c4} Therefore they are being reminded of what they once learned? {It's a} necessity.

That wraps it up.

But what Simmias has now said is puzzling. At 74b2–3, he had said outright that he knows what the equal is. Here (76b4–7) Socrates elicits from him the claim that one who knows about something can give a definition, an account, a λόγος, for it; they further agree that since not all of us can give the required definitions, not all of us know the things for which they are definitions (76b8–c3). But Simmias suggests that once Socrates is gone, there may be no one who can give those definitions (76b10–12). Now

---

[36] Cf. 65d13–e1, 74d6, 75d2, 78d4, d5, 92d9; also *Symposium* 211c8–d1, *Republic* VI 490b3, 507b7, VII 532a7, X 597a2, a4, *Parmenides* 129a2, b7, 133d8, e1, e3, 134a3–4, a6–7, b14, and Aristotle, *Metaphysics* M 4. 1079[b]6. The discussions of this phrase in Shorey (1925), Cherniss (1944) 309–10 n. 211, Else (1936) 43, Crombie (1962/63) II 263–65 (and 251, 253, 287, etc.) are not very helpful; more informative are Kapp (1942) 64, Lacey (1959) 51, Vlastos (1971/72) 454–55 n. 102 = Vlastos (1973b) 261–62 n. 102, and Kahn (1981b) 127–29. "What is equal" translates the phrase as if it were the subject of a definition: "what is equal is what is neither larger nor smaller."

Simmias certainly expects to outlive Socrates. So apparently he considers himself unable to provide definitions. But then why did he say that he knew what the equal was?

There is an obvious answer. Simmias' comments in 76 do not actually contradict what he says in 74. By the time we get to 76, the equal is no longer the sole focus: 75cd has reminded us that the argument is to be generalized to cover all the terms for which Socrates has spent his life seeking out definitions. If we were right in supposing that "equal" is picked because it is one of the easy cases, all we have to suppose is that, while Simmias felt comfortable about defining it, he does not feel similarly comfortable about defining the beautiful or the good.

But that reinforces whatever doubts we may already have about the Standard Interpretation. According to that interpretation, the argument is leading us toward a sort of knowledge that underlies our everyday perceptual practices: our ability to distinguish beautiful things from ugly things, equal ones from unequal ones, and so on, has supposedly been contingent on our ability to recollect Forms from a previous existence, and recollecting is taking place when we make such distinctions. But now it turns out that the knowledge Socrates thinks comes of recollecting involves the ability to answer Socratic questions. This is plainly not the same thing. But it is what a reading of the *Meno* would lead us to expect, and therefore what we think of when Cebes, wittingly or unwittingly, reminds us of the *Meno*.

It is sometimes suggested that the puzzle over Simmias' comments in 76 can be solved by adverting to degrees or sorts of knowledge, or senses of "know."[37] But the argument leaves no room for this dodge. The question is whether what we call learning is recollection. Learning is coming by knowledge. Simmias has already done it, as far as the equal is concerned, so he must have recollected. He is now being asked: is everyone always in possession of all knowledge, or is it so that people have to recollect? The argument selects the latter alternative. The knowledge that Simmias has is not knowledge he has about everything; he can tell from his own case that he has a lot to recollect. But plainly he can make claims about things being beautiful, just, pious and so on. What he cannot do is give an account for those things, and that, he explicitly acknowledges (76b4–7), is required of those who have knowledge.

The present passage reinforces doubts over the Standard Interpretation in another way. Socrates concludes in c4 that people who are unable to give

---

[37] For a clear exposition, see Ackrill (1973) 192 = Ackrill (1997) 28–29.

accounts and *so do not know* (76b4–c3) are being reminded of what they once learned. He has to mean: once they come to be able to give accounts. Socrates can hardly be saying that people are recollecting simply in making judgments about sticks and stones, for then they *would* know: recollection is, we have just been told (75e2–7) just getting back knowledge one has lost.

So the Standard Interpretation fails to connect the talk of recollection here with that in the *Meno*, cannot make sense of a lead premise in the argument, namely (DKC), and cannot make sense of Simmias' admissions. Nothing in the argument requires that Interpretation. So the Alternative Interpretation wins, hands down.

Socrates now draws the expected conclusion: we are, in coming to be able to say what this or that is, reminded of things we once learned (76c6–12), but that can't have been after we became human; so it must have been before that; so our souls must have existed before we were born. Simmias thinks there is a possibility that we learned at the moment of birth (76c14–15), but, Socrates tells him, that has to be when we lost the knowledge, and we couldn't have done both at once (d1–4). Simmias folds (d5–6). This ending is weak, but we need not stop over it. The argument is done, except for a general reflection by Socrates on what it has established.

II.7. 76D–77A: THE UPSHOT OF THE ARGUMENT

Socrates summarizes the position at which they have arrived as follows (76d7–e7):

> If the things we're always chattering about exist, a beautiful and good and every such substance, and to this we refer all the things from our perceptions, finding again what existed before, which is ours, and we compare these with that, it's necessary that, just as these exist, so also our soul existed before, even before we came-to-be; but if these don't exist, this argument has been propounded in vain. Is this how matters stand: there is an equal necessity that these things and that our souls exist even before we come-to-be, and if not the former, neither the latter?

And Simmias assents (76e–77a).

The strongest reading of these claims would have it that the existence of the Forms and the preexistence of the soul are logically equivalent:

(FS) The Forms exist ↔ the soul existed before birth.

But if this is what Socrates means, it is not true: his arguments, even if we grant that they work, have shown nothing of the kind. Rather, they have (under the concession that they work) shown that the existence of Forms is one premise among a number of premises which jointly prove the soul's preexistence. Nothing has been said to show that we could use the preexistence of the soul as one premise among others in deriving the existence of Forms.

The connection between the existence of the Forms and preexistence must be vaguer than (FS) makes it. Perhaps it is this. Our ability to arrive at answers to Socratic "what is it?" questions asked about the equal and the beautiful has been shown to depend on our acquaintance with these things before our birth; for us to have become acquainted with them before birth, (a) they have to have been there, and (b) we have to have been there. As parts of the package that is the Doctrine of Learning as Recollection, these two claims stand or fall together.

We found that, in the *Meno*, if the Doctrine of Recollection were to have any relevance to Socrates' quest for definitions, the objects of that quest would have to have been known before birth. Those objects were called "forms," but nothing was said about what a form was like, or what that initial acquisition of knowledge of them was like: it could have been a matter of sense experience, for all that was expressly said. The *Phaedo* is now explicit about the nature of the objects we recollect, and our previous acquisition of knowledge of them is not a matter of sense experience.

Those objects are now related to the things we see, hear, etc., by having in a superlative degree the same features that these things have. The argument squarely commits Socrates to the idea that the Form for beautiful things is superlatively Beautiful, that for large things superlatively Large, and that for equal things superlatively Equal. This has seemed absurd to philosophers from Aristotle, who rejected the theory partly for that reason, to contemporary philosophers who would prefer to rewrite Socrates' arguments for him so that he is only committed to what we all know and love as "platonism." But we must start with the text of Plato, not with some preordained picture of what Plato must, as the greatest of all philosophers, be saying. I have tried to explain what the text says. Did Plato believe what Socrates is here made to say? Aristotle thought he did, and Aristotle spent about twenty years with the man.

To get to the preexistence of the soul we had to see our ability to define terms as requiring our being acquainted with the objects of those definitions before birth. That in turn demands a peculiar status for those objects. Socrates' own arguments in the course of his attempts to get definitions were already pointing the way toward that status. The devices he had for showing that the beautiful is not a beautiful girl, or gold, or a long and satisfying life, are generalizable to show that the beautiful is nothing on earth. The generalization is the Argument from Relativity, and the conclusion of the Argument from Relativity is the Theory of Forms.

That this is so can be confirmed by a brief digression on the *Symposium*.

CHAPTER 12

The Beautiful in the Symposium

The Argument from Relativity, AR, is not applied to the beautiful in the *Phaedo*. It stands behind the argument of 74a–c, since Socrates thinks AR can be applied to any of a range of terms including the beautiful (76d8, 78d3). The Argument from Relativity does not appear in the *Symposium*, but plainly stands behind Diotima's description of the beautiful in 210e–211a.

12.1. DIOTIMA'S IMMORTALITY

According to Diotima, a human being can only find immortality by leaving behind "another new one such as it itself was" (208a7–b4).[1] Some, according to her, do this bodily, by begetting human offspring (208e); others do it in soul (208e–209a): they are pregnant with "wisdom {φρόνησις} and excellence in general" (209a3–4), and when they come of age, they desire to beget these things (209ab).[2] They seek out beautiful bodies, but prefer the combination of these with beautiful souls as well (209b); with such people they beget poems, as did Homer and Hesiod (209d1–3), and laws, as did Lycurgus and Solon (d4–e2): these win fame for "begetting every sort of excellence" (γεννήσαντες παντοίαν ἀρετήν, e2–3).

This much, she says, even Socrates[3] might be able to grasp (209e5–210a1); she doubts whether he is up to the "final and highest mysteries for the sake of which these exist in the first place," but she is prepared to have a shot at getting them across (210a1–4).

---

[1] Picked up by Aristotle: see *De Anima* B 4. 415ᵃ26–ᵇ7; Diotima's "another such as it itself was" (ἕτερον . . . οἷον αὐτὸ ἦν, 208b1–2) is echoed in 415ᵃ28, as well as in *De Generatione Animalium* B 1. 735ᵃ18 and *Politics* A 2. 1252ᵃ30 (passages referred to in Bury [1932] 117 *ad* 208b).

[2] She assigns both the roles of begetting and of being pregnant to the "father" in this procreative process: see 206c. This does not necessarily make her a women's liberationist: her model for the procreation of matters of the soul pretty clearly involves two men (= adult males, ἄνδρες: cf. 209c1, and see Dover [1980] 151).

[3] Cf. 209e5 κἂν σύ, "even you"; less harshly, "you, too": Dover (1980) 155 prefers this.

12.2. CLIMBING TO THE HIGHER MYSTERIES

The stages in the ascent of the initiate toward the vision of the beautiful are these: he or she contemplates

0. first, one beautiful body (211c3; 210a4–8);
1. then all beautiful bodies (211c3–4; 210a8–b6);
2. then beautiful practices (211c4–5, 210b6–c6);
3. then beautiful studies or knowledges (211c5–6; 210c6–d6);
4. and finally the beautiful itself (211c6–d1; 210d6–211b7).

Stages 0–3 are merely stages of increasing generality that do not involve AR; AR kicks in to get us from stage 3 to stage 4. But let us go over all these stages more slowly.

12.2.1. *From one body to all bodies*

To begin with, the adept-to-be loves one body and begets beautiful discourses or speeches or arguments, λόγοι, with that body (210a5–8).

There are two components here: an emotional one and an intellectual one;[4] the emotional one comes first. It is hardly clear what the content of the λόγοι might be, or what it means to say that the initiate begets beautiful ones with the body of the other. But one is reminded of the *Lysis*: at any rate, it looks as if, at this stage, the trainee is a boy under the tutelage of an older man, and perhaps the λόγοι are intended to induce the sort of confusion in the boy that would lead him to think in terms of beauty in general. For he is supposed to realize that the beauty in one body is sibling to that in another (210a8–b1), that the beauty in all bodies is one and the same (b2–3).[5]

Diotima apparently takes these formulations as two ways of saying the same thing. She cannot, then, be placing great weight on the first: she should not be taken to be saying that each beautiful body has a logically unique instance of beauty that is akin to the logically unique instance of beauty in the next beautiful body over.

As a consequence of his realization, the trainee loves all beautiful bodies, and holds the single one with which he started in contempt (b4–6).

There is an intellectual as well as an emotional component; here the intellectual one comes first. Nothing is said by way of explaining *how* the initiate comes to the realization that the beauty in all bodies is one

---

[4] So also Moravcsik (1971) 286.
[5] Chen (1983) 67 with n. 11, 69–70, and *passim*, seems to ignore this second clause.

and the same: one hopes that the beautiful discourses he begot with the beautiful body of which he was enamored had something to do with it.

12.2.2. *The beauty of the soul*

The summary, at 211c4–5, only mentions beautiful practices at this stage; there is more to it than that. After landing on stage 1 and seeing the identity of the beautiful in all beautiful bodies, Diotima tells Socrates, the initiate must (210b6–c6)

> think the beauty in souls more valuable than that in the body, so that if someone who is decent has, with respect to his soul, even a small flower, {c} it suffices for him to love and have care and to engender[6] such accounts as make the young better, so that he is forced, in turn, to contemplate the beautiful in practices and laws, and to see that this itself is all akin to itself, so that he will think the {beautiful} about the body to be something small.

Nothing is said about what motivates evaluating the beauty of the soul more highly than bodily beauty in 210b6–7;[7] as with much else in this passage, we can see room for argument, and, if Socrates rather than Diotima were in the driver's seat, we would expect argument. But the rest of the description of this stage seems to be discussing the consequences of the initiate's coming to think that psychic beauty is to be preferred. He is, it seems, at stage 2, an older man turned educator: if he sees in the soul of someone young even a little bit of beauty, he is attached to it and tries to beget such λόγοι as will improve him (b8–c3). This requires him to reflect on beautiful practices and laws (c3–4),[8] and he makes the same generalization about these he made at stage 1 with bodies: the beauty in all of them is "akin to itself" (c4–5). But he now thinks all bodily beauty to be pretty trivial (c5–6).

12.2.3. *The beauty of knowledge*

Diotima next introduces knowledge, as something apparently of a different type from practices and laws (210c6–d6):

---

[6] Omitting καὶ ζητεῖν in 210c2 with Bury (1932) 126 and Dover (1980) 156 (who refer the emendation to Ast).

[7] Moravcsik (1971) 288–90 discusses such steps in the ascent as these; he refers to them as "E-steps" ("E" for "Eros"), by contrast with "R-steps" ("Reason"). He thinks Reason has a role to play "in revealing new possible objects of aspiration" (290), but he says nothing about what Reason could actually provide us with at this point.

[8] 210c3 αὖ ("in turn") makes it sound as if we have a new stage here, and it apparently is so taken by Roochnik (1987) 122, but it is clear from the context as well as the summary in 211c4–5 that only one is involved (so Robin [1929] xciii, 68 n. 2).

and after practices {he must} bring in[9] knowledges {τὰς ἐπιστήμας}, so that he may see in turn {the} beauty of knowledges, and may, by looking now toward the beautiful at large, no longer be enslaved to that in the single {case}, like a menial, loving {the} beauty of a boy or of some man or of one practice, mean and narrow-minded, but, turned to the large sea of the beautiful and contemplating it, he may engender many accounts and reflections {διανοήματα} both beautiful and magnificent in unstinting love of wisdom.

The initiate is at this point totally detached from the particular, in the state of φιλοσοφία, "philosophy," the "love of wisdom." Diotima clearly has some of the same traits in her psychological make-up as Socrates: she thinks that philosophy occurs at the level of the general.

The relationship between the introduction of the knowledges and the consideration of complete generality is foggy. It sounds as if, once we have introduced the beautiful knowledges alongside beautiful laws, practices, and bodies, we have before us the full range of application of the term "beautiful." But why should the knowledges complete the range? And why weren't they included among the beautiful things introduced at stage 3?

Also on the emotional end of things, it sounds as if it is the introduction of the knowledges that ensures that the adept is no longer in love with anything particular, even a particular beautiful practice.

Another difficulty is that the initiate should not simply be contemplating these beautiful knowledges as *objects*, as he contemplated the beautiful practices; he should also be *acquiring* these beautiful knowledges. For example, he learns geometry; he adds the beauty of the science of geometry to his list of beautiful things, thereby making the list more comprehensive, but he also now knows geometry. Perhaps this is somehow related to his distancing himself from particulars, if Plato now has the view that knowledge is not really of the particular. But nothing is said here to indicate that he has this view.

12.2.4. *The beauty of it all*

Finally, the initiate turns adept: he sees the beautiful itself. He contemplates the sea of the beautiful and engenders more beautiful λόγοι (210d6–211b7):

---

[9] 210c7 ἀγαγεῖν: the standard construal has the subject shifting at this point: "{his leader must} lead {him} on to knowledges" (see Bury [1932] 126, Dover [1980] 155). This seems to me very difficult. Perhaps in the preceding lines (b6–c6) the role of the adept-to-be has shifted from pupil to teacher: he is now "engendering such accounts as make the young better" (c1–3), having seen in the soul of "someone decent" a "small flower" of beauty. If the adept is now the educator, it is he who is doing the leading in c7.

until, being strengthened and growing there, he may discern a certain single knowledge such that it is of {a} beautiful of the following kind.

{e1/2} Try to hold your mind on me as far as you are capable.

{e2/3} For he who has been educated in erotica up to this point, by gazing on the beautifuls in order and rightly, coming toward the goal of his erotica, will suddenly discern something beautiful, wondrous in its nature {τὶ θαυμαστὸν τὴν φύσιν καλόν},

{e5/6} this, Socrates, {being} that for the sake of which were all his labors hitherto, which, first, {211} always is: it neither comes-to-be nor perishes, neither waxes nor wanes;

{211a2/3} then too, {it is} not beautiful in one way, ugly in another, nor {beautiful} at one time and not at another, nor beautiful relative to one thing, ugly relative to another, nor beautiful at one place, ugly at another, as being beautiful to some and ugly to others;[10]

{a5/6} nor, again, will the beautiful appear to him as some face or hands or anything else of which body partakes, nor as a certain account or a certain knowledge,[11]

{a8/b1} nor as being somewhere in something else, e.g., in an animal, in the earth, in heaven, or in anything else, but itself by itself with itself, always being singular in form,

{b2/3} while all the other beautiful {things} are partakers of that {beautiful} in such a way that, while the others are coming-to-be and passing-away, that in no way comes-to-be any larger or smaller or undergoes anything.

{b5/6} So whenever one who goes up from these {mundane things} through rightly boy-loving begins to discern that beautiful, he must be nearly in contact with his goal.

The relation between this and stage 3 is difficult. In 210d3–e1, it looks as if the trainee comes by various pieces of knowledge and that somehow leads him toward this single knowledge that caps them all. It is as if he generalizes on all the knowledges he has in the same way in which, previously, he generalized on all the beautifuls to get the beautiful itself; when he does this with knowledges, he gets the one knowledge that all of them have, and this turns out to be a knowledge of the beautiful.

---

[10] The text of 210e6–211a5: πρῶτον μὲν ἀεὶ ὂν καὶ οὔτε γιγνόμενον οὔτε ἀπολλύμενον, οὔτε αὐξανόμενον οὔτε φθίνον, ἔπειτα οὐ τῇ μὲν καλὸν, τῇ δ᾽ αἰσχρόν, οὐδὲ τοτὲ μέν, τοτὲ δὲ οὔ, οὐδὲ πρὸς μὲν τὸ καλόν, πρὸς δὲ τὸ αἰσχρόν, οὐδ᾽ ἔνθα μὲν καλόν, ἔνθα δὲ αἰσχρόν, ὡς τισὶ μὲν ὂν καλόν, τισὶ δὲ αἰσχρόν. Bury (1932) 129 proposes to delete the last clause, a4–5 ὡς τισὶ . . . αἰσχρόν ("as being . . . others"); Solmsen (1971) 66 n. 14 says that most scholars seem to agree. I am not sure about the consensus: twentieth-century editions, with the MSS, carry the phrase.

[11] *Contra* Festugière (1954) 80, who translates Plato as saying that there is no definition or knowledge of the beautiful (*il n'y aura d'elle ni définition ni science*; see also Festugière [1936] 228–31, Cross [1954] 442–43 = Allen [1965] 22–23); contrast Bluck (1956) 525 = Allen (1965) 37 and esp. Ackrill (1957) 572–73.

At any rate, the beautiful that he now beholds does possess a kind of absolute generality: it is not beautiful in a particular context, and perhaps ugly in another; it is *the* beautiful *itself*, lifted above every particular context (210e6–211a5): it

(1) always exists;[12]

this is explained as meaning that it does not come into being or go out of it (210e6–211a1);

(2) it is not beautiful only in one respect (211a2),

(3) or beautiful only at one time (a3),

(4) or beautiful only relative to one thing (a3–4),

(5) or beautiful only to some people (a4–5).

The beautiful, in short, is here exempted from the dimensions of relativity that affect every individual beautiful object.

But the beautiful is itself a beautiful *object, something* that is beautiful (210e4–5): it is not simply the universal that attaches to all and only the things that are beautiful. The ascent, up to the last stage, proceeds by generalization. But the last stage, although it presents us with an object that is in a sense general, is not reached by further generalization in the way that the results of the preceding stages were reached. What we have now is *beautiful*, just by itself (cf. 211b1: "itself by itself with itself," αὐτὸ καθ' αὑτὸ μεθ' αὑτοῦ). And this is meant to deny that the beautiful is some other thing, a speech or a woman, that is beautiful: *all* it is, is beautiful.

This passage adds a thesis to the Theory of Forms as we got it from the *Phaedo*. There the contrast was between Forms and perceptible individuals. Here we are to contrast the beautiful not merely with perceptible beautifuls but with beautiful practices, laws, and knowledges: the contrast is between the Form and all of its individual instances. Needless to say, this says nothing about what Plato thought when he wrote the *Phaedo* as opposed to what he thought when he wrote the *Symposium*: he might have intended the Argument from Relativity to cover all the same cases in the *Phaedo*. But he did not say so. Here he does.

Something else may have been added as well. In the *Phaedo*, in the passage which we have yet to examine giving an exposition of the final argument for immortality, Socrates was still prepared to talk as if a Form

---

[12] Roochnik (1987) 125–27 thinks Diotima's speech does not commit her to the objective existence of the beautiful. He says of the Forms (127): "There is no argument which can positively establish their existence independent of the human subjects that are doing the arguing." Apparently Diotima does not agree.

such as the beautiful could be *in* things. But here he apparently gives up on that language (211a8–b2), in favor of saying that other things that are beautiful *partake* of that Form. That language we also find in the *Phaedo*, but it has not there edged out the language of immanence. Here, it seems, it has.

CHAPTER 13

Phaedo *95a–107b: Forms and causes*

In *Phaedo* 86e–88b, Cebes objects that none of the previous arguments for immortality has ruled out the possibility of the soul's wearing out: it might exist before we come-to-be, outlast a number of incarnations, and yet perish in the end. What needs to be shown is "that {the} soul is altogether deathless and imperishable" (88b5–6).

Socrates gets around to this objection in 95a–d, and coming-to-be, perishing, and their causes[1] become the center of his attention. He introduces a theory about these matters, which turns out to be the Theory of Forms again. We are not here primarily concerned with the immortality of the soul. But, just as Socrates and Simmias earlier (76d7–77a5) agreed that the existence of the Forms and the preexistence of the soul somehow went together, so here Socrates is going to be telling us (100b7–9) that the existence of the Forms carries immortality with it. This claim, like the earlier one, can only be understood as highly elliptical.

Socrates does not propound his theory straight off. He first discusses some "mechanistic" (as I'll call them) theories he once held (95e–97b). He rejects all of them,[2] and then (97b–99d) introduces a different sort of theory that we may call "teleological"; this, he seems to say, is the only sort of theory that could ever be really adequate, but he has so far been unable to formulate a satisfactory one. I discuss teleological theories in § 13.1.

In 99d, he turns to the Theory of Forms and gives two versions, one (allegedly) simple and safe (99d–103c, § 13.2), and another more sophisticated but still (allegedly) safe (102c–105c, § 13.3). He finally applies the

---

[1] *Pace* Frede (1980) 222–23 = (1987) 129, there is no discernible difference between αἰτία and αἴτιον in this passage of the *Phaedo*. (Frede is followed in this by Lennox [1985] 197 = [2001] 282; Rowe [1992] 90 n. 2 notes that later occurrences of αἴτιον and αἰτία at 110e2 and 112a7–b2 do not differentiate.)

[2] This rejection involves a sort of "principle of noncontrary causality":

Fx because *Gy* → ¬(*Fz* because con*Gw*)

(see 97a8–b3), and this may in turn derive from a Transmission Theory of Causality.

latter to the question of immortality (105c–107b, § 13.4), with results that plainly please him and the others (although Simmias expresses some slight reservation).

13.1. 97B–99D: ANAXAGORAS, TELEOLOGY, AND MECHANISM

Socrates tells us that he heard somone reading, from Anaxagoras' book, that mind was the cause of all things (97b8–c2). This pleased him: if that is so, he thought, mind would place each thing as it would be best for it (c2–6), so, to find out why things come-to-be as they do, one would only have to find out how it would be best (c6–d5). In the expectation that Anaxagoras would explain all sorts of facts of nature in this way (d6–98b3), he obtained a copy of his own (98b4–6). But Anaxagoras failed to live up to the billing: he made no real use of his mind (b8–9) but reverted to mechanistic causes (b7–c2). Socrates protests that this is like explaining a person's actions in terms of the motions of his body with no regard to his intentions (c2–99a4). Rather, in 99a4–b6, he draws a distinction between that *because* of which someone does what he does and those things in the absence of which "the cause could never be a cause" (99b3–4).

Socrates' format for teleological explanations looks like this:

(TE) x is F because it is best for x to be F.

And he insists that, at least by contrast with mechanistic causes, the final causes that appear in such explanations are the *real* causes (99b2–3).

But, after all this build-up, we are not going to be given teleological explanations. Rather, Socrates goes on to say (99c6–d2):

So, while I should most pleasurably have come-to-be anyone's student as to how it stands with this sort of cause, since I was deprived of this {cause} and came-to-be able neither to discover {it} myself, nor to learn {it} from anyone else, do you want me, he said, to make a demonstration for you of how I've undertaken[3] a second sailing in the search for the cause?[4]

And, of course, Cebes is enthusiastic (99d3). So Socrates is finally about to give his own account of causality. That account will center on the Theory of Forms.

---

[3] 99c8–d2 ἐστερήθην . . . ἐγενόμην . . . πεπραγμάτευμαι: Bedu-Addo (1979a) 105 makes a great deal of the change of tense in this passage; he thinks Socrates is not saying that he is *now* deprived of final causes, only that he once was, and at that time was unable to get at them. But, *pace* Bedu-Addo, nothing Socrates says implies that he *is* now able to handle final causes.

[4] 99d1 τῆς αἰτίας: Bedu-Addo (1979a) 105–7 takes this to be a reference to the good, so that Socrates is expressly saying that his second sailing has the good as its destination.

What is the relationship between that account and teleology? Socrates does not present his own account in the *Phaedo* as giving final causes.[5] Yet he has just placed great importance on final causes: mechanistic "explanations," by comparison, merely give that without which what really is the cause would not be a cause (99b3–4). Here the phrase "what really is the cause" (τὸ αἴτιον τῷ ὄντι, 99b3) refers to the final cause in the case of Socrates' decision to remain in prison; he wants to generalize from such cases to the whole world, and just before the passage just quoted, he berates the mechanists for looking to cosmic rotation or the compacting of air to support the earth in the heavens (99b6–c1): "that, in truth, the good and binding binds and holds together, they do not suppose at all" (99c5–6).

So, when at the end of that passage Socrates speaks of himself as having made a second sailing in search of the cause, there is some presumption that he is speaking of a second stab at locating what really is a cause. This is not quite dictated by the text: from 95e9 on the passage is dealing with "the cause of coming-to-be and passing-away in general," and Socrates might be suggesting retreating to the general level and starting over. He has been so read.[6] But plainly the sort of explanations Socrates thinks he *can* give cannot be *incompatible* with teleological ones; perhaps they even should be on the way to such explanations.

There is a general consideration in support of this. Since there is no further direct reference to final causality, the excursus into final causality in 97–99, in retrospect, sounds like a digression.[7] But it ought to have a point. It has none, if Socrates is *simply* abandoning his quest for final causes in 99cd.[8] So I suppose he must envisage, ultimately, embedding what he is doing in some sort of teleological framework. He does not suggest anything in the *Phaedo* about how that framework might look, and, even if there is pertinent material in the *Republic* (which is not really clear) and in the *Timaeus* (which is clearer), those dialogues are not the *Phaedo*. We have, in short, no reason for supposing that the full-blown theory incorporating

---

[5] Contrast Bedu-Addo (1979b) 123–24, Bedu-Addo (1979a) 111.

[6] See, e.g., Gallop (1975) 176, and further references below.

[7] Goodrich (1903/4) 381b, 382a: an "episode" or "parenthesis."

[8] As he is said to be doing by, e.g., Shorey (1884) 13–14 (= Shorey [1980] I 267–68), Shorey (1924) 6–8 (= Shorey [1980] II 313–15), Shorey (1933) 534, Robinson (1953) 142–43, Murphy (1951) 145–46, Vlastos (1969) 297–98 n. 15 (= Vlastos [1970] 138–39 n. 15 = Vlastos [1973b] 82–83 n. 15), Burge (1971) 1–2 n. 2, Stough (1976) 13–14 n. 18. So far I am in agreement with, e.g., Crombie (1962/63) II 161 and Bedu-Addo (1979a) 104–7, but I cannot see how the method Socrates introduces actually *is* the quest for final causes, as we find in Crombie (1962/63) II 168–69, Gould (1963) 77, Bedu-Addo (1979a) 107–11. Gallop (1975) 176–77 occupies, as do I, middle ground.

teleological explanation along with the Theory of Forms stands in back of what Socrates is saying in the *Phaedo*.

There is a connected question. Socrates has just described the account he is about to give, involving the Theory of Forms and the Method of Hypothesis, as his "second sailing." What was his first sailing?

He has previously described himself as having tried to get (a) mechanistic explanations (96a–97b) and (b) teleological explanations (97b–99c). His first sailing must have been one or both of these two attempts. The most natural option,[9] given the sentence (99c6–d2) in which the reference to the second sailing is embedded, is (b): Socrates has been looking for teleological explanations but has found none, so here comes his second shot.[10]

This does not mean that his second sailing renounces the attempt to find teleological explanations: his second sailing might, for all that has so far been said, be a second attempt at precisely the same thing.[11] He might be suggesting that the attempt to meet questions such as "for the sake of *what* are these things larger than those?" head on failed, and so he was driven to another, less direct route.[12] But the fact is that Socrates does not, in the *Phaedo*, say anything that gets him any closer to answers to such questions.

13.2. 99D–103C: FORMS AS CAUSES – THE SAFE THEORY

Socrates' second sailing turns out to involve two things: first, a method according to which one starts with the safest hypothesis, assumes what harmonizes with it, and assumes false what does not, and second, a specific hypothesis that Socrates takes to be safest: that the Forms exist,[13] and then other hypotheses that he takes to harmonize with this one.

The method we shall refer to as the "Method of Hypothesis," under the assumption that it has something to do with the method that came up in the *Meno*. This is discussed in § 13.2.2. The application of this method to questions of causality, which brings in the Theory of Forms, is taken up

---

[9] Not that everyone would agree: according to Geddes, as quoted in Archer-Hind (1894) 156–57, Socrates' first sailing was his attempt at mechanistic physics.

[10] So also Goodrich (1903/4) 381–83, Murphy (1936) 42–43.

[11] Vlastos (1969) 297–98 n. 15 = Vlastos (1973b) 82–83 n. 15 = Vlastos (1970) 138–39 n. 15 points out that in 99c8 Socrates says "I was deprived of this," where the word "this" (ταύτης) refers back to "this sort of cause" (τῆς τοιαύτης αἰτίας), viz., a final cause, in c7. He concludes that there is "no room" for understanding Socrates' second sailing to be another attempt at final causes. Shipton (1979) 51 n. 17 fails to see the force of this objection; the only way around it, as far as I can see, is to lean on the tenses, as does Bedu-Addo (1979a) 105–6 (see n. 3 above).

[12] So, I take it, Bedu-Addo (1979a) 107.   [13] Tait (1985/86) 468 denies this.

in §§ 13.2.3–13.2.4. First we should consider a question raised by Socrates' opening comments that, once again, looks back toward his first sailing, and forward to his next voyage.

13.2.1. Socrates' previous failure (99d–100a)

He begins his travelogue by saying (99d4–5) that he had previously failed in his attempt to look at τὰ ὄντα, the things that are, the beings. He has previously said that he failed both at mechanism and at teleology: he could now be referring to either or both of these failures. If we think of these as two different unsuccessful attempts to explain how or why perceptible things come-to-be and pass-away, Socrates is referring to his general failure on that score.

Then the beings he failed in his attempt to look at are simply the perceptible things whose coming-into-being and passing-away he set out to explain. At any rate, they are not Forms.[14] Socrates is about to bring the Forms back in on his second sailing; he is going to use them in explaining features of our perceptible world. He can hardly be saying that he has failed in his previous attempts to look at these Forms: he has mentioned no such failed attempts.

He also says (99e1–6) he is now afraid to look at τὰ πράγματα, the objects (e3), directly, with his eyes, since that is potentially soul blinding, so he resorts to images of them in λόγοι, accounts.[15] It sounds as if the beings of d5 are the objects of e3, perceptible things that come-to-be and pass-away: Socrates said earlier (96c4–6) that he was "so badly blinded" (c5–6 οὕτω σφόδρα ἐτυφλώθην; cf. 99b4–6) by his examination of the causes of coming-to-be and passing-away that he had to unlearn various things he thought he knew; he is picking up that metaphor again here. The difficulty that, on this reading, Socrates is representing λόγοι as images of perceptible things is really not much of a difficulty to begin with: it is only if we read this passage supposing that Plato already has in mind the extended metaphor of the divided line in *Republic* VI, and imagining that he would never allow himself any metaphor that conflicted with that one,[16] that we will see any difficulty here. And besides, Socrates immediately (99e6–100a3)

---

[14] Despite Archer-Hind (1894) 97, 156–62, Bedu-Addo (1979b) 113, and perhaps Crombie (1962/63) II 157 (but see 166–167). See also Goodrich (1903/4) 382a and Burnet (1911) 108.

[15] This translation is deliberately vague; alternatives such as "definitions" (Bluck [1955] 113), "propositions" (Hackforth [1955] 133, 138; Sayre [1969] 5 n. 4), and "theories" (Gallop [1975] 51, 178; Grube, in Cooper [1997] 86; Tait [1985/86], 457 and *passim*) may beg questions.

[16] So Archer-Hind (1894) 158; cf. Goodrich (1903/4) 383b.

says that examining things in λόγοι is not really examining them in images any more than examining them "in deeds" (ἐν ἔργοις) is.

13.2.2. The method (100a, 101d–102a)

What Socrates says about his examination of things in accounts is very lean (100a3–7):

At any rate, I started off in this way: having hypothesized each time {an} account which I judge to be most powerful, I posit as being true whatever {things} seem to me concordant with this, both about cause and about all the others, and whatever {things} don't, {I posit} as not true.

Socrates knows this is too little to go on, and Cebes does not understand (100a7–9). But, before considering the example to follow, let us first consider what can be bled out of Socrates' remarks so far.

He now (100a3–4) speaks of "hypothesizing" an account (also in 100b5–6, 101d7), and the noun "hypothesis" appears in the sequel (101d2, 3, 7, 107b5).[17] These words are enough in themselves to connect what is done here with what is said in the *Meno*. There it was something Socrates undertook in the absence of what he really wanted: a definition for excellence on the basis of which he could decide the question of its teachability. Here there is not much about definitions; instead, it seems that what Socrates really wants is an explanation of things' coming-to-be and passing-away that would tell him why it is best for them to do those things in the way that they do. In both cases, it is a method employed in the absence of something preferable.

Socrates "hypothesizes" in each case the account he judges to be the firmest, and then whatever seems to him concordant with this account (τούτῳ συμφωνεῖν)[18] he posits as true, and whatever does not seem concordant he posits as not true (100a3–7).

This is difficult.[19] Positing what is concordant with one's hypothesized account is, one might think, sound practice only if "is concordant with" amounts to "is entailed by"; mere consistency will not do, since, for any true hypothesis, there are any number of things consistent with it but false. But rejecting as false what is not concordant with one's hypothesis is sound practice only if "is concordant with" is read as "is consistent with"; entailment will not do, since, for any true hypothesis, there are any number

---

[17] And earlier: 92d7, 93c10, 94b1, 98a2.   [18] Grube (in Cooper [1997] 86) "agrees with."

[19] See Robinson (1953) 126–27, Ross (1951) 28, Bedu-Addo (1979b) 116–17 (but Bedu-Addo seems to gloss over the difficulty at 117–18).

of things not entailed by it that are nonetheless true.[20] At this rate, we want Socrates to be saying that he takes what is entailed by his fundamental hypothesis to be true and what is inconsistent with it to be false.[21]

But why should we confine ourselves to the options of entailment and consistency? At the time of the writing of the *Phaedo*, no one had yet done any formal logic: there is no reason to think that Plato was in a position to formulate the correlative ideas of logical entailment and logical consistency.[22] The logical relationships he is employing are less stringent than these.

One obvious direction in which the notion of entailment could be loosened up is by retreating to what we might call "enthymematic entailment," where background premises are required to make the inference go. Let us try that for starters.

Socrates assumes the firmest hypothesis he can: the one he takes to be most defensible. Suppose his initial hypothesis is that virtue or excellence is knowledge, (EK). This is a hypothesis Socrates knows needs defense, but it might well seem to him, at some stage, the best he can do. He might, at that point, just put off the actual defense of this hypothesis until later.

He then assumes what is concordant with (EK) and rejects what is discordant with it. To determine what is concordant with it, one of the things to do would be to see what it entails.[23] He might take it that (EK) entails that courage is (a) knowledge, (CK), as well. But (CK) is not entailed by (EK) alone; it is entailed by (EK) together with the claim that courage is an excellence. But since the latter claim is almost unquestionable, it may seem acceptable to speak of (EK) as entailing (CK). What about the claim that excellence is teachable, (ET)? This is entailed by (EK) together with a more questionable claim, that knowledge is teachable. But it still may claim concordance with (EK). So also might the claim (SP) that no

---

[20] Sayre (1969) 22–28 tries to get around this dilemma by confining the claims under consideration in such a way that nonequivalence amounts to inconsistency. He seems to think that this holds in (certain cases in?) geometrical analysis. He considers (27) an equation in three unknowns, and, astonishingly, commits himself to the claim that "any equation expressed in the same terms" will either be equivalent to that one or inconsistent with it. This is manifestly false.

[21] So Hackforth (1955) 139, but he does not seem to see the trouble with interpreting the one occurrence of συμφωνεῖν in 100a5 as "is entailed by" without the negative and "is consistent with" with the negative. Robinson (1953) 128–29 thinks that this is what Plato should have said, but didn't quite, for the sake of "conversational simplicity" (129).

[22] Cf. Tait (1985/86) 465 on Robinson.

[23] This is not enough to guarantee that these entailments are consistent with the original claim or with each other: if the starting hypothesis is internally inconsistent, it entails its own negation. This is of some importance given the sequel, as we shall see. (The objection raised by Robinson [1953] 129–30 against reading "concordant with" as "consistent with" is a red herring, as Robinson himself goes on to show: 131–32.)

one is voluntarily vicious, lacking in excellence, although the background premises here require real work.

But confining "concordance" to "enthymematic entailment" might still be too strict. Socrates might also want to determine what is consistent with his fundamental hypothesis and, while not entailed by it, is relevant to it, or relevantly similar to it: he might ask whether certain claims are defensible given, or are rendered plausible by, his hypothesis, where the connection is even more informal than that of enthymematic entailment.

He says a little more about the relations among the various claims later on. He has introduced the Form the beautiful as something participation in which causes other things to be beautiful, and insists that we avoid giving any other reply to the question why this or that is beautiful (101bc), instead "clutching at" (ἐχόμενος, i.e., holding on to, 101d2) the safety of our hypothesis, and, if anyone should "clutch at" (ἔχοιτο, i.e., attack, 101d4)[24] one's fundamental hypothesis, he has three recommendations as to how to proceed (101d1–102a1).[25]

First, he says, you should check to see if "the things started off {ὁρμηθέντα} from that {hypothesis}"[26] are concordant or discordant with each other (101d3–5).

"Started off" again ought to have something to do with entailment,[27] but it need not be a very strict notion of entailment that is in question. And the same qualifications apply to the terms "concordant" and "discordant" here as before, but it is now even more obvious that "concordant with" cannot be confined to "entailed by," for then to find that the "things started off by" one's hypothesis were concordant with each other would be to find that they entailed each other, and an acceptable hypothesis hardly needs to be one such that the things it "starts off" entail each other.[28] Consistency is more promising than entailment: for a hypothesis to be acceptable, it must be that the further claims to which it gives rise are jointly defensible. If they are outright inconsistent, they are not jointly defensible; but they may also not be jointly defensible if the only plausible way of defending

---

[24] Difficulty has been made over these uses of ἔχειν; emendations have been suggested: cf. Jackson (1882) 148 n. 1, Archer-Hind (1894) 102–3, Burnet (1911) 113 *ad* 101d3, Huby (1959) 14 n. 1, Gallop (1975) 235 n. 67. Gallop says "L.S.J. give no parallel for [the sense] required at 101d3," and is tempted by an emendation. But LSJ list "attack" under the same heading as "cling to" for the middle of ἔχω with the genitive: see *s.v.* ἔχω (A), C2. The verb is simply highly flexible, and emendation is not called for.

[25] Bluck (1955) 13–14, 162, 165–66 supposes 101d–102a to be dealing with Platonic causes whereas 99d–100a was concerned with Socratic λόγοι (see also Bluck [1957] 21 and ff.). But if 101d is *not* dealing with the same claims as 99d, Socrates' exposition is simply a mess.

[26] 101d4–5 τὰ ἀπ' ἐκείνης ὁρμηθέντα. Cf. e2 ὡρμημένων, 100a3 ὥρμησα.

[27] See Robinson (1953) 129.   [28] So also Sayre (1969) 35.

one is inconsistent with the only plausible way of defending the other, and so on.

Socrates' second recommendation (101d6–8) is that, when you finally have to give an account of your hypothesis, you should do it on the basis of another hypothesis that is the best available among hypotheses higher up (ἥτις τῶν ἄνωθεν βελτίστη), proceeding in the same way until you get to something "sufficient" (ἱκανόν, 101d8). Nothing is said about what might constitute sufficiency,[29] or about what makes one hypothesis "higher" than another. A few things are obvious from the context. If Socrates starts from a hypothesis he takes to be "firmest," someone calls that hypothesis in question, and Socrates takes up this challenge, he requires *at a minimum* something which both he and his interlocutor take to be firm, and such that once it is accepted, there is some way of arguing from it as a premise (perhaps with other premises) to the original hypothesis as conclusion.

The third and last recommendation: you must avoid talking about the starting point and what is "started off" from it at the same time if you want to get hold of things (101e1–3). There is nothing to indicate what sort of mistake Socrates has in mind, but it is natural to read him as telling us to keep the preceding two procedures apart: considering the consequences of one's initial hypothesis is one thing, and considering what it is a consequence of is another.

We can only flesh out these airy comments on the method by attending to its application.

13.2.3. *The reintroduction of the Forms (100a–c)*

After the original statement of his method (100a4–7), Socrates pauses to clarify things (a7–9). What he offers by way of clarification is actually the target example of the application of the method, a theory of causality centered on the Forms.

He says that his talk of these entities is only repetition of what he has always been saying, both earlier in the day and earlier than that (100b1–3): so Plato is here, as in 72–78, seeing the Socrates of the earlier dialogues as asking about the Forms that have first come out of the closet in this dialogue. And what he says here is quite reminiscent of what he and Simmias had been saying in 76d7–77a5: they had agreed that the existence of "the things we're always babbling about, a beautiful and good and every such substance" (76d8–9) and the preexistence of the soul stood or

---

[29] Tait (1952) 111–14 explores a number of options.

fell together; now Socrates is telling us that the existence of these "much-babbled" (πολυθρύλητα, 100b5) entities will carry with it the immortality of the soul. Both claims are somewhat elliptical: the logical relationship between the existence of Forms and the immortality of the soul is not one of simple entailment.

Socrates starts by "hypothesizing that there is a beautiful itself by itself and a good and a tall and all the others" (100b5–7): his first hypothesis is the Theory of Forms.

Is it the Forms that are hypothesized, or the claim that they exist? In 100a3–4, what is hypothesized is an "account," whatever that is. The pronominal phrases in a5–8 – Socrates posits as being true "whatever {things}" harmonize with his fundamental hypothesis, etc. – ought to refer to things of the same type as whatever is hypothesized in the fundamental hypothesis. Now the pronominal phrase in 100b1 – Socrates is speaking of "just the {things}" he's never stopped speaking of – is made in the sequel to refer to "those much-babbled {things}," the Forms. But in b5–6 Socrates says that he wants to hypothesize "that {a} beautiful itself by itself is something," etc. So there is, perhaps, a tendency on Socrates' part to slip from talking about hypothesizing claims to talking about the things the claims are about. Perhaps this tendency is regrettable, or dangerous, or something. But until it actually leads to disaster, there is little cause for reproach.

On balance, it is pretty clearly the claims that are hypothesized in the first instance.[30] So Socrates' hypothesis is that claims like

(hb) There is such a thing as the beautiful
(hg) There is such a thing as the good

are true. Let us put down the generalized hypothesis as:

(HF) There is such a thing as the F;

then (hb) and (hg) become instances of this.

If we look back to the account Socrates has given of his method, it is plain that "the strongest account," which, according to that method, one is to begin by positing, is just (HF), the Theory of Forms. We are going to build a theory of causality on that foundation: Socrates has now said (100b3–4) that the Forms illustrate the kind of cause he's concerned with,

---

[30] But Bluck (1955) 161–63 and *passim* insists that it is not propositions that are in question but "provisional notions of Forms." The support for this is extremely vague, and requires us to understand "provisional notions" that are not propositions to have entailments (see also Ackrill [1956] 179).

and further (b7–9) that if their existence is granted, he hopes he can show the soul immortal. So the subsequent theory of causality, and finally the claim that the soul is immortal, are clearly to be things concordant with the fundamental hypothesis (HF), and so are to be accepted along with (HF). There will also be some things rejected as not concordant with the Theory of Forms.

If the fact that the immortality of the soul is "concordant" with the Theory of Forms is to count in its favor, "concordant with" is going to have to mean more than "compatible with." But if it means "entailed by," Socrates is not going to be successful in showing that the immortality of the soul is concordant with the Theory of Forms. For other premises are going to be introduced that are, logically speaking, independent of the Theory of Forms. We are once again driven to the conclusion that "concordant with" means neither "compatible with" nor "entailed by," but something vaguer.

13.2.4. *The application to causes (100c–101d)*

Socrates had earlier said that his method can be applied to causality and to anything else (100a6, § 13.2.2); here the concern is going to be causality. He now says (100c4–6): "it seems to me that, if there is anything else beautiful besides the beautiful itself, it is not beautiful because of any other single {thing} than because it partakes of that beautiful." So it must be concordant with, and so accepted along with, the fundamental hypothesis (HF), that, if there is anything besides the beautiful itself that is beautiful, it is so only because it partakes of the beautiful itself (100c4–6). So we expand our theory as follows.

First, Socrates plainly presupposes that the beautiful itself is beautiful, just as we should have expected given the Argument from Relativity. So we can add to (HF) the Self-Predication

(HFSP) The F is F.

This is not so much an additional hypothesis as part of what is meant by (HF).

But, second, there is an additional hypothesis involving causality, of which Socrates shortly will give further examples, and some elaboration: it is by tallness that tall things are tall, and by shortness that short things are short (100e5–6); ten is more than (πλείω) eight by "manyness" (πλῆθος), plurality (101b4–6); two cubits is taller than one cubit by largeness (101b6–7); the cause of two's coming-to-be is partaking of the dyad and that of one's coming-to-be is partaking of the monad (101c4–7). The general formula (c3–4) looks like this:

(HFC) $x \neq$ the $F \rightarrow$ (x is $F \rightarrow$ x is F because x partakes of the F).

In 100d7–8, e2–3, Socrates shows that he is prepared to abbreviate this to:

(HFCa) $x \neq$ the $F \rightarrow$ (x is $F \rightarrow$ x is F because of the F).

Socrates goes on to tell us what his hypothesis or hypotheses rule out (100c9–d3): this will include the "mechanistic" causes (see especially 100e8–101b2, 101b4–5, b6–7, b9–c2, c7). By contrast with these causes, Socrates says (100d3–8),

simply, artlessly, even perhaps foolishly, I hold this close to myself, that nothing else {d5} makes it beautiful other than the presence {παρουσία} or communion {κοινωνία} or however and in whatever way it comes on[31] of that beautiful; for I don't make any further claims about that, but {I do claim} that {it is} by the beautiful that all beautiful {things are} beautiful.

This, he tells us (d8–e3), is the "safe" way of explaining why something is beautiful.

The "mechanistic" causes, then, are things Socrates rejects as false because they are not concordant with (HF).[32] It sounds in 100d4–5 as if he was saying that *any* explanation other than "*x* partakes of the *F*" is ruled out, but he will shortly be allowing room for other explanations; the most he can mean is that explanations *incompatible* with "*x* partakes of the *F*" are to be ruled out. But here again we must not insist on strict incompatibility: there may only be an incompatibility given some background premises. Let us call this "enthymematic incompatibility," and write "$p \Downarrow q$" for "p is enthymematically incompatible with q." Then Socrates is operating with something like the following Rejection Principle:

(RP) [(x is F because p) $\Downarrow$ (x is F because x partakes of the F)] $\rightarrow$
     $\neg$(x is F because p).

---

[31] 100d6 προσγενομένη: retaining the reading of the MSS and supposing with Bluck (1955) 115 n. 1 that the grammatical mishap (the participle should be προσγενομένου, agreeing with ἐκείνου τοῦ καλοῦ in l. 5) is due to the intervening nouns παρουσία and κοινωνία. Alternatives: emend to προσγενομένου (Cornford [1939] 77 n. 1, Hackforth [1955] 134 n. 1, Rowe [1993] 82, 243), or to προσαγορευομένη (due to Wyttenbach: Burnet [1911] 111, Duke et al. [1995] 158, with papyrus evidence).

[32] According to Sprague (1968) 634, this accounts for the "safety" of Socrates' theory of causality; I doubt this.

The Rejection Principle (RP) is to stand in back of his rejecting such claims as the following ("*" signals rejection):

(*H1) *x* is beautiful because *x* has a rich color
(*H2) *x* is taller than *y* by (because of) a head, etc.

These are plainly not *directly* incompatible with (HF): (*H1) is not the negation of, or equivalent to the negation of, the claim that *x* is beautiful because *x* partakes of the beautiful. Indeed, one might have taken *x*'s rich color as explaining how it is that *x* partakes of the beautiful. There must be background premises at work; what Socrates says next shows this.

He gives two reasons for ruling out the claim that someone is taller than someone else by a head: (1) the taller would be taller and the shorter shorter by the same thing, viz., the head; (2) the taller would be taller by something that is itself short, viz., the head (101a5–b2). When Socrates states these reasons, Simmias laughs (101b3). We must separate the silly from the serious. The pun involved in construing "by a head" in "taller by a head" as if it gave a *cause* is silly. But the rejection of alternatives to "by tallness" is serious if anything in this passage is. And the reasons Socrates gives for rejecting this silly alternative must be serious as well, since in the sequel (101b7–8) he takes it that these reasons generalize to cover the case of ten's being more than eight by two, and two cubits' being taller than one cubit. So we had better look more closely at them.

According to (1), we cannot have something taller and something shorter by, because of, the same thing; Socrates is then presupposing, in general, a Causal Principle to the effect that[33]

(CP1) The cause of something's being *F* cannot also be the cause of something's being con*F*.

According to (2), we cannot have something tall by, because of, something short; Socrates is presupposing that:

(CP2) The cause of something's being *F* cannot itself be con*F*.

Thus generalized, there is no difficulty in applying Socrates' premises to rule out ten's being larger than eight because of two. It is not so easy to apply them to the other cases.

For the "theories" that two comes-to-be through addition or through splitting, we have an earlier passage to go on: 96e–97b shows that Socrates

---

[33] See also Burge (1971) 4–5, Cresswell (1971) 245–46.

would argue as follows. Suppose we say that the (physical) addition of one rock to another is the cause of there being two rocks. Now suppose one of the rocks is split into two: we shall have to say that the splitting of one rock into two is the cause of there being two rocks; the two "explanations" are on a par. But addition is a matter of juxtaposition and splitting a matter of separation, and juxtaposition and separation are contraries. But we cannot have contraries causing the same thing.

This involves a further premise, related to (CP1) and (CP2) but not quite the same as either:

> (CP3) What is caused by something's being *F* cannot be caused by anything's being con*F*.

Perhaps this is close enough to (CP1) to be taken as part of the same package.[34]

But can we attack "theories" to the effect that something is beautiful because of its color or shape using such premises? Let us remind ourselves of what happened to the gold in the *Hippias Major*: we can't suppose that gold makes things beautiful, because if Pheidias had made the eyes in his statue of Athena of gold rather than ivory, that would have been, at least comparatively, ugly (290ab). Under Socrates' present assumptions, in particular, (CP1) above, that would mean gold could not be the cause of anything's being beautiful. It is not hard to imagine cases like this for any given color or shape. So Socrates' premises are usable against these theories as well.

13.2.5. Socratic assumptions

It is usually supposed that the Method of Hypothesis here being introduced is a new departure. But Socrates is made to include it in his autobiography: after he had given up on the investigation of nature, he turned to this method. It is as if Plato were trying to characterize, in his own terms, what Socrates had been up to. So we must ask: how does the method here described relate to the method of Socrates as it appears in Socratic dialogues? In particular, where are there any λόγοι "hypothesized" in those dialogues?

His fundamental hypotheses here in the *Phaedo* are the existential admissions that instantiate (HF). There are such existential admissions strewn

---

[34] It gives us the principle mentioned in n. 2.

throughout the Socratic dialogues. These existential admissions are part of a framework of assumptions that are put to use in refuting attempted definitions. Another piece of the framework is what we were calling a Transmission Theory of Causality. The elements of this theory were these three claims, of which the third is a consequence of the other two:

(TT1) The F is the cause of other things' being F
(TT2) What causes things to be F is itself F and never con$F$
∴ (TT3) The F is itself F and never con$F$

Hypothesis (HFCa) is (TT1), (CP2) is half of (TT2), and (HFSP) is half of (TT3). If we assume (TT1) and (TT2), we have not only (TT3), but all of the (H)'s and all of the (CP)'s as consequences. (TT2) entails (CP2) by simplification, as (TT3) entails (HFSP). (CP1) follows from (TT2): the cause of something's being F, by (TT2), is F and never con$F$, and the cause of something's being con$F$, by (TT2), is con$F$. So the same thing cannot both cause something to be F and cause something to be con$F$. And similarly, the intent of (TT2) is plainly that it is the fact that the cause is itself F that makes it a cause of other things' being F; so neither can we have a cause's being F cause something and another cause's being con$F$ cause that same thing, and that is (CP3).

This interrelationship between the hypotheses of the *Phaedo* and the Transmission Theory of the earlier dialogues is hardly an accident. Socrates is here made to say that, having given up on mechanism, and having failed at teleology, he turned to hypothesizing. The hypotheses he lists as those he turned to are ones he had in fact employed in his quest for definitions.

The *Meno*, of course, bears this out by treating other assumptions in the Socratic framework as hypotheses. But there is one crucial difference between the set of assumptions hypothesized in the *Meno* and the set here: the hypothesis here labeled (HF) has now been elevated, by the Argument from Relativity, to a claim about another world.

Socrates takes great comfort in the "safety" of his theory (100d8–e3; cf. 101d2): it is here being treated as virtually a triviality. Its safety turns on its triviality: beautiful things are beautiful because of the beautiful, however that works. No sane person could deny such a trifling claim. Socrates has said it over and over again, in pursuit of definitions, and his interlocutors, however hostile, stupid, or otherwise perverse they were, never found anything to object to on this score. This was just a preliminary to defining things.

But, we must remember, if this theory requires the Argument from Relativity, it is not as trivial as it is being made to look.

13.2.6. The semantics of the theory (102a–d)

The examples now introduced carry us back to those of 72–78, where Socrates had picked "equal" out of the trio "larger," "equal," and "smaller" (see 75c9); his sample Form now is "largeness." The word μέγας, "large," used of a human being, typically means "tall," and σμικρός, "small", means "short"; these translations fit better here, so let us stick with them from here on.

According to Phaedo, once Socrates had elicited agreement on (HF) (102b1–3), he got Cebes to agree that (102b4–6) "whenever you say Simmias is taller than Socrates but shortler than Phaedo, then you are saying that both are in Simmias {ἐν τῷ Σιμμίᾳ}, both tallness and shortness." The Forms, after 74a, are as transcendent as anyone might wish, but the "language of immanence" is still in play: both tallness and shortness are "in" Simmias, and in Socrates' next speech, Simmias "has" tallness and Socrates shortness (102d2; cf. c4, c7). But, of course, this is metaphor. Socrates has put himself on record as not committed to any particular way of explaining the relationship between Forms and ordinary things (100d6–8: see § 13.2.4); there (d5–6) he had used the terms "presence" and "communion" as illustrative of what the relationship might turn out to be. In 100c5 and 101c3–6 he used the term "partake of" (μετέχειν; cf. "participate in," μεταλαμβάνειν, in 102b2).

He now uses his example to make a further claim about how we talk (102b8–c10):

> But, as a matter of fact, he said, you agree that, as for the {claim} that Simmias exceeds Socrates, it is not so that, as it is spoken in the words, so also the {c} truth holds?[35] For, I suppose, {you agree} it is not that Simmias is of a nature to exceed by his being Simmias, but by the tallness which he in fact has;[36] nor, again, that he

---

[35] 102b8–c1 ἀλλὰ γάρ, ἦ δ' ὅς, ὁμολογεῖς τὸ τὸν Σιμμίαν ὑπερέχειν Σωκράτους οὐχ ὡς τοῖς ῥήμασι λέγεται οὕτω καὶ τὸ ἀληθὲς ἔχειν; This sentence is somewhat difficult. The above translation is pretty much what Rowe (1993) 250 suggests, except that I am taking the articular infinitive τὸ . . . ὑπερέχειν as an accusative of respect. For alternatives see Burnet (1911) 115 *ad* b8, Archer-Hind (1894) 105 *ad* 14, Robin (1926) 76; Fowler (1914) 351, Gallop (1975) 54; and Bluck (1955) 119, Hackforth (1955) 147.

[36] 102c1–3 οὐ γάρ που πεφυκέναι Σιμμίαν ὑπερέχειν τούτῳ, τῷ Σιμμίαν εἶναι, ἀλλὰ τῷ μεγέθει ὃ τυγκάνει ἔχων: Jowett (1953) 460, Bluck (1955) 119, Hackforth (1955) 119, and Gallop (1975) 54 all translate the first clause as if Socrates were saying: "Simmias doesn't exceed because he is of a nature to exceed, that is, because he is Simmias" (Grube [1981] 141 has it right). But that, although it may

exceeds Socrates because Socrates is Socrates, but because Socrates has shortness relative to that one's tallness?

True.

{c7} And again, that it is not that he is exceeded by Phaedo by {virtue of} this, that Phaedo is Phaedo, but because Phaedo has tallness relative to the shortness of Simmias?

It is a bit hard to fix just what Socrates' claim in 102b8–c5 is. He seems to say (b8–c1) that certain words do not express the fact that Simmias exceeds Socrates in accordance with the truth. It is not clear what words are here being pronounced deficient.[37] At first glance, the deficient words are just "Simmias exceeds Socrates."[38] But Socrates was just discussing what is really going on when you say "Simmias is taller than Socrates but shorter than Phaedo" (102b4–5); what you are really saying then is that there are in Simmias both tallness and shortness (b5–6). Then it sounds as if the words he is seeing as inadequate are "Simmias is taller than Socrates" etc.[39]

In 102c1–5, 7–9 Socrates gives reasons for condemning such statements as misleading: Simmias is not taller than Socrates because Simmias is Simmias, or because Socrates is Socrates, and he is not shorter than Phaedo because Phaedo is Phaedo. So he is assuming that, if "Simmias is taller than Socrates" is straightforwardly true, it entails "Simmias is taller than Socrates because Simmias is Simmias." If we generalize this, we get a Theory of Predication according to which the only true predications are essential predications, an Ultra-Essentialist Theory of Predication:

(UETP) x is F → x is F because x is x

Now in fact there is evidence elsewhere that Plato tended toward (UETP):[40] toward saying that the only thing that is F is the F itself. It may lower the pitch of this claim if we phrase it as: the only thing that is *really* F is the F itself, but this is only a matter of tone; the content of the song is the same. Fortunately, however, Ultra-Essentialism plays

---

be what Socrates intended to say, is not precisely what he does say: rather, he rejects "Simmias is Simmias" as an explanation for the fact that Simmias "is of a nature" to exceed. Here "is of a nature" is really too strong: "is of a sort" might be better.

[37] Tait (1985/86) 480–81 takes the reference to be to the words of 102b5–6, but he does not explain how 102c1–2, "for . . . it is not that . . . by being Simmias," c2–3 "nor . . . because Socrates is Socrates," c6–7 "it is not . . . that Phaedo is Phaedo" would then be at all relevant.

[38] See n. 35 for references.

[39] So Gallop (1975) 192, Gallop (1976) 151 n. 6. But I am not convinced that the expression "Simmias exceeds Socrates," as Gallop says in the latter place, "stands for the truth which the words 'Simmias is taller than Socrates' are alleged to misrepresent."

[40] See *Euthydemus* 281e2–5, *Lysis* 220ab, *Hippias Major* 289c, and Simplicius, Diels (1882/95) I 97.25–28.

no discernible role in the argument to follow, and we need not pursue it here.

Cebes endorses Socrates' theory of causality, and Socrates says (102d6–103a2):

> it seems to me not only that the tallness itself will never be at the same time tall and short, but also that the tallness in us never receives the short and will never be exceeded, but one or the other of two things: either it flees, gets out of the way, whenever the contrary, the short, goes toward it, or when this comes toward it, it perishes; but it will not, by enduring and admitting shortness, be other than what it was. Just so I, by admitting and enduring shortness, and still being just what I am, am this same short {person}; but that, which is tall, will not submit to being short; and in the same way the short that is in us will never become or be tall, nor will any of the contraries, still being what it was, become and be at the same time the contrary, but either it withdraws or perishes in undergoing this.

This purported summary may not confuse Cebes, who wholeheartedly agrees (103a3), but it has confused others, from the very moment of its utterance. For at this point an interlocutor whose identity Phaedo is unable to recall intrudes with a suspicion that Socrates' present position contradicts his previous one to the effect that contraries come-to-be from their contraries. Socrates straightens him out, and in the course of doing so says (103b2–11):

> then it was being said that from the contrary *thing* the contrary *thing* comes-to-be, but now, that the contrary *itself* can never come-to-be contrary to itself, neither that in us nor that in nature. For then, my friend, we were talking about the {things} that have the contraries, derivatively naming them after those, but now about those things themselves which, when they are present in {them}, the {things} named get their derivative names; and {we are saying} that these themselves will never admit each other's coming-to-be.

That takes care of the anonymous interlocutor, who falls silent. But there remains a popular confusion over this speech of Socrates and the preceding one, turning on what Socrates means when he speaks of "the tallness in us" in 102d7, "the short that is in us" in e6, and "the {contrary} in us" in 103b5. The first of these locutions contrasts with "the tallness itself" (102d6), and the last with "the {contrary} in nature" (103b5). So, many have inferred,[41]

[41] E.g., Stallbaum (1850) 194; Bluck (1955) 17–18, 118; Hackforth (1955) 147; Keyt (1963) 168; Vlastos (1969) 298 = Vlastos (1970/71) II 140–41 = Vlastos (1973) 84–85; Nehamas (1972/73) 475; Fujisawa (1974) 45, Gallop (1975) 195; Frede (1978) 28; Dorter (1982) 142; 163–64; Matthen (1984) 281; Bostock

Socrates is introducing a third layer of entities between the Forms and the mundane objects that "participate in," or whatever it is that they do (recalling Socrates' studious fence sitting in 100d, § 13.2.4) relative to those Forms. These entities mediate in the process of participation; they are *in* the participants, representing at that level the transcendent Forms.

We should at least be suspicious here. For, after all, we *must* recall Socrates' fence sitting: he had said that, to keep things safe, he would have nothing to say about how the relationship between Forms and mundane objects worked, but, under this interpretation, he certainly does have something to say, and it is far from safe. He will shortly sophisticate the theory on just this point, but then he will take great pains to announce that that is what he is doing. If he already has a new layer of entities in his ontology, he has slipped it in without a whisper.

He would have had to be doing that in 102b, where he says that the claim that Simmias is bigger than Socrates but shorter than Phaedo really amounts to claiming that there are in Simmias both tallness and shortness (b4–6, § 13.2.6). But plainly tallness and shortness in that sentence refer to Forms: Phaedo had just said that everybody present had now conceded the existence of the Forms, and his report of this sentence takes off from that. The fact is that "in" is just one of the words that Socrates uses for the relationship about which he wants to remain noncommittal between Forms and mundane objects. So perhaps we should be more than suspicious about the alleged "Forms in us."

In fact, we should just reject the idea that there are any such things, apart from the Forms themselves. For that idea will not survive a careful reading of what Socrates says to the anonymous interlocutor. He contrasts the earlier claim that contraries come-to-be from their contraries, with the present claim that contraries can never come-to-be contrary to themselves, by saying: earlier we were talking about the things that *have* the contraries (περὶ τῶν ἐχόντων τὰ ἐναντία, 103b6), whereas now we are talking about the contraries *themselves*; and he states the present claim as follows (b4–5):

the contrary *itself* can never come-to-be contrary to itself, neither that in us nor that in nature {αὐτὸ τὸ ἐναντίον ἑαυτῷ ἐναντίον οὐκ ἄν ποτε γένοιτο, οὔτε τὸ ἐν ἡμῖν οὔτε τὸ ἐν τῇ φύσει}.

This clause does *not* contrast "the contrary in us" with "the contrary itself"; it contrasts "the contrary itself in us" with "the contrary itself in nature." And then it is plain that the contrast is not between two different entities,

---

(1986) 179–84. *Contra*: Burnet (1911) 116 *ad* d7, 117 *ad* b5; Verdenius (1958) 232–33; O'Brien (1967/68) 201–3; Guthrie (1975) 353–56. I condense here argument contained in Dancy (1991) 14–18, with a few additional references.

but between a single entity under two different conditions: the contrary itself, the Form tallness or whatever it is, as it is by itself and as it is when it bears whatever relationship it does to Simmias, Socrates, Phaedo, or whoever. The present claim, he says (b8–c2), is "about those things themselves which, when they are present in" mundane objects (περὶ ἐκείνων αὐτῶν ὧν ἐνόντων), give derived names such as "tall" to those objects. These "things themselves" are simply the Forms, here again said to be "present in" their participants.

So Socrates does not tell us that there is a third layer of entities between the Forms and mundane objects; indeed, what he says leaves no room for such a layer.

But then what about Socrates' claim that, at the approach of the short, the tallness in us either "gets out of the way" (φεύγειν καὶ ὑπεκχωρεῖν, 102d9; ἀπέρχεσθαι, 103a1) or "perishes" (ἀπόλλυσθαι, 102e2, 103a1)? The latter option can hardly be available to a Form.[42]

But Socrates soon tells us that the number three "will first perish and undergo anything else before enduring, while still being three, to come-to-be even" (104c1–3). And perishing is no more an option for the number three than it is for a Form; indeed, in 104d5–6 Socrates refers to the number three as "the idea of three" (ἡ τῶν τριῶν ἰδέα). In 102d–103a Socrates is merely stating the abstract possibilities – or, rather, he is stating the abstract possibilities that he will subsequently find useful, for the argument is going to turn on the idea that the soul can only withdraw, not perish, at the approach of death.

That requires an extension of the Safe Theory of Causality.

13.3. INTERMEDIATES AS CAUSES: THE LEARNED SAFE THEORY (103C–105C)

He extends the Safe Theory of Causality; the extension, he thinks, is still safe (105b7–8), but he refers to the earlier Safe Theory as "unlearned" (ἀμαθῆ, 105c1). The new, Learned, Theory requires a new mode of explanation, but no new entities at all.

Socrates begins by distinguishing the hot and the cold from fire and snow, respectively (103c10–d3), but finds that a point can now be made about fire and snow parallel to the one that was just made for such things as the hot and the cold. The original point would have been that the hot must either withdraw or perish at the approach of the cold, and so also the cold at the approach of the hot. The new one is that fire, too, must withdraw

---

[42] Devereux (1994) 68: cf. Fine (1986) 77 n. 12.

or perish at the approach of the cold, and snow likewise at the approach of the hot (103d5–e1); so not only is the Form, the hot, always, under all circumstances, hot, but fire too is always, under all circumstances, hot; and likewise snow is always cold.[43]

We get more examples. Three (ἡ τρίας, "the triad"), as well as the odd, is always odd, as are all the rest of the odd numbers, and two, four, and so on are always even (104ab). Three, "the idea of three" (104d5–6), is conceived as a Form. This is not in conflict with reading fire and snow as ordinary fire and snow, since Socrates has never said that the things he is now finding that bear only one predicate from a contrary pair are all of the same type.

Socrates is led from his numerical examples to a generalization (104b6–c10) which we may paraphrase as follows. Some things, like ordinary kettles and bunches of apples, display, at different times, each of the predicates of a contrary pair. The Form that governs one of a contrary pair of predicates is immune from contrariety with respect to that pair: that much the unlearned Safe Theory gave us. According to the Learned Theory, we are now told, other things too are immune from contrariety with respect to certain pairs of contrary predicates: snow, fire, numbers. Some of these are Forms, others are not.

In the course of characterizing these entities that are immune to contrariety Socrates shows us how the Learned Theory extends the notion of causality beyond the bounds of the Safe Theory, but the sentence in which he gives this characterization is rather a mouthful (104d1–3):

Then, Cebes, he said, wouldn't these be things which, whatever {thing} they occupy,[44] they force {that thing} to have not only its own {i.e., the occupier's}[45] idea, but also always {the idea} of some contrary?[46]

---

[43] Ordinary fire and ordinary snow, *pace* Vlastos (1956b) 93 n. 14 = Allen (1965) 290 n. 2 = Vlastos (1995) 213 n. 14; Keyt (1963) 168 n. 2; O'Brien (1967/68) 220–21. For a little more detail see Dancy (1991) 131 n. 76.

[44] The text for these lines is in n. 46 below. Here I am taking ἅ as subject for ἀναγκάζει, ὅτι as object of κατάσχη: so O'Brien (1967/68) 214. Differently Gallop (1975) 235f. n. 70: ἅ object of κατάσχη, ὅτι subject, giving "which whatever occupies them forces {them} to have." Perhaps what Socrates says in 104d5–7 by way of clarifying his remark slightly favors this, but see O'Brien 216.

[45] Taking αὐτοῦ to refer to ἅ, with Burnet (1911) 119 *ad* d2, O'Brien (1967/68) 215, as against Archer-Hind (1894) 112 *ad* 11.

[46] Reading: Ἆρ' οὖν, ἔφη, ὦ Κέβης, τάδε εἴη ἄν, ἃ ὅτι ἂν κατάσχη μὴ μόνον ἀναγκάζει τὴν αὐτοῦ ἰδέαν αὐτὸ ἴσχειν, ἀλλὰ καὶ ἐναντίου αὐτῷ ἀεί τινος; I have retained αὐτῷ, because it is in the MSS, but Stallbaum (1850) 201, Fowler (1914) 358, Hackforth (1955) 194 *ad* 104d3, Gallop (1975) 236 n. 71, Ross (1951) 32 n. 1 omit it; Robin (1926) 80 and Rowe (1993) 87 print just τῷ; and Bluck (1955) 200 n. 13 suggests αὖ τῷ (so now Duke et al. [1995] 165). Burnet (1911) 120 tries to defend the reading αὐτῷ: "the meaning of ἐναντίου is by no means clear without a dative . . . it is not difficult to interpret αὐτῷ as 'the opposite in question'." This is unconvincing.

Whatever the difficulties with that utterance, the examples Socrates now introduces make the Learned Theory quite clear:[47] the idea of three, which, as we have already seen, is indelibly odd, immune to being even, when it "occupies" something, makes that something odd (104d5–e6); fire is similarly immune to being hot (104e10–105a1), and so on. So we have another safe pattern of explanation, but more sophisticated (105b8–c7):

For if you ask me what it is that, when it comes-to-be in a body, that body is hot, I shall not state to you that safe reply that is unlearned, that it is heat, but one more clever from what {we've said} now, that it is fire; nor, if you ask what it is that, when it comes-to-be in a body, that body will be sick, should I say that it is sickness, but fever; nor, if you ask what it is that, when it comes into a number, the number is odd, should I say oddness, but unit, and other things similarly.

The Learned (but still Safe) Theory employs an intermediary entity that imports the term whose presence is to be explained into the host entity; the explanation appeals to that intermediary.

13.4. 105C–107B: IMMORTALITY AND THE FORMS

And that brings us to the soul. Socrates' strategy for proving its immortality is to make it the intermediary that imports life into the body; then, given that the intermediary must be something that indelibly possesses the predicate it imports, the soul must be indelibly alive, immune to the contrary, death: so it is immortal.

We need not follow Socrates here, for our concern is not with the immortality of the soul, but with the Forms. Earlier in the dialogue, Socrates had said that the immortality of the soul stands or falls with the existence of the Forms; he does not exactly repeat that claim here, but he comes close, and the repeated references to Forms in the course of this argument may create the illusion that there is some essential connection between the Theory of Forms and immortality. There is not. For as soon as Socrates fleshed out the Safe (but unlearned) Theory of Causality into the Learned Theory, he lost all essential reference to Forms. The intermediaries that import predicates into host entities in the Learned Theory are entities that possess the predicates as essential predicates, and that is all that is required. If you explain the presence of heat by appealing to the presence of fire, you have, we may

---

[47] So I cannot agree with Gallop (1975) 235 n. 70 that "much hinges on the grammar and text at 104d1–3."

grant, appealed to the presence of something that is indelibly hot. And that explanation is just as good if your explanation of fire's essential possession of heat is quite alien to the Theory of Forms, or, for that matter, if you have no explanation at all. But the proof of the immortality of the soul depends only on that aspect of the Learned Theory: it depends on nothing specific to the Theory of Forms.

CHAPTER 14

Conclusion

The Socrates of Plato's Socratic dialogues was in quest of definitions because he thought they were required for living right: he supposed that in order to know whether certain actions were courageous, or pious, or admirable, one must know what the courageous, the pious, and the admirable are.

We laid out a theory of definition for Socrates: not necessarily his or Plato's own theory, but one based on the refutations of definitions in Plato's Socratic dialogues. The theory had three main components: the Substitutivity Requirement, the Paradigm Requirement, and the Explanatory Requirement.

The Explanatory Requirement, at first blush, simply demanded that one be able to use the definition for the pious in explaining why one called a given action (or person) "pious": it was a matter of explaining content. But there turned out to be more to it than that: it was required that what one introduces and defines as the pious be itself indelibly pious. That connected the Explanatory Requirement with the Paradigm Requirement. And both were connected with the Substitutivity Requirement, construed as the demand that what is defined as the pious give necessary and sufficient conditions for something's being pious.

That theory has now turned into the Theory of Forms. Substitutivity is obvious enough: the things that partake of the Form, The Pious, have to be all and only the actions and people that are pious. The Paradigm Requirement is now the claim that the separate Form, The Pious, is through and through pious. It is, in fact, this that separates the Form from the pious people and actions, for none of them is indelibly pious; only the Form is. That is the Argument from Relativity.

And the Explanatory Requirement has become a nearly full-blown theory of causality: it is because the pious people and actions enjoy a relationship, that of participation, say, to The Pious that they qualify as pious. The theory is not quite fully blown, since Socrates in the *Phaedo* and *Symposium* (and the same would have been true of the *Republic*, if we had got that far) does nothing to specify what the relationship of participation consists in.

When Plato does come to focus on that relationship, the Theory of Forms gets into deep trouble. This happens in the *Parmenides*. Anyway, so I think. But that is another story.

References

Ackrill, J. L. (1956) Review of Bluck (1955), *Philosophical Quarterly* 6: 178–79.
 (1957) Review of Festugière (1954), *Mind* 66: 572–73.
 (1958) Review of Hackforth (1955), *Philosophical Review* 67: 106–10.
 (1973) "*Anamnesis* in the *Phaedo*: Remarks on 73c–75c," in Lee et al. (1973) 177–95, Ackrill (1997) 13–32.
 (1981) *Aristotle the Philosopher*, Oxford: Oxford University Press.
 (1997) *Essays on Plato and Aristotle*, Oxford: Clarendon Press.
Adam, James (1902) *The* Republic *of Plato*, 2 vols., Cambridge: Cambridge University Press.
Adam, J. and Adam, A. M. (1893) *Platonis Protagoras*, Cambridge: Pitt Press. Reprinted 1905, etc.
Adams, Robert Merrihew (1973) "A Modified Divine Command Theory of Ethical Wrongness," in Gene Outka and John P. Reeder, Jr. (eds.) *Religion and Morality: A Collection of Essays* (Garden City, N.Y: Anchor Press) 318–47. Reprinted in Paul Helm (ed.) *Divine Commands and Morality*, Oxford: Oxford University Press, 1981, 83–108.
Adkins, A. W. H. (1960) *Merit and Responsibility: A Study in Greek Values*, Oxford: Clarendon Press.
 (1972) *Moral Values and Political Behaviour in Ancient Greece from Homer to the End of the Fifth Century*, New York: W. W. Norton and Co.
Allen, R. E. (1960) "Participation and Predication in Plato's Middle Dialogues," *Philosophical Review* 69: 147–83. Reprinted in Allen (1965) 43–60.
 (ed.) (1965) *Studies in Plato's Metaphysics*, London: Routledge and Kegan Paul.
 (1970) *Plato's* Euthyphro *and the Earlier Theory of Forms*, London: Routledge and Kegan Paul.
 (1971) "Plato's Earlier Theory of Forms," in Vlastos (1971) I 319–34.
 (1980) *Socrates and Legal Obligation*, Minneapolis: University of Minnesota Press.
 (1984) *The Dialogues of Plato*, vol. I: *Euthyphro, Apology, Crito, Meno, Gorgias, Menexenus*, New Haven: Yale University Press.
Anton, John P. and Kustas, George L. (eds.) (1971) *Essays in Ancient Greek Philosophy*, Albany: State University of New York Press.
Archer-Hind, R. D. (1894) *The* Phaedo *of Plato*, 2nd edn., London: Macmillan, 1894 (1st edn. 1883). Reprinted New York: Arno Press, 1973.

Ausland, Hayden W. (2002) "Forensic Characteristics of Socratic Argumentation," in Scott (2002) 36–60.

Barker, Andrew and Warner, Martin (eds.) (1992) *The Language of the Cave* (*Apeiron* 25 no. 4), Edmonton, Alberta: Academic Printing and Publishing.

Barnes, Jonathan (1979) *The Presocratic Philosophers*, vol. I: *Thales to Plato*, vol. II: *Empedocles to Democritus*, London: Routledge and Kegan Paul. Reprinted in 1 vol., 1982.

Bedu-Addo, J. T. (1979a) "On the Alleged Abandonment of the Good in the *Phaedo*," *Apeiron* 13: 104–14.

(1979b) "The Role of the Hypothetical Method in the *Phaedo*," *Phronesis* 24: 111–32.

(1983) "Sense-Experience and Recollection in Plato's *Meno*," *American Journal of Philology* 104: 228–48.

Benson, Hugh (1990) "The Priority of Definition and the Socratic Elenchus," *Oxford Studies in Ancient Philosophy* 8: 19–65.

(ed.) (1992) *Essays on the Philosophy of Socrates*, Oxford: Oxford University Press.

(2000) *Socratic Wisdom: The Model of Knowledge in Plato's Early Dialogues*, Oxford: Oxford University Press.

Berg, Jonathan (1991) "How Could Ethics Depend on Religion?" in Peter Singer (ed.) *A Companion to Ethics* (Blackwell Companions to Philosophy), Oxford: Blackwell, 1991, 525–33.

Bergemann, D. (1895) "Gedächtniss-theoretische Untersuchungen und mnemotechnische Spielereien im Altertum," *Archiv für Geschichte der Philosophie* 8: 336–52, 484–97.

Beversluis, John (1974) "Socratic Definition," *American Philosophical Quarterly* 11: 331–36.

(1987) "Does Socrates Commit the Socratic Fallacy?" *American Philosophical Quarterly* 24: 211–23. Reprinted in Benson (1992) 107–22.

(2000) *Cross-Examining Socrates: A Defense of the Interlocutors in Plato's Early Dialogues*, Cambridge: Cambridge University Press.

Bluck, R. S. (1955) *Plato's* Phaedo. London: Routledge and Kegan Paul. Reprinted New York: Liberal Arts Press, 1959.

(1956) "Logos and Forms: A Reply to Professor Cross," *Mind* 65: 522–29. Reprinted in Allen (1965) 33–41.

(1957) "Forms as Standards," *Phronesis* 2: 115–27.

(1959) "Plato's Form of Equal," *Phronesis* 4: 5–11.

(1961) *Plato's* Meno, Cambridge: Cambridge University Press.

Bolotin, David (1979) *Plato's Dialogue on Friendship: An Interpretation of the* Lysis, *with a New Translation*, Ithaca, N.Y.: Cornell University Press.

Bolton, Robert (1993) "Aristotle's Account of the Socratic Elenchus," *Oxford Studies in Ancient Philosophy* 11: 121–52.

Bordt, Michael (1998) *Platon:* Lysis, vol. IV in Ernst Heitsch and Carl Werner Müller (eds.) *Platon: Werke, Übersetzung und Kommentar*, Göttingen: Vandenhoeck and Ruprecht.

Bostock, David (1986) *Plato's* Phaedo, Oxford: Clarendon Press.

(1988) *Plato's* Theaetetus, Oxford: Clarendon Press.

Boter, Gerard J. (1988) "Plato, *Meno* 82c2–3," *Phronesis* 33: 208–15.

Brague, R. (1978) *Le Restant: Supplément aux commentaires du Ménon de Platon*, Paris: J. Vrin.

Brandwood, Leonard (1976) *A Word Index to Plato* (Compendia 8), Leeds: W. S. Maney and Son.

(1990) *The Chronology of Plato's Dialogues*, Cambridge: Cambridge University Press.

(1992) "Stylometry and Chronology," in Kraut (1992b) 90–120.

Brickhouse, Thomas C. and Smith, Nicholas D. (1994) *Plato's Socrates*, Oxford: Oxford University Press.

(2000) *The Philosophy of Socrates*, Boulder, Colo.: Westview Press.

Brown, Malcolm (1967/68) "Plato Disapproves of the SlaveBoy's Answer," *Review of Metaphysics* 21: 57–93. Reprinted (with additions and revisions) in Brown (1971) 198–42.

(ed.) (1971) *Plato's Meno, with Essays*, Indianapolis: Bobbs-Merrill.

(1972) "The Idea of Equality in the *Phaedo*," *Archiv für Geschichte der Philosophie* 54: 24–36.

Bulmer-Thomas, Ivo (1984) "Plato's Astronomy," *Classical Quarterly* 34: 107–12.

Burge, Evan L. (1971) "The Ideas as Aitiai in the *Phaedo*," *Phronesis* 16: 1–13.

Burkert, Walter (1972) *Lore and Science in Ancient Pythagoreanism*, trans. E. L. Minar, Jr., Cambridge, Mass.: Harvard University Press.

Burnet, John (1900/1907) *Platonis Opera*, 5 vols., Oxford: Clarendon Press, 1900 (I), 1901 (II), 1903 (III), 1902 (IV), 1907 (V); often reprinted.

(1911) *Plato's* Phaedo, Oxford: Clarendon Press. Reprinted 1924, etc.

(1914) *Greek Philosophy*, vol. I: *Thales to Plato*, London: Macmillan; often reprinted.

(1924) *Plato's* Euthyphro, Apology of Socrates, *and* Crito, text, commentary, Oxford: Clarendon Press. Reprinted 1957.

Burnyeat, Miles F. (1977a) "Socratic Midwifery, Platonic Inspiration," *Bulletin of the Institute for Classical Studies of the University of London* 24 (1977) 7–16.

(1977b) "Examples in Epistemology: Socrates, Theaetetus and G. E. Moore," *Philosophy* 52: 381–98.

Bury, R. G. (1906) "Platonica," *Classical Review* 20: 12–14.

(1932) *The* Symposium *of Plato*, 2nd edn., Cambridge: W. Heffer and Sons; 1st edn. 1909. Reprinted 1962, 1964.

Butcher, S. H. (1888) "The Geometrical Problem of the *Meno* (p. 86E–87A)," *Journal of Philology* 17: 219–25.

Calvert, Brian (1974) "Meno's Paradox Reconsidered," *Journal of the History of Philosophy* 12: 143–52.

Candlish, Stewart (1983) "*Euthyphro* 6D–9B and its Misinterpretations," *Apeiron* 17: 28–32.

Chance, Thomas H. (1992) *Plato's* Euthydemus: *Analysis of What Is and Is Not Philosophy*, Berkeley: University of California Press.

Chen, Ludwig C. H. (1983) "Knowledge of Beauty in Plato's *Symposium*," *Classical Quarterly* 33: 66–74.

Cherniss, Harold (1937) Review of Buchmann (1936), *American Journal of Philology* 58: 497–500. Reprinted in Cherniss (1977) 261–64.

(1944) *Aristotle's Criticism of Plato and the Academy*, vol. I, Baltimore, Md.: Johns Hopkins University Press. Reprinted New York: Russell and Russell, 1962.

(1959/60) "Plato 1950–1957," *Lustrum* 4: 5–308, 5: 321–648.

(1977) *Selected Papers*, ed. Leonardo Tarán, Leiden: E. J. Brill.

Classen, Carl Joachim (1959) "The Study of Language amongst Socrates' Contemporaries," *Proceedings of the African Classical Association* 2: 33–49. Reprinted, corrected and expanded, in Classen (1976) 215–47.

(ed.) (1976) *Sophistik*, Darmstadt: Wissenschaftliche Buchgesellschaft.

Cohen, S. Marc (1971) "Socrates on the Definition of Piety: *Euthyphro* 10A–11B," *Journal of the History of Philosophy* 9: 1–14. Reprinted in Vlastos (1971) 158–76.

Cook Wilson, John (1903) "On the Geometrical Passage in Plato's *Meno* 86E sqq., with a Note on a Passage in the Treatise de Lineis Insecabilibus (970a5)," *Journal of Philology* 28: 222–40.

Cooper, John (ed.) (1997) *Plato: The Complete Works*, Indianapolis: Hackett Publishing Co.

Cope, Edward Meredith (1877) *The* Rhetoric *of Aristotle*, with commentary; revised edn. by J. E. Sandys, 3 vols., Cambridge: Cambridge University Press. Reprinted Hildesheim: Olms, 1964; New York: Arno Press, 1973.

Cornford, Francis Macdonald (1935) *Plato's Theory of Knowledge: The* Theaetetus *and* Sophist *of Plato*, London: Kegan Paul, Trench and Trubner. Reprinted New York: Library of Liberal Arts, 1957.

(1939) *Plato and Parmenides: Parmenides'* Way of Truth *and Plato's* Parmenides, trans. with introduction and running commentary, London: Routledge and Kegan Paul. Reprinted New York: Liberal Arts Press, 1957.

Cresswell, M. J. (1971) "Plato's Theory of Causality: *Phaedo* 95–106," *Australasian Journal of Philosophy* 49: 244–49.

Croiset, Alfred (1921) *Hippias Majeur, Charmide, Laches, Lysis*, in Croiset et al. (1920/64) vol. II (1921).

Croiset, Alfred and Bodin, Louis (1923a) *Protagoras*, in Croiset et al. (1920/64) vol. III part 1 (1923).

(1923b) *Gorgias; Menon*, in Croiset et al. (1920/64) vol. III part 2 (1923).

Croiset, M., Diès, A., et al. (1920/64) *Platon, Œuvres complètes*, 14 vols. (27 parts). Paris: Société d'Édition "Les Belles Lettres" (Budé).

Crombie, I. M. (1962/63) *An Examination of Plato's Doctrines*, 2 vols., London: Routledge and Kegan Paul.

Cross, R. C. (1954) "Logos and Forms in Plato," *Mind* 63: 433–50. Reprinted in Allen (1965) 13–31.

Dancy, R. M. (1975) *Sense and Contradiction: A Study in Aristotle*. Dordrecht: D. Reidel.

(1984) "The One, the Many, and the Forms: *Philebus* 15b1–8," *Ancient Philosophy* 4: 160–93.

(1987) "Theaetetus' First Baby: *Theaetetus* 151e–160e," *Philosophical Topics* 15: 61–108.

(1991) *Two Studies in the Early Academy*, Albany: State University of New York Press.

Denniston, J. D. (1934) *The Greek Particles*, Oxford: Clarendon Press; 2nd edn., ed. K. J. Dover, 1954; corrected reprint 1959.

Denyer, Nicholas (2001) *Plato: Alcibiades*, Cambridge: Cambridge University Press.

des Places, Édouard (1964) *Lexique de la langue philosophique et religieuse de Platon*, 2 vols., in Croiset et al. (1920/64) vol. XIV parts 1–2.

de Strycker, Émile (1950) "Trois points obscurs de terminologie mathématique chez Platon," *Revue des études grecques* 63: 43–57.

Devereux, Daniel T. (1977a) "Courage and Wisdom in Plato's *Laches*," *Journal of the History of Philosophy* 15: 129–42.

(1977b) "Pauline Predications in Plato," *Apeiron* 11: 1–4.

(1992) "The Unity of the Virtues in Plato's *Protagoras* and *Laches*," *Philosophical Review* 101: 765–89.

(1994) "Separation and Immanence in Plato's Theory of Forms," *Oxford Studies in Ancient Philosophy* 12: 63–90. Reprinted in Fine (1999) vol. I, 192–214.

(1995) "Socrates' Kantian Conception of Virtue," *Journal of the History of Philosophy* 33: 381–408.

Diels, Hermann (1882/95) *Simplicii in Aristotelis Physicorum commentaria*, 2 vols. (Commentaria in Aristotelem graeca 9–10), Berlin: G. Reimer.

(1960) *Die Fragmente der Vorsokratiker*, 3 vols. 9th edn., ed. Walther Kranz. Berlin: Weidmann.

Diès, Auguste (1932) "Introduction," in Croiset et al. (1920/64) vol. VI, pp. v–cli.

Diggle, J. (ed.) (1984) *Euripidis Fabulae*, vol. I, Oxford: Clarendon Press. Corrected reprints 1987, 1989, 1991.

Diogenes Laertius: see Long (1964), Marcovich (1999).

Dittmar, H. (1912) *Aischines von Sphettos*, Berlin: Weidmannsche Buchhandlung. Reprinted New York: Arno Press, 1976.

Dodds, E. R. (1933) *Proclus: The Elements of Theology*, Oxford: Clarendon Press; 2nd edn., 1963.

(1959) *Plato, Gorgias: A Revised Text with Introduction and Commentary*, Oxford: Clarendon Press.

Döring, Klaus (1972) *Die Megariker: Kommentierte Sammlung der Testimonien*, Amsterdam: B. R. Grüner.

Dorter, Kenneth (1982) *Plato's Phaedo: An Interpretation*, Toronto: University of Toronto Press.

(1997/98) "Virtue, Knowledge, and Wisdom: Bypassing Self-Control," *Review of Metaphysics* 51: 313–43.

Dover, K. J. (1968a) *Aristophanes: Clouds*, Oxford: Clarendon Press.

(1968b) *Lysias and the Corpus Lysiacum*, Berkeley: University of California Press.

(1971) "Socrates in the *Clouds*," in Vlastos (1971) 50–77. Abridged reprint of part of the introduction to Dover (1968a).

(1974) *Greek Popular Morality in the Time of Plato and Aristotle*, Berkeley: University of California Press.

(1980) *Plato*: Symposium. Cambridge: Cambridge University Press.

Dreyfus, Hubert (1990) "Socratic and Platonic Sources of Cognitivism," in J.-C. Smith (ed.) *Historical Foundations of Cognitive Science* (Philosophical Studies Series 46), Dordrecht: Kluwer Academic Publishers, 1–17.

Duke, E. A., Hicken, W. F., Nicoll, W. S. M., Robinson, D. B., and Strachan, J. C. B. (1995) *Platonis Opera*, vol. I, Oxford: Clarendon Press.

Dümmler, Ferdinand (1895) *Zur Komposition des platonischen Staats mit einem Exkurs über die Entwicklung der platonischen Psychologie*, Basel: L. Reinhardt. Reprinted in Dümmler, *Kleine Schriften*, vol. I, 229–70, Leipzig: S. Hirzel, 1901.

Dyson, M. (1974) "Some Problems concerning Knowledge in Plato's *Charmides*," *Phronesis* 19: 102–11.

Ebert, Theodor (1973) "Plato's Theory of Recollection Reconsidered: An Interpretation of *Meno* 80a–86e," *Man and World* 6: 163–81.

(1974) *Meinung und Wissen in der Philosophie Platons: Untersuchungen zum 'Charmides', 'Menon' und 'Staat'*, Berlin: Walter de Gruyter.

Edelstein, Ludwig (1962) "Platonic Anonymity," *American Journal of Philology* 83: 1–22.

Else, G. F. (1936) "The Terminology of the Ideas," *Harvard Studies in Classical Philology* 47: 17–55.

Ferejohn, Michael T. (1983/84) "Socratic Virtue as the Parts of Itself," *Philosophy and Phenomenological Research* 44: 377–88.

Festugière, A.-J. (1936) *Contemplation et vie contemplative selon Platon*, Paris: J. Vrin. Reprinted with corrections, 1950.

(1954) *La Révélation d'Hermès Trismégiste*, vol. IV: *Le Dieu inconnue et la gnose*, 2nd edn., Paris: Librairie Lecoffre (J. Gabalda et Cie).

Field, G. C. (1967) *Plato and his Contemporaries*, 3rd edn., London: Methuen; 1st edn. 1930; 2nd edn. 1948.

Findlay, J. N. (1974) *Plato: The Written and the Unwritten Doctrines*, London: Routledge and Kegan Paul.

Fine, Gail (1986) "Immanence," *Oxford Studies in Ancient Philosophy* 4: 71–97.

(1993) On Ideas: *Aristotle's Criticism of Plato's Theory of Forms*, Oxford: Clarendon Press.

(ed.) (1999) *Plato*, vol. I: *Metaphysics and Epistemology*; vol. II: *Ethics, Politics, Religion, and the Soul*, Oxford: Oxford University Press.

Fodor, J. A. (1968) "The Appeal to Tacit Knowledge in Psychological Explanations," *Journal of Philosophy* 65: 627–40.

Forrester, James W. (1975) "Some Perils of Paulinity," *Phronesis* 20: 11–21.

Fowler, D. H. (1987) *The Mathematics of Plato's Academy: A New Reconstruction*, Oxford: Clarendon Press; 2nd edn., 1999.

(1990) "Yet More on *Meno* 82a–85d," *Phronesis* 35: 175–81.

Fowler, H. N. (1914) *Plato*, vol. I: *Euthyphro, Apology, Crito, Phaedo, Phaedrus*, in Fowler et al. (1914/35).

Fowler, H. N. et al. (1914/35) *Plato*, 12 vols. (Loeb Classical Library), Cambridge, Mass.: Harvard University Press; London: William Heinemann.

Frank, Erich (1923) *Platon und die sogenannten Pythagoreer: Ein Kapitel aus der Geschichte des griechischen Geistes*, Halle: Max Niemeyer.

Frede, Dorothea (1978) "The Final Proof of Immortality in Plato's *Phaedo* 102a–107a," *Phronesis* 23: 27–41.

Frede, Michael (1980) "The Original Notion of Cause," in M. Schofield, M. Burnyeat, and J. Barnes (eds.) *Doubt and Dogmatism: Studies in Hellenistic Epistemology*, Oxford: Clarendon Press, 217–49. Reprinted in Frede (1987) 125–50, 369.

(1987) *Essays in Ancient Philosophy*, Minneapolis: University of Minnesota Press.

(1992) "Plato's Dialogues and the Dialogue Form," *Oxford Studies in Ancient Philosophy*, supp. vol., 201–19.

Friedländer, Paul (1958/69) *Plato*, trans. Hans Meyerhoff, 3 vols., vol. I: *An Introduction*, New York: Pantheon Books, 1958 (trans. from German edn. of 1954); 2nd edn., Princeton, N.J.: Princeton University Press, 1969 (based on German edn. of 1964); vol. II: *The Dialogues, First Period*, New York: Pantheon Books, 1964 (based on German edn. of 1957); vol. III: *The Dialogues, Second and Third Periods*, Princeton, N.J.: Princeton University Press, 1969 (based on German edn. of 1960).

Fujisawa, Norio (1974) "Ἔχειν, Μετέχειν and Idioms of Participation in Plato's Theory of Forms," *Phronesis* 19: 30–58.

Furley, David (1976) "Anaxagoras in Response to Parmenides," in Shiner and King-Farlow (1976) 61–85. Reprinted in Furley (1989) 47–65.

(1989) *Cosmic Problems: Essays on Greek and Roman Philosophy of Nature*, Cambridge: Cambridge University Press.

Gadamer, Hans-Georg (1988) "Reply to Nicholas P. White," in Charles L. Griswold (ed.) *Platonic Writings, Platonic Readings*, London: Routledge, 258–66, 299–300.

Gaiser, Konrad (1963) *Platons Ungeschriebene Lehre: Studien zur systematischen und geschichtlichen Begründung der Wissenschaften in der platonischen Schule*, Stuttgart: E. Klett. Reprinted 1968.

Gallop, David (1961) "Justice and Holiness in *Protagoras* 330–331," *Phronesis* 6: 86–93.

(1975) *Plato: Phaedo*, Oxford: Clarendon Press.

(1976) "Relations in the *Phaedo*," in Shiner and King-Farlow (1976) 149–63.

Geach, Peter T. (1956) "The Third Man Again," *Philosophical Review* 65: 72–82. Reprinted in Allen (1965) 265–77.

(1966) "Plato's *Euthyphro*: An Analysis and Commentary," *Monist* 50: 369–82.

Gifford, Edwin Hamilton (1905) *The* Euthydemus *of Plato*, Oxford: Clarendon Press. Reprinted New York: Arno Press, 1973.

Gifford, Mark (2001) "Dramatic Dialectic in *Republic* Book I," *Oxford Studies in Ancient Philosophy* 20: 35–106.

Glaser, Konrad (1935) "Gang und Ergebnis des platonischen *Lysis*," *Wiener Studien* 53: 47–67.

Goodrich, W. J. (1903/4) "On *Phaedo* 96A–102A and the δεύτερος πλοῦς 99D," *Classical Review* 17: 381–84; 18: 5–11.

Goodwin, William Watson (1889) *Syntax of the Moods and Tenses of the Greek Verb*, London: Macmillan. Reprinted New York: St. Martin's Press, 1965.

Gordon, Jill (2003) "Eros and Philosophical Seduction in *Alcibiades* I," *Ancient Philosophy* 23: 11–30.

Gosling, J. (1965) "Similarity in *Phaedo* 73b seq.," *Phronesis* 10: 151–61.

Gould, Thomas (1963) *Platonic Love*, London: Routledge and Kegan Paul.

Grene, D. and Lattimore, R. (eds.) (1959) *The Complete Greek Tragedies*, 4 vols., Chicago, Ill.: University of Chicago Press.

Grote, George (1846/56) *A History of Greece*, 12 vols., New York: P. F. Collier and Son, 1899/1900 (original edn. 1846/56).

Grube, G. M. A. (1926) "On the Authenticity of the *Hippias Major*," *Classical Quarterly* 20: 134–47.

(1927) "Plato's Theory of Beauty," *Monist* 37: 269–88.

(1929) "The Logic and Language of the *Hippias Major*," *Classical Philology* 24: 369–75.

(1935) *Plato's Thought*, London: Methuen. Reprinted Boston: Beacon Press, 1958; reprinted with new introduction and bibliography by Donald J. Zeyl, Indianapolis: Hackett Publishing Co., 1980.

(1981) *Plato: Five Dialogues:* Euthyphro, Apology, Crito, Meno, Phaedo, Indianapolis: Hackett Publishing Co.

Gulley, Norman (1954) "Plato's Theory of Recollection," *Classical Quarterly* 4: 194–213.

(1962) *Plato's Theory of Knowledge*, London: Methuen.

(1968) *The Philosophy of Socrates*, London: Macmillan.

Guthrie, W. K. C. (1956) *Plato:* Protagoras *and* Meno, Harmondsworth, Middlesex: Penguin Books. Reprinted in Hamilton and Cairns (1961) 354–84; Brown (1971) 17–61.

(1969) *A History of Greek Philosophy*, vol. III: *The Fifth-Century Enlightenment*, Cambridge: Cambridge University Press, 1969.

(1975) *A History of Greek Philosophy*, vol. IV: *Plato, The Man and his Dialogues: Earlier Period*, Cambridge: Cambridge University Press.

(1978) *A History of Greek Philosophy*, vol. V: *The Later Plato and the Academy*, Cambridge: Cambridge University Press.

Hackforth, R. (1952) *Plato's* Phaedrus, Cambridge: Cambridge University Press. Reprinted New York: Library of Liberal Arts, 1957.

(1955) *Plato's* Phaedo, Cambridge: Cambridge University Press.

Hamilton, Edith and Cairns, Huntington (eds.) (1961) *The Collected Dialogues of Plato*, New York: Pantheon Books. Reprinted frequently Princeton, N.J.: Princeton University Press.

Hare, J. E. (1981) *Plato*: Euthyphro, Bryn Mawr, Pa.: Bryn Mawr Commentaries.

Hare, R. M. (1964) "A Question about Plato's Theory of Ideas," in Mario Bunge (ed.) *The Critical Approach to Science and Philosophy*, Glencoe, Ill.: Free Press, 61–81.

(1965) "Plato and the Mathematicians," in Renford Bambrough (ed.) *New Essays on Plato and Aristotle*, London: Routledge and Kegan Paul, 21–38.

Heiberg, J. L., ed. E. S. Stamatis (1969/77) *Euclidis Elementa*, 5 vols., Leipzig: B. G. Teubner.

Heidel, W. A. (1900) "On Plato's *Euthyphro*," *Transactions of the American Philological Association* 31: 163–81. Reprinted in William A. Heidel, *Selected Papers*, ed. L. Tarán, New York: Garland Publishing Co., 1980 (no separate pagination).

(1902) *Plato's* Euthyphro, New York: American Book Co. Reprinted New York: Arno Press, 1976.

Heinimann, Felix (1945) *Nomos und Physis: Herkunft und Bedeutung einer Antithese im griechischen Denken des 5. Jahrhunderts*, Basel: Friedrich Reinhardt AG. Reprinted Darmstadt: Wissenschaftliche Buchgesellschaft, 1987.

Hermann, Karl Friedrich (1839) *Geschichte und System der platonischen Philosophie*, vol. I, Heidelberg: C. F. Winter, 1839. Reprinted New York: Arno Press, 1976.

Hicks, R. D. (1907) *Aristotle:* De Anima, Cambridge: Cambridge University Press. Reprinted Amsterdam: Adolf M. Hakkert, 1965.

Huby, Pamela M. (1959) "*Phaedo* 99D–102A," *Phronesis* 4: 12–14.

Huffman, Carl A. (1993) *Philolaus of Croton: Pythagorean and Presocratic*, Cambridge: Cambridge University Press.

Ilting, Karl-H. (1965) "Aristoteles über Platons philosophische Entwicklung," *Zeitschrift für philosophische Forschung* 19: 377–92.

Irwin, T. H. (1977a) "Plato's Heracleiteanism," *Philosophical Quarterly* 27: 1–13.

(1977b) *Plato's Moral Theory: The Early and Middle Dialogues*, Oxford: Clarendon Press.

(1979) *Plato*: Gorgias, Oxford: Clarendon Press.

(1995) *Plato's Ethics*, Oxford: Oxford University Press.

Jackson, Henry (1882) "On Plato's *Republic* VI 509D sqq.," *Journal of Philology* 10: 132–50.

Janko, Richard (1987) *Aristotle:* Poetics I with the Tractatus Coislianus, *a Hypothetical Reconstruction of* Poetics II, the Fragments of the On Poets, Indianapolis: Hackett Publishing Co.

Jowett, Benjamin (1953) *The Dialogues of Plato*, 4 vols., 4th edn., rev. by order of the Jowett Copyright Trustees by D. J. Allan and H. E. Dale, with the assistance of Cyril Bailey, I. M. Crombie, and D. L. Page, Oxford: Clarendon Press.

Joyal, Mark (2000) *The Platonic* Theages: An Introduction, Commentary, and Critical Edition (Philosophie der Antike 10), Stuttgart: Franz Steiner Verlag.

Kahn, Charles H. (1981a) "Did Plato Write Socratic Dialogues?" *Classical Quarterly* 31: 305–20.

(1981b) "Some Philosophical Uses of 'To Be' in Plato," *Phronesis* 26: 105–34.

(1985) "The Beautiful and the Genuine: A Discussion of Paul Woodruff, *Plato, Hippias Major*," *Oxford Studies in Ancient Philosophy* 3: 261–87.

(1986) "Plato's Methodology in *Laches*," *Revue internationale de philosophie* 40: 7–21.

(1988) "Plato's *Charmides* and the Proleptic Reading of Socratic Dialogues," *Journal of Philosophy* 85: 541–49.

(1992) "Vlastos's Socrates," *Phronesis* 37: 233–58.

(1993) "Proleptic Composition in the *Republic*, or Why Book 1 Was Never a Separate Dialogue," *Classical Quarterly* 43: 131–42.

(1996) *Plato and the Socratic Dialogue: The Philosophical Use of a Literary Form*, Cambridge: Cambridge University Press.

(2000) "Some Puzzles in the *Euthydemus*," in Robinson and Brisson (2000) 88–97.

(2001) *Pythagoras and the Pythagoreans: A Brief History*, Indianapolis: Hackett Publishing Co.

Kapp, Ernst (1942) "The Theory of Ideas in Plato's Earlier Dialogues" (ca. 1942, unpublished), in Kapp (1968) 55–150.

(1959) "Deum te scito esse?" *Hermes* 87: 129–32.

(1968) *Ausgewählte Schriften*, ed. H. and I. Diller, Berlin: Walter de Gruyter.

Kerferd, G. B. (1981) *The Sophistic Movement*, Cambridge: Cambridge University Press.

Keyt, David (1963) "The Fallacies in *Phaedo* 102a–107b," *Phronesis* 8: 167–72.

Kirk, G. S., Raven, J. E., and Schofield, M. (1983) *The Presocratic Philosophers: A Critical History with a Selection of Texts*, 2nd edn., Cambridge: Cambridge University Press.

Klein, Jacob (1965) *A Commentary on Plato's* Meno, Chapel Hill: University of North Carolina Press.

Klosko, G. (1983) "Criteria of Fallacy and Sophistry for use in the Analysis of Platonic Dialogues," *Classical Quarterly* 33: 363–74.

Knorr, Wilbur (1986) *The Ancient Tradition of Geometrical Problems*, Boston, Mass.: Birkhäuser.

Kohák, Erazim V. (1960) "The Road to Wisdom: Lessons on Education from Plato's *Laches*," *Classical Journal* 56: 123–32.

Kosman, L. A. (1983) "Charmides' First Definition: Sophrosyne as Quietness," in John P. Anton and Anthony Preus (eds.) *Essays in Ancient Greek Philosophy*, vol. II, Albany: State University of New York Press, 203–16.

Krämer, H. J. (1959) *Arete bei Platon und Aristoteles: zum Wesen und zur Geschichte der platonischen Ontologie* (Abhandlungen der Heidelberger Akademie der Wissenschaften, Philosophisch-historische Klasse, 1959, 6), Heidelberg: Carl Winter, Universitätsverlag. Reprinted Amsterdam: A. M. Hakkert, 1967.

(1990) *Plato and the Foundations of Metaphysics: A Work on the Theory of the Principles and Unwritten Doctrines of Plato with a Collection of the Fundamental Documents* (not published in German; trans. from an Italian translation by J. R. Catan). Albany: State University of New York Press.

Kraut, Richard (1984) *Socrates and the State*, Princeton, N.J.: Princeton University Press.

(1992a) "Introduction to the Study of Plato," in Kraut (1992b) 1–50.

(1992b) *The Cambridge Companion to Plato*, Cambridge: Cambridge University Press.

Kühner, Raphael and Gerth, Bernhard (1898/1904) *Ausführliche Grammatik der griechischen Sprache*, part 2: *Satzlehre*, 3rd edn., 2 vols., Hanover: Hahn. Reprinted 1966.

Lacey, A. R. (1959) "Plato's *Sophist* and the Forms," *Classical Quarterly* 9: 43–52.

(1971) "Our Knowledge of Socrates," in Vlastos (1971) 22–49.

Lamb, W. R. M. (1924) *Plato: Laches, Protagoras, Meno, Euthydemus*, vol. II in Fowler et al. (1914/35).

(1925) *Plato: Lysis, Symposium, Gorgias*, vol. III in Fowler et al. (1914/35).

(1927) *Plato: Charmides, Alcibiades I and II, Hipparchus, The Lovers, Theages, Minos, Epinomis*, vol. XII in Fowler et al. (1914/35).

Lane, Iain (1987) "*Laches*," in Saunders (1987) 69–115.

Ledger, Gerard R. (1989) *Re-Counting Plato: A Computer Analysis of Plato's Style*, Oxford: Clarendon Press.

Lee, E. N., Mourelatos, A. P. D., and Rorty, R. M. (eds.) (1973) *Exegesis and Argument: Studies in Greek Philosophy Presented to Gregory Vlastos*, *Phronesis* supp. vol. 1, Assen: Van Gorcum.

Lennox, James G. (1985) "Plato's Unnatural Teleology," in Dominic J. O'Meara (ed.) *Platonic Investigations* (Studies in Philosophy and the History of Philosophy 13), Washington, D.C.: The Catholic University of America Press, 195–218. Reprinted in James G. Lennox, *Aristotle's Philosophy of Biology: Studies in the Origins of Life Science*, Cambridge: Cambridge University Press, 2001, 280–302.

Levin, Donald Norman (1971) "Some Observations Concerning Plato's *Lysis*," in Anton and Kustas (1971) 236–58.

Levinson, R. B. (1953) *In Defense of Plato*, Cambridge, Mass.: Harvard University Press.

Lisska, Anthony J. (1996) *Aquinas' Theory of Natural Law: An Analytic Reconstruction*, Oxford: Clarendon Press.

Lloyd, A. C. (1976) "The Principle that the Cause is Greater than its Effect," *Phronesis* 21: 146–56.

Long, H. S. (1964) *Diogenis Laertii Vitae philosophorum*, 2 vols., Oxford: Clarendon Press.

Liddell, Henry George, Scott, Robert, Jones, Sir Henry Stuart, McKenzie, Roderick et al. (1940) *A Greek-English Lexicon*, Oxford: Clarendon Press. Reprinted, with a revised supplement, 1996.

Lucas, D. W. (1970) "Euripides," in N. G. L. Hammond and H. H. Scullard (eds.) *The Oxford Classical Dictionary*, 2nd edn., Oxford: Clarendon Press, 418a–421b.

Lutosławski, Wincenty (1897) *The Origin and Growth of Plato's Logic, with an Account of Plato's Style and of the Chronology of his Writings*, London: Longmans, Green and Co. Reprinted Dubuque, Iowa: Wm. C. Brown Reprint Library, n.d.

Lyons, John (1963) *Structural Semantics: An Analysis of Part of the Vocabulary of Plato*, Oxford: Blackwell.

Mackenzie, Mary Margaret (1988) "Impasse and Explanation: from the *Lysis* to the *Phaedo*," *Archiv für Geschichte der Philosophie* 70: 15–45.

Makin, Stephen (1990/91) "An Ancient Principle about Causation," *Proceedings of the Aristotelian Society* 91: 135–52.

Malcolm, John (1968) "On the Place of the *Hippias Major* in the Development of Plato's Thought," *Archiv für Geschichte der Philosophie* 50: 189–95.

(1991) *Plato on the Self-Predication of the Forms: Early and Middle Dialogues*, Oxford: Clarendon Press.

Marcovich, M. (1967) *Heraclitus: Greek Text with a Short Commentary*, editio maior, Merida, Venezuela: Los Andes University Press.

(1999) *Diogenis Laertii Vitae philosophorum*, 2 vols., Stuttgart: B. G. Teubner.

Mastronarde, Donald J. (1994) *Euripides:* Phoenissae, Cambridge: Cambridge University Press.

Matson, Wallace I. and Leite, Adam (1991) "Socrates' Critique of Cognitivism," *Philosophy* 66: 145–67.

Matthen, Mohan (1984) "Forms and Participants in Plato's *Phaedo*," *Nous* 18: 281–97.

McDonough, Richard (1991) "Plato's Not to Blame for Cognitive Science," *Ancient Philosophy* 11: 301–14.

Menn, Stephen (2002) "Plato and the Method of Analysis," *Phronesis* 47: 193–223.

Mills, K. W. (1957/58) "Plato, *Phaedo* 74b7–c6," *Phronesis* 2: 128–47, 3: 40–58.

Mohr, Richard (1984) "Forms in Plato's *Euthydemus*," *Hermes* 112: 296–300.

Moravcsik, J. M. E. (1967) "Aristotle's Theory of Categories," in Moravcsik (ed.) *Aristotle: A Collection of Critical Essays*, Garden City, N.Y.: Doubleday Anchor Books, 1967, 125–45.

(1970) "Learning as Recollection," in Vlastos (1970) I 53–69.

(1971) "Reason and Eros in the 'Ascent' Passage of the *Symposium*," in Anton and Kustas (1971) 285–302.

Moreau, J. (1941): "Le Platonisme de l'*Hippias Majeur*," *Revue des études grecques* 54: 19–42.

Morrison, Donald (1987) "On Professor Vlastos' Xenophon," *Ancient Philosophy* 7: 9–22.

Mourelatos, Alexander P. D. (1984) "Aristotle's Rationalist Account of Qualitative Interaction," *Phronesis* 29: 1–16.

Mueller, Ian (1982) "Aristotle and the Quadrature of the Circle," in Norman Kretzmann (ed.) *Infinity and Continuity in Ancient and Medieval Thought*, Ithaca, N.Y.: Cornell University Press, 146–64.

Murphy, N. R. (1936) "The Δεύτερος Πλοῦς in the *Phaedo*," *Classical Quarterly* 30: 40–47.

(1951) *The Interpretation of Plato's* Republic, Oxford: Clarendon Press.

Nails, Debra (1995) *Agora, Academy, and the Conduct of Philosophy.* Dordrecht: Kluwer Academic Publishers.

(2002) *The People of Plato: A Prosopography of Plato and Other Socratics*, Indianapolis: Hackett Publishing Co.

Napolitano Valditara, Linda M. (1991) "ΤΙ ΕΣΤΙ – ΠΟΙΟΝ ΕΣΤΙ: Un aspetto dell' argomentatività dialettica del *Menone*," *Elenchos* 12: 197–220.

Nehamas, Alexander (1972/73) "Predication and Forms of Opposites in the *Phaedo*," *Review of Metaphysics* 26: 461–91.

(1975/76) "Confusing Universals and Particulars in Plato's Early Dialogues," *Review of Metaphysics* 29: 287–306. Reprinted in Nehamas (1999) 159–75.

(1979) "Self-Predication and Plato's Theory of Forms," *American Philosophical Quarterly* 16: 93–103. Reprinted in Nehamas (1999) 176–95.

(1985) "Meno's Paradox and Socrates as a Teacher," *Oxford Studies in Ancient Philosophy* 3: 1–30. Reprinted in Benson (1992) 298–316; Nehamas (1999) 3–26.

(1986) "Socratic Intellectualism," *Proceedings of the Boston Area Colloquium in Ancient Philosophy* 2: 275–316. Reprinted in Nehamas (1999) 27–58.

(1999) *Virtues of Authenticity: Essays on Plato and Socrates*, Princeton, N.J.: Princeton University Press.

Nestle, Wilhelm (1940) *Vom Mythos zum Logos: Die Selbstentfaltung des griechischen Denkens von Homer bis auf die Sophistik und Sokrates*, Stuttgart: Alfred Kroner; 2nd edn., 1941 (1942 on title page; 1941 on reverse).

Nichols, James H. (1987) "*Laches*" (trans.) and "Introduction to the *Laches*," in Thomas L. Pangle (ed.) *The Roots of Political Philosophy: Ten Forgotten Socratic Dialogues*, Ithaca, N.Y.: Cornell University Press, 240–68, 269–80.

O'Brien, Denis (1967/68) "The Last Argument of Plato's *Phaedo*," *Classical Quarterly* 17: 198–231, 18: 95–106.

Ostenfeld, Erik Nils (1982) *Forms, Matter and Mind: Three Strands in Plato's Metaphysics*, Boston, Mass.: Martinus Nijhoff.

Owen, G. E. L. (1957) "A Proof in the Περὶ ἰδεῶν," *Journal of Hellenic Studies* 77: 103–11. Reprinted in Allen (1965) 293–312; Owen (1986) 165–79.

(1968) "Dialectic and Eristic in the Treatment of the Forms," in G. E. L. Owen (ed.) *Aristotle on Dialectic: The* Topics, Oxford: Clarendon Press, 103–25. Reprinted in Owen (1986) 220–38.

(1973) "Plato on the Undepictable," in Lee et al. (1973) 349–61. Reprinted in Owen (1986) 138–47.

(1986) *Logic, Science and Dialectic: Collected Papers in Greek Philosophy*, ed. M. Nussbaum, Ithaca, N.Y.: Cornell University Press.

Peck, A. L. (1962) "Plato versus Parmenides," *Philosophical Review* 71: 159–84.

Pendrick, Gerard J. (2002) *Antiphon: The Fragments* (Cambridge Classical Texts and Commentaries 39), Cambridge: Cambridge University Press.

Penner, Terry (1973) "The Unity of Virtue," *Philosophical Review* 82: 35–68.

(1987) *The Ascent from Nominalism: Some Existence Arguments in Plato's Middle Dialogues*, Dordrecht: D. Reidel.

(1992) "Socrates and the Early Dialogues," in Kraut (1992b) 121–69.

Phillips, Bernard (1948/49) "The Significance of Meno's Paradox," *Classical Weekly* 42: 87–91. Reprinted in Sesonske and Fleming (1965) 77–83.

Pitt, Valerie H. (1977) *The Penguin Dictionary of Physics*, Harmondsworth, Middlesex: Penguin Books.

Press, Gerald A. (2002) "The *Elenchos* in the *Charmides*, 162–175," in Scott (2002) 252–65.

Prior, William J. (1985) *Unity and Development in Plato's Metaphysics*, LaSalle, Ill.: Open Court Publishing Co.

(1998) "Plato and the 'Socratic Fallacy'," *Phronesis* 43: 97–113.

(2001) Review of Nehamas (1999), *Ancient Philosophy* 21: 182–88.

Randall, John Herman (1970) *Plato: Dramatist of the Life of Reason*, New York: Columbia University Press.

Rankin, H. D. (1983) *Sophists, Socratics and Cynics*, London: Croom Helm.

Rawls, John (1971) *A Theory of Justice*. Cambridge, Mass.: Harvard University Press; rev. edn. 1999.

Reeve, C. D. C. (1989) *Socrates in the* Apology: *An Essay on Plato's* Apology of Socrates, Indianapolis: Hackett Publishing Co.

Richard, Marie-Dominique (1986) *L'Enseignement oral de Platon: Une nouvelle interprétation du platonisme*, Paris: Cerf.

Robin, Leon (1926) *Phédon*, in Croiset et al. (1920/64), vol. IV, part 1.

(1929) *Le Banquet*, in Croiset et al. (1920/64), vol. IV, part 2.

Robinson, David B. (1986) "Plato's *Lysis*: The Structural Problem," *Illinois Classical Studies* 11: 53–83.

Robinson, Richard (1953) *Plato's Earlier Dialectic*, Ithaca, N.Y.: Cornell University Press, 1941; 2nd edn., Oxford: Clarendon Press, 1953. Reprinted (2nd edn.) New York: Garland Publishing Co., 1980.

Robinson, T. M. (1979) *Contrasting Arguments: An Edition of the* Dissoi Logoi, New York. Reprinted Salem, N.H.: Ayer Co., 1983.

(1987) *Heraclitus: Fragments, A Text and Translation with a Commentary*, Toronto: University of Toronto Press.

(1992) "Plato and the Computer," *Ancient Philosophy* 12: 375–82.

Robinson, Thomas M. and Brisson, Luc (eds.) (2000) *Plato*: Euthydemus, Lysis, Charmides, *Proceedings of the V* Symposium Platonicum, *Selected Papers* (International Plato Studies 13), Sankt Augustin: Academia Verlag.

Roochnik, David L. (1987) "The Erotics of Philosophical Discourse," *History of Philosophy Quarterly* 4: 117–29.

Rosen, Stanley (1968) *Plato's* Symposium, New Haven, Conn.: Yale University Press; 2nd edn. 1987.

Ross, W. D. (1924) *Aristotle's* Metaphysics, 2 vols., Oxford: Clarendon Press.

(1951) *Plato's Theory of Ideas*, Oxford: Clarendon Press; corrected 2nd edn. 1953.

(1955a) *Aristotle:* Parva Naturalia, Oxford: Clarendon Press.

Rowe, C. J. (1984) *Plato* (Philosophers in Context 2), Brighton: Harvester Press.

(1986) *Plato:* Phaedrus, *with Translation and Commentary*, Warminster: Aris and Phillips Ltd.

(1992) "Reflections of the Sun: Explanation in the *Phaedo*," in Barker and Warner (1992) 89–101.

(1993) *Plato:* Phaedo, Cambridge: Cambridge University Press.

Rutherford, R. B. (1995) *The Art of Plato: Ten Essays in Platonic Interpretation*, Cambridge, Mass.: Harvard University Press.

Ryle, Gilbert (1939) "Plato's *Parmenides*," *Mind* 48: 129–51, 302–25. Reprinted in Allen (1965) 97–145, with additions 145–47.

(1976) "Many Things are Odd about Our *Meno*," *Paideia* 5: 1–9.

Santas, Gerasimos (1964) "The Socratic Paradox," *Philosophical Review* 73: 147–64. Reprinted in Sesonske and Fleming (1965) 49–64.

(1966) "Plato's *Protagoras* and Explanations of Weakness," *Philosophical Review* 75: 3–33. Reprinted in Vlastos (1971) 264–98.

(1968/69) "Socrates at Work on Virtue and Knowledge in Plato's *Laches*," *Review of Metaphysics* 22: 433–60. Reprinted in Vlastos (1971) 177–208.

(1972) "The Socratic Fallacy," *Journal of the History of Philosophy* 10 (1972) 127–41.

(1973) "Socrates at Work on Virtue and Knowledge in Plato's *Charmides*," in Lee et al. (1973) 105–32.

(1979) *Socrates: Philosophy in Plato's Early Dialogues*. London: Routledge and Kegan Paul.

Saunders, Trevor J. (ed.) (1987) *Plato: Early Socratic Dialogues*, Harmondsworth, Middlesex: Penguin Books.

Savan, David (1964) "Self-Predication in *Protagoras* 330–31," *Phronesis* 9: 130–35.

Sayre, Kenneth M. (1969) *Plato's Analytical Method*, Chicago, Ill.: University of Chicago Press.

Schirlitz, C. (1897) "Der Begriff des Wissens vom Wissen in Platons *Charmides*," *Jahrbuch für classische Philologie* 155: 451–76, 513–37.

Schmid, W. Thomas (1998) *Plato's* Charmides *and the Socratic Ideal of Rationality*, Albany: State University of New York Press.

Schofield, Malcolm (1980) *An Essay on Anaxagoras*, Cambridge: Cambridge University Press.

Scott, Dominic (1987) "Platonic Anamnesis Revisited," *Classical Quarterly* 37: 346–66.

(1995) *Recollection and Experience: Plato's Theory of Understanding and its Successors*, Cambridge: Cambridge University Press.

(ed.) (2002) *Does Socrates Have a Method? Rethinking the Elenchus in Plato's Dialogues and Beyond*, University Park, Pa.: Penn State University Press.

Sedley, David (1989) "Is the *Lysis* a Dialogue of Definition?" *Phronesis* 34: 107–8.

(1998) "Platonic Causes," *Phronesis* 43: 114–32.

Sesonske, Alexander (1963) "Knowing and Saying: The Structure of Plato's *Meno*," *Archiv für Philosophie* 12: 3–13. Reprinted in Sesonske and Fleming (1965) 84–96.

Sesonske, Alexander and Fleming, Noel (eds.) (1965) *Plato's* Meno: *Text and Criticism*, Belmont, Calif.: Wadsworth Publishing Co.

Sharples, R. W. (1985) *Plato:* Meno, Chicago, Ill.: Bolchazy-Carducci Publishers.

(1989) "More on Plato, *Meno* 82c2–3," *Phronesis* 34: 220–26.

Shiner, Roger and King-Farlow, John (eds.) (1976) *New Essays on Plato and the Pre-Socratics, Canadian Journal of Philosophy* supp. vol. 2, Guelph, Ont.: Canadian Association for Publishing in Philosophy/University of Calgary Press.

Shipton, K. M. W. (1979) "A Good Second Best: *Phaedo* 99b ff.," *Phronesis* 24: 33–53.

Shorey, Paul (1884) *De Platonis idearum doctrina atque mentis humanae notionibus commentatio*, Munich: T. Ackermann. Reprinted in Shorey (1980) I 253–313.

(1924) "The Origin of the Syllogism," *Classical Philology* 19: 1–19. Reprinted in Shorey (1980) II 308–26.

(1903) *The Unity of Plato's Thought*, Chicago, Ill.: University of Chicago Press. Reprinted 1960.

(1925) "Emendation of Aristotle's *Metaphysics* 1079B2–6," *Classical Philology* 20: 271–73. Reprinted in Shorey (1980) II 412–14.

(1930) "The Alleged Fallacy in Plato *Lysis* 220 E," *Classical Philology* 25: 380–83. Reprinted in Shorey (1980) II 4–7.

(1930/35) *Plato: The Republic*, vols. V–VI in Fowler et al. (1914/35).

(1933) *What Plato Said*, Chicago, Ill.: University of Chicago Press; 5th impression, 1962.

(1980) *Selected Papers*, 2 vols., ed. Leonardo Taran, New York: Garland.

Silverman, Allan (2002) *The Dialectic of Essence: A Study of Plato's Metaphysics*, Princeton, N.J.: Princeton University Press.

Simplicius: see Diels (1882/95).

Slings, S. R. (1999) *Plato:* Clitophon (Cambridge Classical Texts and Commentaries 37), Cambridge: Cambridge University Press.

Smith, Angela (1998) "Knowledge and Expertise in the Early Platonic Dialogues," *Archiv für Geschichte der Philosophie* 80: 129–61.

Smyth, Herbert Weir (1956) *Greek Grammar*, rev. by Gordon M. Messing, Cambridge, Mass.: Harvard University Press.

Solmsen, Friedrich (1971) "Parmenides and the Description of Perfect Beauty in Plato's *Symposium*," *American Journal of Philology* 92: 62–70.

Sorabji, Richard (1972) *Aristotle*: On Memory, London: Duckworth.

Soreth, Marion (1953) *Der platonische Dialog* Hippias Maior (Zetemata 6), Munich: C. H. Beck.

Sprague, Rosamond Kent (1962) *Plato's Use of Fallacy: A Study of the* Euthydemus *and Some Other Dialogues*, London: Routledge and Kegan Paul.

(1965) *Plato:* Euthydemus, Indianapolis: Bobbs-Merrill.

(1967) "Parmenides' Sail and Dionysodorus' Ox," *Phronesis* 12: 91–98.

(1968) "Socrates' Safest Answer: *Phaedo* 100d," *Hermes* 96: 632–35.

(ed.) (1972) *The Older Sophists*, Columbia, S.C.: University of South Carolina Press.

(1973) *Plato:* Laches *and* Charmides, Indianapolis: Bobbs-Merrill.

(2000) "The *Euthydemus* Revisited," in Robinson and Brisson (2000) 3–19.

Stallbaum, Gottfried (1850) *Platonis Opera omnia* I 2: *Phaedo*, 3rd edn., Gotha: Hennings. Reprinted New York: Garland Publishing Co., 1980.

Stefanini, Luigi (1932/35) *Platone*, 2 vols., Padua: CEDAM, 1932 and 1935; 2nd edn. 1949.

Stewart, J. A. (1909) *Plato's Doctrine of Ideas*, Oxford: Clarendon Press. Reprinted New York: Russell and Russell, 1964.

Stokes, Michael C. (1963) Review of Bluck (1961a), *Archiv für Geschichte der Philosophie* 45: 292–99.

(1986) *Plato's Socratic Conversations: Drama and Dialectic in Three Dialogues*, Baltimore, Md.: Johns Hopkins University Press.

Stough, Charlotte L. (1976) "Forms and Explanation in the *Phaedo*," *Phronesis* 21: 1–30.

Strauss, Leo (1964) *The City and Man*, Chicago, Ill.: University of Chicago Press.

Szlezák, Thomas Alexander (1985) *Platon und die Schriftlichkeit der Philosophie: Interpretationen zu den frühen und mittleren Dialogen*, Berlin: Walter de Gruyter.

Tait, M. D. C. (1952) "A Problem in the Method of Hypothesis in the *Phaedo*," in M. E. White (ed.) *Studies in Honour of Gilbert Norwood, Phoenix* supp. vol. 1, Toronto: University of Toronto Press, 1952, 110–15.

Tait, W. W. (1985/86) "Plato's Second Best Method," *Review of Metaphysics* 39: 455–82.

Tarrant, Dorothy (1920) "On the *Hippias Major*," *Journal of Philology* 35: 319–31.

(1927) "The Authorship of *Hippias Major*," *Classical Quarterly* 21: 82–87.

(1928) *The* Hippias Major *Attributed to Plato*, Cambridge: Cambridge University Press. Reprinted New York: Arno Press, 1976.

(1957) "*Phaedo* 74AB," *Journal of Hellenic Studies* 77: 124–26.

Tarrant, Harold (1993) *Thrasyllan Platonism*, Ithaca, N.Y.: Cornell University Press.

Taylor, A. E. (1926) *Plato: The Man and His Work*, London: Routledge and Kegan Paul; 2nd edn. 1927; 3rd edn. 1929; 4th edn. 1937, reprinted 1948, 1949, 1952, 1956.

Taylor, C. C. W. (1976) *Plato:* Protagoras, trans. with notes, Oxford: Clarendon Press; rev. edn. 1991.

Teloh, Henry (1975) "Self-Predication or Anaxagorean Causation in Plato," *Apeiron* 9 no. 2: 15–23.

(1981) *The Development of Plato's Metaphysics*, University Park, Pa.: Penn State University Press.

(1986) *Socratic Education in Plato's Early Dialogues*, Notre Dame, Ind.: University of Notre Dame Press.

Thesleff, Holger (1982) *Studies in Platonic Chronology* (Commentationes Humanarum Litterarum 70), Helsinki: Societas Scientarum Fennica.

Thompson, E. Seymer (1901) *The* Meno *of Plato*, London: Macmillan. Reprinted Cambridge: Heffer, 1961.

Tigerstedt, E. N. (1977) *Interpreting Plato* (Stockholm Studies in the History of Literature 17), Stockholm: Almqvist and Wiksell.

Tigner, S. S. (1970) "On the Kinship of All Nature in Plato's *Meno*," *Phronesis* 15: 1–4.

Tomin, Julius (1987) "Socratic Midwifery," *Classical Quarterly* 37: 97–102.

Tredennick, Hugh (1954) *Plato: The Last Days of Socrates:* Euthyphro, *the* Apology, Crito, Phaedo, Harmondsworth, Middlesex: Penguin Books; new edn., 1959.

Tuckey, T. G. (1951) *Plato's* Charmides, Cambridge: Cambridge University Press.

Verdenius, W. J. (1958) "Notes on Plato's *Phaedo*," *Mnemosyne*, 4th ser., 11: 193–243.

Versenyi, Laszlo (1975) "Plato's *Lysis*," *Phronesis* 20: 185–98.

Vlastos, Gregory (1954) "The Third Man Argument in the *Parmenides*," *Philosophical Review* 63: 319–49. Reprinted in Allen (1965) 231–63; Vlastos (1995) 166–90.

(1956a) "Introduction" to Vlastos (ed.) *Plato: Protagoras*, Indianapolis: Bobbs-Merrill.

(1956b) "Postscript to the Third Man: A Reply to Mr. Geach," *Philosophical Review* 65: 83–94. Reprinted (augmented) in Allen (1965) 279–91; Vlastos (1995) 204–14.

(1957) "The Paradox of Socrates," *Queen's Quarterly* 64: 496–516. Reprinted as "Introduction: The Paradox of Socrates," Vlastos (1971) 1–21; Vlastos (1995) 3–18.

(1965) "*Anamnesis* in the *Meno*," *Dialogue* 4: 143–67. Reprinted in Vlastos (1995) 147–65.

(1969) "Reasons and Causes in the *Phaedo*," *Philosophical Review* 78: 291–325. Reprinted in Vlastos (1970/71) I 132–66; Vlastos (1973) 76–110.

(ed.) (1970) *Plato: A Collection of Critical Essays*, vol. I: *Metaphysics and Epistemology*, Garden City, N.Y.: Doubleday Anchor.

(1971) *The Philosophy of Socrates: A Collection of Critical Essays*, Garden City, N.Y.: Doubleday Anchor.

(1971/72) "The Unity of the Virtues in the *Protagoras*," *Review of Metaphysics* 25: 415–58. Reprinted in Vlastos (1973b) 221–69.

(1973a) "The Individual as an Object of Love in Plato," in Vlastos (1973b) 3–42.

(1973b) *Platonic Studies*, Princeton, N.J.: Princeton University Press, 1973; 2nd printing, corrected and enlarged, 1981.

(1980) "The Role of Observation in Plato's Conception of Astronomy," in John P. Anton (ed.) (1980) *Science and the Sciences in Plato*, Delmar, N.Y.: Caravan Books, 1–31. Reprinted in Vlastos (1995) 223–46.

(1981) "Socrates on 'The Parts of Virtue'," in 2nd edn. of Vlastos (1973b) 418–23.

(1983) "The Socratic Elenchus," *Oxford Studies in Ancient Philosophy* 1: 27–58. Reprinted (revised) in Vlastos (1994) 1–29.

(1985) "Socrates' Disavowal of Knowledge," *Philosophical Quarterly* 35: 1–31. Reprinted (revised) in Vlastos (1994) 39–66.

(1987) "Socratic Irony," *Classical Quarterly* 37: 79–96. Reprinted (revised) in Vlastos (1991) 21–44, 236–48.

(1988) "Elenchus and Mathematics: A Turning-Point in Plato's Philosophical Development," *American Journal of Philology* 109: 362–96. Reprinted (revised) in Vlastos (1991) 107–31, 269–75.

(1990) "Is the 'Socratic Fallacy' Socratic?" *Ancient Philosophy* 10: 1–16. Reprinted (revised) in Vlastos (1994) 67–86, 138–39.

(1991) *Socrates: Ironist and Moral Philosopher* (Cornell Studies in Classical Philology 50), Ithaca, N.Y.: Cornell University Press.

(1994) *Socratic Studies*, ed. Myles Burnyeat, Cambridge: Cambridge University Press.

(1995) *Studies in Greek Philosophy*, vol. II: *Socrates, Plato, and Their Tradition*, ed. D. W. Graham, Princeton, N.J.: Princeton University Press.

von Arnim, Hans (1914) *Platons Jugenddialoge und die Entstehungszeit der Phaidros*, Leipzig: Teubner. Reprinted New York: Arno Press, 1976.

Wakefield, Jerome (1987) "Why Justice and Holiness are Similar: *Protagoras* 330–331," *Phronesis* 32: 267–76.

Walker, Ian (1984) *Plato's* Euthyphro (American Philological Association, Textbook Series 10), Chico, Calif.: Scholars Press.

Waterfield, Robin (1987) "*Hippias Major*," in Saunders (1987) 213–65.

Watson, Gerard (1973) *Plato's Unwritten Teaching*, Dublin: Talbot Press.

Watt, Donald (1987a) "*Lysis*," in Saunders (1987) 119–61.

(1987b) "*Charmides*," in Saunders (1987) 163–209.

Webster, T. B. L. (1952/53) "Language and Thought in Early Greece," *Memoirs and Proceedings of the Manchester Literary and Philosophical Society* 94: 17–38.

Wedberg, Anders (1955) *Plato's Philosophy of Mathematics*, Stockholm: Almqvist and Wiksell.

Weingartner, Rudolph H. (1973) *The Unity of the Platonic Dialogue: The* Cratylus, *the* Protagoras, *the* Parmenides, Indianapolis: Bobbs-Merrill.

Weiss, Roslyn (1986) "Euthyphro's Failure," *Journal of the History of Philosophy* 24: 437–52.

Wellman, Robert R. (1964) "The Question Posed at *Charmides* 165a–166c," *Phronesis* 9: 107–13.

Westerink, L. G. (1962) *Anonymous Prolegomena to Platonic Philosophy*, Amsterdam: North-Holland Publishing Co.

White, Nicholas P. (1974/75) "Inquiry," *Review of Metaphysics* 28: 289–310.

(1976) *Plato on Knowledge and Reality*, Indianapolis: Hackett Publishing Co.

(1979) *A Companion to Plato's* Republic, Indianapolis: Hackett Publishing Co.

(1987) "Forms and Sensibles: *Phaedo* 74B–C," *Philosophical Topics* 15: 197–214.

Wieland, Wolfgang (1982) *Platon und die Formen des Wissens*, Göttingen: Vandenhoeck and Ruprecht.

Williams, Thomas (2002) "Two Aspects of Platonic Recollection," *Apeiron* 35: 131–52.

Wisdom, John A. T. D. (1969) *Logical Constructions*, New York: Random House.

Witte, Bernd (1970) *Die Wissenschaft vom Guten und Bosen: Interpretationen zu Platons* Charmides, Berlin: Walter de Gruyter.

Wittgenstein, Ludwig (1953) *Philosophical Investigations*, trans. G. E. M. Anscombe, New York: Macmillan; often reprinted.

Wolfsdorf, D. (1998) "The Historical Reader of Plato's *Protagoras*," *Classical Quarterly* 48: 126–33.

Woodbridge, F. J. E. (1929) *The Son of Apollo: Themes of Plato*, Boston, Mass.: Houghton Mifflin Co.

Woodruff, Paul (1978) "Socrates and Ontology: The Evidence of the *Hippias Major*," *Phronesis* 23: 101–17.

(1982) *Plato: Hippias Major*, Indianapolis: Hackett Publishing Co.

(1987) "Expert Knowledge in the *Apology* and *Laches*: What a General Needs to Know," *Proceedings of the Boston Area Colloquium in Ancient Philosophy* 3: 79–115.

Woozley, A. D. (1979) *Law and Obedience: The Arguments of Plato's* Crito, London: Duckworth.

Young, Charles M. (1994) "Plato and Computer Dating: A Discussion of Gerard R. Ledger, *Re-Counting Plato: A Computer Analysis of Plato's Style,* and Leonard Brandwood, *The Chronology of Plato's Dialogues,*" *Oxford Studies in Ancient Philosophy* 12: 227–50.

(1997) "First Principles of Socratic Ethics," in Mark McPherran (ed.) *Wisdom, Ignorance, and Virtue: New Essays in Socratic Studies* (*Apeiron* 30 no. 4), Edmonton, Alberta: Academic Printing and Publishing, 13–23.

(2002) "Comments on Lesher, Ausland, and Tarrant," in Scott (2002) 78–86.

Index of passages cited

General index